ArtScroll Series®

Rabbi Nosson Scherman / Rabbi Meir Zlotowitz

General Editors

CHOFETZ CHAIM

Published by

Me'sorah Publications, ltd

in conjunction with

THE
CHOFETZ CHAIM
HERITAGE
FOUNDATION

A Lesson A Day

THE CONCEPTS AND LAWS
OF PROPER SPEECH
ARRANGED FOR DAILY STUDY

Based on his works, *Sefer Chofetz Chaim* and *Sefer Shmiras Haloshon*
Includes vignettes from the life of the Chofetz Chaim

by Rabbi Shimon Finkelman
and Rabbi Yitzchak Berkowitz

FIRST EDITION
Nine Impressions ... September 1995 — December 2001

SECOND EDITION
Thirteen Impressions ... September 2002 — October 2018
Fourteenth Impression ... June 2020

Published and Distributed by
MESORAH PUBLICATIONS, LTD.
313 Regina Avenue / Rahway, N.J. 07065

Distributed in Europe by
LEHMANNS
Unit E, Viking Business Park
Rolling Mill Road
Jarow, Tyne & Wear, NE32 3DP
England

Distributed in Australia and New Zealand
by **GOLDS WORLD OF JUDAICA**
3-13 William Street
Balaclava, Melbourne 3183
Victoria, Australia

Distributed in Israel by
SIFRIATI / A. GITLER
POB 2351
Bnei Brak 51122
Israel

Distributed in South Africa by
KOLLEL BOOKSHOP
Northfield Centre
17 Northfield Avenue
Glenhazel 2192,
Johannesburg, South Africa

A project of
THE CHOFETZ CHAIM HERITAGE FOUNDATION
361 Spook Rock Road / Suffern, N.Y. 10901 / (845) 352-3505

ISBN 10: 0-89906-321-7 / ISBN 13: 978-0-89906-321-8 (hard cover)
ISBN 10: 0-89906-322-5 / ISBN 13: 978-0-89906-322-5 (paperback)

Typography by CompuScribe at ArtScroll Studios, Ltd.

Printed in PRC
Bound by Sefercraft, Quality Bookbinders, Ltd., Rahway, NJ

בס"ד פ' עקב קדוש השם לפ"ק

בשם ועד הנהלה אנו מביעים הכרת הטוב להנדבנים
והעוסקים במלאכת שמים בלב ונפש להצלחת
המוסד הקדוש הזה. אנחנו מלאי שמחה בהצלחת
המוסד לעורר לבבות אחינו בני ישראל בזהירות
בעניני מצוות הדיבור.

אמרו חכמינו ז"ל כשנברא אדם הראשון העבירו
הקב"ה והזהירו תן דעתך שלא תקלקל ותחריב את
עולמי וכן כל אחד ואחד מוזהר שאכן בכוחו לקלקל
ולהחריב את כל העולם. בס' נפש החיים הרחיב שלא
יאמר האדם מי אני ומה אני, ופורש במשנה דע מה
למעלה ממך שכל מה שנעשה אף בעליונים הכל ממך
על פי מעשי האדם.

באגרת המוסר למרן הגרי"ס זצוק"ל מרחיב
בענין לימוד התורה שמלבד שזה ענין רוחני התבלין
שבה שמעלה האדם וזוכה ליראה ומצילו מחטא יש
עוד מעלה במה שלומד תורת כל עבירה ועבירה.
ומחדש שם שאם לא ישתמש ברפואה גשמית
הלימוד והתבוננות בעצם המצוה אזי גם ברוחניות
שהיא למוד בתורה "לא תתן כחה כל כך ליצר
הרוחני" ונראה בביאור הדברים שכדי שתתעלה על
ידי התורה תבלין צריך להיות מיוסד בקדושה ויסוד
הקדושה הוא שמתעמק ומתחזק בהמצוה ע"י לימוד
שלומד משורש המצוה והלכותי'.

ובכן בואו ונחזיק טובה להגה"צ ראש ישיבת
מאנטשעסטער שתיקן ואיזן ללמוד בהלכות לשה"ר
הלכות ספורות מדי יום ביומו ובמשך הזמן נהי'
בקיאים ונהי' יותר זהירים במצוה זו. בזכות החזקת
מצוה זו נזכה לגאולה שלמה בקרוב.

שמואל קמנצקי

בס"ד

הובא לפני לקט הלכות, קונטרוס אשר הינו חיבור שלם, בהלכות
לה"ר ורכילות, לפי דעתו של מרן רבנו החפץ חיים זיע"א, בלשון
האנגלית. ועברתי בין בתריו, מתחילתו ועד סופו. ואם כי לא בעיון
הראוי לקבוע הלכה בהלכות חמורות כאלו, מצאתיו לפי עניות דעתי
כולו מכוון להלכה. וזאת למודעי – שהדינים מתחלקים ומשתנים הרבה,
מן האסור למותר, ומן המותר לאסור, ומן הנכון לבלתי הגון, ומן מצוה
לעבירה חמורה בשינוי מועט כל דהו. בין בעובדות ובין בתנאים, בשינוי
האישים, ובשינויי המקומות, וכדומה. וממילא קשה לפסוק הלכה ברורה
למעשה, מכל חיבור שהוא, אם לא מי שבקי היטב ולמדן בדינים אלו.
ובפרט בלשון האנגלית, אשר אין מילותיה מוגדרות היטב, לדייק על
ידם, הדיוק המוגדר אשר בלשון הקדוש, אשר ע"י נמסרה לנו תורתנו
הק'. וזה אפי' למי שמבין היטב היטב הלשון ההוא. אך התועלת היוצאת
מן העיון והשינון והחזרה, בלקט הלכות אלו, אין לשער ואין לתאר. ומי
שיקבע זמן קבוע לעיונו בקונטרוס זה, לשנן אותו ולחזר עליו, יהיו
הלכות אלו תמיד לנגד עיניו, ובצירוף מחשבה טובה למעשה, השם
ישמור רגליו מלכד, ולא יכשל חלילה בפליטת אסורה, ואפי' בלתי
הגונה, ומה שיסתפק בו ישאל לרב שיורהו הדרך ילך בה, והמעשה אשר
יעשה.

והוא ית' וית' יראה שאנחנו משתדלים לכלות הקוצים מדברי פינו,
ומבקשים קרבתו ית', יעזור על ידינו, וישמר אותנו בין ברוחניות ובין
בגשמיות, וישוב אלינו במהרה, כמו שהבטחנו.

הכו"ח לכבוד התורה, עמליה ונוטריה

מכתב ברכה מאת
הרב ר' מתתי' סלומון, שליט"א
משגיח רוחני דישיבת בית יוסף דגייטסהד אנגליה

בס"ד

כ"א מנחם אב תשנ"ה לפ"ק

מן הטובות הגדולות שהשפיע השי"ת על דורנו הוא זה ששלח רוח ממרום והתעוררות גדולה בתוך המון בית ישראל ללמוד הלכות לה"ר ורכילות ולחפש תחבולות למעשה איך לקיים נצור לשונך מרע אשר בדור שלפנינו כבר מסר נפשו עליו הסבא קדישא בעל החפץ חיים זצוק"ל. ברם זכר אותו האיש לטוב ה"ה הגה"צ כמוהר"ר יהודה זאב סגל זצוק"ל שאלמלא הוא נשתכח תורת החפץ חיים מדורנו ובכל הזדמנות הי' מעורר ומעודד ללמוד ספר חפץ חיים ולקיים הלכות לה"ר ורכילות בכל פרטיה ודקדוקיה גם הגדיל לעשות לתקן לוח יומי ללימוד ההלכות בכל יום וזכה להפיץ מעיינתו חוצה ונתקבל רעיונו הטהור בכל תפוצות ישראל ותשואות חן חן לו וצדקתו עומדת לעד.

והנה קם חבורה ממזכי הרבים להדפיס הלוח במהדורא חדשה בלשון המדוברת ולעטר כל הלכה והלכה מספר חפץ חיים עם דברי אגדה מספר שמירת הלשון זה מול זה אשר כן הי' רצון החפץ חיים זצוק"ל לחזק לימוד ההלכות ע"י דברי התעוררות ומוסר כדי שתהי' הלימוד על מנת לעשות כאשר מבואר בהקדמה לספר חפץ חיים שם.

מו"ר הגה"צ כמוהר"ר אליהו לופין זצוק"ל הי' תמיד מצטט דברי אבות דר' נתן בפרק כ"ט מי שיש בידו הלכות ואין בידו אגדות הרי הוא דומה למי שיש כלי זין בידו אבל הוא חלש, ומי שיש בידו אגדות ואין בידו הלכות הוא דומה לגבור בלא כלי זין. והי' מסביר דברי המשל כי ההלכות הם חכמת התורה שהוא הכלי זין נגד יצה"ר אבל אם האדם חלש ואינו יכול להרים את הכלי זין שבידו ולהשתמש בו כנגד השונא א"כ מה יועיל לו כלי זינו ורק ע"י התעוררות דברי אגדה מקבל אדם גבורת הלב וגבורת הנפש ואז ירצה ויכול להשתמש בכלי זינו -- אשר הן הן ההלכות -- נגד השונא הגדול השוכן בבתי נפשו (וע' לב אליהו חכמה ומוסר דף קכ"ז).

על כן נחזיקנא טיבותא להאי חבוריא קדשיא שהוסיף בעמלה אומץ וגבורה לכלי זין התקיפים שיסדו קדושים אשר בארץ המה לגרש נגע לה"ר ורכילות ממחנינו -- ובזאת נגמרה ונשלמה המלאכה. יהי נועם ה' עליהם.

יתן ה' שע"י שתיקת ישראל מדבורים אסורים ישתיק ה' וישקיט את המקטרג הגדול מעל כלל ישראל כדברי ח"ח בהקדמתו וישלח לנו משיחו בב"א.

הכו"ח בתקוה שאלי' יעזרו גם יעזבו להיות
שנה זו תחלת גאולה ענני הרבים ה"ל.
מתתי' חיים סלומון.

קריאה גדולה
מגדולי ומאורי הדור

לאחינו בני ישראל הי"ו

לדאבונינו רבתה העזובה והזילזול באיסורי לשון הרע ורכילות, עד שבעיני רבים נדמה הזהירות מאיסור זה כמילי דחסידותא ונעשה כהיתר, כאילו אין איסורים אלו קיימים כלל.

והנה חכמינו בשני התלמודים, מדרשים וזוהר הק' ראשונים ואחרונים החמירו בעוון זה מאוד, והחשיבוהו כחמורה שבחמורות.

ומזעזעים ומחרידים כל לב דברי הרמב"ם פרק ג' מהלכות תשובה הלכה ו' זה לשונו:
ואלו שאין להם חלק לעולם הבא, אלא נכרתין ואובדין על גודל רשעם וחטאתם לעולם ולעולמי עולמים, המינים והאפיקורסין והכופרים בתורה והכופרים בתחיית המתים ובביאת הגואל וכו' וכו' ובעלי לשון הרע וכו' עכ"ל.

אחים יקרים: המציאות קובעת שאין בדורינו מנוס ומפלט להנצל מאיסורי לשה"ר ורכילות בלא לימוד ספרי "חפץ חיים" ו"שמירת הלשון" המכילים דיני לשה"ר ורכילות הלכה למעשה. ודברים מוסריים בוערים כלפידים היוצאים מלב טהור רבן של כל ישראל זיע"א. "מאן בעי חיי" יטעום צוף דבש ספריו הקדושים ללמוד על מנת לקיים. ואכל וחי בטוב בזה ובבא.

עקב זאת הננו קוראים ומכריזים:

א) כל אחד יראה לקבוע זמן ללמוד ספרי "חפץ חיים" ו"שמירת הלשון" הן בצבור בבתי הכנסיות הן בישיבות ובכוללים, הן ביחידות, וכל רב ומנהיג בעדתו ישתדל לייסד שיעורים כאלו במקומו.

ב) כל ראשי ומנהלי הישיבות לצעירים, וכתות הגבוהות בבתי הת"ת ובתי החינוך לבנות יכלילו בסדרי הלימודים בלימוד חובה "חפץ חיים" או עיקרי דינים" [המכיל קיצור ספר חפץ חיים] וספר שמירת הלשון במתכונות יתר הלימודים בעיון ובחזרות בכדי להקנות להתלמידים ולהשריש בליבם הלכות אלו מנעורתם.

[וכמו שכתוב בחפץ חיים סוף כלל ט' ובמשנ"ב סי' שמ"ג ס"ק ג' והסיבה העיקרית לזילזול בחטאי הלשון, היא ההרגל לזה מקטנתו ע"ש]

והשי"ת יערה עלינו רוח טהרה בקרבינו וישמור מצרות נפשנו, כמאמר הכתוב "שומר פיו ולשונו שומר מצרות נפשו" ויחיש גאולתינו במהרה. שלה' שבט תשל"ו.

חיים שמואלביץ	יעקב ישראל קניבסקי	ישראל אלטר	מנחם מנדל טאוב
ראש ישיבת מיר	בעל "קהילת יעקב"	אדמו"ר מגור	בן הק' מראזלא אדמו"ר מקאליב
אברהם וינברג	יחיאל מיכל פיינשטיין	יחיאל יהושע	מאיר חדש
אדמו"ר מסלונים	ראש כולל "בית יהודה"	בן לאאמו"ר וצללה"ה אדמו"ר מביאלא	מנהל רוחני דישיבת חברון
בנימין יהושע זילבר	ישראל אבוחצירא	יוחנן טברסקי	משה שמואל שפירה
בעל מקור הלכה וע"ס	רבן ומאורן דיהודי צפון אפריקה	אדמו"ר מרחמסטריבקה	ראש ישיבת "באר יעקב"
חיים יוסף הלוי דינקלס	יהודה ש. צדקה	מרדכי שלום יוסף	מרדכי שרעבי
בעל "דעת יוסף"	ראש ישיבת "פורת יוסף"	מבוהר"ר אהרן אדמו"ר מסדיגורה	זקן המקובלים
חיים פנחס שיינברג	יוסף אדלער	משה מרדכי בידרמן	שמואל הלוי ואזנר
ראש ישיבת "תורה אור" בעל טבעת החושן	גאב"ד טורדה	אדמו"ר מלעלוב	גאב"ד ור"מ זכרון מאיר

Dedicated to the memory of

הגאון הצדיק הרב יהודא זאב
בן הגאון הצדיק הרב משה יצחק הלוי סג"ל זצוק"ל

HaRav Yehuda Zev Segal, זצ"ל,
The Manchester Rosh Yeshiva

The Sages of the Talmud are referred to throughout Jewish literature as *"talmidei chachamim,"* which translated literally means "students of the wise." Rabbi Simchah Zissel Ziv, known as the *Alter* (Elder) of Kelm, explained that throughout their days these brilliant, learned men were also students, striving constantly to reach new heights in their comprehension of G-d and His Torah. It is this constant striving, with the fervor of a child, that is the true indication of wisdom.

The *keruvim,* two golden figures which stood atop the Holy Ark in the *Beis Hamikdash,* had the faces of children. This, says the Alter, was to teach each member of the Jewish People, great and small alike, to consider himself as a child, always ready to learn.

This wholehearted devotion to learning, driven by the expectation that each new day would bring new insights and new light, characterized the life of Harav Yehuda Zev Segal, זצ"ל, the Manchester Rosh Yeshiva. To the last day of his life, his energetic approach to each moment of life equalled the vigor of a young man at the peak of his powers. Though he had labored his whole life in Torah, he never rested on his accomplishments; he pressed forward with undiminished energy.

His was a character constantly in the process of refinement. When he exhorted those at his Yeshiva to stay far from anger, pride, flattery and idle talk, he spoke to himself. Though his ways exemplified the Torah's ideals, he was not set in his ways. His heart was always open and ready, like a child's, for possibilities for self-improvement.

R' Segal was known throughout the world for his deep-rooted love and concern for every Jew — as attested to by the thousands who sought his help in times of trouble. On one such occasion, he received a transatlantic call from a heartbroken father telling him of the loss of a child. Throughout the fifteen minutes of the phone call, he wept, pierced by the pain of a man he did not know, because he took every Jew's pain as his own.

What many sought from R' Segal, aside from his advice and sympathy, was the awesome power of his prayer. Here, too, he exhibited a childlike purity of purpose. He recited every prayer, no matter how simple, from a *siddur,* pointing to each word as he prayed. He beseeched Hashem on behalf of all those who sought His help, his heart overwhelmed by the troubles of others, many of whom he had never met. Each Yom Kippur, when the *aron kodesh* stood open, he would plead on behalf of all who were childless, pouring out his heart with tears of anguish.

His incredible *ahavas Yisrael* (love of his fellow Jew) was grounded in the laws of *Shmiras Haloshon,* the *mitzvah* that, perhaps more than any other, characterized his life's work. To know him and observe the way in which he conducted his life was to see living proof of how, by embracing the Torah's laws on speech, man can truly reflect the Divine image in which he was created.

Considered by many "the Chofetz Chaim of this generation," Rav Segal used every opportunity to raise consciousness about *Shmiras HaLoshon.* Those who came to him for help were invariably told to turn their attention to this *mitzvah* as the surest way to arouse Hashem's compassion.

To inspire his generation toward greater progress in *Shmiras Haloshon,* he developed a daily calendar for learning *Sefer Chofetz Chaim* and *Sefer Shmiras Haloshon.* That calendar is the basis for the worldwide *Shmiras Haloshon Yomi* program.

Rav Segal was the inspiration, heart and soul of the Chofetz Chaim Heritage Foundation. As its founding rabbinic advisor, he lent his profound love and knowledge of this *mitzvah* to the organization's efforts. His unstinting encouragement and wise counsel provided the basis for dozens of *Shmiras Haloshon* programs that have succeeded in heightening awareness of the *mitzvah* throughout the Jewish world.

Two weeks before his passing, Rav Segal asked the Chofetz Chaim Heritage Foundation to produce the *sefer* you now hold, which he saw as a vital step in making these works of the Chofetz Chaim accessible to all. These were his last instructions to us.

Some time before his passing, R' Segal made two requests regarding his burial. Of all his myriad achievements he considered his *Shmiras Haloshon* calendar as his "passport to the World to Come," and asked that a copy of the calendar be buried with him.

And, he gave instructions as to where he wished to be buried. This learned, revered and beloved man, the spiritual father and teacher of thousands, chose to be laid to rest not among the great and famous, but among the children. Though his reason for this request is not known to us, it surely seems fitting that a man whose radiant countenance reflected purity and innocence should be buried among the most pure and innocent of our people.

May the learning

and Shmiras Haloshon

engendered by this book

be a זכות

לע״נ

אליעזר בן משה ז״ל

קאניא בער בן יעקב אלימלך ז״ל

בתיה ביילע בת ברוך הכהן ע״ה

לעילוי נשמת

ר' פנחס בן ר' יהושע אליעזר בראקער ע"ה
נפטר כ"ח אייר תשנ"ד

ואשתו מרת שיינדל בת ר' יצחק מאיר ע"ה
נפטרה י"ח שבט תשנ"א

ת.נ.צ.ב.ה.

Dedicated in memory of our parents

Pincus and Sonia Broker ע"ה

Pincus Broker exemplified humility and Torah scholarship. His quiet strength brought him through the Holocaust and enabled him to help save the lives of sixteen others in an underground bunker he had built. At the end of the war, with the great Torah centers of Europe lying in ruins, he came to New York to continue his learning. He began a new life based on his old ideals, placing little value on material things. Sharp in mind and unassuming in character, he passed his love of learning on to his children.

Sonia Broker was a descendant of the Gerrer Chassidic dynasty. She built a new life in America upon the inspiration she drew from her own family, most of whom perished in the Holocaust. As a mother she was selfless and joyful, uplifting all who knew her with her energy and enthusiasm.

Together they built a home based on love of Torah and Ahavas Yisrael. This sefer, which will further the ideals by which they lived, is dedicated to them.

Dr. Moshe and Aviva Broker   Izzy and Sharon Broker
Sara and Jay Pernikoff

Dear Reader:

Ahavas Yisrael and *Shmiras Haloshon* are the key to the hopes and dreams of *Klal Yisrael.* The Chofetz Chaim Heritage Foundation is an educational foundation working to eliminate hatred and divisiveness from our midst and make *Shmiras Haloshon* the norm. It is our hope that these efforts will strengthen the unity of our people, thereby bringing the Final Redemption.

Our foundation disseminates this important information in several ways. We organize lectures and assemblies around the country. We have *Shmiras Haloshon Telephone Shiurim* (Lectures) in 14 cities across the country. We have sold thousands of tapes on the philosophy and *halachah* of this topic, and we have distributed literally hundreds of thousands of brochures and flyers to schools, camps and cities nationwide.

We are only missing one thing.

You.

We invite each of you to join us in building together a world of *Ahavas Yisrael* and *Shmiras Haloshon.*

Your involvement is crucial.

Because each person who becomes aware of the meaning, the power and the proper observance of *Shmiras Haloshon* adds new strength to the Jewish people's centuries-old push toward the Redemption.

Together, with your help, we can get there.

The Chofetz Chaim Heritage Foundation

❧ *Table of Contents*

A Note to the Reader:

Sefer Chofetz Chaim is the code of laws relating to proper speech written by Rabbi Yisrael Meir Kagan of Radin, who was known as the "Chofetz Chaim." *Sefer Shmiras Haloshon*, also compiled by the Chofetz Chaim, contains the philosophical teachings relating to proper speech.

In *A Lesson A Day*, each left handed page offers a selection of laws from *Sefer Chofetz Chaim*; the right handed page offers a selection from *Sefer Shmiras Haloshon*.

Hebrew terms transliterated in this book are defined in the Glossary at the book's conclusion. The following terms are basic to this volume and are used frequently:

Hashem — lit., *the Name*, a reference to G-d.

Loshon Hora — *evil talk*. In its general sense, the term refers to various forms of speech prohibited by the Torah. Specifically, it refers to speech which is derogatory or harmful in nature.

Shmiras Haloshon — lit., *guarding of the tongue*, the quality of exercising caution in matters of speech so that one's words are in consonance with the Torah's commandments relating to speech.

⇒〇⇐

For Halachic questions regarding Shmiras Haloshon, readers may contact a *poseik* at the Shmiras Haloshon Sh'eila Hotline (718) 951-3696 Monday-Thursday 9 -10:30 PM and Motzaei Shabbos.

⇒〇⇐

Note: *The dates of each day's dedication do not necessarily indicate the Yartzeit of the individual.*

✒ *Introduction*

When one explores the *mitzvah* of proper speech, and the concomitant transgression of *loshon hora*, one fact becomes eminently clear: we are not dealing with business as usual. The cosmic repercussions of this issue are so intense that they have literally shaped the destiny of our people. It is hard to imagine that any religion would make so dramatic a statement as to say that G-d Himself has chosen not to sit in His home on this earth, that His people have been in exile for 2,000 years, because of the words that come out of our mouths.[1]

The power we wield when we speak is far beyond what we can perceive. Imagine going to an automatic teller machine at your local bank, inserting the plastic ATM card and making a simple transaction, only to be told upon exiting that you had actually just transferred $17 billion from the treasury of one country to that of another and left a devastating bankruptcy in your wake. We think we're only exchanging a few words, when in fact we're moving worlds.

What we will find as we explore the philosophy and laws of proper speech is that what appear to be benign pieces of information are actually the tremendously potent key factor in our relationship to Hashem and in living our lives as Jews. *Loshon hora* is so powerful, in fact, that it can erase the merits of a lifetime of Torah learning and *mitzvah* observance.[2]

Just as the negative consequences of speech can be so vast, the positive consequences of proper speech are even greater. The Vilna Gaon says that proper speech is the single biggest factor in determining one's portion in the World to Come.[3] The Chofetz Chaim tells

---

1. *Nesivas Olam*, *Nesiv Haloshon*, Maharal.
2. *Sefer Shmiras HaLoshon*.
3. *Igeres HaGra*, Vilna Gaon.

us that adherence to these laws empowers our prayers,[4] validates our Torah learning, accesses G-d's Divine Protection[5] and invokes the many blessings that G-d, in His kindness, is waiting to shower upon us.[6]

From this, it is clear that proper speech is so vital to our lives that it is almost life itself. And that is why King David declared, "Who is the man who desires life? Guard your tongue from evil." (*Tehillim* 34:14).

So, to those who are searching for a life of peace and closeness to G-d in this world, and a good life in the World to Come, join us as we explore the Chofetz Chaim's masterpiece, the definitive guide to living as a Jew.

---

4. *Sefer Shmiras HaLoshon, Shaar HaZechira.*
5. Ibid.
6. *Sefer Shmiras HaLoshon* Part 2, Chapter 11.

✒Acknowledgments

Our gratitude to Hashem *Yisbarach* is inexpressible for His having permitted us to produce this *sefer* and spread the importance of *ahavas Yisrael* and *Shmiras HaLoshon.*

We would like to thank the following people for their outstanding work and tremendous devotion to the cause of *Shmiras HaLoshon.* They are the backbone of our organization and we are extremely grateful to them for joining forces with us.

HaGaon Harav Yehuda Zev Segal, זצ״ל**,** the founding Rabbinic Advisor of our organization, was one of the precious resources of our generation. His love and concern for every Jew can only be compared to that of the Chofetz Chaim himself. This *sefer* is his inspiration, for he asked us to produce it in his last conversation with us.

HaRav Shmuel Kamenetsky, שליט״א**,** is the Chairman of our Rabbinical Board. He is our source of inspiration and guidance, always taking time out of his busy schedule to answer our questions and to give us direction and advice.

HaRav Hillel Zaks, שליט״א**,** Rosh Yeshiva of Yeshivas Chevron in Jerusalem gave of his time and energy and provided guidance for an accurate presentation of the laws of *Shmiras HaLoshon.*

HaRav Aryeh Beer, שליט״א**,** graciously took time to review the Overview and offer crucial advice.

For **Rabbi Shimon Finkelman,** who prepared the material from *Sefer Shmiras HaLoshon* and wrote the vignettes, and **Rabbi Yitzchak Berkowitz**, who compiled the Laws from *Sefer Chofetz Chaim* and wrote the accompanying Hebrew notes, this work was a labor of love. Their dedication to this project carried the day.

Chana Nestlebaum has been the voice of our organization for the last six years. Her words have inspired and enlightened people all over the world. It was only fitting that in this *sefer*, her pen should write the Overview. The Overview itself was culled from many sources including tapes (distributed by our organization) of addresses by the following distinguished *rabbanim* שליט״א: Rabbi Avraham Pam, Rabbi Moshe Eisemann, Rabbi Berel Wein, Rabbi Mendel Kessin, Rabbi Paysach Krohn, Rabbi Dovid Gottlieb, Rabbi Yissocher Frand, Rabbi Avrohom Maimon, and Rebbetzin Tzipporah Heller, תחי׳.

Mrs. Shaindy Appelbaum was the editorial coordinator of this *sefer.* More than anyone, she pulled this project together and made it happen.

The role she played in the publication of this *sefer* was so important and vital it is inconceivable that we could have done it without her.

Rabbi Yehuda Samet and **Rebbetzin Yehudis Samet** reviewed the manuscript and offered meaningful advice, as did several other *talmidei chachamim* in Jerusalem.

Rabbi Nosson Scherman and **Rabbi Meir Zlotowitz**, General Editors of ArtScroll/Mesorah, are responsible for giving thousands of English-speaking people the opportunity to learn from the Chofetz Chaim's *sefarim*. A special thanks to **Rabbi Avrohom Biderman** who has been a crucial link in producing this *sefer*, and to the typesetting/graphics department at ArtScroll.

Our thanks to Rabbi Nisson Wolpin for his advice and editorial expertise; **Gary Sternberg** for design work; **Ms. Chaya Richmond**, for typing the original manuscript of the Laws section; the **office staff of Yeshivah Aish HaTorah** in Jerusalem, for their efforts sending and processing faxes; and the **office staff of Camp Agudah** in upstate New York for all their help during the final hectic weeks before publication.

Rabbi Yissocher Frand and **Rabbi Paysach Krohn** deserve a great debt of gratitude. We have all been inspired by their words regarding *Shmiras HaLoshon* during the last six years.

If you have participated in a *Shmiras HaLoshon* event over the last few years it is because of the selfless dedication of our superb coordinators and office staff: **Raizy Friedman, Sorelle Gelber, Ita Grinblat, Adrienne Hafif, Esther Klein, Shaindy Nussencweig, Judy Oelbaum, Tova Rokowsky, Chaya Suri Rawicki, Chavi Twersky** and many others.

Others that have played an important role in our organization are **Shmuel Borger, Yehuda Bunker, Chaim Shmuel Friedman, Mordechai Golding, Baila Jacobs, Joelle Silverman, Zalman** and **Chani Umlas,** and **Kalman Zeines.**

Our organization's success is due to friends across the United States who have brought our programs to their *shul*, school or community. To our chapter members, the *Rabbanim*, principals, and lay people who have lifted the banner of *Shmiras HaLoshon*, thank you so much.

To all of the above as well as those who have supported us financially — the major supporters who wish to remain anonymous, the families who have helped bring this book to publication by sponsoring a day, our *Agudas Hashomrim* members and the many others that have supported us, may the great *zechus* of *Shmiras HaLoshon* stand by you, your families and all of *Klal Yisrael*.

The Chofetz Chaim Heritage Foundation

❧ An Overview /
The Beauty of Shmiras HaLoshon

This is not a book about your tongue.

It is a book about your essence — the person Hashem created you to be. The Torah's laws of speech, whose observance is capsulized by the timeless term *Shmiras HaLoshon,* constitute G-d's plan for how people should live with each other. They are the tools that the Torah has given us to remove anger, bitterness and jealousy from our hearts, and to eliminate strife, hurt and divisiveness from the Jewish people.

The Torah's laws of speech, whose observance is capsulized by the timeless term Shmiras HaLoshon, constitute G-d's plan for how people should live with each other.

When we examine the workings of our words, we come to see that they, more than any other human capacity, define us. What we say and how we say it is who we are. Angry, hurtful words define an angry, hurtful person. Kind, considerate words define a kind, considerate person.

This can be seen by considering the unique nature of the tongue: it is partly hidden and partly revealed. It is usually not seen, but it is heard. *Maharal* concludes that Hashem designed the tongue to reflect its function, which is to reveal the hidden self — one's thoughts, ideas and personality. The tongue takes these hidden elements from within the person and, through words, brings them into the open.

The laws of proper speech are Hashem's specific, practical directives for how to use this defining capacity. They teach us how to look at people, speak to people, and speak about people. They reflect the Torah's wisdom, which sees the impact and ripple effect of every negative interaction. The Torah understands that at the core of virtually every broken friendship, shattered career or divorce is a seed of

The laws of proper speech are Hashem's specific, practical directives for how to use this defining capacity. They teach us how to look at people, speak to people, and speak about people.

hatred, a seed usually planted by a hurtful word. The Torah's laws reflect Hashem's knowledge that much of the pain and anguish of life can be averted by restraining ourselves from sowing these seeds.

It is actually a simple principle: If one removes negativity, gossip, slander and divisiveness from one's vocabulary, one automatically and dramatically improves one's own life and the lives of everyone in one's environment.[1]

If one removes negativity, gossip, slander and divisiveness from one's vocabulary, one automatically and dramatically improves one's own life and the lives of everyone in one's environment.

Right here in this world, in everyday life, the rewards of *Shmiras HaLoshon* shine brightly enough for anyone to see. When King David wrote,"Who is the man who desires life?" he was speaking of the beauty and peace *Shmiras HaLoshon* imprints upon life in this world.

To understand why the Torah focuses so intently on speech, one need take only a cursory look at how words act upon the world. One person can enter a room, speak a few angry words, and quickly set everyone around him on edge. A few careless words between friends can be all that's needed to forever alter the tenor of their relationship. One derogatory word, which labels another person as slow, sloppy or spoiled, can make that perception true in the minds of all who hear it.

Words of encouragement can dispel despair, even for someone in a terribly difficult situation.

Or, words can effect miracles. Words of encouragement can dispel despair, even for someone in a terribly difficult situation. Words have the power to take what is ordinary and make it holy. They turn a glass of wine into *kiddush,* a loaf of bread into an offering, a man and woman into a couple united through the sanctity of Jewish marriage.

---

1. There are times when *loshon hara* is permitted or even required, i.e, when warning a person about potential harm, for example a potential business or marriage partner. On the other hand, secondhand information and baseless impressions have momentous implications. The questions of when you are allowed or even required to speak *loshon hora* are complicated. A rabbinic authority with expertise in the field of *Shmiras HaLoshon* should be consulted in any of these cases.

But more than anything, words are the sole medium through which the Jew fulfills the purpose for which he was created — to communicate Hashem's greatness and presence in this world.

The Torah teaches us that the words we choose determine how we experience our lives. By taking hold of our power of speech, we take hold of life itself. But Hashem does not simply hand us this tremendous power and leave us to discover how it works. He gives us detailed instructions, in the form of the laws of *Shmiras HaLoshon*. More than a body of *halachah*, *Shmiras HaLoshon* is G-d's human relations training program that teaches us how to interact with others in the best possible way. One who follows it faithfully immediately perceives the work of Divine intelligence, reflecting Hashem's perfect understanding of human nature.

Take Hold of Life

Shmiras HaLoshon is G-d's human relations training program that teaches us how to interract with others in the best possible way.

Although most Jews are generally aware of the Torah's prohibitions against *loshon hora*, this devastating force has somehow glided through the centuries disguised as a relatively harmless aspect of human nature. But the toxicity of *loshon hora* isn't hard to grasp. One need only examine the aspects of human nature that fuel it: arrogance, anger, jealousy, a critical attitude and a negative outlook. That is the formula that energizes *loshon hora* and sets it flying.

Conversely, when one follows kind, gentle words back to their source, one finds them embedded in the most wholesome aspects of man's personality: humility, a willingness to avoid disputes, recognition of Hashem's image in others, a focus on the good, and *ahavas Yisrael*, love of one's fellow Jew.

And that is why *Chovos HaLevavos* says that, "The

Inside Loshon Hora

When one follows kind, gentle words back to their source, one finds them embedded in the most wholesome aspects of man's personality.

A mouth that spews venom can only be the outlet of a heart that produces it.

mouth is the quill of the heart." The mouth expresses the contents of the heart. A mouth that spews venom can only be the outlet of a heart that produces it.

The Torah hones in on this tightly intertwined bond between the words and the heart, directing every Jew to work to replace the dark with the light, the low with the lofty.

> *"Which man desires life (hechofetz chaim) who loves days to see good? Guard your tongue from evil" (Tehillim 34:13)."*

To See Good

Why did King David add the words,"to see good" in his famous verse on *Shmiras HaLoshon*? The answer is that seeing good, seeing the good in others and in life, is the engine that drives *Shmiras HaLoshon.*

"To see good" is the goal. But the Torah does not leave it at that. It paves the road to that goal with practical steps, which are the laws of proper speech. By practicing these laws, every Jew becomes trained to see the good in others.

Getting There

The Chofetz Chaim says that when one observes the laws of *Shmiras HaLoshon*, one inevitably evolves into a better person. That is because in every interaction, one is focused on not causing others pain. Time after time, day after day, the person who is careful with speech calls that imperative into play. It informs his decisions about what he says and what he thinks. Eventually, it becomes who he is.

> *"For Hashem loves His people, and the stronger one loves G-d's people, the stronger is G-d's love for him (cf. Mesilas Yesharim 19)."*

G-d explicitly directs His people to love each other, to cultivate in themselves a bond with all of *Klal Yisrael*. So fundamental is the requirement, that He conditions His own love upon it. Hashem concerns Himself not only with how the Jewish people serve Him, but also how they serve and support each other. In fact, a Jew cannot consider himself a true servant of G-d if he is not also a lover of people.

The Binding Thread

Each Jew is integral to the whole and no one is expendable. *Chazal* illustrate this point in a discussion of the incense that was burned as an offering in the *Beis HaMikdash*. Hashem instructed the *Kohanim* to prepare it from a blend of spices. All of these spices were fragrant except for one, which had a pungent, unpleasant aroma. But if the incense were prepared without all of its ingredients, including the malodorous one, it was unusable.

Like the incense, *Klal Yisrael* must also come to Hashem as a whole, a blend of all its ingredients. That is G-d's prerequisite for a relationship with His people. And through the laws of Torah, He provides each Jew with the means of cultivating this sense of love and unity. From that stream of *ahavas Yisrael*, the laws of *Shmiras HaLoshon* flow.

Like the incense, Klal Yisrael must also come to Hashem as a whole, a blend of all its ingredients.

"The nation which I created for Myself, My praises it should recite (Yeshayahu 43:21)."

Hashem created the Jewish people so that it would sing His praises through prayer, Torah study and other *mitzvos*. The mouth is the primary instrument by which this purpose is fulfilled. The mouth, therefore, defines the Jew.

The Essence of Speech

"Whoever guards his mouth, his mouth becomes like a vessel of the Holy Temple."

Used for the purposes Hashem intended, the mouth attains the status of a holy object. Like a *kli shoreis*, a vessel of the *Beis HaMikdash,* which enabled the sacrifices to make their journey from earth to Heaven, the mouth enables words of prayer and learning to ascend. But it possesses even more power than that, because it is also the means by which man is able to draw the holiness of Heaven down to earth. A loaf of bread becomes sanctified through the utterance of a ten-word blessing. The pronouncement of 121 words constitutes the key part of creating a holy bond of marriage between a man and woman. With 54 words, a glass of wine is elevated to the status of *kiddush*. Through the mouth, each Jew has been given the power to imbue his world with holiness.

The mouth is the means by which man is able to draw the holiness of Heaven down to earth.

However, like a *kli shoreis*, the mouth can become impure and thus unfit to fulfill its function. Were one to place an unkosher offering in a *kli shoreis* of the *Beis HaMikdash,* the *kli shoreis* would be defiled. It would be rendered useless as an instrument for serving Hashem. In exactly the same way, when one uses his mouth to speak the forbidden words of *loshon hora*, it, too, becomes defiled. That is why *loshon hora* incapacitates the Jew, rendering him unable to effectively produce the words of prayer and learning for which he was created.

Loshon hora incapacitates the Jew.

A Bridge Between Heaven and Earth

Humans are made of earth. Any human body can be reduced to a small pile of the earth's minerals and elements. Yet, this seemingly insignificant entity has an exalted function — it acts as a vessel for the *neshamah* (soul), the Heavenly spark with which G-d imbued man. The mouth is the intersection of this physical and spiritual essence. It ushers man's G-dly essence into the physical world in the form of the words it speaks. The ability to speak is a bridge between the physical, earth-bound human and the spiritual being. It provides man with the capacity to activate his spiritual self.

When Hashem took the dust of the earth, formed man, and breathed into him a G-dly soul, He created a unique creature containing within himself both the spiritual and the physical. It is that duality that endows man with free will. Were he bound strictly by the physical world, he would have no more free choice than the animals. Were he connected solely to the spiritual world, he would have no more free choice than the angels. Because man lives in both worlds, he has the ability to make choices. It follows then that the mouth, where these two worlds intersect, is where free will is most clearly evident.

When one chooses to use his power of speech unwisely, the choice he is really making is not simply between speaking *loshon hora* or exercising restraint. It is between exercising his G-dly self or his earthly self. His own relationship to himself is altered by the choice. If he chooses incorrectly, he declares himself unfit for his highest purpose and has altered his own essence. He has become like a chair with no seat, a cup with no bottom — a utensil unable to do what it was created to do.

When one chooses to use his power of speech unwisely, the choice he is really making is not simply between speaking loshon hora or exercising restraint. It is between exercising his G-dly self or his earthly self.

Redefining Reality

Speech also has another awesome power, and that is to literally redefine reality. Thoughts exist in a separate, private sphere. Once articulated, the thought is no longer a private matter. It becomes an item on the world's agenda — something to be agreed with or argued; proven or disproven; attended to or ignored.

A person may work side by side with someone for years, and during the entire time harbor the thought that the colleague is "annoying." For all those years, the thought has no power to affect anything or anyone beyond the person thinking it. Then, one day, this person enters into a conversation with a third co-worker, and offers his assessment of the other man as "annoying." The instant that thought is released into the world, it sets out on a path of destruction. Now another person's attention has been drawn to this man's allegedly "annoying" mannerisms. He loses a little respect for him, identifies him as a little less competent, a little less appealing.

Inevitably, this new assessment affects their relationship. It creates a bias in the third person's mind which he will now confirm every time the "annoying" person does or says anything. And it may go much further. This third person may well share his new-found perception with others, thereby altering their perceptions as well. It is not even necessary that they believe what they hear. Even if they never seriously think about the statement, it seeps into the subconscious and colors their future assessments of this person's behavior. The situation could easily evolve into one in which the colleague tagged as "annoying" feels inexplicably distanced from others. His livelihood, his self-esteem, even his outlook on life could suffer from the voicing of that one word, "annoying."

Even if they never seriously think about the statement, it seeps into the subconscious and colors their future assessments of this person's behavior.

Words are the seal. Like the seal with which Hashem finalizes His judgments on Yom Kippur, words give finality to the thoughts and judgments they are expressing. Once spoken, the judgment stands.

"Whoever speaks loshon hora raises his sins to the Heavens" (Arachin 15b).

"No word is lost, for all is recorded. Angels are sent to every person to note each and every word, and they never part from him. 'For the bird of the sky transmits the voice and the accompanying angel testifies.' (Koheles 1:20)... (Excerpts from a letter by the Vilna Gaon)

O ne's words have a profound impact in Heaven as well, because our Sages state that the words spoken here on earth are the tools through which an accusation is lodged before the Heavenly Court.

Satan, the Heavenly Prosecutor, is always ready with his accusation, but he needs a second witness to set the judicial process in motion. Hashem has granted each Jew the power to act as a witness and thus take part in opening a case against another Jew. *Loshon hora* has the drastic effect of turning oneself into Satan's corroborating witness. The speaker of *loshon hora* feeds Satan what he needs to begin prosecution. In fact, the *Zohar* states that the very words which Satan uses in making his accusation are the words that one Jew has spoken against another. Speaking *loshon hora*, therefore, not only opens the case against a fellow Jew, but literally puts accusatory words into Satan's mouth.

Loshon hora has the drastic effect of turning oneself into Satan's corroborating witness. The speaker of loshon hora feeds Satan what he needs to begin prosecution.

Hashem has granted Satan yet further prosecutorial power. Once he has met the requirements for opening one case, he has the floor. From there, he is able to conduct a free-ranging trial of the past deeds of the accused, the speaker of *loshon hora*, and the listener as well.

That is because the Heavenly Court functions on the principle of *midah k'neged midah* (measure for measure), a perfect form of justice. This justice system dictates that what the speaker of *loshon hora* has caused for another Jew comes back to him in equal measure. Because he has created a prosecution against another Jew, he too is prosecuted. And because he judged another harshly, he too is subject to harsh judgment. Thus, every time a Jew casually passes judgment on another Jew — once, twice, 20 times a day — he takes the fateful step of summoning himself to Court to be judged for his deeds.

This justice system dictates that what the speaker of loshon hora has caused for another Jew comes back to him in equal measure.

The listener is the third defendant placed in jeopardy by this one act of *loshon hora*. Because he has listened to *loshon hora*, to accusations against another Jew, Hashem agrees to listen to accusations against him, measure for measure.

"Judge your fellow man favorably" (Avos 1:6).

Heavenly justice is harsh for one who has judged harshly. For one who trains himself in compassion and understanding, *midah k'neged midah* wields tremendous positive power. *Shelah* states that for judging favorably one earns for himself a magnificent portion in the World to Come.

Most people, with rare exceptions, are more than willing to view their own shortcomings as excusable. Hashem asks that Jews do this for each other, too. The Torah teaches that if one sees a fellow Jew apparently transgressing, he must find excuses for him — he didn't understand the seriousness of what he was doing; he was unaware that it was wrong; the temptation was irresistible.

By judging each Jew favorably, one deprives *loshon hora* of a place to take root. Negative judgments are the fertile soil in which all *loshon hora* grows. Without them, there are no negative thoughts to articulate. Therefore, there's no need to restrain one's tongue.

And, because of midah k'neged midah, the person who judges favorably finds favorable judgment for himself in Heaven. By viewing others with compassion, he earns Hashem's compassion.

And, because of *midah k'neged midah,* the person who judges favorably finds favorable judgment for himself in Heaven. By viewing others with compassion, he earns Hashem's compassion. By defending those who are being maligned, he creates defenders for himself in Heaven. By refraining from *loshon hora*, he keeps his own case out of the Heavenly Court, removed from strict justice. Instead, he is judged by Hashem as a father judges a child, with love, mercy and understanding (see *Shabbos* 151b).[1]

1.Note: The principle of *dan l'kaf zechus* does not restrain one from taking action in situations in which clear harm or wrong is being done, as in cases of abuse. The Torah absolutely prohibits a Jew from standing by while others are being endangered and requires that one take constructive action to prevent harm from occurring or continuing.

Words: A Study in Contrasts

Loshon hora is a weapon manufactured solely from words, yet the Torah considers the harm those words create to be massive. So sharp a wedge does loshon hora drive between a Jew and Hashem that it even deprives him of Divine assistance in a time of need. And the sheer number of Torah directives relating to speech has no direct parallel in any other function.

Words Move Worlds

Obviously, loshon hora must be doing more harm, on a far grander scale, than the average person can readily perceive. Because people speak many times a day, every day of their lives, and most of what's said appears to create no discernible consequences, it becomes easy to perceive speech as a relatively benign force.

Words of loshon hora do more harm, on a far grander scale, than the average person can readily perceive.

> "At the time of the [destruction of the] second Beis HaMikdash the people toiled in Torah, performed mitzvos and acts of kindness, [yet the Beis HaMikdash] was destroyed because of baseless hatred." (Yoma 9b).

Loshon hora destroyed the Beis HaMikdash and keeps it in ruins today. The Beis HaMikdash was the Shechinah's dwelling place among Hashem's chosen people. The Jews at the time of the Second Beis HaMikdash were learned and fervently devoted to Hashem, and yet, because of divisiveness among His people, Hashem allowed His house to be destroyed. The reason for this national disaster, whose effects we still suffer, is sinas chinam, baseless hatred, which has its expression in loshon hora.

Loshon hora destroyed the Beis HaMikdash and keeps it in ruins today.

Maharal explains that a common thread running through every kind of loshon hora is its capacity to cause division and separation. This factor stands in stark opposition to the goal of the Jew, which is to achieve unity between the Jewish people and Hashem Himself, Who is "One and there is no Oneness like Him in any way" (from the Thirteen Principles of Faith).

The mitzvah of Shmiras HaLoshon is an expression of the unity of the Jewish people.

The *mitzvah* of **Shmiras HaLoshon** is an expression of the unity of the Jewish people. Seeing the good in others stems from seeing their common bond as Jews created in Hashem's image. Being sensitive to the feelings of others arises from recognizing each Jew as a part of oneself.

Our Sages state that taking on the observance of this *mitzvah* and strengthening it throughout *Klal Yisrael* is the most effective means of laying the foundation of a new *Beis HaMikdash*.

> ...What more is there to say about this sin (loshon hora) which is the severest of all sins? Man's ultimate task is not to sin with his mouth. The Sages say that one's good deeds and Torah knowledge cannot offset the damage that one does with speech ... (Excerpts from a letter by the Vilna Gaon).

> "Just as the learning of Torah equals all other mitzvos combined, so does speaking loshon hora equal all sins combined" (Yerushalmi Peah 1:1).

Words can unravel one's Torah and mitzvos

Loshon **hora** engenders an almost limitless quantity of sins. Each word of such conversation is a sin of its own.[1] Each carries the full weight of the transgression of *loshon hora*, setting into motion all of its destructive power. Thus, just one conversation can produce hundreds of sins.

> "There are those who acquire wealth but in truth have nothing" (Proverbs 13:7).

_____

1.See *Chovas HaShmirah* (by the Chofetz Chaim), ch.1 paragraph 3 and ch.3 paragraph 4.

Weighed down by these sins, the speaker of *loshon hora* enters the World to Come with an even greater deficit, because his words have erased so much of his *mitzvos* and learning that would otherwise stand as a precious merit. The Chofetz Chaim explains the above verse from *Proverbs* as an illustration of this point. It speaks of a man who has devoted his 120 years on earth to Torah and *mitzvos,* building a vast reserve of wealth for the next World. But when he reaches his destination, and his accounts are considered, he discovers that actually he has nothing at all. Because of the *loshon hora* he had spoken, his merit had evaporated without a trace. After a lifetime of labor, he arrives in eternity empty-handed.

Not only does *loshon hora* deprive a Jew of the fruits of his labors in Torah, it actually causes those *mitzvos* to be exchanged for sins. *Chovos HaLevavos* describes the process: If someone is learned and distinguished, and has achieved status in the community whereby his words carry weight, his speaking *loshon hora* will deprive him of all the *mitzvos* he has done to reach his position. Because the position has been used to do harm, the *mitzvos* that got him there will no longer be his. Instead, they will accrue to the person his words have harmed. This is the victim's compensation for the pain, loss of face, or financial loss that the speaker of *loshon hora* has caused him. In effect, the speaker's *mitzvos* have been transferred to his victim. And in their place are the many transgressions involved in the one sin of *loshon hora.*

> *"For every moment one guards one's tongue, he earns reward that is beyond the comprehension of angels" (Vilna Gaon citing Midrash)."*

> *...The principle way of meriting the World to*

Come is through guarding one's mouth, which is greater than Torah learning and mitzvos because the mouth is the Holy of Holies..." *(Excerpts from a letter by the Vilna Gaon).*

Shmiras HaLoshon builds a beautiful, radiant share in the World to Come, the reward for each moment of restraining one's mouth from speaking *loshon hora*. Were every Jew able to preview the reward that comes to those who restrain their tongues, the resolve to refrain from speaking *loshon hora* would be unshakable. In his works, the Chofetz Chaim refers repeatedly to the Sages' statement, that Hashem's Divine light, hidden away from the time of creation and reserved only for *tzaddikim,* is rewarded to one who turns aside from the temptation to speak *loshon hora*. Every time he is tempted but exercises restraint, he merits this reward.

Were every Jew able to preview the reward that comes to those who restrain their tongues, the resolve to refrain from speaking loshon hora would be unshakable.

This light, explains the Chofetz Chaim, is Hashem's radiance, whose beauty is incomprehensible even to angels. For one whose eye is on Heaven, the possibility of meriting this light is the only incentive needed to try, at every moment, to guard one's tongue.

When one guards his speech and engages others in conversations that are positive and constructive, the merit of *Shmiras HaLoshon* is multiplied many times because, by exercising restraint in speech, one draws others to this *mitzvah* as well.

The View from Within: How Words Affect Our Lives

The same words that sweep through the Heavens are also capable of penetrating the deepest levels of man. Even in the most seemingly meaningless chatter, the words that pass between people work powerful changes on them and within them. What a person says, what he hears and what others say about him can surely change the course of his life, and even alter his substance.

To see this at work, one must zoom in closely and watch. Like the time-lapse photography that shows a flower blooming, the activity of words in our world is indiscernible from minute to minute, but shows up with startling clarity when viewed over time.

Loshon hora diminishes its victim in the eyes of others. That could mean a lost job or business opportunity, a wounded or ruined marriage, a feud among friends or neighbors, a devalued reputation. Once spoken, the words carve their own path, destroying in ways the speaker can never predict.

Words have a profound affect on others.

As damaging as *loshon hora* can be to the external factors of another person's life, it has the even more disastrous potential for demolishing a person's interior landscape. The self-image is a malleable entity. People pick up clues as to their own worth through the way others treat them. If they receive honor, they feel honorable. If they are ignored, they feel invisible. That is why, when *loshon hora* reaches back to its subject, the harm it does is so severe.

The self-image is a malleable entity. People pick up clues as to their own worth through the way others treat them.

For the disparaging words to reach back to the subject, it isn't necessary that there be a direct report of what was said and who said it. It can become obvious in an indirect way, by the changed manner in which others treat him. Either way, his vision of himself is altered. Another Jew has essentially reached inside this person and robbed him of some aspect of his self-image. Something inside him is gone.

Shmiras HaLoshon increases the level of mutual respect among one's friends, family and co-workers. By focusing on the good in others, one illuminates it and highlights it for everyone to see.

Shmiras HaLoshon increases the level of mutual respect among one's friends, family and co-workers.

Moreover, the same wit and insight that can be used to critique another person and violate his sense of self can also serve the purpose of building it, reflecting back to him the best Hashem has placed within him.

Words are a barometer of ego

Loshon hora reflects the belief that everyone and everything should conform to one's own standard. It arises out of an intolerance of differences between oneself and others — someone else's customs as opposed to one's own, someone else's opinion as opposed to one's own, someone else's financial approach as opposed to one's own. The underlying basis for focusing on these differences is the sense that one's own way is the right way.

It is the egocentric need to assert the superiority of one's own way of doing things, which is, at its heart, a denial of the uniqueness with which Hashem has endowed each human being. That is the mechanics of *loshon hora.*

> *"Just as people's faces don't resemble each other, so too their thought processes don't resemble each other" (Bamidbar Rabbah 21:2).*

Shmiras HaLoshon is the prism through which one can see the validity in the various paths and opinions among well-meaning people. Even without agreeing or seeing the value of someone else's way of thinking, one can accept it as valid. The *Beis Yisrael,* Rabbi Yisrael Alter of Ger, commented on the *Words imbue children with their understanding of the world.* above Aggadic teaching, saying that one should accept differences in thought as readily as he accepts differences in appearance.

Loshon hora bequeaths to one's children a discontented attitude toward life. Through their parents' example, they learn to become critical and cynical, a lesson that will color every relationship in their lives. And they become inclined toward *loshon hora*, a habit which will cripple their efforts to live as Torah Jews.

Shmiras HaLoshon instills in children confidence in the fundamental goodness of the world and other people. They learn to judge others favorably, forming a habit that enhances every relationship in their lives. And they develop the character traits that will equip them for their lifetime endeavor of serving Hashem.

Loshon hora coarsens the speaker. Without looking any further into *loshon hora's* destructive power, the Torah proscribes it for one overriding, basic reason. Demeaning others is self-demeaning. It is a lowly activity that coarsens the character and has no place among the traits of a Jew. As Hashem's people, Jews are held to a higher standard of behavior that simply doesn't allow for an act as unrefined as "peddling" derogatory information about another person.

Words define one's relationship to oneself.

Moreover, *loshon hora* breeds unhappiness in the speaker. The momentary gratification of engaging in gossip is far outweighed by the damage *loshon hora* does to one's perception of the world. A speaker of *loshon hora* trains himself in bitterness and complaining. In his eyes, he is surrounded by irritating, inconsiderate, flawed people who make his world a disappointing, uncomfortable place. He makes it his habit to look past the G-dly image of his fellow Jew, and gaze intently at his every flaw. His perceptions fill his heart with anger and disdain, and his mouth gives form and life to those feelings.

Further damage, on a much deeper level, accrues to the speaker of *loshon hora*. That is because his words, and the sense of power they confer upon him, foil the soul's constant striving to rise toward its Source. By pushing others down, *loshon hora* provides one with the illusion of becoming more elevated.

The speaker of *loshon hora* is motivated by this very powerful human need to feel important. So, he sets himself up as the other person's superior by standing in judgment. "The other person is bad. Therefore, I am better. Her children are rude, therefore mine are polite. His business is mismanaged, therefore mine is well run." Instead of striving honestly to lift himself, the speaker of *loshon hora* attains his height by looking down upon those he has cast to the ground.

Shmiras HaLoshon refines the speaker and brings into full bloom the traits with which Hashem has endowed Klal Yisrael — kindness, compassion and mercy.

Shmiras HaLoshon refines the speaker and brings into full bloom the traits with which Hashem has endowed *Klal Yisrael* — kindness, compassion and mercy.

And, these laws bring lasting happiness to those who embrace them. They are the palette from which a joyful, appreciative view of the world is painted. Through these laws, one trains oneself to focus on the good that, by definition, characterizes every aspect of Hashem's creation.

One who adheres to the laws of *Shmiras HaLoshon* elevates himself in a real way, even while he elevates all those around him. By seeing the good, he moves in harmony with his *neshamah* onto ever higher planes.

In place of the illusory power conferred by becoming the source of gossip, the person who guards his speech builds real power. This is the power of self-discipline, the knowledge that one has control over his impulses, that he has the inner strength to restrain himself, measure his words and act in accordance with the highest aspects of himself.

Words determine how others see us.

Loshon hora lowers one's standing with family and friends. People who feel they gain acceptance by being the one who knows the inside information are observing a short-term phenomenon. In any situation, there are likely to be people present who are interested in hearing *loshon hora*. The speaker will, indeed, capture their attention with his report. However, the Chofetz Chaim tells us that every person who hears this *loshon hora* will have formed an opinion of the speaker as someone not to be trusted. Everyone senses that a person who will talk about one friend will talk about others. In the end, people become more guarded and distant from the speaker of *loshon hora*. The closeness he feels is a false one, based on momentary interest in his words.

Everyone senses that a person who will talk about one friend will talk about others.

Shmiras HaLoshon creates a greater sense of closeness and trust with one's friends and neighbors. Without *loshon hora*, without *onaas devarim* (causing hurt through the spoken word), without creating enemies and derogating others, there is still much to be said. The words that remain are those that can be spoken gently, that relate positive judgments and cement the bonds among friends.

Loshon Hora obscures the Divine image in another person. When one person hears *loshon hora* about another, his vision of that person is instantly altered. He now knows something about that person that reduces his estimation of him. The effect may be totally subconscious, but it is real and immediate. The listener's capacity to see the Divine light in another Jew has been damaged.

Words reveal or obscure the Divine image in man.

Shmiras HaLoshon turns each Jew into an instrument for revealing the Divine image in others, and in himself. In a very real way, he augments the Divine light present in this world, heightening its level of sanctity and bringing it closer to perfection.

Loshon Hora: A Well-Stocked Arsenal

In its broader sense, the term *"loshon hora"* refers to four destructive forms of speech. In this verbal arsenal, each weapon inflicts harm in its own way, but all use the same ammunition — the words we speak about each other and to each other.

In its narrower sense, *loshon hora* refers specifically to derogatory or harmful speech which is related to a third party. When Neighbor A says to Neighbor B, "Neighbor C is such a cold, unfriendly person," A and B have engaged in *loshon hora* — A as the speaker, and B as the listener, who is also guilty of a second transgression if he believes A's statement.

Rechilus, the second form of *loshon hora*, literally means "peddling." One who engages in *rechilus* peddles a tale, informing one person of a negative statement that has been made about him by another person. Relating back to the example above, *rechilus* would occur if, after having their *loshon hora* conversation, Neighbor B went to Neighbor C and told him, "Neighbor A tells me that you're unfriendly toward him."

Rechilus, the second form of loshon hora, literally means "peddling."

The defining trait of *rechilus* is that it causes animosity between people. Neighbor C, who may never have harbored any ill feelings toward Neighbor A, has now been turned against him, and B's report is the sole reason for that change.

A third form of *loshon hora* is *motzi shem ra,* slander. While the first type of *loshon hora* applies to statements that are true, *motzi shem ra* refers to negative statements that are false. Among the three neighbors, *motzi shem ra* would occur if Neighbor A told Neighbor B something untrue about Neighbor C, for instance, that he never returns what he borrows, when in fact that isn't true.

The Torah looks upon this pain as a real wound, in complete opposition to the common belief that words cannot hurt

Onaas devarim, the fourth type of *loshon hora*, is defined as causing pain with words. The Torah looks upon this pain as a real wound, in complete opposition to the common belief that words cannot hurt. In the Torah's acute awareness of the power of words, it sees *onaas devarim* as every bit as real as, and in some ways more serious than, the physical or financial harm individuals can inflict upon each other.

In reality, many difficult situations arise in life. The need to reproach someone who is heading in the wrong direction, to correct a child, to instruct or perhaps even fire an employee, are all real needs to which one must attend. However, the prohibition against *onaas devarim* tells every Jew to use the softest possible approach to such situations, to use the kindest possible words and manner to convey the message.

Onaas devarim does not, however, always arise out of necessary situations. Often, it is simply the product of insensitivity, or the mistaken belief that opinions on such matters as physical appearance, a new purchase, a spouse, someone else's background or perceptions, and so forth, are open fields for frank discussion.

There are scores of sensitive subjects which, when approached in an insensitive way, can leave people feeling insecure, inept or somehow diminished. There are also scores of methods for conveying disdain. Such phrases as "I told you so," sarcastic jokes or comments, quotes and aphorisms that point out another's deficiency, even certain gestures and facial expressions, can all serve as weapons of *onaas devarim.*

The potential is there, for anyone who lacks a basic sensitivity, to cause pain in many everyday interactions, leaving a battlefield of emotional carnage in his wake.

B esides these forms of *loshon hora*, the Chofetz Chaim discusses other types of speech that a Jew must avoid. Words of anger, arrogance, deceit, lying and false flattery are all within this category. Each

Other Prohibited Speech

uses the gift of speech in a way that violates the sanctity of the mouth and distorts the character traits that define the Jewish people.

The Road to Peace and Unity

> *"Hashem said to Israel: 'My beloved children, what do I ask of you? Only that you love one another and respect one another"*
> *(Tana Dvei Eliyahu Rabbah ch. 28).*

Streng-
thening the
Bond

In addition to all the many compelling motivations mentioned above for observing the laws of *Shmiras HaLoshon,* there is still one more. Through *Shmiras HaLoshon*, every Jew can forge a deeper bond with G-d. The following allegory illustrates how:

There is a friend whose friendship you especially treasure. One day, in the course of a conversation, he reveals to you a secret, a piece of private information that he requests should go no further than your ears.

Later that day, you meet someone who is also close to your confidante. The first friend's name comes up, and you both speak with warmth and interest about your mutual acquaintance.

Your secret pops, like a temporarily submerged buoy, to the top of your consciousness. Here stands someone who would love to know this secret, an interesting piece of innocent, harmless news.

As the words form in your mouth, you face a choice. You can massage this relationship with the

At the moment
you choose loyalty
over gratification,
you strengthen
and deepen the
bond with your
friend, whose
secret you've pro-
tected.

balm of an interesting piece of information. Or you can keep faith with the first friend, who trusted you with his secret. At the moment you choose loyalty over gratification, you strengthen and deepen the bond with your friend, whose secret you've protected.

This describes the inner workings of *Shmiras HaLoshon*. When you see a fellow Jew doing something wrong, which is the trigger that sets off much *loshon hora*, G-d makes a request of you. He asks that later in the day, when you come across a mutual friend, you should keep the wrongdoing to yourself. Through the laws of *Shmiras HaLoshon*, He implores you, "Please, please don't repeat what you've seen."

There's no doubt that G-d knows the wrongdoing that has occurred; He sees the deeds of everyone. But because you also know, it is as if you and Hashem share a secret, a secret about one of Hashem's children. And like any loving father, Hashem does not want to hear people demeaning His children. So, through the laws of proper speech, He asks you not to spread this information, not to compromise His child's reputation. And at the moment you choose to keep His secret, at the moment you choose loyalty to Hashem over your own gratification, you have immeasurably enhanced and deepened your bond with G-d. That is *Shmiras HaLoshon*.

Our Sages have outlined in clear detail the great rewards that accrue to the person who guards his tongue. Not only does he self-actualize as a Jew, but he creates for himself a tremendous vehicle for bringing blessing into his life and good into his world.

The ultimate blessing

Every person seeks peace. Everyone wants a harmonious home, pleasant relations with friends and colleagues, and a calm, peaceful heart. Our Sages state that peace is the ultimate blessing, the container in which all other blessings are held. Nothing is whole, nothing is perfect unless it is accompanied by peace. That is why the *Shemoneh Esrei*, *Bircas Hamazon* and *Kaddish* all end with a prayer for peace.

Shmiras HaLoshon is the means Hashem has

"Seek peace and pursue it" (Tehillim 34:15).

given us with which to pursue peace with one another. When a Jew chooses to follow this path in dealings with his fellow man, he arrives at peace. Within his own heart, peace and contentment grow as well. Less negativity in his outlook and less strife with others automatically imbue his heart with tranquility.

Peace is the container in which all other blessings are held.

Kindness through Words

As effective as *Shmiras HaLoshon* is in bringing good into one's life, it is perhaps even more powerful as a means of bringing good to others. Every day, people produce thousands of words. Each of these words has the potential to become a vehicle of *chesed,* an act of kindness in and of itself. When one speaks to family, friends, even strangers, in a gentle, considerate way, one's words become conductors of tremendous positive power. They can alleviate loneliness, build self-confidence, uplift, encourage, instruct and advise.

Words can alleviate loneliness, build self-confidence, uplift, encourage, instruct and advise.

When greeting an acquaintance, words can make that person feel sincerely acknowledged. When asking a child, a spouse or a colleague to perform a task, the words and tone can make the individual feel needed and appreciated. When it becomes necessary to reproach someone, words can convey loving concern for his welfare. And when speaking to someone who is facing difficulties, words can make him feel understood and supported.

To use words to actively effect good in the world is to speak *loshon tov* (good or positive talk). It is a form of *chesed,* pure and simple. Like visiting the sick, feeding the hungry and clothing the poor, *loshon tov* is a means for emulating Hashem's kindness and compassion.

But this is a form of *chesed* which is virtually limitless. One needs no extra time or money to devote to it. It's a *mitzvah* that can be performed in almost every conversation, every day of one's life. Simply by becoming aware of the words and tone of voice one uses, by tuning in to the needs of the people to whom one speaks, a person can generate immeasurable good into this world.

By tuning in to the needs of the people to whom one speaks, a person can generate immeasurable good into this world.

O ur Sages state that the compassion a person shows in judging and speaking of others favorably arouses Heaven's compassion towards himself. That is why the Chofetz Chaim singles out *Shmiras HaLoshon* as the key for attaining Hashem's mercy, and recommends that every Jew put special focus on this *mitzvah* as Rosh Hashanah approaches.

"One who has compassion for others is granted Heavenly compassion" (Shabbos 151b).

It is Hashem's desire to shower His people with His limitless store of mercy. When people act compassionately by using their words for good, they allow Hashem's compassion to flow from its Source into their lives. *Shmiras HaLoshon* not only opens the gates of Heaven to one's prayers, it manifests Hashem's protection upon His beloved nation by drawing upon them a generous measure of His limitless mercy.

Shmiras HaLoshon opens the gates of Heaven to one's prayers.

Every effort one expends in learning about *Shmiras HaLoshon*, understanding this *mitzvah* and living in accordance with its laws, initiates a wellspring of Divine compassion and is an inestimable source of merit for a life of health, happiness and peace.

Prayer for *Siyata D'Shmaya* (Divine Assistance) in Matters of Speech

In his work *Chovas HaShmirah* (The Obligation of Guarding [one's tongue]), the Chofetz Chaim recommends that one recite a daily prayer for Divine assistance in fulfilling the requirements of proper speech. Noting that *Sifre* (*Devarim* 24:9) cites a Scriptural source for verbal remembrance of the prohibition against speaking *loshon hora*, the Chofetz Chaim comments that recital of this prayer is a form of remembrance, which in itself helps one maintain vigilance in *shmiras haloshon*.

The following prayer is drawn from the much lengthier prayer formulated by the Chofetz Chaim. It was prepared by the Manchester Rosh Yeshivah, Rav Yehudah Zev Segal, *zt"l*.

רִבּוֹנוֹ שֶׁל עוֹלָם, יְהִי רָצוֹן מִלְּפָנֶיךָ אֵל רַחוּם וְחַנּוּן שֶׁתְּזַכֵּנִי הַיּוֹם וּבְכָל יוֹם לִשְׁמוֹר פִּי וּלְשׁוֹנִי מִלָּשׁוֹן הָרָע וּרְכִילוּת. וְאֶזָּהֵר מִלְּדַבֵּר אֲפִילוּ עַל אִישׁ יָחִיד, וְכָל שֶׁכֵּן עַל כְּלַל יִשְׂרָאֵל אוֹ עַל חֵלֶק מֵהֶם, וְכָל שֶׁכֵּן מִלְּהִתְרַעֵם עַל מִדּוֹתָיו שֶׁל הַקָּדוֹשׁ בָּרוּךְ הוּא. וְאֶזָּהֵר מִלְּדַבֵּר דִּבְרֵי שֶׁקֶר, חֲנוּפָה, מַחֲלוֹקֶת, כַּעַס, גַּאֲוָה, אוֹנָאַת דְּבָרִים, הַלְבָּנַת פָּנִים, לֵצָנוּת, וְכָל דִּיבּוּר אָסוּר. וְזַכֵּנִי שֶׁלֹּא לְדַבֵּר כִּי אִם דָּבָר הַצָּרִיךְ לְעִנְיָנֵי גוּפִי וְנַפְשִׁי, וְיִהְיוּ כָל מַעֲשַׂי וְדִבּוּרַי לְשֵׁם שָׁמַיִם.

Master of the Universe, may it be Your will, Compassionate and Gracious God, that You grant me the merit today and every day to guard my mouth and tongue from [speaking] loshon hora and rechilus. And may I be zealous not to speak ill even of an individual, and certainly not of the entire Jewish people or a portion of it; and even more so, may I be zealous not to complain about the ways of the Holy One, Blessed is He. May I be zealous not to speak words of falsehood, flattery, strife, anger, arrogance, hurt, embarrassment, mockery, and all other forbidden forms of speech. Grant me the merit to speak only that which is necessary for my physical and spiritual well-being, and may all my deeds and words be for the sake of Heaven.

CHOFETZ CHAIM
A Lesson A Day

✍ *Loshon Hora: A Definition*

*L*oshon hora (lit., evil talk) is defined as information which is either derogatory[1] or potentially harmful[2] to another individual. A derogatory statement about someone is *loshon hora,* even if it will definitely not cause that person any harm.[3] To focus on the shortcomings of another person is in itself wrong.[4]

A statement that could potentially bring harm to someone — be it financial, physical, psychological or otherwise — is *loshon hora,* even if the information is not negative.[5]

(It should be noted that the term *loshon hora* refers even to true statements which are derogatory or harmful. Negative statements that are untrue or inaccurate are termed *hotzaas shem ra,* slander — see Day 31.)[6]

Footnotes for *Sefer Chofetz Chaim* section begin on page 416

Doing a mitzvah in this world causes a spiritual light to rest upon one's soul; it is from this light that the soul draws eternal vitality.

1 Tishrei · The Manchester Rosh Yeshiva הרב הצדיק הגאון נ"לע
יהודא זאב בן הגאון הצדיק הרב משה יצחק הלוי סג"ל זצוק"ל
Dedicated by מכירי טוב, London, England
1 Nissan · לע"נ מאיר בן אשר לייב מינץ
Dedicated by his family

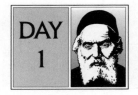

◢ Food for the Soul

*One who guards his mouth and tongue, guards his soul
from tribulations   (Mishlei 21:23).*

*Which man desires life, who loves days of seeing good?
Guard your tongue from evil and your lips from speaking deceit...   (Tehillim 34:13-14).*

Why do the above verses single out *shmiras haloshon*, guarding
one's tongue, as the key to a good life in both worlds?

The human body is composed of 248 organs and 365 sinews.
Corresponding to this are the 248 spiritual organs and 365 spiritual
sinews of the soul. As Scripture states: "You clothe me with skin and
flesh, cover me with bones and sinews" (*Iyov* 10:11). The various
parts of the body are referred to as "clothing" and "covering" for they
clothe and cover the soul within man. Each physical organ corresponds to a specific aspect of the soul.

Hashem has given us 248 positive commandments and 365 negative commandments which relate to the particular parts of the body
with which they are performed.[1] By performing a given *mitzvah*
through a given organ, a spiritual light comes to rest upon the corresponding component of the soul; it is from this light that this
component draws eternal vitality.

Thus, when a person fulfills all the Torah's commandments, he
transforms himself into an *adam hashaleim,* man of spiritual perfection, whose every fiber is sanctified unto Hashem.

The converse is true as well. If a person commits a transgression
and does not repent for it, then the component of the soul which
corresponds to that prohibition will suffer accordingly.

---

1. See opening introduction to *Sefer Chareidim.*

SEFER CHOFETZ CHAIM
LOSHON HORA: Laws of Derogatory Speech

✍ *Breach of Halachah*

It is forbidden to relate that someone has been remiss in matters of Jewish observance — be it a transgression prohibited by the Torah, a rabbinical prohibition, or even a breach of custom. Such statements are derogatory by the Torah's standards, and thus are forbidden.[7]

Therefore, it is forbidden to mention an incident in which one of the people involved transgressed a *halachah,* even in a society where that particular *halachah* is commonly ignored.

It is the power of speech which defines man's essence and distinguishes him from other creatures.

לע״נ מרים שרה גיטל בת ר׳ אליקום חנוך פייבוש ע״ה · 2 Tishrei
Dedicated by her children
לע״נ ר׳ נתן בן שמואל מאיר ע״ה Nussen Schon · 2 Nissan
Dedicated in loving memory of my uncle, by Nechy Freidmann

✍ *The Essential Quality*

It is every person's hope and prayer that he or she be healthy, that every organ of the body function as it should. Similarly, it should be every person's hope and yearning that his or her soul, which lives on eternally, be spiritually healthy. It is therefore imperative that one strive throughout his lifetime to faithfully observe all 613 *mitzvos*, which provide the components of the soul with eternal life and vitality.

Shmiras haloshon is especially crucial to one's spiritual well-being. People who habitually speak *loshon hora,* and accept as fact the evil talk of others, corrupt their power of speech and hearing on this world — and their souls will surely be affected in a parallel way in the next world. How great will be their shame in the next world! For it will be obvious to all that their deficiencies resulted from the sin of *loshon hora* and their having been the cause of strife on this world.

The Torah states: "And HASHEM (God) formed man from the dust of the ground, and He blew into his nostrils the soul of life, and man became a living being" (*Bereishis* 2:7). *Targum Onkelos* translates the verse's last phrase as, "and man became a speaking spirit." It is the power of speech which defines man's essence and distinguishes him from other creatures.

Thus does Scripture state: "One who guards his mouth and tongue, guards his soul from tribulations" (*Mishlei* 21:23). *Shmiras haloshon* is singled out because speech is man's essential quality. Impairment of this power deprives the soul of its essential quality in the next world and is the source of its ultimate tribulation.

David therefore declares, "Which man desires life, who loves days of seeing good? Guard your tongue from evil and your lips from speaking deceit..."

✑ Lack of Commitment

It is forbidden to say that an individual lacks commitment in fulfilling a particular commandment. Therefore, it is forbidden to say that a man sets aside little time for daily Torah study, or that he does not go out of his way to help others.

This would apply even if the speaker and listener themselves study little or are not known for their benevolence, and will openly admit to this without shame. Since the Torah commands us to make Torah study and *chesed* performance priorities in our lives, it is forbidden to say that someone else lacks dedication in these areas.[8]

It is Satan's desire that we speak loshon hora so that our prayers will be rejected Above.

לע"נ הבחור שלום דוד ע"ה בן 3 Tishrei · Sholom Weinraub
מרדכי זיסל יבל"ח
Dedicated by his parents, brothers and sisters
לע"נ אמי מורתי מירל בת משה ע"ה 3 Nissan · Mrs. Mina Willner
Dedicated by Rabbi & Mrs. Eric Willner, Brooklyn, NY

✍ *Purpose of This Volume*

There are many factors which can cause a person to speak *loshon hora.* The three primary factors are:

(1) A lack of awareness of what a Jew is and is not permitted to say. It is in response to this that we have compiled *Sefer Chofetz Chaim*, which is a code of laws of proper speech.

(2) Satan's powerful efforts in this area, as he seeks to indict us Above and to cause our prayers to be rejected (as stated in the holy *Zohar*, which will be cited in a forthcoming chapter).

(3) Ignorance of the methods through which one can succeed in avoiding the urge to gossip. As Scripture states, "For with strategies shall you wage war for yourself" (*Mishlei* 24:6).

It is in response to the second and third factors that we have authored this work *(Sefer Shmiras Haloshon)*, a compilation of Aggadic teachings from the Talmud, *Midrash* and the holy *Zohar*, which speak of the great reward, in this world and the next, for guarding one's tongue, and of the retribution that can result from the terrible sin of speaking *loshon hora.*

We have also labored, with the help of Hashem, to compile from the thoughts of our Sages many methods and suggestions for how to escape the snare of the sin of *loshon hora.* It is our hope that this will inspire and aid the reader to overcome his inclination to speak the forbidden, so that he can develop the precious, sterling quality of *shmiras haloshon.*

Because this present work contains many topics that are of vital interest, it is therefore exceedingly precious to me. Therefore, I have given it a title of its own,[1] *Shmiras Haloshon*, based upon the verse, שמר פיו ולשונו, שמר מצרות נפשו, *One who guards his mouth and tongue, guards his soul from tribulations* (*Mishlei* 21:23).

---

1. I.e. Though this compilation of Aggadic teachings and insights is actually another section of *Sefer Chofetz Chaim*, the author gave it a title of its own.

ד תשרי
4 TISHREI / CYCLE 1

ד ניסן
4 NISSAN / CYCLE 2

SEFER CHOFETZ CHAIM
LOSHON HORA: Laws of Derogatory Speech

❧ *Relative Statements*

Certain statements are *loshon hora* when said regarding one person, yet are perfectly acceptable when said regarding someone else. For example, to say that a businessman studies Torah five hours a day is obviously not derogatory. However, to say this of a *kollel* member who is assumed to be spending his entire day engrossed in Torah study would be derogatory. Similarly, it would be forbidden to relate the amount of *tzedakah* given by an individual, if that amount is considered respectable only for a man of lesser means.[9]

[There may be factors which would prohibit relating such information even when it is clearly complimentary. For example, people who give charity generously often do not want that fact to become public knowledge. See Day 34.]

If a person is not knowledgeable of the laws of a given prohibition, then no amount of mussar will help him.

4 Tishrei · Israel Kirshenbaum לע״נ ישראל זאב בן אליהו שמואל ע״ה
Dedicated by Rochie & Les Kirshenbaum and family
4 Nissan · Sandra Asch לע״נ שרה פייגל בת אברהם
Dedicated by Shimon & Miriam Apisdorf and family, Baltimore, MD

DAY 4

๑ *The Imperative of Halachic Study*

Knowledge of the Aggadic teachings regarding *loshon hora* must be complemented by study of the laws of proper speech. In the words of *Midrash Mishlei* (1:2): " 'To know wisdom and *mussar* [inspirational, ethical instruction]' (*Mishlei* 1:2) — If one has wisdom [i.e. knowledge of *halachah*] then he can study *mussar*, but if he lacks wisdom, then he cannot study *mussar*." The *Midrash's* intent is clear: If a person is not knowledgeable in the laws of a given topic, then no amount of *mussar* will help him.

For example: If a businessman thinks that a given practice is not robbery, [when, in fact, it is] then what good will it do to inform him of the severity of the sin of robbery? The same applies to all other negative commandments. Therefore, one must study the Torah's laws to know what is permitted and what is forbidden, and he must also learn the *mussar* teachings which inspire a person to fear Hashem. Through study of such teachings, one arouses his soul toward observance of Torah, aside from fulfilling the positive commandment, "Fear HASHEM, your God" (*Devarim* 10:20).

And so it is with regard to *shmiras haloshon.* Of what benefit will all the *mussar* in the world be, if one convinces himself that a given forbidden statement is not in the category of *loshon hora*?! Or, if he tells himself that the laws of *loshon hora* do not apply when speaking of a certain individual [when, in fact, they do]?!

Therefore, it is imperative that one know what is and what is not in the category of *loshon hora* according to *halachah.* This study should be complemented by inspirational study of the relevant Aggadic teachings.

ה תשרי
5 TISHREI / CYCLE 1

ה ניסן
5 NISSAN / CYCLE 2

SEFER CHOFETZ CHAIM
LOSHON HORA: Laws of Derogatory Speech

ஐ *Character*

It is forbidden to say that someone possesses a negative character trait. For example, it is forbidden to say that an individual is quick-tempered, argumentative, stingy, arrogant, etc.[10]

To say that someone is of *bad* character is forbidden as it is a derogatory statement. However, to indicate that someone is of *average* character (for example, that he does not overlook the wrong done to him) — while not complimentary — is also not derogatory and may be permissible.[11] In common situations where the term "average" has negative connotations, such a statement would also constitute *loshon hora.*

On the basis of the principle of relative statements discussed in Day 4, the claim that a person known for his piety is, in actuality, no better than average, is certainly *loshon hora.*[12]

The quality of shmiras haloshon is within everyone's reach.

יהושע אליעזר בן ברכה לרפואה שלמה · 5 Tishrei
לע"נ יחיאל בן מנדל ע"ה · 5 Nissan
Dedicated by his wife and children

DAY 5

❧ *Claims and Counter-Claims*

> *R' Yochanan ben Dehavai said: Do not distance your-*
> *self from a quality that is without limit and from a labor*
> *that is without end.*
>
> *To what can this be compared? To someone who took*
> *water from the ocean and cast it onto dry land. The*
> *ocean did not appear any less full and the land did not*
> *become filled [with water]. The man grew frustrated. His*
> *employer said: "Foolish one! Why are you upset? Each*
> *day you will receive a gold coin for your work."*
>
> *(Avos D'R' Nosson 27:3).*

The "quality" to which the sage refers is *shmiras haloshon*. The evil inclination seeks to discourage us from striving to develop this quality, by way of the following argument: "What benefit will you have from studying the laws and concepts of proper speech? Are you really capable of guarding your tongue all your life? Try to avoid speaking *loshon hora* for even a day or two! And do you really think that you can avoid *everything* that one is forbidden to speak? Why, you are a man of the world, you have dealings with scores of people!

"Don't even attempt to acquire this quality — it simply cannot be done. Guarding one's tongue requires constant vigilance. It is relevant countless times a day, every day of a person's life, and it applies to virtually every situation that can occur between man and his fellow."

R' Yochanan ben Dehavai teaches us that this is simply not true. One should *not* distance himself from this quality which, indeed, is "without limit,"[1] as we shall explain.

---

1. "A labor without end" of which the passage speaks is that of Torah study.

ו תשרי
6 TISHREI / CYCLE 1

ו ניסן
6 NISSAN / CYCLE 2

SEFER CHOFETZ CHAIM
LOSHON HORA: Laws of Derogatory Speech

➳ *Content and Intent*

Previously, we saw that a statement which is essentially derogatory is forbidden, regardless of the speaker's opinion regarding that statement. Conversely, it is forbidden to utter a statement which, essentially, is not derogatory, if either the speaker or the listener considers it derogatory.[13]

An illustration of this would be where an individual's mode of dress is being discussed. Although there may be nothing wrong with the way the person dresses, nevertheless, it is forbidden to say that the individual dresses in that manner, if either the speaker or listener has an unfavorable impression of those who dress that way.

For each moment that a person refrains from speaking the forbidden, he merits a hidden light that no angel can fathom.

6 Tishrei · Liesel Weis (née Moeller) לע״נ מרת אסתר בת החבר ר׳ יצחק
Dedicated by her husband and children
6 Nissan · Mr. Jack Glogower לע״נ ר׳ יצחק מאיר בן ר׳ צבי

❧ *Beyond Comprehension*

Let us address the contention that it is virtually impossible to faith-fully observe the laws of *shmiras haloshon* for more than a day or two:

Even if this were correct, is it reason enough to ignore this *mitzvah*? Imagine a person walking along the seashore, who sees that the sea has washed ashore precious gems. Would such a person — even if he were wealthy — refrain from picking up any gems because he knows it will be impossible to gather them all?

It is exactly the same regarding *shmiras haloshon.* It is well known that the Vilna Gaon (in his famous letter) quotes the *Midrash* which says that for each moment in which a person refrains from speaking the forbidden, he merits a hidden light that no angel can fathom. Note that the *Midrash* does not speak of refraining from forbidden speech for a month, a week, or an hour — but for only a moment!

Scripture states: "If you will seek it like silver and hunt for it like hidden treasures, then you will understand the fear of HASHEM, and knowledge of God you will find" (*Mishlei* 2:4-5). One must strive to attain spiritual goals in the way that he would seek the greatest valuables that this world has to offer. This is the intent of the statement, "Do not distance yourself from a quality that is without limit." Avoiding forbidden speech brings infinite merit; if we will only pursue this quality, and not tell ourselves that it is out of our reach, then we will have achieved that which no angel can fathom.

ז תשרי
7 TISHREI / CYCLE 1

ז ניסן
7 NISSAN / CYCLE 2

SEFER CHOFETZ CHAIM

LOSHON HORA: Laws of Derogatory Speech

❧ *Matters of Taste*

It would seem that there is nothing derogatory about a statement of taste. To say, "I don't like dry wine," is a description of the speaker's preferences and not a critical evaluation of the wine.

Ostensibly, then, one should be allowed to say that he does not like the oratory style of a given lecturer. In fact, however, such statements are generally prohibited, for they imply that the speaker lacks effectiveness.[14]

> *The longer one persists in guarding his tongue, the easier it becomes.*

7 Tishrei · May today's learning create נחת and joy for הקב"ה
Dedicated by משפחת וייס
7 Nissan · Harav Yaakov Kamenetsky הרהג' מרן ר' יעקב בר' בנימין
קמנצקי זצ"ל
Dedicated by his children, grandchildren and great grandchildren

DAY
7

✍ *Breaking Bad Habits*

In truth, there is no basis for the contention that the average person cannot avoid forbidden speech for more then a day or two. It is a proven fact that the longer one persists in guarding his tongue, the easier it becomes.

To gossip is a habit, and habits, as time goes on, become a part of a person's nature. But bad habits can be broken, especially when one becomes aware that a given habit involves numerous Torah prohibitions and is described by our Sages in most severe terms. Such an awareness, coupled with a bit of zealousness, goes a long way. One who would speak whatever came to mind without a moment's hesitation, will now find himself weighing his words before expressing them.

One should not grow frustrated if, after he resolved to avoid forbidden speech, his evil inclination got the better of him and he spoke *loshon hora.* Even if this happens time and again, nevertheless, he should not despair. Rather, he should forever strengthen himself to avoid improper speech, and persevere. This is how one should conduct himself his entire life.

This is the intent of the Talmud's statement, "One should forever arouse his good inclination to subdue his evil inclination" (*Berachos* 5a). Life is an ongoing struggle with one's evil inclination. One must forever be poised for battle and never be discouraged by failure. With knowledge of what the Torah requires of us and proper resolve, our efforts will ultimately succeed.

ח תשרי
8 TISHREI / CYCLE 1

ח ניסן
8 NISSAN / CYCLE 2

SEFER CHOFETZ CHAIM
LOSHON HORA: Laws of Derogatory Speech

❧ Past History

Another area involving *loshon hora* is that of past history. It is forbidden to relate something about an individual's past which either the speaker or the listener considers shameful, though in reality it is not shameful at all.

Our Sages teach that "at the place where *baalei teshuvah* (returnees to the path of Torah) stand, perfect *tzaddikim* (those who have always been righteous) cannot stand" (*Berachos* 34b). Thus, there is nothing shameful about being a *baal teshuvah*. Nevertheless, it is forbidden to relate that someone is a *baal teshuvah* if either the speaker or listener looks down at such people.[15] (Related laws regarding *baalei teshuvah* are discussed in Day 20.)

You stumbled this morning and spoke the forbidden? Then strengthen yourself once more, and succeed in the afternoon.

יצחק יוסף בן שרה רייזא לרפואה שלמה · 8 Tishrei
Dedicated by Worcester friends and family
8 Nissan · May Kasten לע״נ מנוחה פרידא בת יעקב יהודה
Dedicated by the Kasten, Hirsh & Schenk families

DAY 8

~ *Do Whatever You Can (I)*

A Torah scholar once posed the following question: If one has failed to concentrate while reciting the *Shemoneh Esrei* prayer and finds himself near its conclusion, with what approach can he inspire himself to pray the remainder of the prayer with proper concentration? The scholar offered a solution by way of a parable:

A young girl was standing in the marketplace with a large basket of apples for sale. Suddenly, a thief approached and began to snatch apples out of the basket. The girl became confused and stood helplessly, not knowing what to do. Someone who was watching from a distance called out to her, "Why are you standing still? What are you waiting for —that he should grab everything? Just as he is grabbing, so should you grab —whatever you can get will still be yours!"

And so it is regarding prayer. If one was overcome by lethargy and mindless daydreaming at the start of the *Shemoneh Esrei,* and suddenly finds himself near the prayer's end without having "grabbed any apples," this does not mean that he should give up and leave himself with nothing. Rather, he should strive with all his inner strength to concentrate on the remaining blessings.

And so it is, exactly, with *shmiras haloshon.* You stumbled this morning and spoke the forbidden? Then stand ready this afternoon to overcome your evil inclination and refrain from forbidden talk. And if you fail in the afternoon, nevertheless, strengthen yourself to do battle once more tomorrow. Surely Hashem will help you to succeed, for "one who seeks to purify himself is granted Heavenly assistance" (*Shabbos* 104a).

ט תשרי
9 TISHREI / CYCLE I

ט ניסן
9 NISSAN / CYCLE 2

SEFER CHOFETZ CHAIM
LOSHON HORA: Laws of Derogatory Speech

❧ Self-Incrimination

It is forbidden to relate derogatory information about someone even when the speaker mentions that he himself has the very same shortcoming or is guilty of having committed the same act. This is derived from God's rebuke of the prophet Yeshayah for his having referred to himself as "a man of impure lips dwelling among people of impure lips" (*Yeshayahu* 6:5).[16]

Loshon hora cannot be spoken even when it is clear that one is not speaking out of malice or with intention to malign. Thus, one cannot relate negative information about his loved ones.[17]

If one feels that he cannot fulfill all the fine points of a given mitzvah, nevertheless, he should strive to fulfill it to the best of his ability.

לע"נ מרת חיה איטא ענגעל ע"ה בת ר' 9 Tishrei · Honey Engel
קלונימות קלמן זילבער נ"י, נלב"ע בדמי ימיה
לע"נ יצחק בן שמואל ורחל ע"ה 9 Nissan · Isaac ben Rachel Salem
Dedicated in loving memory by his wife Mary and his entire family

DAY
9

✒ Do Whatever You Can (II)

"**D**o you really think that you can avoid *everything* that must not be spoken? Why, you are a man of the world, you have dealings with scores of people!" This was another argument cited above, which can lead a person to totally ignore the concept of *shmiras haloshon.*

Again, we respond with an analogy: Let us suppose that I was hurrying somewhere to engage in a business enterprise. A man asks me, "Why do you hurry? Do you think that this enterprise will make you one of the world's richest men, like So-and-so?" Surely I would reply, "Is that a reason not to seek a livelihood for myself?!"

If this response is correct when material matters are concerned, then surely it applies when spiritual matters are at stake. If one feels that he cannot abide by the laws of forbidden speech with all their details and fine points, does this mean that he should refrain entirely from caring for his soul? Is it reason to allow oneself to, Heaven forbid, be counted among the *ba'alei loshon hora* (habitual gossipers) who will not merit to bask in the glory of the Divine Presence (*Sotah* 42a)?

Reishis Chochmah (*Sha'ar HaAhavah* ch. 54) relates that R' Moshe Cordovero[1] saw the author of *Shushan Sodos* in a dream [following the latter's passing], and he was shining like the light of a torch. The deceased revealed that this was in merit of his having avoided idle chatter while on this world. Should such merit be totally forfeited because one feels that to acquire it in its entirety is out of reach?

The wisest of men declared, "Whatever you are able to do with your might, do it" (*Koheles* 9:10), meaning that even if one feels he cannot fulfill a given *mitzvah* in all its fine points, nevertheless, he should strive to fulfill it to the best of his ability. It is in this vein that our Sages derived from the verse, "Then Moshe set aside three cities" (*Devarim* 4:41), that although those three cities could not afford refuge [to one who murdered inadvertently] until the three cities in the Land of Canaan had been set aside —and Moshe knew that he would not be permitted to enter the Land of Israel and set them aside —nevertheless, Moshe said: "I will accomplish whatever is in my power to accomplish."[2]

---

1. Sixteenth-century Kabbalist, author of *Tomer Devorah.*
2. See *Rashi,* ad loc.

י תשרי
10 TISHREI / CYCLE 1

י ניסן
10 NISSAN / CYCLE 2

SEFER CHOFETZ CHAIM
LOSHON HORA: Laws of Derogatory Speech

❧ With Permission

It is forbidden to speak derogatorily about someone even when the subject has made it known that he does not mind if such things are said of him.[18]

As mentioned above, to speak negatively of one's fellow is shameful in itself, regardless of the subject's feelings. Speaking *loshon hora* is contrary to man's exalted status as the only creature who was fashioned *b'tzelem Elokim,* in the Divine image — and this is not altered by the fact that one has been granted permission to speak derogatorily.

A person who scrupulously refrains from hurting others through words will surely not do so through action!

10 Tishrei · May today's learning be a זכות for our משפחה
Dedicated by Asher Zelig Menachem Berkovits and family, Lakewood, NJ
להגדיל תורה ולהאדירה · 10 Nissan
Dedicated by Dov & Malki Levine, Shifra and Yisroel Meir, Brooklyn, NY

DAY 10

≈ Key to Spiritual Success

"Which man desires life, who loves days of seeing good? Guard your tongue from evil and your lips from speaking deceit. Turn from evil and do good, seek peace and pursue it" (*Tehillim* 34:13-15). The commentators explain that the term "life" refers to that of the World to Come, while "days" refers to man's years on this world which are only "days" by comparison to the eternal life of the next world.

We are commanded to fulfill 613 *mitzvos*; regarding all of them Hashem says to us, "See that I have placed before you today life and that which is good ... that you should love HASHEM, your God, to go in His ways and to observe His commandments" (*Devarim* 30:15-16). Why, then, does David, in the above verse, say that the quality of one's life in both worlds is primarily dependent on guarding one's tongue? In the opening passages of this work we have offered one answer to this question. Below, we offer more on the subject:

In the preface to *Sefer Chofetz Chaim,* we explained how the bitter sin of *loshon hora* can involve transgression of numerous positive and negative commandments, to a degree that is not found with any other sin. Thus, *shmiras haloshon* is a key to fulfillment of one's obligations both toward Hashem and toward his fellow Jew.

When a person is careful not to speak disparagingly of his fellow, or to embarrass him; when he demonstrates caution in avoiding comments that can aggravate dispute; and when he is careful to avoid transgression of other commandments related to evil talk, both positive and negative, then he will surely avoid more blatant sins. If one accepts upon himself to scrupulously avoid causing harm or shame through the spoken word, surely he will not do so through action!

Thus, one who zealously refrains from speaking *loshon hora* will, through such self-discipline, come to fulfill all his obligations toward his fellow.

יא תשרי
11 TISHREI / CYCLE 1

יא ניסן
11 NISSAN / CYCLE 2

SEFER CHOFETZ CHAIM
LOSHON HORA: Laws of Derogatory Speech

ᕱ *Common Knowledge*

A derogatory statement is considered *loshon hora* even when the information is common knowledge, for as stated above, to speak negatively of one's fellow is shameful in itself.[19]

Negative information about Jews appearing in newspapers may not be repeated. Newspapers often publish articles based on hearsay and thus, one is not even permitted to *believe* such information if the newspaper is its only source. Even after one has verified the information, he may nevertheless not repeat it.

The antithesis of Torah study, the greatest of all mitzvos, is loshon hora.

11 Tishrei · David ben Garaz לע״נ דוד בן גראז
Dedicated by the Franco family
11 Nissan · לכבוד הרב יוסף קאלאצקי שליט״א ותלמידיו
Yad Avraham Institute כולל יד אברהם

DAY
11

✒ *Equal to All*

Talmud *Yerushalmi* (*Pe'ah* 1:1) states that the reward for studying Torah is equivalent to that of all other *mitzvos* combined, and the punishment for speaking *loshon hora* is equivalent to that of all other sins combined. Thus, the antithesis of Torah study, the greatest of all *mitzvos*, is *loshon hora*. Their respective primacy can be explained as follows:

Of the four basic elements of nature —fire, wind, water and earth —the intangible (fire and wind) are far more powerful than the tangible (water and earth). Fire can engulf material objects and totally destroy them, and the power of wind is awesome, as it is written, "A great and mighty wind which breaks apart mountains and shatters stones" (*I Melachim* 19:11).

The same is true in the spiritual realm. Torah study impacts in the Upper Worlds in a way that no other *mitzvah* can. This is because all other *mitzvos* are related to the physical — for example, to fulfill the *mitzvah* of *tzitzis*, one dons a garment, a material object; a *lulav* is held, a physical act; a *shofar* must be blown, etc. Torah study, however, is performed through the power of speech, which, essentially, is a function of the soul.[1] This is why the reward of Torah study is equivalent to that of all other *mitzvos* combined.

The converse is true of sin. The spiritual damage caused by *loshon hora* is infinitely greater than that caused by other transgressions, because it is committed through the power of speech. Its effect in the Upper Spheres is awesome. Therefore, its punishment is equivalent to that of all other sins combined.

---

1. As mentioned above, *Targum Onkelos* translates "and man became a living being" (*Bereishis* 2:7), as "and man became a speaking spirit."

יב תשרי
12 TISHREI / CYCLE 1

יב ניסן
12 NISSAN / CYCLE 2

SEFER CHOFETZ CHAIM
LOSHON HORA: Laws of Derogatory Speech

❧ *Ambiguous Statements*

A Jew is responsible for exercising caution in speech and not making statements which can be misinterpreted as being derogatory.[20]

An example of an ambiguous statement that should not be said is, "He's a well-meaning fellow," which can mean, "He's well-meaning but not very intelligent," or, "He's well-meaning but his actions are wrong." If one simply means, "He's well-meaning and sincere," then this should be made clear.

Hashem acts towards us in the way that we act toward others.

לע״נ ר׳ יונה צבי בן ר׳ יוחנן הערצאג ז״ל · 12 Tishrei
Dedicated by the Herzog family, New York
12 Nissan · May today's learning be a זכות for our משפחה
Dedicated by Yehuda Levine & family

DAY 12

❧ *Measure for Measure*

The way in which one acts towards others determines the way in which Heaven will act towards him. For example, if one strives to overlook the hurt caused him, and if he acts towards others with kindness and compassion, then he awakens the Attribute of Compassion in Heaven. Hashem will judge him with mercy and he will be shown kindness from Above. As our Sages state: "Whoever has compassion towards others will be shown compassion from Above" (*Shabbos* 151b); and "Whoever refrains from exacting his measure [of retribution from others for the wrong they caused him] will have all his sins forgiven" (*Rosh Hashanah* 17a). Moreover, in his merit, Divine compassion will manifest itself upon the Jewish nation as a whole.[1]

However, if it is one's way to be absolutely unrelenting towards others and to treat them without compassion, then he lends strength to the Attribute of Justice —toward himself specifically, and to the entire Jewish nation as well. Heaven will be unrelenting regarding that person's sins, for "With the measure that a person measures do they [i.e. Heaven] measure him" (*Megillah* 12b).

Our Sages state: "Jerusalem was destroyed only because its inhabitants limited their decisions to the [letter of the] law of Torah" (*Bava Metzia* 30b). This seems difficult, for Scripture records many sins of which that generation was guilty. Our discussion sheds light on the matter. Had the people overlooked the wrong caused them, then Hashem would have forgiven them as well. However, they were absolutely unrelenting toward each other, demanding from one another whatever they could possibly extract according to the law —and Heaven judged them accordingly.[2]

---

1. See *Zohar* to *Parashas Emor*.
2. See *Toldos Adam* 1:2.

יג תשרי
13 TISHREI / CYCLE 1

יג ניסן
13 NISSAN / CYCLE 2

SEFER CHOFETZ CHAIM
LOSHON HORA: Laws of Derogatory Speech

✑ Obvious Intent

While statements which have a negative connotation are prohibited, this would not apply where the listener can be expected to understand that nothing derogatory was intended.[21]

Therefore, *halachah* permits making an ambiguous statement if:

(1) Nothing derogatory is intended; and

(2) the unintended meaning of the statement is only mildly derogatory; and

(3) the statement is made in the presence of three people or in the presence of the person being discussed.

As an illustration, the early commentators offer the statement, "In that house, something is always cooking on the stove." This could mean that this family's door is always open to guests, or it can mean that the family is overindulgent. If the statement were to be made in the presence of three, one can safely assume that it would eventually become known to the family of whom it was said. Such being the case, the listeners would assume that the speaker intended it as a compliment. It would also be permissible to make such a statement in the presence of the family of whom it is said, since it would be obvious to all that there was no derogatory intent.

Those who speak loshon hora cause the Accuser to speak against the Jewish people.

DAY 13

❧Awakening the Accuser

Sifre[1] states that Hashem, as it were, does not want to associate with gossipers and rescue them from troubles. *Zohar* states (*Parashas Shelach*): "R' Shimon said: Of everything is the Holy One, Blessed is He, forgiving — except for *loshon hora.*" The reason for this is perfectly clear.

When a Jew speaks *loshon hora*, he causes accusation in Heaven toward the Jewish people. In the words of *Zohar (Parashas Pekudei)*, this sin "brings plague, sword and murder to this world. Woe to those who awaken this evil force, who do not guard their tongues and pay no heed to this! They do not realize that the ways of Heaven are reflective of the ways on this world, both for good and for bad. [Through evil talk,] Satan is aroused to voice accusation against the entire world."

A father's great love for his child can impel him to make allowances for the child's bad behavior. When a father is forced to rebuke his child, he does it lovingly, with abundant compassion. However, if people come to the father and report that they witnessed how the child quarreled with others over nothing, and that he embarrassed and ridiculed his peers, the father will have no alternative but to take strong measures to ensure that his child mend his ways.

Hashem loves the Jewish people with a deep, unfathomable love. In the words of the prophet: "Is Ephraim My most precious son or a delightful child, that whenever I speak of him I remember him more and more? Therefore, My inner self yearns for him, I will surely take pity on him..." (*Yirmiyahu* 31:19-20).

Of course, Hashem is well aware of all that transpires both in public and in private, as it is written, " 'Can a man hide in a hidden place so that I will not see him' says HASHEM?" (*Yirmiyahu* 23:24). Nevertheless, out of His great love for Israel, He is slow to anger and seeks to find merit for His nation, as it is written, "He gazes at no iniquity in Yaakov..." (*Bamidbar* 23:21; see *Rashi*). In His infinite wisdom, Hashem has decreed that His judgment of man reflect the intercessions and accusations of the Heavenly angels. When the Accuser [i.e. Satan] comes before Him to relate the sins of His people, then He feels compelled, as it were, to respond.

And it is those who speak *loshon hora* who cause the Accuser to speak against the Jewish people.

---

1. Cited in *Yalkut Shimoni, Parashas Ki Seitzei, 933.*

 יד תשרי
14 TISHREI / CYCLE 1

יד ניסן
14 NISSAN / CYCLE 2

SEFER CHOFETZ CHAIM
LOSHON HORA: Laws of Derogatory Speech

❧ *"Your People"*

The Torah states: לא תלך רכיל בעמיך, *Do not go as a gossipmonger among your people* (*Vayikra* 19:16). From the word בעמיך, *among your people,* our Sages derive that it is forbidden to speak *loshon hora* about a Jew only when he is עושה מעשה עמך, *one who acts in the way of your people.*

It is not shameful to focus on the shortcomings of a wicked person. The term "wicked person" refers to a מומר להכעיס, *malicious offender.* However, one who sins out of ignorance or temptation *is* in the category of *amecha* and it is forbidden to speak *loshon hora* about him (unless it is for a constructive purpose, as will be discussed later).[22]

Middah k'neged middah (measure for measure) is the rule of Heaven in all instances.

לע״נ שמואל זאב בן ישראל יצחק הלוי · 14 Tishrei
14 Nissan · Rabbi Avraham Y. Hirsch בן יצחק אברהם הרב לע״נ
ר' בנימין זצ״ל
Dedicated by his children: Hirsch, Chopp, Lapa, & Axelrod families

**DAY
14**

✎ Silencing the Accuser

As mentioned above, Hashem acts towards the Jewish people in the way that we act towards one another. Thus, if Jews live in peace and harmony with one another, then in Heaven, Satan is not able to indict them. Hashem has implanted in Satan's nature an inability to indict His beloved nation in any way under such conditions. *Midrash Shir HaShirim* states that this applies even when the Jewish people are guilty of the worst sins, such as idol worship. Thus it is written, "Bound [to one another in peace but attached] to idol worship is Ephraim — let him be" (*Hoshea* 4:17).

Middah k'neged middah (measure for measure) is the rule of Heaven in all instances. When a person restrains himself from speaking disparagingly of his fellow and arousing bad feelings towards him, then in Heaven the Accuser is unable to open his mouth to accuse.

The converse is true when *loshon hora* is spoken, and this evokes Divine wrath toward the speaker. As our Sages comment on the words, ובידו רצפה, *and in his hand was a coal (Yeshayahu* 6:6), Hashem told the angel: "רצוץ פה, *Break the mouth* of the one who spoke ill of my children!" (*Yalkut Shimoni* 406).

✿ Other Forms of Negativity

While the Scriptural prohibition against *loshon hora* applies only to speaking about the living, our Sages prohibit making slanderous remarks about the deceased.[23]

It is also forbidden to speak negatively of our beloved land, *Eretz Yisrael.* As the Torah relates, the generation that merited to be liberated from Egypt spent forty years in the Wilderness and died there because of דבת הארץ, *evil speech concerning the Land* (See *Bamidbar* chs. 13-14).[24]

In truth, it is proper to avoid focusing on the negative unnecessarily even when discussing non-sacred objects. The early commentators tell of the wise man and his students who came upon the carcass of an animal. When the students commented on its foul odor, the wise man responded, "But see how white are its teeth!"[25]

Those who refrain from speaking ill of others can rest assured that their entreaties carry great weight in Heaven.

15 Tishrei · Fay Kasmer Broome לע״נ צפורה בת משה דוד
Dedicated by Bernard H. Broome
15 Nissan · The Manchester Rosh Yeshiva לע״נ הגאון הצדיק הרב
יהודא זאב בן הגאון הצדיק הרב משה יצחק הלוי סג״ל זצוק״ל
Dedicated by Osher and Goldie Sternlicht, London, England

✒ *A Dreadful Scenario*

Picture the following scenario: A Jew is instructed to enter the Temple of God, stand before the Holy Ark and accuse his fellow Jews of whatever sins he knows them to be guilty of. Without a doubt, even the lowest among us would endanger his own life rather than carry out this dreadful order.

Yet people fail to realize that this is exactly what they are doing when they speak *loshon hora*! As stated in *Tanna D'Vei Eliyahu* (I, 18:64): "When the wicked speak *loshon hora*, it ascends before the Throne of Glory..."

It is therefore not difficult to understand the gravity of this sin, and the heavy price that the speaker is liable to pay, both in this world and the next. Therefore, David cautions us that if we seek to enjoy the bliss of eternal life in the next world and desire good days in this world, our first step must be to guard our tongues.

On the holy day of Yom Kippur we beseech Hashem: הס קטגור וקח סנגור מקומו, *Silence the Accuser and let the Defender take his place.* How can one utter these words without feeling shame and humiliation, if through his own *loshon hora* the Accuser is aroused and endowed with the strength to accuse?

Conversely, those who are successful in their efforts to refrain from speaking ill of others can rest assured that their entreaties before Hashem to "silence the Accuser" carry great weight in Heaven.

May Hashem cause love, peace and brotherhood to dwell amongst His people.

✥ The Listener

Once something is defined as derogatory, it is forbidden to relate it other than for constructive purposes and under specific conditions which will be discussed later. One may not share negative information about people with friends and family, including one's spouse. It must be underscored that relating *loshon hora* to one's spouse is no less forbidden than when relating it to anyone else. To focus on another's shortcomings is undignified and wrong.[26]

Man is superior to other creatures only if he uses his power of speech in a constructive manner.

לע"נ אהרן בן יצחק מאיר ז"ל · 16 Tishrei
Dedicated in loving memory by Esther Statman, Stanley Statman,
Shirley Heller-Klausner
לע"נ הב' קלמן פלטיאל בן ר' שמעיה ז"ל · Kalman Fried · 16 Nissan
Dedicated in memory of a beloved son by Mrs. Bella Fried,
London, England

~ Man's Superiority

The person who restrains himself from speaking the forbidden merits the *hidden light* [אור הגנוז] which was stored away for the righteous at the time of Creation.[1] Conversely, regarding the sin of *loshon hora*, our Sages state (*Yerushalmi Pe'ah* 1:1): "Punishment for this sin is exacted from the person on this world, while its principal [i.e. primary punishment] remains for him in the World to Come."

This is yet another reason why David declares: "Which man desires life... Guard your tongue from evil."

Consider the following: Man is superior to all other creatures by way of his Heavenly soul, which the Creator has endowed with intellect that is granted expression through the power of speech. As mentioned above, the Torah defines man's essence by calling him a "living being," which *Onkelos* translates as "a speaking spirit" (*Bereishis* 2:7). But man can claim superiority only if he uses his power of speech in a constructive manner. If he uses this power wickedly, then all other creatures, who cannot speak and cause the destructiveness that only words can cause, are actually *superior to him*.

Thus does Scripture state: מי האיש, *Which* man [*desires life... guard your tongue...*], for it is this quality that makes one deserving of being called an איש, *man*.

---

1. See *Rashi* to *Bereishis* 1:4.

יז תשרי
17 TISHREI / CYCLE 1

יז ניסן
17 NISSAN / CYCLE 2

SEFER CHOFETZ CHAIM
LOSHON HORA: Laws of Derogatory Speech

~ Repentance

We have seen that to speak derogatorily of one's fellow is to degrade one's own status as a creation *b'tzelem Elokim* (in God's image).

For one who speaks *loshon hora,* the *teshuvah* (repentance) process is the same as for all sins between man and his Creator: confession, sincere regret, and the resolution never to speak *loshon hora* again.

One is not required to discuss the matter with the subject of one's sinful words and seek his forgiveness, unless actual harm was caused. (*Teshuvah* for having caused harm through *loshon hora* will be discussed later.)[27]

The way to ensure ourselves of eternal reward for all our good deeds is by avoiding loshon hora.

❧ Forfeiting Eternity

Rabbi Raphael Hamburger[1], in his work *Marpei Loshon,* offers another insightful explanation of the verses, "Which man desires life ... guard your tongue from evil ..." He bases his thoughts on the following passage from *Sefer Chovos HaLevavos* (*Sha'ar HaKeniah*, ch. 7):

> On the Day of Judgment, many people will find themselves credited with meritorious deeds which they did not do. "These are not mine!" each one will declare. He will be told, "These are the deeds of those who spoke disparagingly of you [and thereby caused their merits to be transferred to your account]." And the one who spoke disparagingly will be told, "These deeds were taken from you when you spoke against So-and-so."
>
> Conversely, some will find acts of guilt on their account which they never committed. When each one will protest, "These are not mine!" he will be told, "These were taken from the account of So-and-so, against whom you spoke ..."

The above is found in other sacred works as well.

A person may spend a day or two earning for himself eternal bliss through Torah and *mitzvos,* only to exchange these merits for his neighbor's sins by speaking against him. A few more days might go by as he accrues more reward, only to lose it all in the same manner when another opportunity for evil talk comes his way. This pattern might continue until his day of death, when he departs this world stripped of all his "possessions," that is, the Torah and *mitzvos* in which he invested much time and effort.

Therefore, David first exhorts us, "Guard your tongue from evil," and only then does he say, "Turn from evil and do good." The way to ensure that the reward of *mitzvah* observance remains ours for all eternity is by refraining from speaking ill of our fellow Jew.

---

1. Eighteenth-century Torah luminary.

יח תשרי
18 TISHREI / CYCLE 1

יח ניסן
18 NISSAN / CYCLE 2

SEFER CHOFETZ CHAIM

LOSHON HORA: Laws of Harmful Speech

∞ Definition

Thus far we have focused on statements which are derogatory in nature. The second category of *loshon hora* involves statements that could potentially cause harm to a person, be it physical, emotional or financial.[28]

The Talmud teaches that *gramma b'nizakin assur,* it is forbidden to cause a person damage indirectly. Thus, any form of speech, even if not derogatory, but which may cause harm to someone, constitutes *loshon hora* and is forbidden.[29]

> *One who speaks loshon hora destroys three people: the subject of his evil words, his listener and himself.*

לע״נ הרב מנחם מרדכי בן ר׳ מיכאל · 18 Tishrei
Dedicated by the Weldler family
לע״נ צבי בן רב נפתלי הערץ Hirsch Bassman · 18 Nissan
Dedicated by his wife and children

DAY 18

❧ *A Triple Tragedy*

M idrash Shochar Tov (Tehillim 52:2)[1] states:

It was taught in the academy of R' Yishmael: Whoever relates *loshon hora* commits grave sins which equal the Three [Cardinal] Sins of idolatry, immorality and murder.[2] [This can be deduced as follows]: Regarding *loshon hora* it is written, "May HASHEM cut off all equivocating lips, the tongue which speaks haughty words [גדולות]" (Tehillim 12:4). Regarding idolatry it is written, "I implore! This people has committed a great sin [חטאה גדולה]" (Shemos 32:31). Regarding immorality it is written, "How can I perpetrate this great evil? [הרעה הגדולה]" (Bereishis 39:9). And regarding murder it is written, "Is my sin too great [גדול] to be borne?" (Bereishis 4:13). [Thus, the plural form גדולות is found only with regard to *loshon hora*.]

Alternatively: When someone commits murder, he kills a single soul, but one who speaks *loshon hora* destroys three: the subject of his words, his listener and himself. From where do we see this? From Doeg, who spoke *loshon hora* concerning Achimelech (I Shmuel chs. 21-22) and thereby destroyed Shaul, who accepted the report; Achimelech, about whom it was spoken; and himself. Shaul, who accepted it, [died because of it] as it is written: "Shaul died for the faithlessness with which he acted towards HASHEM" (I Divrei HaYamim 10:13); Achimelech [died because of it], for about him it was said [by Shaul], "Die, you shall die, Achimelech (I Shmuel 22:16); and Doeg was banished from the World [to Come], as it is written, "Likewise, God will shatter you for eternity" (Tehillim 52:7). And what caused this? *Loshon hora.*

---

1. See also *Arachin* 15b.

2. The *Midrash* cannot mean that speaking *loshon hora* is a greater sin than any of the Three Cardinal Sins, for they carry the death penalty while speaking *loshon hora* does not. The *Midrash* means that speaking *loshon hora* can lead to the transgression of *many* severe sins (Maharsha).

❧ *Embarrassing Remarks*

One who conveys information to others has no control over who will hear it and in what setting it will be repeated. Whatever one says concerning another person may very well be repeated in the presence of that person.

It is therefore forbidden to say anything about a person that might embarrass him if it were to be repeated in his presence, even if the information is not derogatory.[30]

It is forbidden to relate that an individual is a *baal teshuvah* if the person is sensitive about this fact. This is true even in a community where *baalei teshuvah* are highly respected.

The exceptional Torah knowledge of the children in Shaul's generation could not gain his armies victory in battle — such is the power of loshon hora.

19 Tishrei · May the *shmiras haloshon* engendered by today's learning be a זכות for our parents
Dedicated by Heshy & Perel Kulefsky
19 Nissan · May today's learning be a זכות for Rabbi Chaim Boruch Katz and family, Brooklyn, NY
Dedicated by his children and grandchildren

~ *Words of Defeat*

*S*ifre states[1]:

> With ten trials did our ancestors test [God in the Wilderness],
> but their judgment was sealed only on account of the sin of
> *loshon hora*, as it is written, "They have tested Me these ten
> times and did not heed My voice" (*Bamidbar* 14:22),[2] and it is
> written, "You have made HASHEM weary [i.e. unrelenting]
> with your words" (*Malachi* 2:17).

The generation of the wicked King Achav was plagued by idol
worship; yet they were victorious in war in merit of their not informing on one another (*Yerushalmi Pe'ah* 1:1). This is evident from
the fact that no one revealed to Achav that Ovadiah, aided by others, was sustaining one hundred prophets of Hashem against the
king's wishes.[3] However, in the days of the righteous Shaul, when
informers such as Doeg[4] and the Ziphites[5] were found among the
Jews, their armies fell in battle. The fact that there were children in
Shaul's generation who were knowledgeable in forty-nine facets of
Torah was not enough to gain them victory. Such is the power of
loshon hora.

---

1. See also *Arachin* 15a.

2. God uttered these words after the Spies had spoken their slanderous report of the
land. The Talmud (*Arachin* 15a) enumerates the ten tests.

3. See *I Melachim* ch. 18.

4. *I Shmuel* ch. 22.

5. Ibid. ch. 23.

❧ *Baalei Teshuvah*

Above (Day 8), we saw that one may not mention that someone is a *baal teshuvah* if either the speaker or listener considers this derogatory (which, in fact, it is not). Based on the prohibition against relating negative information or information that could cause harm or hurt, it is permissible to relate that a person is a *baal teshuvah* only if, in addition to the speaker and listener not considering this to be derogatory, the *baal teshuvah* himself is open about his past and if this fact were mentioned in his presence he would not feel hurt; or (in a case where the *baal teshuvah* is sensitive about his past) the listener is known to be discreet and the information will never be passed on to others.[31]

Jerusalem was destroyed because of the gossipers who caused baseless hatred to reign.

לע"נ ישראל חיים בן אהרן ז"ל - ד' חול המועד סוכות · 20 Tishrei
הונצח על ידי בנו, אהרן יהושע דוד ברוין
לע"נ ר' מרדכי בן מנחם מנדל ז"ל · Mordechai David · 20 Nissan
Dedicated by Mr. & Mrs. Menachem Shayovich

DAY
20

~ The Shechinah Departs

The sin of *loshon hora* causes the *Shechinah* (Divine Presence) to remove itself from our midst.

The *Midrash* (*Devarim Rabbah* 5:10) states:

> R' Mona said: Whoever speaks *loshon hora* causes the *Shechinah* to ascend from this world. As David said: "My soul is among lions, I lie with men who are aflame, people whose teeth are spears and arrows, and whose tongue is a sharp sword. Be exalted above the heavens, O God, above all the earth be Your glory" (*Tehillim* 57:5-6).
>
> David's intent was: "Master of the Universe: Why is Your Presence manifest on this world [when such sinners are present]? Remove it to Your heavenly abode."

Regarding the gossiper does Hashem say: "He and I cannot dwell together in this world" (*Arachin* 15b). Furthermore, the second Destruction occurred because of the gossipers who caused *sinas chinam* (baseless hatred) to reign among the people (*Yoma* 9b).

One who causes strife among friends is despicable in the eyes of Hashem, and his sin is too great to bear. King Solomon said: "Six things are hated by HASHEM, and the seventh is despised by Him. Haughty eyes, a tongue of falsehood, hands which shed innocent blood... and one who incites quarrels among brothers" (*Mishlei* 6:16-19). Our Sages state that the seventh sin is the worst of all.[1]

---

1. *Vayikra Rabbah* 16:1. *Yefei Toar* (ad loc.) explains that evil talk can ultimately lead to murder and other heinous sins. Thus, it is potentially the worst sin of all (see comment of *Maharsha* cited in Day 18)

כא תשרי
21 TISHREI / CYCLE 1

כא ניסן
21 NISSAN / CYCLE 2

SEFER CHOFETZ CHAIM
LOSHON HORA: Laws of Harmful Speech

☙ Ruining Opportunities

Any information that, although not derogatory, could harm an individual's opportunity for a job or a *shidduch* should it become known, may not be related. This form of loshon hora is common when people are approached for information regarding a shidduch or a job interview.

It is forbidden to talk of an individual's physical weakness or lack of intelligence even if neither the speaker nor the listener views these shortcomings as negative. Sharing such information could prove harmful.[32]

The gossiper looks over his shoulder to make sure that his target is not listening. But why isn't he worried that Hashem is listening?!

21 Tishrei · The Manchester Rosh Yeshiva הרב הצדיק הגאון לע"נ
יהודא זאב הלוי סג"ל זצוק"ל
Dedicated by Mordche Bunem Brandeis and family, Manchester, England
21 Nissan · Mrs. Shoshana Appelbaum בת וויטא שושנה לע"נ
ר' ישראל הלוי ע"ה
Dedicated by her husband Nute Tsvi Appelbaum and family

❧ Seeming Denial

Our Sages state:

> R' Yehoshua ben Levi said: The term תורה, Torah, appears five times in the chapters which discuss the *metzora* [whose affliction is punishment for having spoken *loshon hora*].[1] This teaches that one who speaks *loshon hora* is considered as if he had transgressed the Five Books of the Torah (*Vayikra Rabbah* 16:6).

> R' Yochanan said in the name of R' Yose ben Zimra: Whoever speaks *loshon hora* is considered as if he had denied the existence of God, as it is written, (*Tehillim* 12:5), "Those who have said, 'With our tongues we shall prevail, our lips are with us, who is master over us?' " (*Arachin* 15b).

Sefer Yereim explains that when someone wants to speak *loshon hora*, he first casts a glance in all directions to make sure that the subject of his evil words is not present. His seeming lack of concern that his words will be noted Above conveys an impression that, to his mind, Heaven is not cognizant of what he is about to say. This is why speaking *loshon hora* is akin to denial of belief in God.

What more must be said concerning the severity of speaking *loshon hora*? There is no recourse but to engage the evil inclination in battle, so that one will not become caught in the net of this bitter sin. Those who will emerge victorious will reap the inestimable fruits of their efforts, both in this world and the next.

---

1. *Vayikra* 13:59; 14:2; 14:32; 14:54; 14:57.

Sefer HaAkeidah (cited by *Maharzu* to *Vayikra Rabbah*) notes that the subject of *loshon hora* is prominently mentioned in all Five Books. The Book of *Bereishis* (ch. 3) relates how the Serpent, through cunning and deception, caused Adam and Eve to sin; the Book of *Shemos* (2:15) relates how Moshe was forced to flee Egypt because of the treachery of Dasan and Aviram; the Book of *Vayikra* (chs.13-14) details the laws of *tzaraas* which is a Divinely inflicted retribution for speaking *loshon hora,* and it also contains the primary prohibition against speaking *loshon hora* (19:16); the Book of *Bamidbar* relates the episodes of Miriam's *tzaraas* (ch. 12), the Spies' slander (chs. 13-14), and Korach's rebellion (ch. 16); and the Book of *Devarim*, in its opening verse, alludes to episodes in which the Jews in the Wilderness were guilty of sinful talk (see *Rashi* ad loc.).

כב תשרי
22 TISHREI / CYCLE 1

כב ניסן
22 NISSAN / CYCLE 2

ᔟ *Disparagement and Ridicule*

Making a statement about a product that would discourage people from buying it constitutes speaking *loshon hora* as it could harm the livelihood of either the manufacturer or the storekeeper who sells it. (In certain situations, however, this would be permissible, as will be discussed later.)[33]

Similarly, it is forbidden to make a cynical comment about a speaker that could either discourage people from attending his lectures, or weaken the impact of his message.[34]

As with any *mitzvah,* a child should be trained to avoid speaking *loshon hora* as soon as he reaches the age of understanding in this regard. It is common for children to denigrate the food they are served, causing hurt to the cook. Children should be trained to avoid making such comments.[35]

The best craftsman cannot perform his task properly if his tools are flawed and of poor quality.

לע"נ גולדע דבורה בת משה אליהו · 22 Tishrei - Gussie Kleinman
Dedicated by Ruth R. Levine, Dover NH, in memory of Bubbe's Yiras Hashem
22 Nissan · לע"נ אבינו הרה"ג ר' בן ציון יחיאל מיכל בן הרה"ח
ר' נח יעקב פוקסמן זצ"ל
הונצח על ידי נח יעקב ושמואל נחום פוקסמן ומש',
ושרה לאה בריס ומש'

❧ *Tools Without Flaw*

Through *shmiras haloshon* a Jew perfects the primary tool of his service of Hashem — his power of speech. By not using his tongue for forbidden talk, he ensures that his words of Torah study and prayer will ascend before Hashem and achieve their desired results.

The Sages refer to speech as the Jew's אמנות, *craft*. When a king wants an item made for his personal use, he will choose only the finest craftsman to accomplish this task. He will seek someone who can create products of rare beauty, fit to be placed upon the royal table.

Yet even the world's greatest craftsman will not be able to satisfy the king if he lacks the necessary tools. If he is forced to use tools that are damaged and of poor quality, the finished product will quite likely be rejected by a commoner, and surely by a king.

If, however, the master craftsman is provided with the very best tools, then the final product will be a thing of beauty and bring the king much satisfaction.

There is no greater satisfaction to the King of kings, as it were, than when his "craftsmen" — the Children of Israel — go about their Divine service with "tools" that are free of spiritual imperfection. And it is only through *shmiras haloshon* that this can be achieved.

כג תשרי
23 TISHREI / CYCLE 1

כג ניסן
23 NISSAN / CYCLE 2

SEFER CHOFETZ CHAIM
LOSHON HORA: Laws of Harmful Speech

✺ When the Subject Approves

U nlike statements that are derogatory, a non-derogatory but potentially harmful statement *can* be made about a person if it is clear that he does not object.

If someone regularly talks about his inability to remember even his own phone number, it would not be forbidden for others to repeat that statement, provided that neither the speaker nor the listener thinks any less of the person on account of his poor memory.

Certainly, if a person explicitly grants permission for others to disclose potentially harmful information about himself, they are permitted to do so, provided that the information is not derogatory.[36]

Through shmiras haloshon, a Jew forever enhances the spiritual power of his words.

23 Tishrei · Yehuda Borish לע״נ יהודה יונתן ע״ה בן אליהו ראובן ונחמה
Dedicated by Mishpachas Yosef Leib & Nechama Homburger
Spring Valley, NY
23 Nissan · Mrs. Leah Epstein לע״נ לאה בת אלחנן צבי
Dedicated by the Oppenheimer family, Monsey, NY

~ *Powerful Words*

The power of speech is the great tool with which man can build heaven and earth, as it is written, "And I have placed My words in your mouth ... to implant the heavens and to set a base for the earth ..." (*Yeshayahu* 51:16). The prophet speaks in a most literal sense, for through the sacred words of Torah study and prayer that a Jew utters on this earth, exalted worlds and angels are created Above. With regard to the latter, the Mishnah states: "He who fulfills even a single *mitzvah* gains for himself a single advocate" (*Avos* 4:13). By "advocate," the Mishnah means that these angels will intercede on the person's behalf before the Heavenly Throne.

The level of sanctity of these worlds and angels is contingent upon two factors: the spiritual readiness of the person at the time he performed the *mitzvah*, and the quality of the medium through which the *mitzvah* was performed. A person who avoids *loshon hora* and utilizes his power of speech in a positive way is forever enhancing the spiritual power of his words. Thus, the Torah study and prayer which emanate from his lips are endowed with an exalted spiritual light. Conversely, if a person defiles his mouth with words of gossip, mockery, falsehood and the like, with what sort of sanctity can his words of study and prayer be endowed? He is a craftsman who has severely damaged his indispensable tool. His only recourse is to mend his ways and refine his power of speech.

SEFER CHOFETZ CHAIM

LOSHON HORA: Laws of Harmful Speech

◂ *Public Knowledge But Harmful*

We have seen that it is forbidden to speak in a derogatory manner even if the information being conveyed was already known to the listener. This is because the act of speaking negatively is inherently wrong.

Conversely, it stands to reason that a non-derogatory but potentially harmful statement *can* be made in the presence of anyone who is already aware of the information, unless the speaker emphasizes some point that the listener may not have realized previously. This is because the statement will not be cause for any harm which otherwise would not have come about.

Rambam takes this a step further, stating that if a potentially harmful statement was made in the presence of three people, the three are permitted to relate the information in conversation with others.[37] This is because each of the three can assume that the other two will probably make the information public anyway. However, this would *not* be permissible if either:

(1) one of the three is known to be discreet or especially careful regarding the laws of forbidden speech, or

(2) the person's intent in relating the information is to publicize the matter yet further.

According to the Chofetz Chaim, *Rambam* permits any of the three to repeat the information even if it is derogatory.[38]

(Continued on page 406)

> **The metzora must seek the prayers of others, because his own prayers would be rejected in Heaven.**

24 Tishrei · Ira Warren Sohn לע״נ יצחק זאב בן נפתלי
Dedicated by Dr. & Mrs. Norman Sohn
24 Nissan · Abraham (Red) Sommerstein לע״נ אברהם צבי בן נפתלי זאב
Dedicated by Andrea, Robin, Ivy, Wendy, Arthur & John Sommerstein,
Lynn, MA

≈ The Metzora's Cry

*Z*ohar *(Parashas Metzora)* states:

> The prayer of one who speaks *loshon hora* will not come before the Holy One, Blessed is He, for a *ruach tamei* (impure spirit) hovers over it. When he repents, and [sincerely] accepts upon himself the [various aspects of] repentance, then what is written of him? "On the day of his purification, he shall be brought before the *Kohen*" *(Vayikra 14:2).*[1]

The above lends added clarity to the Torah's instruction that the *metzora* (one who is afflicted with *tzaraas* for having spoken *loshon hara*[2]) call out to those who pass by, "[I am] contaminated, contaminated!" (ibid. 13:45) so that they will pray for him. Since his own prayers will not be accepted Above, the Torah therefore advises him to request that others pray on his behalf.

Scripture declares: "Take note of God's work! For who can straighten what he has twisted?" *(Koheles 7:13).* We can interpret this as follows: *Take note of God's work!* Ponder well the Heavenly fruits of a Jew's prayer on this earth: prayer can radiate spiritual light and create exalted edifices in the Upper Worlds. Ensure, then, that your prayers be uttered with proper readiness, and by a mouth that is pure and unsullied by sin. *For who can straighten what he has twisted?* If one's prayer will be lacking, then its spiritual products in the Upper Worlds will be lacking as well. This will bring eternal distress to one's soul, for these are not earthly structures, which can be repaired or improved by a second craftsman.

As Hillel declared: "If I am not for myself, who will be for me?" *(Avos 1:14).* Only the person himself has the power to correct his past mistakes — through proper repentance and a firm resolve to live by the laws of proper speech.

---

1. Homiletically, this means that having repented and achieved purification, the *metzora* is assured that his prayers will, once again, gain acceptance Above.

2. Contrary to its common translation, *tzaraas* is not leprosy or some other bodily disease, but the physical manifestation of spiritual malady. As R' Samson Raphael Hirsch demonstrates, if *tzaraas* were some biological disorder and the *metzora's* confinement were to prevent contagion, then some of its related laws are inexplicable. For example, if the symptoms of *tzaraas* are found on a newlywed during the festive week following marriage, the *Kohen* does not pronounce the person *tamei* (impure) so as not to interfere with the festivities. Also, the Torah states that if one's entire body is covered with *tzaraas*, he is *tahor* (pure), but if one spot on his body heals, then he is *tamei.*

❧ *Harming the Wicked*

We have seen that it is permissible to speak disparagingly concerning a *rasha,* wicked individual.

With regard to potentially harmful speech, it is obvious that one may not say anything that could cause physical, financial or phychological harm to any person unless the Torah permits harming him. Just as it is forbidden to steal from a sinner, so too it is forbidden to speak about him in a way that could cause him financial loss.[40]

Can one transform an accuser into an advocate?

25 Tishrei · Sol Brevda לע״נ שלום בן אליה
Dedicated by Mrs. Frances Brevda, Brooklyn, NY; Isaacson family,
Baltimore MD; Meyers family, Rego Park, NY
25 Nissan · May today's learning be a זכות for Shimon Aryeh Leib
Goldstein, Yerushalayim

⚯ *Points to Ponder*

The following is drawn from the writings of the holy *Alshich*:

How can one speak before the King of kings with a mouth which utters forbidden talk? Would not God, as it were, respond, "Who is this shameful person who dares to beg forgiveness of his sins with a lowly tongue? Would he dare serve an earthly king with vessels which are covered with grime? Surely the king would punish him severely for such disgraceful service!"

How can one contemplate singing the praises of *Psalms* before the "One Who spoke and the world came into being" with a tongue which speaks evil talk? Should not one refrain from bringing an unclean object into the Sanctuary of God — out of respect for the Glory that dwells there? Can one not feel a sense of shame, having taken that which was given him to serve his Creator, and transformed it into something despicable? Can one hope to seek God's favor with a mouth that is impure? Can one transform an accuser into an advocate?

≈ About Children

It is forbidden to speak *loshon hora* about children. While most people understand that "kids are kids" and the Torah does not hold children responsible for their actions, if one speaks about a child in a manner that either the speaker or listener sees as derogatory, then the laws of *shmiras haloshon* have been violated.[41]

It is also forbidden to say or write something about a child that potentially could prove harmful to him.[42]

A teacher who is prepared to enter a negative comment on a student's record should pause to contemplate the effect that entry might have on the student's future educational and employment opportunities.

Likewise, teachers should exercise caution and fairness when conveying their feelings concerning a student to his teacher for the coming year.

There is no comparison between breath that is tainted by sin and breath that is free of sin.

26 Tishrei · Rabbi Yitzchok Kirzner זצ"ל לע"נ הרב יצחק ליב בן הרב זעליג זצ"ל
Dedicated by צפורה בת גרשון אליהו
26 Nissan · Charlie Klugmann לע"נ ר' משלם בן החבר משה
Dedicated by the Klugmann & Rubinfeld families

✒ Pure and Untainted

The Talmud states:

> Reish Lakish said in the name of R' Yehudah Nesiah: "The world is sustained only in the merit of the breath [of Torah study] of school children."
>
> Said R' Pappa to Abaye: "And what is with yours and mine [i.e. our Torah study]?"
>
> Abaye replied: "There is no comparison between breath that is tainted by sin and breath that is free of sin" (*Shabbos* 119b).

If the Sages were, to their minds, guilty of forbidden speech, it could only have been an inadvertent and rare occurrence. Yet they declared their words of Divine service to be tainted because of this. How much more so is this true of one who habitually speaks the forbidden — especially *loshon hora*, which causes ill will and strife among Jews.

✤ Repentance

If one has uttered a potentially harmful statement about someone, he has committed a sin that is both *bein adam la'Makom*, between man and Hashem, and *bein adam la'chaveiro*, between man and his fellow. Confession, regret and resolution for the future can only serve as *teshuvah* (repentance) for one's sins before Hashem. For sins against man, one must approach the person and beg forgiveness.[43]

This only applies to a situation where one's speech has already caused damage. If a potentially damaging statement was made but no actual harm has resulted as of yet, it is the speaker's responsibility to do his best to prevent this from happening.[44]

A practical way of accomplishing this would be to approach anyone who has heard the harmful information, and explain that it was inaccurate.

The awesome sanctity of Torah is an unchanging fact; the greater the purity of one's speech, the more he is bound up with the light of the Torah he learns.

27 Tishrei · Sidney I. Broome לע"נ ישראל יצחק בן ר' אברהם שלמה
Dedicated by Bernard H. Broome
27 Nissan · David Aharon Sklar לע"נ דוד אהרן ז"ל בן יעקב משה
Dedicated by the Sklar family, Israel

❧ *The Poor Man's Treasure*

A very noteworthy concept can be derived from the Talmud's teaching that the world exists in the merit of the Torah study of children, and that their study is superior to that of the generation's leading sages. This concept can be better understood with a parable:

A poor man found a very rare, precious gem, which was commonly found only in the crowns of kings. This was a gem which could be used for a variety of very important purposes, a fact of which the poor man had no notion. The king of that country asked the poor man to give him the gem, and in return, rewarded him with great wealth and a position of prominence. Thus, the poor man received great reward not for what he knew, but for what he possessed.

Torah study is the rare, precious gem and the young children, who are unaware of the Torah's awesome sanctity and the depth of its wisdom, are like the poor man who does not perceive the gem's true worth. Though they lack this understanding, nevertheless, they are personally sanctified and sustain the world through their study. This is because the awesome sanctity of Torah is an unchanging fact and is not dependent on any mental or other preparation on the part of the student. Whenever anyone studies Torah, he is naturally bound up with its sanctity. Thus does the prophet allude to the study of Torah when he says, "... whenever I speak of him I remember him more and more. Therefore, My inner self yearns for him..." (*Yirmiyahu* 31:19).

However, when a person defiles his power of speech by speaking that which is forbidden, then the degree of spiritual light which he draws from the study of Torah is diminished.

We can now better understand the Sages' discussion cited above. R' Pappa asked Abaye, "What of our Torah study? Do not the sacred thoughts which are so essential to our study make it superior to that of young children?" Abaye responded, "There is no comparison between breath that is tainted by sin and breath that is free of sin," meaning that the purity of the children's study outweighs whatever it lacks.

כח תשרי
28 TISHREI / CYCLE 1

כח ניסן
28 NISSAN / CYCLE 2

SEFER CHOFETZ CHAIM

LOSHON HORA: Laws of Harmful Speech

❧ Unknowing Victim

A person who has caused harm to his fellow must ask forgiveness even if the victim is unaware that he has been harmed.[45]

A case in point is where an employee was being considered for promotion but was never informed of this possibility. If someone violated the laws of *loshon hora* and made a statement to the employer which resulted in the promotion not being granted, he must approach the victim, explain what has happened, and beg forgiveness.

However, Rabbi Yisrael Salanter is reported to have held that if relating the incident to the victim would cause him anguish, one would have to forego that aspect of the *teshuvah* process.

When business matters are concerned, people are careful to remove any possible impediment to success. Should we be any less vigilant in our spiritual pursuits?

28 Tishrei · Meshulem Rosenfeld לע"נ משולם פייש בן שמעון
Dedicated by Baila, Arieh Leib & Suri Rosenfeld, Aharon & Chanie
Dier and Moshe & Faygie Kramer
28 Nissan · Mrs. Anna Kantor לע"נ העניל בת הירש לייב
Dedicated by Allen, Susan and Ariella Black

✒ *Comparisons*

L et us consider the above: The Sages of the Talmud were mighty cedars, whose thoughts were constantly bound up with Hashem. They were forever contemplating His greatness and His commandments, and their speech was exceedingly sacred and pure. If, in the course of speaking, it happened by chance that an improper word escaped their lips, surely they immediately engaged in an appropriate form of repentance. Nevertheless, even this rare improper utterance did damage to the sanctity of their power of speech, so that it was diminished from its previous level.

What of ourselves, then, whose level of study in no way compares to that of the Sages of the Talmud? If we will defile our mouths with words of *loshon hora,* mockery, strife and the like — what sort of sanctity will be manifest through our Torah study?

Let us compare our approaches to spiritual and material pursuits. When, for example, business matters are concerned, one does not cease from pondering ways by which to improve his enterprises and increase his profits. He is careful to remove any possible impediment to success. And no person of sound mind would intentionally do anything that could harm his very source of livelihood.

Yet with spiritual pursuits the opposite is often the case. We ourselves bring about the ruination of the remnant that still remains with us — the bit of Torah study and prayer that we have. How? Through forbidden speech.

כט תשרי
29 TISHREI / CYCLE 1

כט ניסן
29 NISSAN / CYCLE 2

SEFER CHOFETZ CHAIM

LOSHON HORA: General Rules

❧ Other Means of Communication

Having concluded our discussion of the two basic categories of *loshon hora* (derogatory or harmful information), it is important to note several rules that apply equally to both:

Loshon hora is not limited to speech. Included in this prohibition is communication of derogatory or harmful information through any means. Therefore, writing *loshon hora,* or using code, sign or body language (e.g. a cynical smile or rolling one's eyes upward in exasperation) that communicates something negative or harmful is forbidden.[46]

To show others a letter or article that would reflect badly on its author is forbidden, as is revealing the identity of the author of a work that is known to be of poor quality.[47]

It is also forbidden to show photographs of people which they would find embarrassing.

When a Jew studies Torah, he perfects his entire being —but this can be forfeited through speaking loshon hora.

---

29 Tishrei · Mrs. Norma Kletzel לע״נ נחמה בת הר״הג רב צבי הירש
Dedicated by her children & grandchildren
29 Nissan · May today's learning be a זכות for שירה ברכה בת
מיכאל נתן שתחי׳

DAY 29

❧ Forfeiting the Greatest of Treasures

Speaking *loshon hora* can cause the inestimable merit of one's Torah study to be forfeited. In the words of *Midrash Shochar Tov* (*Tehillim* ch. 52):

> Let not your mouth bring guilt on your flesh, and do not tell the emissary that it was an error. Why should God be angered by your speech and destroy the work of your hands? (Koheles 5:5).

> Let not your mouth bring guilt on your flesh —by speaking *loshon hora*.

> Why should God be angered by your speech and destroy the work of your hands? — for you will lose the little Torah which you have to your credit.

The intent of this *Midrash* is that, as already discussed,[1] speaking *loshon hora* causes the speaker's merits to be transferred to the Heavenly account of the person against whom he spoke.

When a Jew studies Torah, he perfects his entire being, for he draws upon himself a spirit of sanctity, which gives vitality to his body in this world and to his soul in the next world. Thus do the Sages teach (*Eruvin* 54a): "One who feels pain in his head should study Torah... One who feels pain in his throat should study Torah... One who feels pain in his entire body should study Torah, as it is written (*Mishlei* 4:22), 'And a cure for his entire flesh.' "

And all this can be lost through speaking *loshon hora*.

---

1. See Day 17.

ל תשרי
30 TISHREI / CYCLE 1

ל ניסן
30 NISSAN / CYCLE 2

SEFER CHOFETZ CHAIM
LOSHON HORA: General Rules

❧ *Without Names*

All forms of *loshon hora* are prohibited even when no names are mentioned, if it will be possible for people to determine who is being discussed.[48]

Furthermore, if names are omitted but the story will reflect badly on an entire group of people, it may not be spoken. Speaking critically about an unnamed student at a yeshivah is often taken as a statement about the entire student body or as a reflection on yeshivah students in general. If this is the implication, the statement is a more serious form of *loshon hora,* for it reflects on a multitude of Jews.

Surely there is infinite reward for man who, through his own free choice, refrains from speaking the forbidden.

לע"נ ר' משה יעקב בן ר' נחום ז"ל · 30 Tishrei · Jacob M. Shayovich
Dedicated by Mr. & Mrs. Mark Kutoff and family, Minneapolis, MN
לע"נ ר' יוסף ז"ל בן הרה"ג ר' מרדכי פארהאנד זצוק"ל · 30 Nissan
Dedicated by his sons · Vienna, New York, London

❧ *Rewards*

*Z*ohar states (*Parashas Chukas*) that one who is zealous in avoiding forbidden speech becomes enveloped in a spirit of sanctity.

Midrash Tanchuma (*Tehillim* 52:2) states: "The Holy One, Blessed is He, said: 'If you seek to escape [the punishments of] *Gehinnom*, distance yourself from *loshon hora*. Through this, you will be deemed meritorious in this world and the next.' "

The Torah states: "You shall not eat flesh of an animal that was torn in the field; to the dog shall you throw it" (*Shemos* 22:30). In fact, it is permitted to dispose of such meat in other ways as well. However, the Torah says to throw such meat to dogs as a way of reward for their not having howled at any Jew on the night of the Exodus (ibid. 11:7), for Hashem does not deprive any creature of its just reward. Surely, then, there is infinite reward reserved for man, who, through his own free choice, refrains from speaking the forbidden (*Mechilta, Parashas Mishpatim* 20).

א חשון
1 CHESHVAN / CYCLE 1

א אייר
1 IYAR / CYCLE 2

SEFER CHOFETZ CHAIM
LOSHON HORA: General Rules

❧ Slander

All forms of *loshon hora* are prohibited even when the information is true and accurate. (Only in very specific circumstances is it permissible to say something that would otherwise be considered *loshon hora;* this will be discussed later.)

Slander, which is information that is not true, referred to as *hotzaas shem ra* (lit., spreading a bad name), is worse than *loshon hora* which is derogatory but true.[49]

To relate derogatory information that is essentially true but includes either exaggerations or even slight altering of facts is also considered *hotzaas shem ra.*[50]

One who speaks ill of others becomes contemptible even to those who listened to his evil talk and accepted it as truth.

לע"נ ר' מרדכי בן ר' אהרן זצ"ל · 1 Cheshvan
Dedicated by his children, Rabbi & Mrs. Aharon Yona Piller
and family, Wickliffe, OH
לע"נ הגאון הצדיק הרב יהודא זאב Yeshiva Rosh Manchester The · 1 Iyar
בן הגאון הצדיק הרב משה יצחק הלוי סג"ל זצוק"ל
Dedicated by Chevras Shmiras Haloshon, Golders Green, London, England

DAY 31

✐ *The Quality of Peace*

Through *shmiras haloshon* one is blessed with the precious quality of peace. By refraining from speaking ill of others, one ensures that he will not be the object of their enmity; to the contrary, others will love him and confide in him, and surely will not speak ill of him.

Peace is precious, for in its merit, God does not allow Satan to harm the Jewish people, even when idolatry is found among them (*Bamidbar Rabbah* 11:16).[1]

One who accustoms himself to speaking favorably of others merits that God refers to him as שלום, *Peace*, which is one of God's own Names.[2] Conversely, with regard to the gossiper, the Sages state: "One who dines with his fellow and then speaks disparagingly of him is referred to by the Holy One, Blessed is He, as רע, *evil,* as it is written, "Deceit in the heart of those who plot evil" (*Mishlei* 12:20).

One who belittles others will, in the end, be the object of scorn — aside from the retribution that he will incur. The early commentators find an allusion to this in the verse, "Just as he inflicted a wound upon a person, so will be inflicted upon him" (*Vayikra* 24:20). Moreover, by speaking *loshon hora*, one becomes an object of contempt even in the eyes of his listener, who accepted his sinful words as truth. As the Sages put it, "False witnesses are contemptible even in the eyes of those who hire them" (*Sanhedrin* 29a). And his listeners will forever suspect that he might one day speak ill of them.

---

1. See Day 19.
2. As derived from *Shoftim* 6:24.

ב חשון
2 CHESHVAN / CYCLE 1

ב אייר
2 IYAR / CYCLE 2

SEFER CHOFETZ CHAIM

LOSHON HORA: General Rules

⚞ *Non-Kosher Entertainment*

It is forbidden to relate a story for entertainment purposes only, if it contains derogatory or harmful information.[51]

To relate an amusing incident that would cause embarrassment to any of the people involved if told in their presence constitutes speaking *loshon hora.* Many a humorous situation is actually quite painful to the person involved.

Wherever peace is found, fear of God is found; wherever peace is lacking, fear of God is lacking.

2 Cheshvan · Harav Chaim Gorfinkel לע״נ הרב חיים בן ר׳ שלמה הלוי ז״ל
Dedicated by the Garfinkel & Kaplinsky families, Brooklyn, NY; the
Landesman family, Silver Spring, MD
2 Iyar · The Manchester Rosh Yeshiva לע״נ הגאון הצדיק הרב יהודא זאב
בן הגאון הצדיק הרב משה יצחק הלוי סג״ל זצוק״ל
Dedicated by Mr. Margulies and family, Monsey, NY

DAY
32

ᴤ Peace is Precious

S efer Ma'alos HaMiddos (24) states:

Know, my son, that peace is an exalted quality, for it [Peace] is one of the Names of God ... Wherever peace is found, fear of God is found; wherever peace is lacking, fear of God is lacking.

Our Sages state: Peace is precious, for God altered the truth for the sake of peace between Avraham and Sarah. Sarah [in expressing disbelief that she would yet bear a child] said, "And my master [Avraham] is old" (Bereishis 18:12), but Hashem [in relating her statement to Avraham] said, "And I [Sarah] am old" (ibid. v. 13).

After Yaakov died, the brothers sent Yosef a message: "Your father gave orders before his death, saying, 'Thus shall you say to Yosef: O please, kindly forgive the spiteful deed of your brothers...' " (ibid. 50:16). We do not find any indication in the Torah that Yaakov did, in fact, give such instructions, for he did not suspect Yosef [of bearing any ill will toward his brothers. Yet the brothers, out of fear that Yosef had not forgiven them, altered the truth for the sake of peace].

Peace is precious, for in times of war, we must first seek peace, as it is written: "When you draw near to a city to wage war against it, you shall call out to it for peace" (Devarim 20:10).

Peace is precious, for it is with the blessing of peace that we conclude Bircas Kohanim (The Priestly Blessing), as it is written, "... and [may Hashem] establish peace for you" (Bamidbar 6:26).

Peace is precious, for it is with a request for peace that we conclude our daily prayer [i.e. the Shemoneh Esrei], as is derived from the verse: "HASHEM will give might to His people, HASHEM will bless His people with peace" (Tehillim 29:18).[1]

Moreover, on the great day of consolation at the End of Days, the first good tidings will be of peace, as it is written, "How beautiful ascending the mountains are the footsteps of the herald, making heard, 'Peace!' " (Yeshayahu 52:7).

---

1. See Megillah 18a.

ג חשון
3 TISHREI / CYCLE 1

ג אייר
3 NISSAN / CYCLE 2

SEFER CHOFETZ CHAIM
Avak Loshon Hora

ᴥ *Negative Allusions*

There are times when a speaker makes a positive statement about a person and intends it as such, but negative and harmful information can be inferred from his words. The Torah would not consider one who does this to be a *holech rachil,* peddler of gossip, since both his intent and his words are clearly sincere and positive.

Rabbinically, however, this too is prohibited, under a category referred to as *avak loshon hora,* the "dust" of *loshon hora,* that is spread by way of carelessness.

A common form of *avak loshon hora* is where one sincerely praises another person, but in doing so, alludes to a shortcoming of that individual.

"Who would have believed that he would have come this far?" clearly suggests something negative about the person. Such a statement can cause the person embarrassment when said in his presence, and can be harmful to him even when he is not present. Hence, it is forbidden.[52]

If someone bears you ill will, greet him with peace, for this will awaken a positive feeling within him.

לע״נ חיים ראובן בן ישעיהו בוייער · 3 Cheshvan
3 Iyar · Mrs. Gloria Schwartzberg לע״נ גיטל פרידע בת בנימין
Dedicated by the Slater family, Monsey NY

⚓ When Foes Become Friends

S*efer Ma'alos HaMiddos* continues:

> The Talmud states that no man —even a gentile in the marketplace —ever preceded Rabban Yochanan ben Zakkai in extending a greeting of peace (*Berachos* 17a).
>
> Our Sages taught: "Initiate a greeting of peace to every person" (*Avos* 4:20). What is meant by "every person"? Even if you know that someone bears you ill will, nevertheless, initiate a greeting of peace toward him. This will awaken a feeling of love for you within him. And even if he will not humble himself to make peace with you, God will humble him before you [so that he will not cause you any harm]. An allusion to this is found in Scripture, "But if he does not make peace with you ... HASHEM shall deliver him into your hand" (*Devarim* 20:12-13).
>
> Illustrative of the above is the story of David and Shaul. David sought peace with Shaul, while Shaul, far from being appeased, pursued David with the intent of harming him. Thus did David say, "I am peace —but when I speak, they are for war" (*Tehillim* 120:7). In two separate episodes, Hashem gave Shaul over into David's hands [and David could have easily killed him].[1] Yet, it did not enter David's mind to cause Shaul any harm, for man must love peace and pursue it.

---

1. See *I Shmuel*, chs. 24 and 26.

∝ *Harmful Praise*

Praise which has absolutely no negative connotations can, at times, fall under the category of *avak loshon hora.* It is forbidden to publicize a person's hospitality or generosity if this will cause the insincere and undeserving to take advantage of the person, causing him monetary loss and emotional discomfort.[53]

> **Never
> despair
> and say,
> "It is
> impossible
> to make
> peace!"**

✍ *Don't Despair*

S*efer Ma'alos Hamiddos* continues:

> David said, "Seek peace and pursue it" (*Tehillim* 34:15), meaning: Seek peace for your friends and pursue it among your enemies; seek peace where you dwell and pursue it in other places; seek peace with your body and pursue it with your resources;[1] seek peace for yourself and pursue it for others; seek peace today and pursue it tomorrow.
>
> Never despair and say, "It is impossible to make peace!" Rather, pursue peace until you attain it. How should you "pursue peace"? Speak words of peace when a feud has erupted, and put aside personal pride for the sake of the community. This was the way of Moshe, our Teacher, as it is written, "So Moshe stood up and went to Dasan and Aviram" (*Bamidbar* 16:25).[2]
>
> To pursue peace is to put aside one's personal affairs in order to make peace between husband and wife, man and his neighbor, teacher and student. Even to arrange a meal between feuding parties as a way of reconciling them is to pursue peace.

---

1. I.e. there are times when one must be willing to suffer monetary loss in order to maintain peace. In his conclusion of *Sefer Shmiras HaLoshon* (Part I), the Chofetz Chaim writes that a person can avoid minor monetary disputes by deciding in his mind to set aside a certain sum each year as "peace money." This will allow him to relent easily when such disagreements arise. The Chofetz Chaim reasons that just as the average Jew is willing to extend himself in order to fulfill *mitzvos* such as *arba minim* on Succos or matzah on Pesach —which can involve considerable expense — so too should he be willing to spend money so that he can reap the priceless benefits of avoiding strife and *loshon hora*, overlooking the hurt caused him, and pursuing peace.

2. Dasan and Aviram had joined with Korach in a rebellion against Moshe's leadership.

SEFER CHOFETZ CHAIM

Avak Loshon Hora

☙ *Praise in the Presence of Adversaries*

Praising a person in a situation where someone present is likely to temper such praise with criticism is another form of *avak loshon hora*. It is forbidden to praise someone in the presence of anyone who is known to dislike him, as it is common for such people to respond by mentioning the person's shortcomings.[54]

Therefore, it is wrong to praise someone in the presence of a large group of people, since there is a reasonable chance that at least one person in the group dislikes him.[55]

Likewise, it is forbidden to praise a businessman in the presence of his competitors even if they claim to harbor no ill will towards him.

Excessive praise should always be avoided for it can often cause people to respond negatively even when they have no particular dislike for the person being discussed.[56]

Shabbos candles take precedence over Kiddush wine, for their light fosters peace and harmony in one's home.

5 Cheshvan · Natalie Rebecca Shipman לע"נ הילדה חיה שושנה רבקה
ע"ה בת ר' שמואל הלוי נ"י
Dedicated to a special daughter and sister by the Shipman family,
London, England
5 Iyar · Rachel Wacks לע"נ מרת רחל בת ר' צבי ז"ל
Dedicated by her family, Manchester, England

❧ *Exceedingly Precious*

Sefer Ma'alos HaMiddos continues to demonstrate that the attribute of peace is exceedingly precious:

> After creating heaven and earth, God's next task was the creation of light (*Bereishis* 1:3), and light represents peace, as it is written, "Who forms light and creates darkness, makes peace and creates evil" (*Yeshayahu* 45:7). The Sages rule that when one has to choose between purchasing Shabbos candles or wine for *Kiddush*, Shabbos candles take precedence, for their light brings harmony to one's home (*Shabbos* 23b).
>
> The Mishnah (*Gittin* 5:8) lists a number of enactments which were instituted to promote harmony among the community: "These things were declared [by the Sages] because they are among the ways that foster harmony: A *Kohen* reads first [from the Torah scroll in the synagogue], and after him a *Levi*, and after him a *Yisrael,* because this is [one of the] ways that foster harmony ..."[1] And so it is written, "Her [the Torah's] ways are ways of pleasantness, and all her paths are peaceful" (*Mishlei* 3:17).
>
> The *Midrash (Bamidbar Rabbah* 15:13) enumerates thirteen items which are exceedingly precious to Hashem, as evident by Scripture's use of the term לִי, *for Me*, in connection with them, thus signifying their being God's prized possessions. Yet, only with regard to peace is the term לִי, *for Me,* used twice, as it is written, "If he would grasp My fortress, he would make peace for Me, peace would he make for Me" (*Yeshayahu* 27:5).

---

1. By creating an immutable order for the Torah reading, the Sages prevented quarreling among the community (*Rashi*).

ו חשון
6 CHESHVAN / CYCLE 1

ו אייר
6 IYAR / CYCLE 2

SEFER CHOFETZ CHAIM
Avak Loshon Hora

◌ *Obvious Implications*

There is a form of *avak loshon hora* that can re-sult from one's keeping the laws of forbidden speech. If one says that he is reluctant to discuss a particular individual so as to avoid speaking *loshon hora*, he is, in effect, communicating that he knows something negative about that person.

"I'd rather not discuss So-and-so," is *avak loshon hora.*[57]

When faced with such a situation, a person must either attempt to divert the conversation to another topic or indicate that he does not know any perti-nent information about the person under discussion.

When does Hashem manifest His Presence among His people? When they are united.

6 Cheshvan · David M. Kasten לע״נ הרב דוד יחיא-ל מיכל בן יהושע חיים
Dedicated by the Kasten, Hirsh & Schenk families
6 Iyar · Cantor Martin Horowitz לע״נ מרדכי מאיר בן צבי הירש הלוי
Dedicated by Mina, Howard, Sharon Millendorf & Mrs. Clara Horowitz

❧ *Spiritual Blessings*

*S*efer Ma'alos HaMiddos continues:

When Hashem rewards the wicked in this world for whatever good they have done [reserving their punishment for the World to Come], He grants them wealth, property, longevity, honor, and other benefits — but He does not grant them tranquility, as it is written, " 'There is no peace,' says my God, 'for the wicked' " (*Yeshayahu* 57:21). Conversely, peace is a reward reserved for the righteous, as it is written, "And the deed of righteousness will be [rewarded with] peace" (ibid. 32:17).

It is through [one's ways of] peace and brotherhood that others are inspired to repent and draw near to the One Above, as it is written, "I create fruit of the lips: 'Peace, peace, for far and near,' says HASHEM, 'and I shall heal him' " (ibid. 57:19).

Peace is precious, for regarding all but one of the journeys and encampments in the Wilderness, the Torah writes ויסעו, *they journeyed,* and ויחנו, *they encamped,* in the plural form, symbolizing the strife that plagued them. It is when the Jews arrived at Sinai that the Torah states: *And Israel camped there opposite the mountain* (*Shemos* 19:2), with the verb ויחן [lit. *and he camped*] in the singular. "Said the Holy One, Blessed is He: 'The moment when they shall receive the Torah has arrived' " (*Vayikra Rabbah* 9:9), for as long as peace dwelled amongst them, the Divine Presence dwelled amongst them. Thus it is written, "He [God] became King over Jeshurun when the numbers of the nation were gathered — the tribes of Israel in unity" (*Devarim* 33:5). When is God Israel's King in the fullest sense, and when does His Presence dwell among them? — when they are united.

Precious is peace, for it is through peace that the world endures, as the Sages state (*Avos* 1:18): "The world endures on three things — justice, truth and peace, as it is said, 'Truth and the verdict of peace are you to adjudicate in your gates' " (*Zechariah* 8:16).

SEFER CHOFETZ CHAIM

Avak Loshon Hora

❧ Constructive Negatives

Below we will see that in certain situations one may — and sometimes must — provide people with negative information that is important for them to know, either to avoid being harmed or for some other constructive purpose.

Whenever faced with such a situation, one must explain why he is saying something that would ordinarily be prohibited, so that the listener understands that the prohibitions regarding *loshon hora* are not being transgressed. To say anything that the listener thinks is *loshon hora* when, in fact, it is not, constitutes speaking *avak loshon hora*.[58]

Hashem allowed His sacred Name to be erased in order to restore peace between husband and wife.

לע״נ דבורה בת דוב בעריש הלוי ז״ל · 7 Cheshvan
לע״נ תעאה בת אשר ע״ה Thea Plaut · 7 Iyar
Dedicated in loving memory by Dr. & Mrs. Asher Plaut and family

✍ Love Peace and Pursue It

*S*efer *Ma'alos HaMiddos* concludes its discussion of the quality of peace with the following:

Our Sages state: Peace is precious, for one who erases a single letter of God's Holy Name transgresses a Torah prohibition,[1] yet in order that peace be restored between husband and wife, the Torah commands, "The *Kohen* shall inscribe these curses on a scroll and erase it into the bitter waters" (*Bamidbar* 5:23).[2] [The Scriptural verses written upon the scroll contain the Name of God.] Said the Holy One, Blessed is He, "Let My Name, which was written in sanctity, be erased upon the water!" (*Vayikra Rabbah* 9:15).

Our Sages (ibid.) further state: Peace is precious, for all the good blessings and consolations that the Holy One, Blessed is He, brings upon Israel conclude with peace. The blessings of the evening *Shema* conclude with, "Who spreads the shelter of peace." The *Shemoneh Esrei* concludes with, "He Who makes peace in His heights, may He make peace on us..." *Bircas Kohanim* concludes with, "May HASHEM... establish peace with you."

Therefore, my son, be zealous regarding this trait. Love peace and pursue it, for there is infinite reward for those who do so.

---

1. *Devarim* 12:3.

2. This verse is from the Torah portion dealing with the laws of the *sotah*, a married woman who is suspected of immorality and is forbidden to live with her husband until she undergoes the procedure detailed in the Torah. The *sotah*'s drinking of the bitter waters in which the scroll's verses are erased determines whether or not she sinned; if, indeed, she had been guilty of immorality, she would miraculously die a gruesome death upon drinking the water. If she would not die, her innocence would be proven and she would be permitted to live with her husband once again.

ח חשון
8 CHESHVAN / CYCLE 1

ח אייר
8 IYAR / CYCLE 2

SEFER CHOFETZ CHAIM
LOSHON HORA: General Rules

✒ *The Habitual Speaker of Loshon Hora*

The primary prohibition against speaking *loshon hora* is: לא תלך רכיל בעמיך, *Do not go as a gossip-monger among your people* (*Vayikra* 19:16). However, the Chofetz Chaim demonstrates that this sin can involve the transgression of numerous positive and negative commandments. The *baal loshon hora,* habitual speaker of *loshon hora,* can easily accumulate a multitude of transgressions at a rate unparalleled by any other sin. That is why the Sages say that speaking *loshon hora* is worse than even the most severe sins.[59]

Furthermore, it is virtually impossible for the habitual speaker to ask forgiveness of everyone who was affected by his sinful speech; thus, he will find it difficult if not impossible to achieve full repentance for his sins.[60]

The Sages caution us to avoid associating with a *baal loshon hora,* and not to live in the vicinity of such people.[61]

To love and pursue peace is to secure for oneself a place in the World to Come.

---

8 Cheshvan · May today's learning be a זכות for Shmuel Yerucham
Goldstein and family, Har Nof, Yerushalayim
8 Iyar · Bessie Panish לע״נ בתיה בת מאיר
Dedicated in memory of our mother and grandmother by Harry,
Stuart, & Mark Panish and their families

❧ Disciples of Aharon

The greatness of peace can be seen from the following incident recorded in the Talmud (*Ta'anis* 22a):

> R' Beroka of Bei Chozai would frequent the marketplace of Bei Lefet. The prophet Eliyahu often appeared to him. Once, R' Beroka said to Eliyahu: "Is there anyone in this marketplace who is destined for the World to Come?"
>
> In the meantime, two other people entered the marketplace. Eliyahu said to R' Beroka, "These ... are destined for the World to Come." R' Beroka approached them and asked, "What do you do?" They replied, "We are comedians and we go to cheer up those who are depressed.[1] Additionally, whenever we see two people involved in a quarrel, we strive hard to make peace between them."

"Hillel said: 'Be among the disciples of Aharon, loving peace and pursuing peace, loving people and bringing them closer to Torah' " (*Avos* 1:12). To be among the disciples of Aharon is to secure for oneself a place in the World to Come.

With regard to the other source of merit of the two men, one should note the importance of helping others to rid themselves of their anguish and worries. To do so is to fulfill the *mitzvah*, "You shall love your fellow as yourself" (*Vayikra* 19:18). Moreover, this brings immeasurable pleasure to Hashem, as it were.

We can liken this to a father whose son is experiencing worry and suffering. Surely the father will experience great relief and joy if someone offers his son moral support, and he overcomes his distress. Similarly, the Jewish people are considered Hashem's children.[2]

---

1. They devoted their comic talents solely for such situations, and thus acted for the sake of Heaven.
2. *Devarim* 14:1; see *Bava Basra* 10a.

≈ Like Any Other Prohibition

A s with any Torah prohibition, one cannot justify speaking *loshon hora* on the basis of personal need or practicality. A Jew must be prepared to forego his comfort, social status, and even livelihood rather than transgress Torah Law.[62] Needless to say, it is forbidden to speak *loshon hora* to gain popularity or win friendship.

One must not succumb to social pressure and engage in gossip, in the same way that one would not compromise his *kashrus* standards due to social pressure.[63]

It is forbidden to comply with an employer's demand that one reveal information which is *loshon hora* — even if such failure means the loss of one's job.[64]

Similarly, the commandment to honor one's father and mother does not justify speaking *loshon hora*. One must respectfully refuse a parent's request that derogatory or harmful information be related.[65]

Why must the metzora live in isolation? Because he caused friction between those who had loved one another.

9 Cheshvan · The Manchester Rosh Yeshiva לע״נ הגאון הצדיק הרב
יהודא זאב בן הגאון הצדיק הרב משה יצחק הלוי סג״ל זצוק״ל
הונצח על ידי האחים חיים יהושע הכהן וויוסף אברהם הכהן אסט,
לונדון, ענגלאנד
אריה בן אליהו ישעיהו נ״י for זכות a 9 Iyar · May today's learning be

❧ *The Metzora's Isolation*

"He who slanders his neighbor in secret — him will I cut down" (*Psalms* 101:5). The Talmud (*Arachin* 15b) interprets the latter half of the verse as a reference to the terrible affliction of *tzaraas*.[1]

The Talmudic sage Reish Lakish sees the term מצרע (one who is afflicted with *tzaraas*) as a contraction of מוציא שם רע, *one who spreads slander.* "Whoever speaks *loshon hora* will have afflictions [of *tzaraas*] visited upon him" (ibid.).

This indicates the extreme severity of this sin, for the Torah is unusually stringent with regard to the laws of *tumah* (ritual impurity) as pertaining to the *metzora*. In the Wilderness, three distinct boundaries existed within the Jews' encampment, each representing a different level of sanctity. From among the various types of ritually impure, only the *metzora* was forbidden from entering all three camps. As the Torah states: "He shall dwell in isolation; his dwelling shall be outside the camp" (*Vayikra* 13:46).

"Why was the *metzora* singled out to live in isolation? Because [through his evil speech] he caused a husband to separate from his wife, and friends to become distant from one another" (*Arachin* 16b).

"R' Yehoshua ben Levi said: Why was the *metzora* singled out to bring two birds for his purification? Said the Holy One, Blessed is He: 'His sin was one of [sinful] chatter, therefore, let him bring an offering of chirping birds' " (ibid.).

---

1. See second footnote to Day 24.

י חשון
10 CHESHVAN / CYCLE 1

י אייר
10 IYAR / CYCLE 2

SEFER CHOFETZ CHAIM

LOSHON HORA: General Rules

⌇ Fighting Fire With Fire

We have seen that one must be prepared to make sacrifices so that the laws of forbidden speech not be violated.

In the world of business, when one's product is maligned by competitors, the natural and predictable reaction is to respond in kind. Such is not the way of the Torah. There is no basis for the notion that one who has been the object of *loshon hora* can respond with a counter-offensive of defamation.[66]

The metzora's isolation and disgrace humbled him, and inspired him to regret his sin.

---

10 Cheshvan · Mrs. Rena Lillian Freeman לע״נ רחל לאה בת זאב ע״ה
Dedicated by the Freeman, Brecher & Shapiro families
10 Iyar · May today's learning be a זכות for our משפחה
Dedicated by Yehuda Levine & family

❧ *Humbled and Contrite*

The Torah teaches that the punishment of *tzaraas* can take on a number of forms, and each is intended as a Divine calling to the afflicted individual. In the words of *Rambam* (*Hilchos Tumas Tzaraas* 16:10):

> The term *tzaraas* encompasses a number of phenomena which are totally distinct from one another. It refers to the whitening of human skin; the falling out of human hair from the head or beard; a change of color of a garment; and a change of color of the wall of a house.[1]
>
> These [phenomena] . . . did not fall within the laws of nature. Rather, each was a sign and wonder among the people of Israel to caution them with regard to *loshon hora.*
>
> If a person would speak *loshon hora*, then the walls of his house would change color [and the house would be pronounced *tamei* (impure) by the *Kohen*]; if he repented, the walls would revert back to their original state [and would be purified]. If he persisted in his wickedness until his house would have to be destroyed, then the hides upon which he would sit or lie would change color [and be declared *tamei*]; if he repented, then the hides would undergo ritual purification. If he persisted in his wickedness until the hides would have to be burned, then the clothing he wore would change color; if he repented, then the clothing would undergo purification. If he persisted in his wickedness until they would have to be burned, then his skin color would change and he would be declared a *metzora*. He would have to remain apart [from his fellow Jews] and his condition would become known to all, so that he would no longer take part in the conversations of the wicked, which are filled with frivolity and *loshon hora.*

(Continued on page 406)

---

1. The laws of the various forms of *tzaraas* are detailed in the Torah portions of *Tazria* and *Metzora* (*Vayikra* chs. 13-14).

יא חשון
11 CHESHVAN / CYCLE 1

יא אייר
11 IYAR / CYCLE 2

SEFER CHOFETZ CHAIM
Laws of Toeles

❧ Toeles — Constructive Purpose

Based on the rule that one must endure social and financial loss rather than speak *loshon hora,* it would seem that there should be no halachic justification to speak *loshon hora* for a constructive purpose (*l'toeles*). Why then does the *halachah* permit constructive statements to be made?

We have noted that all forms of *loshon hora* fall under one of two categories:

(1) derogatory statements;

(2) statements which have the potential to cause the subject harm.

Derogatory speech was explained as being lowly in that the speaker focuses on the negative aspects of someone's character or behavior.

There are times when discussing someone's shortcomings is clearly constructive, and the responsible thing to do. This is true either: when one is attempting to assist the person he is speaking about, or when he is trying to protect others from that person. In such cases, though negative traits or actions are being mentioned, the statements made do not constitute *loshon hora.* Destructive speech is *loshon hora;* constructive speech is not.[67] Similarly, there is no such thing as "constructive *rechilus*" (gossip); a statement can be classified as *rechilus* only if it is destructive.

(Continued on page 406)

> **When Hashem visits punishment upon an individual, He does it for the person's benefit.**

לע״נ מנשה בן נג׳י גבאי ז״ל · II Cheshvan
Dedicated by his wife Orna & daughters Natalie Michal, Rivka
Na'ama & Nethanella Rachel Hadassa
II Iyar · William Goldbaum לע״נ זאב וולף בן יצחק אייזיק
Dedicated by families: Goldbaum, Reinin, Platt, Bittelman & Gross

DAY
41

☙ *To Inspire Repentance*

God would take note of the *metzora*'s repentance and would heal him of his affliction. The *Kohen* would go outside the Israelite Camp to examine the *metzora*. Having been declared healed by the *Kohen*, the *metzora* would begin the purification process, which included the offering of Temple sacrifices, as detailed in the Torah.[1]

Having benefited from God's infinite kindness in being cured of his affliction and restored to a state of *taharah* (ritual purity), the person would, upon returning home, surely uphold his earlier resolutions. He would beg forgiveness of those he wronged and strive with all his strength to avoid speaking *loshon hora* in the future. Thus, he would be completely cleansed of his sin.

One may wonder why in our day the affliction of *tzaraas* is not manifest upon those who habitually speak *loshon hora*. The *Chidah*[2] offers the following explanation:

When God visits punishment upon an individual, He does it for the person's benefit, to purify him of his sins and to stir him towards repentance. Now, it was only during the Temple era that a *metzora* could attain *taharah* (purification). Today, however, when due to our sins there is no Temple, no sacrifice, and no way for the *Kohen* to perform the other components of the purification process, if God were to afflict a person with *tzaraas*, he would remain in his impure state for the rest of his life, without any possibility of ridding himself of it. Therefore, in the absence of the Temple, the impurity of this affliction clings only to the soul, but is not manifest on the person's body.

---

1. *Vayikra* ch. 14.
2. R' Chaim Yosef David Azulai (חיד״א) in his *Sefer Nachal Kidumim*.

יב חשון
12 CHESHVAN / CYCLE 1

יב אייר
12 IYAR / CYCLE 2

✒ *Parameters*

The most common constructive purposes which justify speaking negatively about a person fall under four categories:

(1) To help the person about whom one is speaking (e.g. to discuss a person's faults with someone else in order to help the person improve).[68]

(2) To help those who are being adversely affected by the person's behavior:

(a) providing help for people physically, psychologically or financially victimized by him;[69]

(b) protecting people from falling victim to his behavior in the future[70] — including warning the unsuspecting who are seriously considering entering into an unhealthy social or business relationship with him.[71]

(3) To help put an end to a dispute in which the person is involved and which threatens to divide the community.[72]

(4) To help others learn from the person's mistakes.[73]

The gossiper should bemoan the state of his soul.

12 Cheshvan · Miriam Posner (Weilgus) לע"נ מרים בת שמחה משה הלוי
Dedicated by Dr. Louis & Chanie Malcmacher and children
12 Iyar · Irwin Heller לע"נ חיים יצחק ישראל ז"ל בן ברוך הלוי
Dedicated in loving memory by his son Aaron S. Heller ז"ל and family

DAY
42

⚘*Affliction of the Soul*

The fact that *tzaraas* is a spiritual malady which afflicts the soul [aside from afflicting the body] is stated in the *Midrash*:

שמר פיו ולשונו שמר מצרות נפשו, *One who guards his mouth and tongue, guards his soul from tribulations (Mishlei* 21:23).

מצרות נפשו [lit., *his soul from tribulations* can be read homiletically] מצרעת נפשו, *[One who guards his mouth and tongue guards] his soul from tzaraas (Yalkut Shimoni, Parashas Metzora).*

Thus, one who is in the habit of speaking *loshon hora* should bemoan the state of his soul. Though Hashem has mercy on him and does not reveal his disgrace in this world, such will not be the case in the World to Come. There, the shame of his malady will be revealed to all. *Alone will he sit Above, outside the camp of Israel*[1] — unless he repented properly before departing this world.

---

1. Based on *Vayikra* 13:46.

יג חשון
13 CHESHVAN / CYCLE 1

יג אייר
13 IYAR / CYCLE 2

SEFER CHOFETZ CHAIM
TOELES: Seven Conditions

❧ Preconditions

The fact that a situation falls under one of the previously listed categories does not necessarily mean that discussing it constitutes constructive speech. No less than 7 conditions must be met before a critical statement about an individual may be said.

Condition #1: The first set of conditions deals with verification of facts. It is absolutely forbidden to make any critical statement about a person on the basis of information obtained through hearsay. Only through first-hand information may one assume that a Jew's character or behavior is wanting.[74] (An exception would be where one seeks to protect someone from potential harm; such instances would permit one to pass on second-hand information. This will be discussed later.)[75]

Condition #2: Even if one has witnessed seemingly unacceptable behavior, he must not hastily pass judgment on what has occurred. An incident taken out of context can be terribly misleading, both as a reflection on an individual's character as well as in determining who is right in a dispute between parties. Circumstances must be carefully investigated before one can be sure that he understands a situation correctly. Above all, before concluding that a person has, in fact, transgressed Jewish law, one must be knowledgeable of the relevant *halachos.*[76]

The sufferings of poverty take the place of tzaraas.

13 Cheshvan · Wohlberg לע״נ יהושע בירך בן ישראל שלמה
Dedicated by Moti & Estee Salamon
13 Iyar · Mrs. Gertrude Rietman לע״נ גיסא בת יוסף פישל
Dedicated by the Siegal, Gawartin & Kenzer families

❧ *Poverty*

A bove, we discussed the question of how it is that in our day those who habitually speak *loshon hora* are not afflicted with *tzaraas*. Another answer to this is found in *Sefer Davar Kedushah*, who cites *Sefer HaKaneh:*

The sufferings of poverty take the place of *tzaraas*, for by being dependent upon others for survival, the poor man becomes rid of any arrogance — a prime cause of *loshon hora*.[1] Moreover, the poor man is actually afraid to speak disparagingly of others, lest they learn of his remarks and cease to assist him.

Tikkunei Zohar, as well, states that this sin can lead to poverty. Therefore, one who seeks to avoid material strain should be zealous in *shmiras haloshon*.

---

1. See Day 134.

יד חשון
14 CHESHVAN / CYCLE 1

יד אייר
14 IYAR / CYCLE 2

SEFER CHOFETZ CHAIM
TOELES: Seven Conditions

๛ *End Result*

Before relating negative information *l'toeles,* for a constructive purpose, one must carefully consider whether or not his words will, in fact, bring about the desired result. Speaking negatively *l'toeles* is justified only if there is a reasonable chance that the desired result will be accomplished.[77]

This point is of particular importance when one seeks to discourage a potentially harmful friendship, business association or *shidduch* (marriage match). Often, a final decision has already been made, and speaking negatively of the other party will serve no constructive purpose.[78]

It would have been fitting to conceal the episode of Miriam's tzaraas. The Torah records it, and commands us to recall it, to emphasize the severity of loshon hora.

14 Cheshvan · Alice Rothschild לע״נ יענדעלע בת ר׳ ארי׳ ע״ה
Dedicated by Kurt & Edith Rothschild and family
14 Iyar · Samuel Rosengarten לע״נ ר׳ שמואל בן ר׳ מנחם מנדל הכהן ע״ה
Dedicated by his children

DAY 44

❧ *Miriam's Affliction*

The Torah relates (*Bamidbar* ch. 12) how Miriam criticized her brother Moshe for not living with his wife after the Torah was given through him. Miriam did not realize that a man of Moshe's humility and selflessness would not have done so unless he had been commanded to be in a constant state of readiness to receive prophecy. Miriam was punished with *tzaraas*, and was subsequently healed through the prayers of Moshe.

The Torah states: "Beware of a *tzaraas* affliction, to be very careful and to act; according to all that the *Kohanim*, the Levites shall teach you ..."(*Devarim* 24:8). The very next verse exhorts the Jewish people to "Remember what HASHEM, your God, did to Miriam on the way when you were leaving Egypt.' *Sifre* comments:

> Why are these two verses juxtaposed? — to teach that Miriam was punished [with *tzaraas*] only because she spoke *loshon hora*. It is a *kal v'chomer* (a fortiori): If Miriam, who spoke against her younger brother, was punished [so severely], then how much more so one who speaks against someone greater than himself. Alternatively: If Miriam, whose words were heard by no one other than the Holy One, Blessed is He, as it is written, "And HASHEM heard" (*Bamidbar* 12:2), was punished [so severely] then how much more so one who speaks disparagingly of his fellow in public.

Ramban comments: "[With this verse,] we are commanded to make known [the episode of Miriam] to our offspring and to relate it to future generations. It would have been fitting to conceal this episode so as not to speak the disgrace of the righteous; nevertheless, Scripture commands that we make it known and revealed, so that we be well versed in the prohibition of forbidden speech, which is a great sin and brings about many bad happenings, yet is transgressed frequently."

טו חשון
15 CHESHVAN / CYCLE 1

טו אייר
15 IYAR / CYCLE 2

SEFER CHOFETZ CHAIM
TOELES: Seven Conditions

✎ *Reprove First*

Condition #3:

Before speaking about a person with others, one must first discuss the issue with that person himself. Trying to persuade the sinner to change his ways is a course which must be pursued before bringing anyone else into the picture.[79] (This would not apply if speaking to the sinner might make it difficult, if not impossible, to achieve the desired result through any other means.)[80]

There is no natural way for the metzora to rid himself of his affliction; his only hope is teshuvah.

15 Cheshvan · Henry Gleitman לע״נ יחזקאל בן דוד אריה
Dedicated by the Gleitman family, Brooklyn, NY
15 Iyar · In honor of the Pressman family לכבוד משפחת פרסמן
Dedicated by Yakov & Judy Pressman

DAY 45

✍ *Remembrance*

Remember what Hashem, your God, did to Miriam on the way, when you were leaving Eygpt (Devarim 24:7).

In this verse, the Torah instructs us to remember four factors in the episode of Miriam's sin and subsequent punishment: 1) *Remember what HASHEM, your God, did* — remember the punishment which He inflicted. 2) *Remember* upon whom it was inflicted — *to Miriam*. 3) *Remember* where this occurred — *on the way*. 4) *Remember* at which juncture in our history it occurred — *when you were leaving Egypt*.

Each of the above factors is significant, and its remembrance is of great benefit.

As mentioned above, Miriam was punished with *tzaraas* for speaking wrongly of her brother Moshe. The *metzora,* upon being declared healed by the *Kohen*, must undergo a purification process which includes the taking of two birds. One bird is slaughtered, while the other is set free upon the open field. The *Midrash* explains this as an allusion: Just as a slaughtered bird cannot return to life, so too there is no natural way for the *metzora* to become rid of his *tzaraas;* his only hope is *teshuvah* (repentance). And just as the bird which is set free is allowed to return to its previous way of life, so too can the *metzora's* repentance result in a complete cure so that he can return to normal living among his brethren.

As mentioned above, the *tumah* (impurity) of *tzaraas* is extremely severe. The *metzora* must live in solitude, his clothing rent and his hair disheveled like a mourner, unlike any other *tamei* (impure person). Anyone who stands under the same roof as the *metzora* contracts *tumah*.[1] Moreover, the Sages liken a *metzora* to a dead person (*Nedarim* 64b).[2]

Remember what HASHEM, your God, did to Miriam...

---

1. Aside from a *metzora,* only a human corpse can transmit *tumah* in this way.
2. This lends added meaning to the above comparison to a slaughtered bird.

טז חשון
16 CHESHVAN / CYCLE 1

טז אייר
16 IYAR / CYCLE 2

SEFER CHOFETZ CHAIM
TOELES: Seven Conditions

◄§ *A Last Resort*

Condition #4:

If, in addition to personal reproof, any other option exists that could preclude the necessity to speak negatively of someone, it must be pursued. Negative speech, even for a constructive purpose, is lowly if it can be avoided.[81]

In the same vein, when speaking negatively is necessary, one must carefully calculate just how much must be related in order to achieve the desired result. To relate any unnecessary negative information would be to speak *loshon hora.*[82]

Furthermore, even if it is clear that someone must be made aware of certain derogatory information about another person, one should choose the least blatant means by which to communicate that information. Directing someone to where he will become aware of information on his own is preferable to expressing it verbally.[83]

In comparing two candidates for a position, stressing the strengths of one is often sufficient without actually articulating what the other lacks. In all cases, the least negative course is the one to follow.[84]

Miriam's intentions were purely for the sake of Heaven. Yet this did not save her from affliction for having spoken against her brother.

16 Cheshvan · Sol Firestone לע״נ שמואל בן אריה לייב
Dedicated by Ezra & Miriam Firestone
לע״נ מרת אידל ברייער בת ר׳ אברהם שרייבער · 16 Iyar
Dedicated by the Breuer family, London, England

DAY
46

~A Timeless Message

R*emember* upon whom the punishment of *tzaraas* was inflicted — upon the righteous Miriam, in whose merit the miraculous well poured forth water from the time the Jews departed Egypt until her death almost forty years later. She was a prophetess, as it is written, "Miriam the prophetess, the sister of Aharon ..." (*Shemos* 15:20). Her criticism was directed toward her brother, whom she loved like her very own self, and for whom she endangered her life when she stood by the riverbank when Moshe was placed in the river as an infant (ibid. ch. 2). She did not speak disparagingly of Moshe; she merely accorded him the status of other prophets.[1] She did not speak in Moshe's presence, which might have caused him embarrassment, nor did she utter her words in public. Whatever she said was spoken between herself and her righteous brother Aharon. Her intentions were purely for the sake of Heaven. Moreover, Moshe, upon being informed of her words, bore her no ill will, as it is written, "Now the man Moshe was exceedingly humble ..." (*Bamidbar* 12:3). Despite all of the above, Miriam was punished with *tzaraas*.

Remember upon whom it was inflicted.

The Torah relates, "The people did not journey until Miriam was [cured and] brought in [to the camp]" (*Bamidbar* 12:15). Miriam's exceptional merits were not enough to allow her punishment to be deferred until the nation had arrived at their next destination, where her condition would have drawn less attention. She was punished on the way, and her disgrace became known to all.

Remember where the episode of Miriam's affliction occurred.

---

1. Thus, she faulted him for not living with his wife as other prophets did.

יז חשון
17 CHESHVAN / CYCLE 1

יז אייר
17 IYAR / CYCLE 2

SEFER CHOFETZ CHAIM

TOELES: Seven Conditions

✎ *Be Accurate*

Condition #5:

While derogatory information may be related for a constructive purpose, slander cannot be justified. One does not have the right to exaggerate or alter facts for a constructive purpose, nor may one omit details that minimize the severity of the person's actions.[85]

Indiscriminate use of superlatives such as "very" can easily distort facts way out of proportion. This is, in fact, a most common form of slander that people engage in, albeit unwittingly. Conversely, one must omit authentic details that make the story sound even worse if the result can be attained without their being mentioned.

We are obligated to take a lesson from both the episode of Miriam and that of the spies.

17 Cheshvan · Jack Weinberg לע״נ יוסף בן ישראל
Dedicated by Michael Weinberg in memory of his father
17 Iyar · Mrs. Sarah Weintraub לע״נ שרה דבורה בת ר׳ חיים מרדכי
Dedicated by her children, grandchildren and great grandchildren

DAY
47

✥ *Learning from Past Mistakes*

R*emember* at which juncture in our history the episode of Miriam's affliction occurred — *when you were leaving Egypt.*

Miriam's words were spoken at the start of the Jews' second year in the Wilderness, when knowledge of the severity of *loshon hora* was not widespread among the people.[1] Miriam's affliction made such knowledge known to all, making them fully accountable for transgressing this sin. This explains the juxtaposition of this episode with that of the Spies who spoke shamefully of the precious Land of Israel.[2] The grievous sin of the Spies and those who accepted their slanderous report was compounded by the fact that they did not take a lesson from what happened to Miriam.[3]

We cannot in any way compare ourselves to the righteous Miriam, whose merits, as mentioned above, could not save her from affliction. Moreover, we are obligated to take a lesson both from the episode of Miriam and that of the Spies. Therefore, if one will be guilty of Miriam's sin, or worse yet, if he will intentionally seek to degrade or embarrass his fellow Jew, surely he will not escape a most severe punishment — and it may not be long in coming, as was the case with Miriam.

Remember what HASHEM, your God, did to Miriam on the way, when you were leaving Egypt.

---

1. The *tzaraas* which Moshe himself suffered for having doubted that the Jews would believe him when he returned from Midian to lead them (see *Shemos* ch. 4) was healed almost immediately and was viewed as a sign rather than a punishment.

2. The episode of the Spies is discussed below (Days 49-52).

3. See *Rashi* to *Bamidbar* 13:2.

יח חשון
18 CHESHVAN / CYCLE 1

יח אייר
18 IYAR / CYCLE 2

SEFER CHOFETZ CHAIM
TOELES: Seven Conditions

✍ Intent

Condition #6:

Having ascertained that 1) the negative information is accurate, 2) the perpetrator was not justified, 3) reproof has proven unsuccessful, 4) there are no other options, and 5) the information will be related accurately, two more conditions must still be met before the information can be conveyed.

The speaker must be certain that his sole intent is *l'toeles,* for a constructive purpose. If he knows that in his heart he is pleased to cast the perpetrator in a bad light, he is not permitted to speak — even though the purpose cannot be accomplished any other way.

It is lowly to enjoy speaking negatively — even for a constructive purpose.[86]

If a word is worth one coin, silence is worth two.

This is especially challenging when one is required to speak about a person whom he does not like. It is necessary to first eradicate any negative feelings towards that person; only then can the negative information be related.[87]

18 Cheshvan · Mrs. Nechama Yoselovsky לע״נ מרת נחמה בת
ר׳ מאיר הכהן ע״ה
Dedicated by the Yoselovsky family, Lakewood NJ
18 Iyar · לע״נ אריה לייב בן יצחק מאיר

DAY 48

❧ *The Best Medicine*

King Solomon taught:

> Let not your mouth bring guilt upon your flesh, and do not tell the emissary that it was an error. Why should God be angered by your speech and destroy the work of your hands? (*Koheles* 5:5).

The Sages expound (*Koheles Rabbah* 5:3):

> *Let not your mouth bring guilt upon your flesh*: Do not let your mouth speak *loshon hora*, for this sin will bring affliction [i.e. *tzaraas*] upon your entire flesh.

> *Let not your mouth bring guilt upon your flesh*: This refers to Miriam, regarding whom it is written, "... and behold! Miriam was afflicted with *tzaraas* like snow" (*Bamidbar* 12:10).

> *... and do not tell the emissary*: This refers to Moshe, as it is written, "He [God] sent an emissary and took us out of Egypt" (ibid. 20:16).

> *... that it was an error*: as it is written, [Aharon said to Moshe:] "[I beg you, my lord, do not cast a sin upon us,] for we have been foolish and we have sinned" (ibid. 12:11).

> *Why should God be angered by your speech*: by the *loshon hora* which you spoke of Moshe, as it is written, "The wrath of HASHEM flared up against them, and He left" (ibid. v. 9).

> *... and destroy the work of your hands*: R' Yochanan said: She [Miriam] sinned with her mouth, yet all her limbs were afflicted, as it is written, "The cloud had departed from atop the Tent, and behold! Miriam was afflicted with *tzaraas* like snow" (ibid. v. 10).

> R' Yehoshua taught: "If a word is worth one coin, silence is worth two."[1] Rabbi [Yehudah the Prince] said: "The best medicine of all is silence," as stated (*Avos* 1:17) in the name of Rabban Shimon ben Gamliel: "All my days I have been raised among the Sages and I have found nothing better for oneself than silence."

---

1. Speech that is proper and correct is of value. But the prevention of improper speech is worth twice as much (*S'fas Emes* to *Megillah* 18a; see *Maharsha*).

יט חשון
19 CHESHVAN / CYCLE 1

יט אייר
19 IYAR / CYCLE 2

SEFER CHOFETZ CHAIM

TOELES: Seven Conditions

∝ *Harmful Information*

Condition #7:

As noted above, the permissibility of speaking negatively for a constructive purpose is based upon the principle that it is not lowly to relate negative information for a positive reason.

This applies only to information which is derogatory but harmless. However, it is forbidden to relate harmful information for a constructive purpose. The only exception to this rule is where one has determined that *halachah* allows for the subject to be harmed in that manner.[88]

The evil inclination employs contrasting approaches to entice people to sin.

19 Cheshvan · May today's learning be a זכות for Eliezer Gavriel Goldstein, Yeshivas Ponevez, B'nai Brak
19 Iyar · Leonard Peretz לע״נ אליעזר יעקב בן גרשון
Dedicated by the Faska family

◆ *The Sin of the Spies*

In the second year of the Jews' sojourn in the Wilderness, Moshe sent twelve great men, one from each tribe, to scout out the Land of Canaan in advance of Israel's conquest of it. When they returned from their mission, ten of the Spies delivered a slanderous, demoralizing report about the Land and the Jews' ability to conquer it. The people accepted this report as fact and wept throughout the night.

> R' Yochanan said: The Spies returned on the eve of Tishah B'Av. The Holy One, Blessed is He, said, "You wept in vain. I will establish it [i.e. this night] for you as a time of weeping for all generations" (*Ta'anis* 28b).

God decreed that, because of this sin, the Jews would wander in the Wilderness for forty years and all adult males of that generation would not enter the Land (see *Bamidbar* chs. 13-14).

How could the Spies, each one a leader among his people, have sinned so grievously? Where did they go wrong?

The evil inclination uses contrasting approaches to entice people to sin. At times, it fills a person's heart with arrogance, so that the person becomes convinced that he is among the God-fearing, or even among those who have true love of God, a yet higher level. The person therefore sees no reason for self-improvement and is content with his mediocre service of Hashem.

The evil inclination also employs an opposite approach. It can cause a person to dwell upon his past sins, though he has long repented and has ceased to repeat them. The person finds himself in a constant state of spiritual despair. When the opportunity for a *mitzvah* presents itself, the person tells himself, "Such acts are befitting the righteous, not sinners like myself."

It was such an attitude that was at the root of the Spies' error, as we shall explain.

כ חשון
20 CHESHVAN / CYCLE 1

כ אייר
20 IYAR / CYCLE 2

SEFER CHOFETZ CHAIM

TOELES: Seven Conditions

☙*In Summation*

It is permissible to speak negatively about a person:

(1) to help the person, or

(2) to help anyone victimized by the person, or

(3) to resolve major disputes, or

(4) to enable others to learn from the mistakes of that person, provided that:

(1) one's remarks are based on first-hand information and careful investigation, and

(2) it is apparent that this person is wrong, and

(3) the person has been spoken to but refuses to change his behavior, and

(4) the statement to be made will be true and accurate, and

(5) the intent of the speaker is for a constructive purpose only (and there is a reasonable chance that the intended goal will be accomplished), and

(6) there is no alternative means by which to bring about the intended result, and

(7) no undue harm will be caused by the statement.

The illustrations presented below (as well as those to be discussed in the section on *rechilus* [gossip]) serve to clarify the application of these conditions.

> **The Spies resorted to slander, casting aspersions upon our precious Holy Land.**

20 Cheshvan · Sarah bat Flora Shalam לע"נ שרה בת אברהם ופלורה ע"ה
Dedicated in loving memory by her husband Sasson and her entire family
20 Iyar · Ethel Rajch לע"נ עטיל בת חיים גבריאל
Dedicated by Mr. & Mrs. Juda Herbst and family

DAY
50

❧Despair and Slander

After the Spies had scouted out the Land, they became filled with despair. They told themselves, "Conquest of this land requires great and awesome merit. Our generation, which made the Golden Calf[1] and committed other sins, surely lacks such merit." They convinced themselves that Hashem's promise to grant them the Land was conditional on their being *tzaddikim*, righteous people, and they felt sure that such was not their status.

The Torah relates: "Calev silenced the people toward Moshe saying, 'We shall surely ascend and conquer it, for we can surely do it!' " (*Bamidbar* 13:30). Our Sages explain that Calev at first posed as an ally of the Spies, so that they and the people would hear him out. He began, "Is that all that the son of Amram has done to us?" Expecting a condemnation of Moshe, the people grew silent. Calev then continued, "He took us out of Egypt, split the sea, brought us the manna, and gathered together the quail" (*Rashi* from *Sotah* 35a). Calev's intent was: Had Hashem led the Jews according to the strict measure of justice, they would never have been granted the miracles which they had already witnessed and benefited from. Even as the sea split, some demonstrated a weakness of faith, as it is written, "They rebelled at the sea, the Sea of Reeds" (*Tehillim* 106:7). The people had complained before being granted the manna, and at other times as well. Calev assured the people that just as they had earned God's compassion in the past, so too would they witness the fulfillment of His promise to bring them safely into *Eretz Yisrael*.

The Spies, however, were not convinced. Lest the people be swayed by Calev's words, the Spies resorted to slander, casting aspersions upon the precious, sacred Land that was to have been their eternal inheritance.

---

1. *Shemos* ch. 32.

◄Helping Others to Improve

The first category of constructive purpose is to help the person about whom one is speaking. There is a tendency among many to ignore the misconduct of others in favor of a "live and let live" attitude. Let us first understand why the Torah rejects this attitude.

Every person is born with character flaws. It is our mission in life to change, to grow, to strive for perfection and spirituality. We all want to rid ourselves of our imperfections; people *do* want to be good. What makes life so challenging is that negative character traits are blinding. We either lose sight of what our goals should be or rationalize to the point that we simply cannot differentiate between right and wrong.

One of the greatest gifts Hashem has blessed us with is companionship: friends, family, people around us who are close enough to care, yet distant enough to be objective. To abstain from speaking up and offering one another reproof and guidance amounts to depriving one another of one of the most valuable tools for personal growth. We *must* get involved and, when necessary, even enlist the involvement of others in helping people through the struggles of life. Remaining silent when reproof is called for is not *shmiras haloshon,* it is depriving one's fellow of his lifeline to self-improvement.

> *As long as a person does not flout Hashem's will, he can still hope for His compassion.*

דאבא לאה בת שרה לרפואה שלמה · 21 Cheshvan
שרה רבקה בת פרץ ומלכה בת יהושע מאיר Dedicated by
לע"נ ר' ישראל מדרכי בן ר' יקותיאל יהודא זלצר · 21 Iyar

◄❧*More Lessons*

After hearing the slander of the other Spies, Calev and Yehoshua bin (son of) Nun responded to their sinful words:

> *The Land that we passed through, to spy it out — the Land is very, very good! If HASHEM desires us, He will bring us to this Land and give it to us ... But do not rebel against HASHEM! You should not fear the people of the Land, for they are our bread. Their protection has departed from them; HASHEM is with us — do not fear them! (Bamidbar 14:7-9).*

They meant the following: The Spies' contention that Hashem's promise of the Land was conditional on their being *tzaddikim* was patently incorrect. Hashem does not say to a person, "I will help you, but only if you will be a *tzaddik.*" Rather, Hashem says, "I will not help you if you rebel against Me." This is the intent of the words, "But do not rebel against Hashem." As long as a person does not flout Hashem's will, he can still hope for His compassion.

As to the Spies' fearful descriptions of the mighty Canaanites, Calev and Yehoshua responded, "...for they are our bread." Would a person be frightened by a giant-sized loaf of bread? Similarly, they argued, Hashem would not offer the Canaanites any protection from the Jews, and as such they would be easily devoured, as it is written, "You will devour all the people that HASHEM, your God, has delivered to you" (*Devarim* 7:16). Indeed, Scripture indicates that when the Jews, led by Yehoshua, crossed the Jordan River and began their conquest, they found the giants of Canaan to be the most faint-hearted of all.[1]

The lessons to be learned from this tragic episode are crucial to us all.

---

1. See *Yehoshua* 11:21 and *Shoftim* 1:10.

SEFER CHOFETZ CHAIM

TOELES: For the Subject's Benefit

❧*Passing Judgment*

B efore assuming that a person's actions merit *tochachah,* reproof, one must be absolutely certain that he has, in fact, sinned.

From the command בצדק תשפט עמיתך, *Judge your fellow favorably* (*Vayikra* 19:15), we learn that if a person appears to be committing a transgression which is totally out of character for him, we are to seek to understand what transpired in a positive light. If there is any way to interpret his actions as not involving transgression, we are required to do so.[89]

If it is absolutely clear that the person did sin in a manner which is out of character for him, then we must assume that he immediately regretted his actions, and has already repented. To discuss the incident with anyone constitutes speaking *loshon hora.*[90]

Every Jew, without exception, is capable of spiritual growth and success.

22 Cheshvan · Mrs. Sarah Bergman לע״נ שרה בת יוסף
Dedicated by Mr. Morris Fialkoff and Mr. & Mrs. Herman Fialkoff
לע״נ הרהח׳ ר׳ ישראל בן הרהח׳ ר׳ ברוך דוד · 22 Iyar

◄*Most Crucial*

DAY 52

When a person grows lax in his commitment to Torah study, his commitment to general *mitzvah* observance grows lax as well. When this person is asked why he, a God-fearing Jew who knows that "one hour of spiritual bliss in the World to Come is better than the entire life of this world,"[1] shows such weakness of commitment, he might very well reply: "Such striving is for *tzaddikim,* people who distance themselves from the pleasures of this world and dedicate every fiber of their being to service of Hashem. It is for them that the great rewards of the next world are reserved. Plain people like myself, however, cannot hope for such reward."

The above argument echoes that of the Spies. Our response to it is similar to that of Calev and Yehoshua, as related above.

Hashem does not demand of every Jew that he separate himself from mundane life to engage in spiritual strivings all day and night. A Jew who chooses to enter the world of business has fulfilled his spiritual obligations if he sets aside a fixed, significant amount of time each day for the study of Torah and if he conducts his business endeavors in strict accordance with the related Torah laws. As the Talmud states: "When a person departs this world, the Heavenly Court asks him, 'Did you conduct your business affairs in good faith? Did you have fixed times for Torah study?' " (*Shabbos* 31a).

Hashem is not overbearing with His children. Every Jew, without exception, is capable of spiritual growth and success. Most crucial, however, is that which Calev and Yehoshua underscored: *"But do not rebel against HASHEM!"* One dare not blatantly ignore any *mitzvah,* be it positive or negative. One who is sincere in his Divine service will surely succeed.

If one has been lax in his study, or with any other *mitzvah,* he need not despair. Hashem, Who loves kindness and seeks to confer merit upon His people, has granted us the great gift of *teshuvah* (repentance), which preceded Creation. Through *teshuvah,* any Jew can attain the greatest heights.

---

1. *Avos* 4:22.

כג חשון
23 CHESHVAN / CYCLE 1

כג אייר
23 IYAR / CYCLE 2

SEFER CHOFETZ CHAIM

TOELES: For the Subject's Benefit

✑The Occasional Sinner

If a person whose actions may have involved a given transgression is known to commit that particular sin at least occasionally, then the commandment, "Judge your fellow favorably," does not require that one seek a positive explanation for what he did. However, it is meritorious to give the person the benefit of the doubt and assume that this time he did not sin. Reproof would not be necessary.[91]

If it is absolutely clear that the person did commit a sin, then the *mitzvah* to reprove does apply and one should, in a respectful and caring manner, help the person to overcome his evil inclination by offering reproof.

There are times when it would be more effective for someone else, such as a close friend or *rav,* to reprove the individual. Theoretically, it should be permissible for the one who witnessed the transgression to inform the friend or *rav* of it and ask that he handle the situation. However, we have learned that one may not act on hearsay, which would mean that one cannot possibly offer reproof unless he personally witnessed the transgression. Consequently, it would be one's responsibility to find an effective means of reproving himself, or to ask the *rav* to either personally investigate the situation or tactfully discuss the matter with that individual without making accusations.

David was unaware that he had sinned. Yet, he accepted Shimi's blasphemy as a manifestation of Divine judgment against himself.

23 Cheshvan · Malka Schwartz לע"נ מלכה בת ישעיהו
Dedicated by Sholom & Devorah Herzig
23 Iyar · The Sanzer Sofer לע"נ ר' משה בר' יהושע באדנער זצ"ל
Dedicated by his son-in-law, daughter and family, Rumpler

⁓David's Acceptance

The Sages teach that one who speaks *loshon hora* is fit to be stoned (*Arachin* 15b). The following lends support to this statement of the Sages, whose teachings are true and everlasting:

In an incident recorded in the Book of *Shmuel*, King David was, according to the Sages, guilty of accepting *loshon hora*.[1] In the very next incident, David, as he fled during the rebellion of his son Avshalom, was cursed and stoned by Shimi ben Geira. The word הנה, *and behold,* with which this second narrative begins (*II Shmuel* 16:5), indicates a connection between the two episodes. This implies that for transgressing the *loshon hora* prohibitions one is fit to be stoned, as David was (by Shimi) after he had been guilty of such an infraction.

Parenthetically, the above is indicative of David's exalted holiness and righteousness, for Scripture makes clear[2] that David was as of yet unaware that he had sinned in accepting a slanderous report. Yet when one of his officers suggested that Shimi be punished for his blasphemous behavior, David responded, "Hashem told him [i.e. inspired him] to curse" (ibid. v. 11). David, without knowing how and when he had sinned, recognized the fact that Hashem would not have permitted Shimi to act as he did had he, David, not been deserving of such disgrace. Therefore, he would not allow his men to attack Shimi.

---

1. See *II Shmuel* 16:4 and *Shabbos* 56a.
2. *II Shmuel* 19:30. See footnote to *Sha'ar Zechirah* ch. 8.

❧The Habitual Sinner

In the case of a habitual sinner who ignores a particular commandment altogether, one is to assume that even a questionable act is, in fact, a transgression of that commandment. "Judge your fellow favorably" demands fairness, not naiveté.[92]

Having concluded that the person *did* transgress, one must then seek to understand *why* he frequently commits this sin. It may be due to ignorance — he may be totally unaware that the act is forbidden, or he might not realize the severity of the prohibition. Should this be the case, one must find some way of enlightening the person without hurting his feelings. Discussing his behavior with others constitutes speaking *loshon hora.* (This situation is common among those who were raised in communities where there is widespread violation of certain laws. In such instances, people mistakenly view those who observe these laws as *machmirim,* individuals who are stringent beyond the letter of the law.)[93]

The reward for those who refrain from evil speech is beyond comprehension, and the sins of the gossip-monger outweigh the very worst transgressions.

24 Cheshvan · Leon Schottenstein בן לע"נ ר' ארי' ליב בן
אפרים אלעזר הכהן ז"ל
Dedicated in loving memory by Tuvia & Lea Schottenstein and children,
24 Iyar · לע"נ יוסף שלום בן חיים אלטר

❧ Most Severe

R' Yehoshua ben Levi said: Whoever relates *loshon hora* accumulates sins which reach the heavens, as it is written (*Tehillim* 73:9), "They direct their mouths to the heavens, their tongue struts on earth" (*Arachin* 15b).

As mentioned above,[1] the sin of *loshon hora* can result in an accumulation of sins greater than the Three Cardinal Sins. This refers not only to the sins' severity, but to their punishment as well. As *Talmud Yerushalmi* states (*Pe'ah* 1:1)[2], "There are four sins for which retribution is exacted in this world while the principal [i.e. primary punishment] remains for the World to Come: idol worship, immorality, murder — and *loshon hora* is equal to them all."

In *Tanna D'Vei Eliyahu* (I, ch. 15) we read: "Those who strike their fellow stealthily [through *loshon hora*],[3] those who desecrate the Name in public, those who belittle their neighbors with words, and those who incite strife, their end will be that of Korach; regarding them does the Torah state: 'The earth covered them over [and they were lost from among the congregation]' " (*Bamidbar* 16:33).

---

1. Day 18.
2. Cited by *S'mag*, prohibition 9.
3. The Torah states: "Accursed is one who strikes his fellow stealthily; and the entire people shall say, ' Amen.' " (*Deuteronomy* 27:24). *Rashi* interprets this as referring to the sin of *loshon hora*.

≈Social Pressure

A מומר לתאבון (lit., *rebel due to temptation*) is someone who regularly submits to temptation in violating a specific *mitzvah.* While the prohibition against gossipmongering does apply with regard to speaking about him (as he is not a heretic), his situation differs drastically from one who occasionally transgresses a given *mitzvah* but basically is committed to its observance.

As we have learned, the primary prohibition against speaking *loshon hora* is לא תלך רכיל בעמיך, *Do not go as a gossipmonger among your people* (*Vayikra* 19:16). One who embarrasses his fellow Jew transgresses the prohibition לא תונו איש את עמיתו, *A man shall not aggrieve his fellow* (*Vayikra* 25:17).

Our Sages interpret the term עמך, *your people,* in the first prohibition as excluding only a מומר להכעיס, (lit., *rebel whose intent is to spite*), one whose lack of regard for a given prohibition causes him to regularly transgress it. However, the term עמיתו, *his fellow,* in the second prohibition, excludes even the מומר לתאבון. Thus, it is forbidden to speak *loshon hora* about a מומר לתאבון but it is permissible to exert social pressure on him in order to induce him to mend his sinful ways.

(Continued on page 407)

Those who habitually speak loshon hora will find no cure for themselves at the End of Days.

---

25 Cheshvan · May today's learning be a זכות for חנה יהודית זכות
בת מנחם מנדל שתחי׳
25 Iyar · לע״נ יצחק ישכר מנחם מענדיל ז״ל בן הרב אברהם בנימין
זילברברג זצ״ל

DAY 55

❧ *The Time Is Now*

The serpent, whose deceitful words created a barrier between God and man, was cursed: "And dust shall you eat all the days of your life" (*Bereishis* 3:14). The Talmud (*Berachos* 12b) interprets the phrase "all the days of your life" in another verse of the Torah (*Devarim* 16:3) as referring to the Messianic era.[1] Thus, at the End of Days, all creatures will be cured of their maladies except for the serpent. And just as "the snake bites because it was not charmed" [i.e. cured of its curse] so too "there will be no advantage [i.e. remedy] for the master of the tongue" (from *Koheles* 10:11). Those who habitually speak *loshon hora* will, like the serpent, find no cure for themselves at the End of Days (*Midrash Aggadas Bereishis* 79:2 and *Pirkei D'R' Eliezer* ch. 52). Their only hope is to repent now.

The gossiper brings suffering not only upon himself, but upon the community as well: "R' Shimon ben Pazi said: Rain is withheld only because of those who speak *loshon hora*, as it is written (*Mishlei* 25:23), 'The north wind prevents the rain and [God shows] an angry countenance [when there is] secretive talk' " (*Ta'anis* 7b). *Zohar* states that this sin brings death and destruction to the world.

Therefore, one who cares for his own well-being and that of his fellow men will strive to acquire the golden quality of *shmiras haloshon*.

---

1. This teaching is also found in the Passover *Hagaddah*.

❧Public Announcements

Traditionally, Jewish communities have used so-cial pressure in dealing with the publicly observant whose private behavior includes blatant violation of basic *halachah.*

If all else fails, it is permissible to publicize the fact that an otherwise observant Jew is guilty of im-morality on a regular basis, if the disclosure will prompt him to repent.[95]

Similarly, rabbinical courts have the authority to post signs informing the public of someone's re-fusal (*siruv*) to comply with a court ruling. Social pressure is often the only means through which rabbinical courts can enforce their decisions.[96]

When a Jew speaks loshon hora, his every word is recorded by a Heavenly angel.

26 Cheshvan · May today's learning be a זכות for our son Eli Meir נ"י
Dedicated by Rabbi & Mrs. Avrohom Chaim Feuer, Monsey, NY
26 Iyar · Carol Colen לע"נ צירל בת חיים ע"ה
Dedicated by Judy Colen

◄ Evil Epitomized

The Talmud states (*Sotah* 42a): "Four groups will never be allowed to stand in the presence of the *Shechinah* (Divine Presence): scoffers, liars, flatterers, and those who speak *loshon hora* ... [With regard to this last group it is written] (*Tehillim* 5:5), 'For you are not a God who desires wickedness, no evil, רע, sojourns with you.' " The wickedness referred to here is that of *loshon hora*, as the psalmist goes on to say, "For in their mouth there is no sincerity, their inner thought is treacherous" (ibid. v. 10). The habitual speaker of *loshon hora* is called רע, *evil*, as the Sages state: "R' Chama bar Chanina said: Whoever converses with his neighbor, dines with him and then speaks *loshon hora* against him, is called רע, *evil*, by Hashem" (*Aggadas Mishlei* 12:1).

Whatever words a person utters on this world are recorded Above. In the *Midrash* we find (*Devarim Rabbah* 6:5):

Let not your mouth bring guilt on your flesh ... (*Koheles* 5:5). How is this? When the mouth speaks *loshon hora*, it sins against the body by bringing punishment upon it.

... and do not tell the emissary that it was an error. Do not say: "I will go and speak *loshon hora* and no one [but the listener] will know of it!"

Says the Holy One, Blessed is He: "Know that I will send an angel who will stand next to you and record every word that you speak against your fellow."

~Loshon Hora and the Non-Observant

Based on the rules we have just studied, the rules of *loshon hora* vis-a-vis the totally non-observant Jew become clear.

(1) The average non-observant Jew today has been deprived of a meaningful Jewish education. Whether or not he has been exposed to Orthodox Jewish life, society has prevented him from taking Torah seriously. *Rambam* compares such a person to a *tinok shenishbah,* a kidnapped Jewish child whose kidnappers reared him with non-Torah ideals, and whose transgressions are committed out of ignorance. Such a person may be in the category of both עמך, *your people* and עמיתו, *his fellow.* It is our obligation to educate him with love, care and sensitivity and it is strictly forbidden to speak *loshon hora* against him.[97]

What more need be said concerning this most severe of sins?

(2) A non-observant Jew who did receive a meaningful Jewish education, has been taught Torah values and knows that what he is doing is wrong, but claims that observance is too difficult, is a *rebel due to temptation.* He is considered part of עמיך, *your people,* which means that *loshon hora* may be spoken of him only if it is for a constructive purpose.

(continued on page 407)

❧The Gaon's Will

In his ethical will to his family, the Vilna Gaon wrote:

One will stand judgment for every utterance; even a light remark will not be ignored.... The sin of forbidden speech is the worst of all, as our Sages have stated: "These are the sins whose fruits [i.e. secondary punishments] are exacted from the person in this world, while the principal [i.e. primary punishment] remains for him in the World to Come ... and *loshon hora* is equivalent to them all." What more need be said concerning this most severe of sins? To the verse, "All man's toil is for his mouth" (*Koheles* 6:7), the Sages comment (*Koheles Rabbah* 6:6) that all the *mitzvos* and Torah study of a person are not sufficient to negate that which he utters [sinfully]. They further state: "Which craft should man pursue in this world? He should strive to emulate a mute [to avoid evil talk] (*Chullin* 89a), and press his lips together like two millstones [which grind against one another]."

... Not a single [such] utterance escapes from being recorded Above. Heavenly angels are forever being sent to each person to record his every utterance. "For a bird of the sky will carry the sound, and a winged creature will relate the matter" (*Koheles* 10:20). "Let not your mouth bring guilt on your flesh and do not tell the emissary that it was an error" (ibid. 5:5).

כח חשון
28 CHESHVAN / CYCLE 1

כח אייר
28 IYAR / CYCLE 2

SEFER CHOFETZ CHAIM

TOELES: For the Subject's Benefit

❧Avoiding Flattery

Even where it is permissible to speak negatively for a constructive purpose, one must avoid insincere flattery. It is forbidden to be critical of someone when he is not present, yet demonstrate approval of his behavior in his presence. If the concern is that the person's feelings not be hurt, then the solution is to express respect and concern for him as a person, but clear disapproval of his behavior.

If one is certain that reproof will be ignored, and is therefore prepared to publicize the person's behavior as an attempt to induce him to change his ways, one must nevertheless approach the sinner first, so as not to be suspected of insincerity.[100]

In the above case, where it is clear that the person will not be moved by rebuke, one can remove the need for first speaking to him by dispelling any possible suspicions concerning one's own sincerity. For example, if one speaks against the perpetrator in public (in the presence of three) rather than speaking to individual members of the community in private, it becomes clear to all that the speaker could not be attempting to gain favor with the perpetrator by showing acceptance of his behavior. Similarly, if the speaker is known to be zealous and outspoken and would not be suspected of flattery, he could resort to private discussion. Also, if it is clear to all that the perpetrator is a difficult personality, and publicly criticizing his behavior could be dangerous, then one may speak against him in private without fear of personal suspicion.

One who follows the teachings of Torah will avoid any possibility of baseless hatred.

מרים בת רבקה שרה לרפואה שלמה · 28 Cheshvan
Dedicated by the Gold family, New York and Toronto
28 Iyar · David Klugmann לע״נ החבר דוד בן החבר משה ע״ה
Dedicated by the Klugmann family

DAY
58

~A Proper Outlook

Anyone who sincerely strives to emulate Aharon *HaKohen*, who loved and pursued peace[1], must refrain from speaking *loshon hora* and from accepting as truth the *loshon hora* related to him by others.[2] To accept gossip as truth is to be led along the path of *sinas chinam* (baseless hatred), quarreling and strife.

When a person is told that So-and so has spoken or acted negatively toward him and he accepts this report as fact, he will inevitably quarrel with that person. In the end, the two will become bitter enemies, to the point that each will seek the downfall of the other and will rejoice over the other's misfortune.

Now, would the listener react in the way dictated by Torah, all this would not occur, for upon hearing the report, he would think to himself that perhaps the information is entirely false, or at least laced with falsehood in a way that totally alters the true nature of what had occurred. Or, perhaps the speaker had omitted certain key details which, had they been mentioned, would have cast the matter in an entirely different light. As we all know, even a change of nuance can alter a word portrait drastically.

Would the listener follow the way of Torah, he would seek some source of merit for the alleged perpetrator. Perhaps whatever had been done was committed without intent to harm. Any and all of the above possibilities would preclude ill feeling and ensure that strife not come between the two parties.

---

1. *Avos* 1:12.
2. As prohibited by the verse, "Do not accept a false report" (*Shemos* 23:1).

≈Character Deficiencies

Helping one's fellow to improve his character also falls within the realm of *toeles,* constructive purpose. If an acquaintance requires character refinement, then the *mitzvah* to reprove one's fellow Jew requires one to bring the matter to that person's attention with care and sensitivity. However, if one feels incapable of offering reproof and knows that others are also aware of this person's character deficiencies, he is permitted to discuss the matter with them and seek their advice or involvement, if necessary. Though we have seen that it is lowly and forbidden to speak negatively of someone even with those who are already aware of the information, constructive speech is not at all lowly.[101]

Should one find it necessary to consult with someone who is unaware of this person's deficiencies for guidance in how to approach the person, he may do so, for this too constitutes constructive speech. However, if it is possible to discuss the issue without mentioning names, then this course must be followed.

We have already seen (Day 53) that if one seeks the active involvement of someone who is unaware of the situation, that individual would have to investigate the matter personally and verify the facts before taking definitive action.

* When this month has only 29 days, the lesson for 30 Cheshvan should also be studied today.

A gossiper has no credibility and his words cannot be accepted as truth.

לע"נ ר' אהרן הלל הלל ז"ל בן הרה"ג ר' מרדכי פארהאנד זצוק"ל · 29 Cheshvan
Dedicated by Mrs. Martha Vorhand and children, London, England
29 Iyar · The Manchester Rosh Yeshiva לע"נ הגאון הצדיק הרב יהודא זאב
בן הגאון הצדיק הרב משה יצחק הלוי סג"ל זצוק"ל
הונצח על ידי תלמידו יחזקאל פרוידענבערגער ומשפחתו, לונדון, ענגלאנד

**DAY
59**

◆❃No Credibility

When one is told *loshon hora* and attempts to follow the Torah's command to reject it as false, the evil inclination often counters with the following argument: "How can you not accept this report as fact? Dare you accuse the speaker of lying, of transgressing the prohibition, 'Distance yourself from falsehood'? " (*Shemos* 23:7).

The response to this is as follows: If you were to see a Jew [who is knowledgeable in the laws of Jewish observance] flagrantly violate Torah law, would you then accept as fact whatever information he has to offer about others? Certainly not! Surely one cannot trust the word of one who openly flouts Hashem's will.

A Jew who speaks ill of his fellow has transgressed "You shall not be a gossipmonger among your people" (*Vayikra* 19:16), a most severe prohibition. As the *halachah* makes clear, this prohibition is violated even when the report is true. Thus, the speaker is guilty of severe transgression and, as such, has no credibility.

❧*Problem Students*

The dedicated teacher often finds it necessary to discuss the progress and difficulties of students with parents, colleagues and principals. A lack of clear guidelines with regard to *loshon hora* can create either a free-for-all atmosphere, where people talk about anyone with anyone, or, at the other extreme, a simplistic approach to *shmiras haloshon* which could inhibit the teacher's effectiveness as an educator.

Generally speaking, the area of *chinuch* (child education and upbringing) constitutes a constructive purpose which would permit relating negative information concerning a student. However, the specific conditions which permit speaking negatively for a constructive purpose must never be overlooked.

Verification of facts is crucial. For a teacher to play amateur psychologist and hastily diagnose the student as having some complex disability or disorder without pursuing the matter properly constitutes recklessness — and the consequences can be devastating. To communicate one's evaluation under such circumstances would be *hotzaas shem ra* (slander). It is an unfortunate fact that certain problematic children have not succeeded only as a result of having been misunderstood by a teacher, whose labeling tainted the image of that student in the eyes of all his future teachers.

(continued on page 407)

When this month has only 29 days, the lesson for 30 Cheshvan should be learned together with 29 Cheshvan.

To reject loshon hora as false is a great source of merit.

---

30 Cheshvan · May today's learning be a זכות for our משפחה
Dedicated by Yehuda Levine & family
1 Sivan · In honor of our dear husband and father Mr. Eli D. Cohen נ"י
Dedicated by his wife Esther and their children

DAY
60

﹏Source of Merit

To reject *loshon hora* as false is an exceedingly great source of merit — especially if the subject of the report is respected as a man of spiritual stature. *Tanna D'Vei Eliyahu* (II, ch. 7) states:

> It is said of Yeravam ben Yoash that he was a man who accorded the prophets honor. Therefore, those nations which the Holy One, Blessed is He, did not give over into the hands of Yehoshua bin Nun or David, King of Israel, He gave over into the hands of Yeravam ben Yoash, as it is written, "He [Yeravam] returned the borders of Israel from the approach to Chamas until the sea of Aravah ..." (*II Melachim* 14:25). Why did Yeravam, who was an idol worshiper, merit this? Because he did not accept *loshon hora* regarding the prophet Amos.[1]...At that moment [when he rejected the report against the prophet], God said, "Though the generation is guilty of idol worship and its leader is guilty of idol worship, nevertheless, the land which I promised to Avraham, Yitzchak and Yaakov will be given over into his [Yeravam's] hands."

---

1. See *Amos* ch 7.

א כסלו
1 KISLEV / CYCLE 1

ב סיון
2 SIVAN / CYCLE 2

SEFER CHOFETZ CHAIM

TOELES: For the Subject's Benefit

➼*With No Alternative*

If after giving a situation much thought, a teacher comes to the conclusion that a particular student has a behavioral or learning problem and feels that it will not be possible to deal with the problem without the involvement of the principal, his colleagues, or the student's parents, then the teacher should speak to the necessary party without delay.

Condition 5 of constructive speech (see Day 50) is that the speaker's intent be purely for constructive reasons and not out of anger or frustration. This could be extremely trying when the student in question is disruptive and frequently upsets the teacher.

Difficult as it is, teachers must not take students' behavior personally. The disruptive student is, in most cases, not fighting the teacher; he is struggling with himself as he deals with the challenges of life.

When a person is known to refrain from listening to loshon hora, gossipmongers will avoid speaking in his presence.

1 Kislev · Mrs. Vicki Press לע"נ האשה וויטציא בת הרב יהודה לייב
Dedicated by Melech & Zlata Press and family
2 Sivan · Rhea Silverman לע"נ ריבה בת ר' יעקב ע"ה
Dedicated by Steve Rosenberg and family, New York

DAY 61

⊸Pure and Wholesome

By rejecting *loshon hora* as false, one ensures that his study of Torah and fulfillment of other *mitzvos* remain wholesome and untainted.

One who is in the habit of listening to *loshon hora* is liable to lose thousands of *mitzvos* which he could have performed — specifically, the many responses of אמן and אמן יהא שמה רבא, and the many minutes of Torah study that can be lost while listening to gossip. Generally speaking, gossipmongers are eager to sell their "wares" to anyone who is willing to listen and at any time, even in the synagogue while prayers are in progress and in the study hall while Torah is being learned. They carry on conversations while *Kaddish* is being recited, during the *chazzan's* repetition of the *Shemoneh Esrei,* and during the public Torah reading.

When a person is known to refrain from listening to *loshon hora*, gossipmongers will avoid speaking in his presence, even when their words are intended for others to hear and not for him.

One who seeks to be completely innocent of the sin of accepting *loshon hora* should, on a steady basis, speak to the members of his immediate family regarding the imperative of *shmiras haloshon.* He should tell them of both the great reward for being zealous in matters of speech and the severe retribution that one may incur for transgressing the sins of speaking and accepting *loshon hora.*[1]

---

1. See *Sefer Chofetz Chaim*, Part I, 8:13-14; and Part II, 7:5.

ב כסלו
2 KISLEV / CYCLE 1

ג סיון
3 SIVAN / CYCLE 2

SEFER CHOFETZ CHAIM
TOELES: For the Subject's Benefit

❧Harming A Student

Finally, a teacher must be careful not to cause his student undue harm. *Halachah* permits a teacher to strike a child for educational purposes,[102] and embarrassment may also be justified, if it is for the student's benefit. (The Talmud states that striking one's older child is prohibited as it may incite him to hit back.)[103] However, in today's era of brazenness, corporal punishment even in early childhood often teaches violence rather than discipline, and must be carefully evaluated. Verbal abuse by a teacher can have a decidedly negative effect on his students and may undermine all efforts at educating the students regarding *shmiras haloshon*.

In any situation where embarrassment or physical punishment might result from the teacher relating the student's problem to others, he may do so only if the consequences are necessary for the student's growth and development. As mentioned above (Day 26), teachers must also bear in mind the long-term effects of relating or recording negative information about a student.

One should train himself to avoid idle conversation in the synagogue and study hall.

2 Kislev · Mr. Milton Schwartzberg לע״נ מיכל וואלף בן קלמן
Dedicated by the Slater family, Monsey, NY
3 Sivan · Mollie Freedman לע״נ מלכה בת שלמה לוי
Dedicated in loving memory by her daughter Rosella Freedman

☙ Sound Advice

I offer the following advice to anyone who seeks to guard his tongue from speaking the forbidden: Train yourself to refrain from engaging in any conversation while in a *beis midrash* (study hall) or *beis haknesses* (synagogue). The benefits of this practice are many:

(1) One fulfills the great *mitzvah* of displaying respect for the awesome sanctity of these places.[1]

(2) His Torah study is untainted by disruption (see Day 61) and his prayers are likewise uninterrupted and not lacking even one *Amen* or *Yehei Shemei Rabbah*, each a priceless irreplaceable treasure. Conversely, to disregard these responses is a serious sin.

(3) The average Jewish male spends approximately four hours a day in the *beis haknesses* for the three daily prayers. (This figure takes into account the fact that most people remain in the synagogue [studying and praying privately] for a while after the prayer has ended.[2]) He spends another two hours in the *beis hamidrash* studying Torah — a total of six hours, or one-fourth of each twenty-four period. Thus, one who scrupulously avoids idle conversation in halls of Divine service is assured of having spent at least one-fourth of his lifetime on this earth engaged in Torah study and prayer and having avoided all forms of forbidden speech.

(4) Having trained oneself to avoid conversation for these six hours, one will find it relatively easy to refrain from speaking *loshon hora* the remainder of the day.

---

1. The Torah states, "Observe My Sabbaths and revere My sanctuary — I am HASHEM" (*Vayikra* 26:2). The status of the synagogue and study hall as "miniature sanctuaries" demands proper reverence. "Regarding synagogues, one may not conduct himself with levity in them, one may not eat in them, nor may one drink in them, nor may one adorn himself in them, nor may one stroll around in them, nor may one enter them in the summer to escape the heat or in the rainy season to escape the rain ..." (*Megillah* 28a). Included under "levity" is mundane conversation, such as matters pertaining to business (see *Shulchan Aruch, Orach Chaim* 151:1).

2. The Chofetz Chaim wrote these words in the late 1800's.

ג כסלו
2 KISLEV / CYCLE 1

ד סיון
3 SIVAN / CYCLE 2

SEFER CHOFETZ CHAIM
TOELES: For the Victim's Benefit

◈*Informing*

The second category of constructive purpose is to help those who are being (or have been) adversely affected by the subject's behavior.

If one has personally witnessed a Jew causing monetary damage to another, to ensure that the victim will be compensated is a constructive purpose. It would therefore be permissible to relate what has transpired. After ascertaining that the facts are correct, and after having spoken with the perpetrator, one must determine what will result from relating the information and whether or not *halachah* justifies effecting that result.[104]

In a civilized society, the straightforward way of dealing with crime is to inform the authorities. However, reporting one's fellow Jew to secular officials may result in his facing punishment undeserved according to Torah. Imprisonment, for example, is not an acceptable means of punishment for monetary infractions, by Torah standards. Providing information that might lead to a Jew's imprisonment could therefore constitute *malshinus* (the act of being a *malshin,* informer). Only if it is clear that an individual is dangerous and poses a threat to others can he be spoken against for the sake of protecting others from harm. Such matters are extremely sensitive and complex, and demand consultation with a competent *halachic* authority.[105]

To engage in conversation while the Torah reading is in progress involves numerous grave transgressions.

3 Kislev · Mrs. Shaindel Hilsenrath   לע"נ שיינדל בת יצחק הלוי ז"ל
Dedicated by the Hilsenrath children and grandchildren
4 Sivan · Chaya Liebe Beyman   לע"נ חי' ליבא בת החבר ר' שלמה
Dedicated by the Ferber, Beyman and Wikler families

❧Talking During the Torah Reading

Unfortunately, idle conversations often begin with stories that are filled from beginning to end with *loshon hora.* When held in the synagogue, such conversations usually begin prior to the Torah reading, but when the reading commences, the speaker continues his narrative so that he speaks *loshon hora* even as the words of our holy Torah are being read. Often, this person is among the distinguished members of the congregation whose seat is at the eastern wall, so that his sin is committed in full view of everyone. In this way, one is guilty of desecrating Hashem's Name in public, meaning, in the presence of ten Jews, a most severe form of *chilul Hashem.*[1]

Note how many prohibitions this man has transgressed:

(1) The prohibition against speaking *loshon hora*, aside from numerous other commandments both positive and negative [which one might transgress when speaking *loshon hora*].

(2) The sin of "You shall not desecrate My Holy Name" (*Vayikra* 22:32), which, as mentioned above, was transgressed in public.

(3) He has ignored the Torah reading; even if he has missed a single verse or even a single *word*, his sin is enormous. For our Sages consider it a serious sin even to leave the synagogue while the Torah reading is in progress;[2] how much more so regarding one who is present in the *beis haknesses* (synagogue) and whose craving for idle conversation and *loshon hora* causes him to ignore the word of the Living God! Often, this occurs on Shabbos, when the sin is far greater than on a weekday, as is stated in many holy works.

To all of the above is added the sin of engaging in idle conversation in the *beis haknesses* or *beis midrash*, which is a great sin as stated in *Shulchan Aruch*[3] — and certainly when such conversation is in the form of *loshon hora!*

---

1. See *Sefer HaMitzvos* of *Rambam* 63.
2. See *Berachos* 8a.
3. *Orach Chaim* 151:1.

ד כסלו
4 KISLEV / CYCLE 1

ה סיון
5 SIVAN / CYCLE 2

SEFER CHOFETZ CHAIM

TOELES: For the Victim's Benefit

◈Initiating A Din Torah

The Torah requires that monetary disputes be adjudicated by a *beis din,* rabbinical court.[106] It is permissible to exert social pressure on an individual to convince him to agree to participate in a *din Torah* (court case) before a *beis din.* However, social pressure that could cause embarrassment is not an option if the person is in the category of *amisecha,* your fellow (see Day 55). A person who erroneously believes that he is justified in taking someone else's money must be set straight, but he is not a *mumar* (rebellious sinner). Embarrassment is not a recourse, but one may discuss the matter with anyone who can influence the person and explain that the person is involved in a monetary dispute and should be persuaded to come before a *beis din.*

Unlike an individual a *beis din* may publicize the fact that an individual refuses to abide by its ruling or has ignored a summons to appear before it.[107] As previously mentioned, social pressure is often the only means by which rabbinical courts can enforce their decisions.

The Torah places great emphasis on caring for the needs of others.

לע"נ אליהו בן משה חיים Eliyahu Pollak · 4 Kislev
Dedicated by the Pollak, Taplin, Goldberg, Pollak, Tropper & Abel families
לע"נ שמואל יצחק בן יהודה ארי' ז"ל Mr Samuel Becher · 5 Sivan
Dedicated by his children

DAY
64

▰*Causing Others To Sin*

Our Sages speak harshly of a חוטא ומחטיא, *sinner who causes others to sin.* "Causing another to sin is worse than killing him. For by killing him, one denies him this world, but by causing him to sin, one denies him both this world and the next" (*Sifre, Devarim* 23:8). Thus, to relate forbidden information and cause another to listen to and accept *loshon hora* is to commit a most serious offense [aside from the transgression of numerous Scriptural laws for speaking the forbidden[1]].

One should also take note of the emphasis which the Torah places on caring for the needs of one's fellow. For example, we are forbidden to ignore another Jew's lost object. Even if the object is worth but a few cents, and even if the owner is unaware of its loss, nevertheless, we are commanded to pick it up and return it to him.[2] Now, if the Torah commands us to be so concerned with our fellow's material possessions, which have value only in this temporal world, how much more must we be concerned with matters affecting his soul, which lives on eternally. We dare not harm him spiritually by causing him to sin!

---

1. As detailed in the preface to *Sefer Chofetz Chaim.*
2. *Devarim* 22:1-3.

ה כסלו
5 KISLEV/ CYCLE I

ו סיון
6 SIVAN / CYCLE 2

SEFER CHOFETZ CHAIM
TOELES: For the Victim's Benefit

✥Taking The Law Into One's Hands

We have seen that it is permissible for a *beis din*, rabbinical court to use certain forms of social pressure to persuade an individual to abide by its ruling. However, it is forbidden to use social pressure in order to bypass the court process and force a thief to return what he stole. It is wrong to cause the community to take a stand in a monetary issue on the basis of an individual's word alone; only through the *psak* (ruling) of a *beis din* may the community take a stand. Thus, it is correct to ensure that the parties come before a *beis din*, but it is forbidden to personally orchestrate the enforcement of what one believes to be justice.[108]

Listening to gossip might be enjoyable, but it is certainly not worth the heavy price.

5 Kislev · May today's learning be a זכות for our משפחה
Dedicated by Yehuda Levine & family
6 Sivan · The Manchester Rosh Yeshiva לע״נ הגאון הצדיק הרב
יהודא זאב בן הגאון הצדיק הרב משה יצחק הלוי סג״ל זצוק״ל
Dedicated by Mr. & Mrs. Chaim Lefkovits and family, Brooklyn, NY

DAY
65

◈A Swindler Comes to Town

People who speak *loshon hora* tend to rationalize their sinful behavior with the contention that the listener wanted to hear the gossip and that he obviously enjoyed it. Moreover, the two remained good friends after their discussion. Could one really be guilty of causing his listener harm when he obviously had such a good time? The fallacy of such thinking can be explained with the following parable:

A swindler came to a certain town and disguised himself as a respected leader of the community. When a visitor arrived in the town, the swindler welcomed him like an old friend and invited him to a local inn where the two could enjoy each other's company. At the inn, the swindler said, "It's been so many years since the last time we saw one another. My joy is indescribable. This calls for a celebration! Please, go to the counter and tell the manager to serve us the very best of everything he has to offer! Of course, I'll pay the bill."

The two wined and dined until they had both eaten more than their fill. At that point, the swindler slipped out the door, leaving his "guest" with the enormous bill to pay. The poor fellow explained to the manager what had transpired, but to no avail. "All I know," said the manager, "is that you came to the counter and ordered all that food and drink. Whatever happened between you and that other fellow is of no concern to me. Pay up!"

One who listens to *loshon hora* is like the visitor in our parable. The listener is happy and feels no enmity toward the speaker, who seems to be entertaining him free of charge. The listener sees the speaker as his dear confidant, who tells him private information that he might not divulge to others. But all this is only on this world, while "the shop is open, and the Merchant extends credit" (*Avos* 3:20). In the next world, however, where "the ledger is open ... and the collectors make their rounds," one will have to stand judgment for having listened to and accepted forbidden talk. Every word that he listened to will be recorded there, and he will have to pay a very heavy price.

ו כסלו
6 KISLEV/ CYCLE 1

ז סיון
7 SIVAN / CYCLE 2

SEFER CHOFETZ CHAIM

TOELES: For the Victim's Benefit

≈ Accusations Against the Beis Din

If one witnessed a crime which subsequently came before a *beis din,* rabbinical court, and the accused was acquitted of any wrongdoing, it is forbidden to voice criticism of the *beis din's* ruling. One must assume that a court comprised of Torah scholars has done its best to ascertain the facts according to the methods prescribed by *halachah* (i.e. testimony of two valid witnesses), and has ruled in accordance with Jewish law as detailed in *Shulchan Aruch.* If one was the sole witness to a crime, then his testimony is invalid, no matter how convincing are his arguments. Furthermore, one must come to terms with the reality that humans are limited in their ability to determine and carry out absolute justice, and ultimately, it is in Hashem's power to correct social injustice.

Words cannot adequately depict the depth of the gossip-monger's crime.

Certainly one who loses a court case cannot possibly be objective in his evaluation of the *beis din's* ruling. The practice of raising questions as to the competence of the *beis din,* or accusing the judges of bias, is blatant *hotzaas shem ra* (slander).[109]

Nevertheless, if one suspects that the ruling was the result of an error in the legal process, he could seek the advice of a rabbinic authority and ask that he investigate the matter.

---

6 Kislev · Aaron Holand לע״נ אהרן בן גבריאל
Dedicated by Sharon & Manny Saltiel
7 Sivan · May the increased unity in *Klal Yisrael,* created by this undertaking, stand as a זכות for our משפחה and hasten the coming of משיח

❧ *Beyond Description*

O ur Sages teach: "*Loshon hora* kills three: the speaker, the listener, and the person being discussed" (*Yerushalmi Pe'ah* 1:1).

A gossipmonger causes many to sin all at once, for it is his way to
assemble a crowd around himself to hear his latest piece of gossip.
The gossipmonger is deft in the art of making his reports intriguing
and convincing, so that his listeners accept his words as fact and, in
most cases, spread the news to others. Moreover, those who take
pleasure in listening to gossip often adopt the ways of the gossipmonger, as they spread gossip, both new and old, to others.

Words cannot adequately depict the depth of the gossipmonger's
sin. His words bring untold harm to himself and to all those who accept and relate *loshon hora* because of him. His crime is often
compounded as he spices his words with mockery and lies, which
even if not disparaging are nonetheless forbidden.

The Mishnah states: "Scripture punishes one who joins transgressors like the transgressors themselves" (*Mishnah Makkos* 1:7). Surely
whoever willingly joins the gossipmonger's group will stand judgment for this, and will be inscribed Above as belonging to a
"fraternity of wickedness" (*Tzavaas R' Eliezer* 7).

ז כסלו
7 KISLEV / CYCLE 1

ח סיון
8 SIVAN / CYCLE 2

SEFER CHOFETZ CHAIM
TOELES: For the Victim's Benefit

≈The Rights Of The Victim

We have seen (Days 63-66) that even when it is clear to someone that one person has wronged another financially, he may not attempt to effect justice outside the confines of *halachah*. This applies not only to a witness, but also to the victim himself.

If one feels that he has fallen victim to another person's dishonesty, and after verifying the facts concludes that he has a valid claim against that person, he must not publicly speak against that person for the sake of attaining restitution. Rather, he should confront the individual privately and, if necessary, consult a *rav*. If possible, the name of the accused should not be mentioned.[110]

A witness may not divulge to the victim the identity of the perpetrator, if the victim could be expected to employ halachically unacceptable tactics to retrieve his money.[111]

A wise man will consider the ramifications of his actions before he acts.

7 Kislev · Mrs. Dina Gross לע״נ דינה טילא בת משה
Dedicated by the Golberger families Brooklyn & Spring Valley, NY
8 Sivan · Chana Strenger לע״נ חנה בת מנחם מענדל הכהן
Dedicated by Yoily & Toby Steinberg in memory of her mother

❧Idle Conversations

A distinguished Torah scholar offered the following advice: On Shabbos afternoons in the summertime, when *Shalosh Seudos* often ends well before dark and people go outside to enjoy the fresh air, never stand outside a synagogue or study hall and carry on a conversation with someone. When such conversations do take place, what usually happens is that the two people are joined by a third, then a fourth ... until a large group has congregated. Each person proceeds to relate whatever interesting developments occurred in his business, on his street, or elsewhere during the week that passed. Inevitably, such discussions lead to *loshon hora* and light-headedness. And who are to blame? The two who initiated the discussion. A wise man will consider the ramifications of his actions *before* he acts.

Our Sages teach: "The righteous seek to find favor in the very area in which they sinned" (*Tanchumah, Parashas Beshalach* 24). Therefore, the first step for one who has caused others to accept or speak *loshon hora* is to accustom himself *not* to sit among groups who engage in idle discussion, contrary to his habit thus far. According to *Shelah*, this suggestion is alluded to in the verse: לא תלך רכיל בעמיך, *Do not be a gossipmonger among your people (Vayikra* 19:16). This can be interpreted homiletically: רכיל, *Gossipmonger*: לא תלך בעמיך, *do not walk among your people* [i.e. among groups where you are liable to repeat past sins].

Additionally, one should use his power of speech to arouse his brethren to strengthen their commitment to Torah and *mitzvah* observance, and he should strive to bring peace among Jews.

ח כסלו
8 KISLEV / CYCLE 1

ט סיון
9 SIVAN / CYCLE 2

SEFER CHOFETZ CHAIM
TOELES: For the Victim's Benefit

✎*Psychological And Emotional Damage*

An important area of speech which is considered constructive is that which helps to relieve someone of psychological or emotional damage caused by others.[112]

It is permissible for anyone who is suffering emotionally or psychologically to seek appropriate help even if this involves discussions of people and events that would otherwise constitute *loshon hora*. If possible, names should be omitted, and only pertinent information should be shared.

The Chofetz Chaim speculates that it may be considered constructive for a person troubled by an issue to unburden himself to someone even if only to relieve himself of stress.[113] Obviously, this applies to especially difficult situations and not to the daily vicissitudes of life.

One should flee from a group of idle chatterers like from a fire.

---

8 Kislev · Saul Freedman   לע״נ ישראל בן עקיבה
Dedicated in loving memory by his daughter Rosella Freedman
Rebbetzin Libby Zohn   לע״נ ליבא בת הרב אלחנן צבי
9 Sivan · Dedicated by the Gartenhaus family of Lakewood, NJ

◄Run for Your Life

Anyone whose heart is touched by fear of God should not sit himself among a group unless he is certain that its members are
careful in matters of speech. One should flee from a group of idle
chatterers like from a fire. Why should one sit himself among people
when he knows that he will be obligated to reprove them for speaking the forbidden? And if he will listen to their talk and remain silent,
then he too will incur punishment. In the words of *Rabbeinu Yonah*
(*Sha'arei Teshuvah* 3:197):

> Suppose a person hears others speak *loshon hora*, or vulgar-
> ities, or he finds himself among scoffers who speak
> disgracefully about the Torah and its *mitzvos*. Knowing that
> these people are stubborn and defiant, and that they will ig-
> nore any reproof, he chooses to remain silent. He will be
> punished for not rebuking them, for people may interpret his
> silence as agreement with what they have spoken. He is
> therefore obligated to respond to their words and rebuke
> them sharply, to demonstrate respect for the Torah and
> *mitzvos* which they have shamed, or for the righteous indi-
> vidual against whom they have spoken. This obligation is
> one of the factors which require a person to leave the com-
> pany of the wicked, lest he listen to their evil talk and refrain
> from responding. Thus did King Shlomo state: "Do not envy
> men of evil, do not desire to be with them. For their hearts
> think of plunder, and their lips speak of wrongdoing" (*Mishlei*
> 24:1-2).

ט כסלו
9 KISLEV / CYCLE I

י סיון
10 SIVAN / CYCLE 2

SEFER CHOFETZ CHAIM
TOELES: For the Victim's Benefit

❧ *Verbal Abuse*

It is permissible to speak negatively about some-one who was guilty of verbal abuse, in order to comfort his victim. The pain and humiliation caused by insulting speech can be minimized by pointing out to the victim that the perpetrator lacks intelligence or discretion and that people do not take him seriously.[114]

At a later point in time, it would be important to help the victim understand the nature and problems of the perpetrator so that he can learn how to deal with the person and prevent recurrence of such incidents.

It is enough to suffer retribution for one's own sins; must one suffer for the sins of others as well?

לע"נ נפתלי חיים בן שמואל · Nathan Borsten · 9 Kislev
Dedicated in loving memory of her brother by Polly & Milton Herman, Silver Spring, MD
לע"נ רב אברהם אהרן בן ר' שלמה זלמן הלוי · Malinowitz · 10 Sivan
Dedicated by his children

DAY
69

∾Keep Your Distance

The anguish one will experience in the next world for having sat in the company of gossipers can be better understood with a parable:

A group of men were enjoying each other's company when police suddenly appeared to arrest one of them, a man of ill repute, for allegedly having committed a crime. The man was led off in chains and brought before the authorities, who interrogated him thoroughly. Seeing how the accused steadfastly maintained his innocence, the authorities ordered that all those who were with him at the time of his arrest be taken into custody as well. They too were subjected to intense interrogation, in the hope that at least one of them would provide information which would prove the accused's guilt. These men were well aware that they themselves were not being accused of any wrongdoing. Yet they experienced deep regret for having associated with the accused. Had they kept distant from him, they would not have suffered the humiliation, intimidation and fear to which they were subjected.

When in the end they were released unharmed, they made sure to never again associate with that individual.

How careful one must be to avoid gossipers! When one feels his resolve weakening, out of fear of being labeled an outcast, he should tell himself: "It is enough that I will have to stand judgment for my own sins; need I suffer for the sins of others as well?"

❧Serious Threats

The Torah commands us: לא תעמד על דם רעך, *Do not stand aside while your fellow's blood is being shed* (*Vayikra* 19:16). We are obligated to spare no effort in preventing our fellow Jew from suffering physical, emotional, or monetary damage.

In a situation where a potential victim is unaware that he is being threatened, one is required to warn him even though this will reflect negatively on the person or persons responsible. Speech of this sort is not merely permissible, it is obligatory.[115] Nevertheless, one must be certain that conditions which render speech constructive have been appropriately met (see Days 42-50).

Strife inevitably leads to a host of severe transgressions.

10 Kislev · Mrs. Sylvia Montag לע״נ שרה פעסיל בת אברהם אלי׳הו
Dedicated by the Montag family, Brooklyn, NY & the Franco family, Long Branch, NJ
11 Sivan · Mrs. Felicia Peltzman לע״נ פייגא בת ר׳ ישראל ע״ה
Dedicated in loving memory of our dear mother by Rochel Leah and Yaakov Dov Stanger and family, Teaneck NJ

≈Strife

It is obvious that one should do everything in his power to avoid becoming involved in strife and dispute. For Jews to feud with one another is a dreadful sin that is often accompanied by a host of other severe transgressions. These are: speaking *loshon hora* and *rechilus*;[1] becoming overcome with baseless hatred (*sinas chinam*); causing hurt through words (*onaas devarim*); embarrassing one's fellow; seeking revenge; bearing a grudge; expressing a wish for another's misfortune; and actively seeking to deny him his livelihood. At times, strife also leads to *chilul Hashem*, desecration of Hashem's Name, an exceedingly severe sin.

Strife often leads to the sin of flattery, as the disputants fawn upon others in order to gain their support, and to mockery, as each side ridicules the other in order to draw people into its camp. Our Sages state that initially Heaven exacts suffering as punishment for mockery; ultimately, the consequences of this sin can be devastating (see *Avodah Zara* 18b).

Even if initially a disputant intends to avoid engaging in the kind of sinful behavior described above, he will ultimately transgress some or all of these sins. This unfortunate truth is known to all.

The evil inclination has two prime avenues through which he draws even men of spiritual stature into this morass: anger and a desire to triumph. When a person is overcome by these destructive emotions, then what is clearly wrong and contrary to Torah becomes the proper path. He will find a myriad of reasons why the negative behavior described above is permissible and even desirable. In the end, he will become convinced that it is a *mitzvah* to defame his adversary and absolutely forbidden to show him any mercy.

---

1. Evil talk that breeds ill will among Jews. See Laws of *Rechilus* in this work.

☙*Possible Harm*

U nlike other cases of constructive purpose, protecting someone from possible harm is permissible even when no firsthand information is available. If one happens to hear that one Jew is plotting to harm another, it is permissible to advise the potential victim to beware of the suspected plotter. In such a case, where the suspicions are based on hearsay, the information must not be presented as fact. It should be clearly stated that the concerns stem from unconfirmed secondhand information that may or may not be true.[116]

The Chofetz Chaim maintains that although one who fails to warn his fellow Jew of impending danger is in violation of, "Do not stand aside while your fellow's blood is being shed," this does not apply when one is unable to personally verify that danger does, indeed, exist. Nevertheless, it is proper to convey even secondhand information if this might spare someone harm.[117]

[One must be certain to comply with the seven rules of *toeles* when relating the necessary information.]

Any attempt to fully describe the destructiveness of strife will be insufficient.

❧ Self-Destruction

In his last will and testament, *Rambam* writes: "Prophets prophesied and wise men spoke many words of wisdom regarding the wickedness of strife — and they did not plumb its full depth." Thus, any attempt to fully describe the great destructiveness of strife will be insufficient. We will therefore offer only brief citations concerning this matter, and allow the man of intellect to ponder it further.

The *Midrash* states:

> R' Berechiah said: How destructive is strife! The Heavenly Court does not exact punishment [from the living] until the age of twenty;[1] the [Jewish] courts on this earth do not punish until the age of thirteen [for a male]; yet in the dispute involving Korach, infants were swallowed up into the abyss, as it is written, "... with their wives, children, and infants ... The earth opened its mouth and swallowed them and their households .... they and all that was theirs descended alive to the pit" (*Bamidbar* 16:27, 32-33).
>
> The Sages taught: Four are classified as "wicked": one who extends his hand to strike his fellow, even if he does not actually strike him; one who borrows and does not repay; a brazen person who has no sense of shame before those of greater stature than himself; and one who engages in strife. Regarding this last sinner, it is written, "Turn away now from the tents of *these wicked men* [i.e. Korach and his group]" (ibid. v. 26).

How much inner shame should one feel for having been the cause of dispute! Would a person not be unforgiving if someone called him a *rasha* (wicked person) even in private, with no one else present? Should not a person be overcome with shame for having *caused himself* to be deserving of this description?!

---

1. See *Shabbos* 89b and *Rashi* to *Bereishis* 23:1.

יב כסלו
12 KISLEV/ CYCLE 1

יג סיון
13 SIVAN / CYCLE 2

SEFER CHOFETZ CHAIM
TOELES: For the Victim's Benefit

❧Overhearing a Threat

A n obvious case where conveying negative information is required is where a person is overheard plotting to harm someone. While we have seen that when a Jew may be in danger, even secondhand information can be related, it is imperative that one first determine that the plot is apparently serious and not a bad joke.[118]

The condition that one first reprove the person against whom he intends to speak (see Day 45) applies only if one believes he can change the alleged plotter's attitude. Otherwise, warning him would only induce him to modify the plot to ensure that it not be uncovered.[119]

The remaining conditions are required here no less than in an ordinary case of constructive speech: One's intent must be solely to avert harm (and not, for example, for the pleasure of thwarting the plotter); if an alternative exists — including not revealing the identity of the plotter — then that avenue must be pursued. Also, one must be reasonably sure that the plotter will not be caused undue harm. If the potential victim is known to be hot-tempered and can be expected to take revenge, he cannot be spoken to. Alternative means would have to be found to protect the victim without endangering the plotter. (The case of one who overhears a plotter will be discussed in greater detail in the laws of *rechilus*.)

Strife is the cause of immeasurable heartache and suffering.

12 Kislev · Bertha Leah Winer לע"נ ברכה לאה בת יוסף אריה
Dedicated by יוסף אריה בן חיים יהושע
13 Sivan · Rabbi Abe Dekoven לע"נ הרב אברהם חיים בן יהודה ליב ז"ל
Dedicated by his wife Marilyn, daughters and family, Chicago, IL

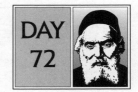

DAY 72

❧*The Work of Satan*

Much of Satan's efforts are directed toward inciting strife, and toward ensuring that once a feud has erupted, it does not end quickly. The Talmud relates:

> There were two people whom Satan regularly incited, so that at every twilight period [on the eve of Shabbos] they fought with one another. R' Meir visited there and restrained them for three such twilight periods until he made peace between them. He subsequently heard Satan say: "Woe, that R' Meir has removed that one [i.e. Satan] from his house [i.e. from the place where he was previously welcome]!" (*Gittin* 52a).

The *Midrash* states that the word מחלקת *(dispute)* is an acronym for מכה, *plague;* חרון, *wrath;* לקוי, *affliction;* קללה; *curse;* תכלית, *conclusion;* for ultimately, strife brings destruction upon man.

The greater the stature of the disputant, the greater is his sin.[1] This is why the Torah underscores the fact that those who joined Korach in his rebellion were "leaders of the assembly, those summoned for meeting, men of renown" (*Bamidbar* 16:2).

---

1. See *Tanna D'Vei Eliyahu Rabbah* ch. 18.

יג כסלו
13 KISLEV / CYCLE 1

יד סיון
14 SIVAN / CYCLE 2

SEFER CHOFETZ CHAIM
TOELES: For the Victim's Benefit

◄Consumer Protection

Consumer protection is an important — but sensitive — area which allows for information to be conveyed *l'toeles*, for a constructive purpose.[120]

If a storekeeper hands a customer too little change, or charges him for something he did not purchase, one must not assume that the storekeeper is dishonest or careless — we all make mistakes. If this happens often, one must bring the matter to the storekeeper's attention and inform him that if the practice continues, one will have no choice but to inform his clientele. If the situation still does not change, one is required to warn people to count their change carefully and examine their receipts for any mistakes. It is forbidden to insinuate that the man is dishonest even if one has reason to suspect so, since it is sufficient for people to think that he is careless (or has problems with his arithmetic) for them to take the necessary precautions.[121]

It would also be forbidden to inform hot-headed individuals who, for example, might vandalize the store in the name of justice.

Hashem is relenting regarding the most severe sins, but not regarding strife.

לע"נ החבר מרדכי בן החבר גרשון ז"ל · 13 Kislev · Max Rothschild
Dedicated by Kurt & Edith Rothschild and family
14 Sivan · Wohlberg לע"נ ישראל שלמה בן יהושע בירך
Dedicated by Mr. & Mrs. Martin Dov Berger, Kew Gardens Hills, NY

ᴥ*When Heaven is Unrelenting*

Our Sages state (*Mishnas R' Eliezer* ch. 4):

In three instances the Holy One, Blessed is He, relented regarding idol worship, but was unrelenting regarding strife.

Idol worship was initiated in the days of Enosh, as the Torah states: "Then to call in the Name of HASHEM became profaned" (*Bereishis* 4:26). God spared that generation [from total destruction] only because harmony prevailed among the people. In the generation of the Flood, however, strife was prevalent, as is evident from the robbery that was found among them. It was this which sealed their fate, as it is written, "The end of all flesh has come before Me, for the earth is filled with robbery through them; and behold, I am about to destroy them from the earth" (ibid. 6:13).

In the Wilderness, God was forgiving of the sin of the Golden Calf, but He was unrelenting when strife was found among the people. Wherever strife was found, a great punishment followed. Particularly illustrative of this is the episode of Korach.

When the idol of Michah was erected, God granted time for repentance, because peace reigned among the people. Thus it is written, "And the sons of Dan erected the idol, and Yehonasan, son of Gershom, son of Menashe, he along with his sons, were priests for the tribe of Dan until the [people of] the land were exiled" (*Shoftim* 18:30). However, when the Ten Tribes initiated a feud with the tribes of Yehudah and Binyamin, each side became a source of punishment for the other, as it is written, "Aviah [King of Yehudah] and his people smote them mightily. Five hundred thousand chosen men fell slain from Israel" (*II Divrei HaYamim* 13:17). And when the tribes of Yehudah and Binyamin sinned, the Ten Tribes came and attacked them, as it is written, "In that Pekach son of Remaliahu slew one hundred and twenty thousand in one day" (ibid. 28:6)

Thus, feuding parties become tools of punishment against one another.

יד כסלו
14 KISLEV / CYCLE 1

טו סיון
15 SIVAN / CYCLE 2

SEFER CHOFETZ CHAIM
TOELES: For the Victim's Benefit

✒A Better Deal

It is permissible to inform friends and neighbors of a store where they can obtain items of better quality or at better prices than at the store where they usually shop.

Here too certain conditions have to be met:

One should know the information firsthand. (If one cannot verify the information firsthand, he would have to say, "I have heard, but have not verified that ..." [see Day 43].) He must be certain that the quality of the other merchandise is superior (brand names are not necessarily better); where there is a significant difference in price, one must verify that the less expensive item is not inferior in quality to the more expensive one.

There must also be no suspicion that the preferred store is dealing in stolen merchandise, as *Halachah* prohibits purchasing stolen goods.

In conveying the information, it is important not to imply that the first storekeeper is overcharging or is guilty of selling inferior products; one must convey the pertinent information without being judgmental. Furthermore, since people often view high pricing in a negative way, the information may be considered derogatory and could only be conveyed for a constructive purpose. Consequently, one may only relate the information to people who may be interested in making a purchase. Discussing the matter for the sake of making conversation might constitute *loshon hora*.

(Continued on page 408)

> *When there is peace among God's legions on this world, there is peace among the Heavenly legions.*

14 Kislev · Rebbitzen Chana Gorfinkel לע״נ הרבנית חנה בת הרב אלחנן צבי
Dedicated by the Garfinkel, Kaplinsky and Landesman families
15 Sivan · Dr. Mordechai Hirsch לע״נ החבר מרדכי בן החבר שמעון הירש
Dedicated by the family

ᐒ*Peace in Two Worlds*

Sefer Ma'alos HaMiddos (24) states:

How damaging is strife! — it can imperil one's very life. It was the feud between the shepherds of Avraham and the shepherds of Lot that caused Lot to move away from Avraham and settle in Sodom[1] where he almost perished along with the rest of the Sodomites.

Our Sages state (*Derech Eretz Zuta ch. 9*): "A home in which there is strife will ultimately be destroyed; a synagogue in which there is strife will see its congregants dispersed, and ultimately will be made desolate; a city in which there is strife will become a place of bloodshed. Two Torah scholars in a single city or two rabbinical courts in a single city who feud with one another — their end will be death. Moreover, strife between rabbinical courts brings destruction to the world. For when there is peace among God's legions on this world, there is peace among the Heavenly legions, as it is written, "Who builds His upper chambers in the Heavens, and His union is established upon the earth" (Amos 9:6). When are His upper chambers "built"? When "His union is established on this earth," meaning, when the Jewish nation is united in peace.

---

1. *Bereishis* 13:7-13.

☙ Unsafe Products

It is permissible to warn people that a product is dangerous — that is, if the warning is truly warranted. Countless items are potentially dangerous if misused, and many processed foods are unhealthy if consumed in large quantities; in such cases, labeling the item "dangerous" is wrong. Labeling an item as unsafe is justified only if such a declaration is considered reasonable by normal standards. (See Day 43, condition 2.) Furthermore, if the information is not known firsthand, this must be mentioned when relating the information (see Day 43).

If the manufacturer is Jewish, he must be spoken to first (see Day 45). Failure to fulfill the above conditions would render the statement *loshon hora*, as it would cause harm to the manufacturer, as well as to the consumer who will needlessly avoid the product.

The sin of shaming Torah scholars led to the destruction of Jerusalem.

לע"נ אהרן שמואל אליהו בן Aaron Samuel Heller · 15 Kislev
חיים יצחק ישראל ע"ה
Dedicated by Shirley & Arnold Klausner, Esther Statman
לע"נ דוב בעריש בן חיים אשר ז"ל Benny Wiener · 16 Sivan
Dedicated by Pinchas & Sherie Gross and
Yitzchak & Marsha Kasdan and families, Silver Spring, MD

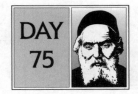

DAY 75

⌒Disparaging a Torah Scholar

While it is a sin to quarrel with any Jew, the sin is greater when one initiates a feud with a Torah scholar. And when one's adversary is his own Torah teacher, the sin is magnified manifold.

It is the way of warring parties to disparage one another, and it is regarding one who disparages a Torah scholar that our Sages apply the verse, "For he scorned the word of HASHEM and broke His commandment; that person will surely be cut off, his sin is upon him" (*Bamidbar* 15:31).[1]

The Talmud relates (*Shabbos* 119b) that the sin of shaming Torah scholars led to the destruction of Jerusalem, as it is written, "But they mocked the messengers of God, despised His words and scoffed at His prophets, to a point that the anger of HASHEM rose against His people, without any possibility of abatement" (*II Divrei HaYamim* 36:16).

The Talmud further states: "R' Yehoshua ben Levi said: Whoever speaks disparagingly of a deceased Torah scholar descends into *Gehinnom*" (*Berachos* 19a).

---

1. See *Sanhedrin* 99b and *Yoreh De'ah* 243:6.

↵*Kashrus*

A most sensitive area of constructive speech is that of kashrus.

Raising doubts regarding the reliability of a *hechsher* (rabbinical endorsement) without reliable information constitutes speaking *loshon hora*. If one has reason to suspect that a *hechsher* is inferior, the matter should be discussed with a competent *rav*, who can offer guidance as to how one should proceed. Even if one *rav* suggests that a *hechsher* not be relied upon, this does not necessarily mean that the *hechsher* is definitely unreliable. It is the *rav* of the community who should decide the status of a *hechsher* for his constituents, or else direct them to a recognized *posek* (halachic authority) for his decision.

In a case of a questionable product manufactured by a local Orthodox Jew who assumes responsibility for his product and does not operate under a *hechsher*, extreme caution must be exercised before declaring the product non-kosher. Only the local *rav* or *posek* is in a position to decide the halachic status of the item, after taking all factors into consideration. Causing a Jew to close down his business is a very serious matter and preventing such a situation may even outweigh the observance of *chumros* (unrequired halachic stringencies) generally kept by the community.[123]

> **To initiate a dispute against one's rabbi or Torah teacher is to play with fire.**

16 Kislev · Doris Bell לע״נ שרה דברא בת ירחמיאל יהודה ז״ל
Dedicated by her niece Marilyn, great nieces, nephews and family, Chicago, IL
17 Sivan · Chana Sacks לע״נ חנה בת נחום לייב
Dedicated by the Sacks family

☙Playing with Fire

The Talmud states:

> R' Chisda said: One who argues against his Torah teacher
> [and incites others to join him] is considered as if he argued
> against the Divine Presence, as it is written [regarding
> Korach's rebellion against Moshe], "... when he [Korach] con-
> tended against HASHEM" (*Bamidbar* 26:9). R' Chama bar
> Chanina said: One who initiates a dispute with his Torah
> teacher is considered as if he had initiated a dispute with the
> Divine Presence, as it is written, "They are the waters of
> strife, where the Children of Israel contended with HASHEM[1]"
> (ibid. 20:13) ... R' Chanina bar Pappa said: One who voices
> complaints against his teacher is considered as if he voiced
> complaints against the Divine Presence ... R' Avahu said:
> Whoever is skeptical of his teacher is considered as if he
> were skeptical of the Divine Presence.

The above infractions are listed in descending order of severity.
We see, however, that even to view the conduct or teachings of
one's Torah teacher with skepticism is in itself a severe sin.

How foolish are those who are quick to initiate disputes against
the rabbi or *av beis din* (head of the rabbinical court) of their city, and
ignore the severe punishment which they are likely to incur, both in
this world and the next!

The verse, "You shall honor the presence of a sage" (*Vayikra* 19:32)
requires us to show respect for Torah scholars.[2] Commenting on this
verse, the *Midrash* (*Bamidbar Rabbah* 15:13) speaks harshly of one
who fails to accord his rabbi proper respect. Surely, to initiate a dispute between the local community and its rabbi is a sin of far greater
severity and demands far greater retribution.

---

1. In fact, they had directed their complaints toward Moshe.
2. See *Kiddushin* 32b.

יז כסלו
17 KISLEV / CYCLE 1

יח סיון
18 SIVAN / CYCLE 2

SEFER CHOFETZ CHAIM
TOELES: For the Victim's Benefit

~Shifting the Blame

Yet another situation where negative speech may be in order is where one is the victim of false accusation and wishes to divulge the identity of the real culprit to vindicate himself. Whether or not this is permissible depends on the nature of the crime.

If the crime is of a type that would halachically require the observer to inform either the victim or others of the culprit's identity, he should do so.

If there is no constructive purpose in revealing the culprit's identity other than to vindicate oneself, it would be forbidden for the accused to name the culprit. The accused should declare his innocence and refrain from incriminating anyone else.[124]

In a situation where only two people are possible suspects, which means that a denial on the part of one is tantamount to an accusation against the other, it is permissible to deny the charges provided that the act committed was indeed improper. However, if the alleged offense was, in fact, an innocent statement or action, the accused should not deny it. Denial would implicate the other person who, in this case, is guilty of no real crime.[125]

It is a *middas chassidus* (measure of piety) to accept the blame in all cases, unless revealing the identity of the guilty party serves a constructive purpose.[126] Also, one should not accept the blame for an act which would reflect badly on the community or on observant Jews in general, as this would constitute a *chilul Hashem,* desecration of God's name.

> *Tragically, it is the way of quarrelers to involve their wives and children in their disputes.*

17 Kislev · Eleanor Klugmann Levovitz לע"נ חוה בת ר' יהודה הכהן
Dedicated by the Klugmann & Rubinfeld families
18 Sivan · Berger הלוי לע"נ אפרים בן ישראל
Dedicated by the Berger & Freifeld families Brooklyn & Queens, NY

DAY 77

ᔆThe Tragedy of Strife

There is something most astonishing about those who are bent toward strife.

If the child of one of these people would be slightly injured by someone, even unintentionally, the father would castigate the culprit with fury. If the child would be hurt intentionally and become bedridden because of his wounds, the angry father would publicly denounce the attacker — even after the child had recovered — as a cruel, violent individual. The father would not rest until he felt that he had dealt the guilty party a blow commensurate with his callous deed. The man of strife would harbor eternal hatred toward the person who caused his child harm.

As stated above[1], even infants may be included in Divine retribution meted out to those who are parties to strife. Yet the man of strife does not consider for a moment that he himself brings untold harm — and even death, Heaven forfend — upon his children because of his sinful ways. Tragically, it is the way of quarrelers to involve their wives, children and other relatives in their disputes. Such was the way of Dasan and Aviram, as the Torah states: "Dasan and Aviram went out erect at the entrance of their tents, with their wives, children and infants" (*Bamidbar* 16:27).

Thus, it is written, "The children gather the wood, but it is the fathers who ignite the fire" (*Yirmiyahu* 7:18). The evil inclination blinds these people, so that they and their loved ones stumble into the abyss below.

---

1. See Day 71.

✒*Quest for Truth or Personal Feud*

The Mishnah (*Avos* 5:20) contrasts *machlokes l'sheim shamayim*, a dispute for the sake of Heaven, with one that is not. The former is epitomized by the disputes of Hillel and Shammai whose differing views in matters of *halachah* are reverently studied and pondered generation after generation as eternal components of the Oral Law. The latter is epitomized by the dispute of Korach, whose personal feud against Moshe *Rabbeinu* earned him an untimely death and eternal dishonor. As the Chofetz Chaim notes in his preface to *Sefer Chofetz Chaim*, one whose sinful talk fuels strife transgresses the prohibition, "that he not be like Korach and his assembly" (*Bamidbar* 17:5; see *Sanhedrin* 110a).[127]

To the Jew, intellectual disagreement in a common search for truth is an integral part of life. As a spiritual, thinking people, Jews are forever involved in discussion of ideas.

Conversely, personal bickering, jealousy, and competition are signs of immaturity and weakness. They have no place in the world of the Jew.

The difficulty, however, lies in our tendency to transform every dispute into an ideological one. Korach, too, came with a philosophy: that all Jews are equally holy, and thus there is no justification for one family, Aharon and his *Kohanim* descendants, to be above everyone else.

(continued on page 408)

Better to experience embarrassment on this world than to be shamed in the World to Come.

18 Kislev · Mrs. Chana Flamm לע״נ חנה בת יהושע הערץ
Dedicated by the Flamm family, Brooklyn, NY
19 Sivan · Rabbi Shlomo Yisroel Gelber לע״נ שלמה ישראל ב״ר יוסף יהודה ז״ל
Dedicated by the Gelber family

❧ *At All Costs*

If one finds oneself embroiled in feud, he dare not rest until he has fully extricated himself from it. One must strive with every ounce of resolve to remove himself from strife, no matter how difficult this may be.

The Torah relates that initially Ohn ben Peles was among the leaders of Korach's camp in his rebellion against Moshe (*Bamidbar* 16:1). Yet he managed to separate himself from Korach's group and thus was not punished when their time came.[1]

Do not be convinced by the evil inclination's arguments and incitements that, for example, it is below one's dignity not to follow through in a dispute until victory is achieved. Better to experience embarrassment on this world than to be shamed in the World Above in the presence of the entire Heavenly Assembly.

Our Sages state: "Better that a person be called a fool all his life than to be considered a wicked person even for a moment before the Omnipresent" (*Mishnah Ediyos* 5:6).

---

1. See *Sanhedrin* 109b.

✒ Rabble-Rousers

The Talmud teaches that one is permitted to speak *loshon hora* about *baalei machlokes*, men of strife, who are at the forefront of a community feud. The purpose of speaking out against such individuals is to encourage other members of the community to dissociate themselves from them. Isolating instigators of a dispute can help restore tranquility to a community torn by strife. The undisputed *rav* of a community could, for example, urge his constituents to refrain from conversing with certain individuals, so as not to give them an opportunity to develop a following to create strife.

However, disparagement of one party in a dispute by the other usually results in mudslinging which further escalates the dispute. That is not at all what the Sages had in mind when they permitted speaking against *baalei machlokes*.[128]

Never lend support to either party in a feud.

19 Kislev · Chana Schonberg לע״נ חנה בת משה
Dedicated by her children
לע״נ יעקב בן ר׳ יונה צבי ע״ה · 20 Sivan
Dedicated in memory of my beloved father R' Yakov Herzog ע״ה

DAY
79

Don't Get Involved

Above, we discussed the seriousness of initiating and pursuing strife. One must also beware not to lend support to either party in a feud, lest he suffer along with them when their time of retribution arrives. As the Mishnah states: "Scripture punishes an accomplice to transgressors like the transgressors themselves" (*Mishnah Makkos* 1:7).

The *Midrash* states (*Bamidbar Rabbah* 18:3): "Take heed of the severity of strife, for when one is an accomplice to strife, the Holy One, Blessed is He, brings about his end, as it is written [regarding those who sided with Korach], 'A flame came forth from HASHEM and consumed the two hundred and fifty men who were offering the incense' " (*Bamidbar* 16:35).

The Talmud states: "Rav said: Whoever maintains a dispute transgresses a negative commandment, as it is written, '... that he not be like Korach and his assembly ...' " (ibid. 17:5). Rav Asi said: Such a person is fit to be afflicted with *tzaraas*"[1] (*Sanhedrin* 110a). In a previous chapter we cited the words of *Sefer HaKaneh* which state that at times God substitutes poverty for *tzaraas*, thus placing the sinner at the mercy of his fellow men.

---

1. See Days 39-48.

כ כסלו
20 KISLEV/ CYCLE 1

כא סיון
21 SIVAN / CYCLE 2

⊸Learning from Others' Mistakes

We have seen (Day 11) that it is forbidden to discuss someone's faults even with people who are aware of these deficiencies, for to focus on a person's weaknesses is lowly.

However, when teaching or offering guidance, one may make use of real-life illustrations of improper behavior in other people and even refer to those people by name, provided that the listeners are already familiar with the behavior of these people. The use of actual situations to which the listener can relate will deliver a message that mere discussion cannot convey. Reference to negativity here is constructive and is not considered lowly.[129]

Therefore, it is permissible to make reference to the life-style of a non-observant Jew to emphasize weaknesses in his behavior and its consequences, though his lack of observance is rooted in ignorance. However, one should be careful not to condemn the person.[130]

One may not use examples from the past history of a *baal teshuvah* without his permission. Constructive intent is not a license for possible embarrassment.

It is also wrong to use examples from the life-styles of different ethnic groups within the Jewish nation unless it is clear that neither speaker nor listener is unsympathetic towards that group.

Rather than anticipate the taste of victory in dispute, one should ponder the shame and retribution that may be his lot.

20 Kislev · Yankel Schonberg לע״נ יעקב יצחק בן נפתלי בנימין
Dedicated by his children
21 Sivan · Julius Cooper לע״נ יהודה בן יוסף מיכל
Dedicated by his children

DAY
80

⤚The Pursuer's Lot

Scripture states: "God always seeks the pursued" (*Koheles* 3:15). The *Midrash* comments (*Vayikra Rabbah* 27:5):

> R' Yose ben Nehurai said: The Holy One, Blessed is He, always exacts retribution from the pursuers for the blood of the pursued.
>
> R' Elazar said in the name of R' Yose ben Zimra: So it is with Temple offerings. God said: The ox is pursued by the lion, the goat by the leopard, the sheep by the wolf; do not bring offerings from the pursuers, but only from the pursued.

One must refrain from assisting in a feud, lest Hashem hold him accountable for the hurt caused the other party. Rather than anticipate the glory of triumph when his side emerges victorious, let him instead picture the shame and retribution that may be his lot.

One who scrupulously avoids dispute is truly honored by others, as it is written, "It is an honor for a man to refrain from quarreling" (*Mishlei* 20:3). The *Midrash* comments (*Yalkut HaMechiri, Mishlei* 26:14): If personal dignity demands that one refrain from becoming involved in personal feud, then certainly it demands that one avoid becoming entangled in someone else's feud! Of those who take the opposite path, Scripture states: "Like someone who grabs hold of a dog's ears is a passerby who becomes involved in a quarrel not his own" (*Mishlei* 26:17).[1]

---

1. The man who grabs hold of a dog's ears has only himself to blame for the bite that is sure to come (*Rashi*).

כא כסלו
21 KISLEV/ CYCLE 1

כב סיון
22 SIVAN / CYCLE 2

SEFER CHOFETZ CHAIM
TOELES: Relationships

✑*Breaking up a Harmful Friendship*

Another form of constructive speech is that which prevents or breaks up a relationship that is harmful to at least one of the parties. It is correct to suggest that someone distance himself from a person or persons who may have a negative influence upon him. Similarly, it is proper to inform a parent that someone may be having a negative influence on his child. All preconditions must, of course, be fulfilled — including verification of facts and constructive intent (see Days 43-50). If the information is not firsthand it may nevertheless be conveyed, provided that it is clearly being presented as secondhand information.[131]

With regard to the requirement of accuracy of the information, the Chofetz Chaim suggests that exaggeration may be permissible if that is the only way to convince the person or parent to end the relationship.[132]

The Chofetz Chaim adds that it is imperative to explain why conveying the information does not constitute speaking *loshon hora*, especially when speaking to a child.[133]

If a father commands his son to transgress even a Rabbinic decree, his order must be ignored, for both father and son are obligated to honor the word of Hashem.

לע"נ החבר ר' שלמה בן ישראל מאיר ע"ה · 21 Kislev
Dedicated by the Ferber, Beyman and Wikler families
לע"נ ר' יהושע מאיר בן ר' רפאל ז"ל · 22 Sivan · Yehoshua Freshwater
Dedicated by the Freshwater families, London, England

✍*Father and Son*

E ven if the quarreler is one's close relative, including his own father, he should, nevertheless, be exceedingly careful not to join
the feud.

Even if it appears that one's father is correct in his contentions,
one should seek to quell the dispute, rather than to strengthen his
father's hand against his adversary. Aside from the *mitzvah* of making peace between Jews, one should realize that it is impossible to
see things objectively when one of the parties involved is one's parent. *Sifre* interprets the phrase, "...your friend who is like your own
soul" (*Devarim* 13:7) as a reference to one's father, whom one loves
like his own self. Thus, deciding between the positions of one's father and his adversary is akin to deciding between the positions of
oneself and one's own adversary.

If a father instructs his son to assist him in his dispute, his order
must not be obeyed. For, as the *halachah* states (*Yoreh De'ah* 240:15),
if a father commands his son to transgress even a Rabbinic decree,
his order must be ignored, for both father and son are obligated to
honor the word of Hashem. This is especially true with regard to the
severe sin of engaging in strife.

ᴥPotentially Harmful Relationships

The next set of rules concerns information which, if provided, could prevent a potential relationship (e.g. business partnership, *shidduch* [marriage match], hiring a worker) from materializing.[134]

In these cases, *Halachah* differentiates between three situations:

(1) where one suggests the relationship;

(2) where one is called on to answer questions from one party concerning the other;

(3) where one is in a position to volunteer information to either one of the parties about the other, though it has not been requested.

These three situations involve different Torah commandments and therefore are to be dealt with using varying criteria.

When suggesting that someone consider entering into a relationship with someone else, one must be mindful of the commandment לפני עור לא תתן מכשל, *Before a blind person do not place a stumbling block* (*Vayikra* 19:14), which our Sages interpret as an admonition not to offer עצה שאינה הוגנת, *advice which is not proper*.

It is absolutely forbidden to suggest someone as a possible employee, business partner or marriage partner if one is aware that:

(Continued on page 408)

The opening chapter of Tehillim sings the praises of those who were not drawn after their father's quarrel.

22 Kislev · David Garfinkel לע"נ דוד בנימין בן חיים מאיר ז"ל
Dedicated in loving memory of our grandfather by the Victor, Gibber and Katz families
23 Sivan · Sylvia Bartzoff Havivi לע"נ צביה בת חיים אליעזר וגולדה
Dedicated by her sons, Eliezer & Abraham Havivi

DAY
82

✍The Sons of Korach

The sons of Korach were not drawn after their father's rebellious ways, and thus were saved from the terrible punishment which befell him. As the *Midrash* comments (*Yalkut Shimoni, Parashas Korach*, ch. 16):

> *Praiseworthy is the man (Tehillim 1:1)*: These are the sons of Korach.
>
> *... that walks not in the counsel of the wicked*: who did not follow their father's counsel, as it is written, "[Moshe told the people:] 'Turn away now from the tents of these *wicked* men ...' " (*Bamidbar* 16:26).
>
> *... and stood not in the path of the sinful*: as it is written, "As for the fire-pans of these *sinners* against their [own] souls" (ibid. 17:3).
>
> *... and sat not in the sessions of scoffers*: This refers to Korach who scorned Moshe and Aharon.

The *Midrash* (*Yalkut Shimoni* 752) relates that at one point the sons of Korach were in a dilemma. They were sitting with their father when Moshe appeared. They said to one another: "What shall we do? If we rise out of respect for Moshe, we will, in effect, be showing disrespect for our father, and we are commanded to honor father and mother. If we do not rise, we will have transgressed the command to rise before a sage." They decided to rise out of respect for Moshe. It was in this merit that they were saved, for at that moment thoughts of repentance stirred in their hearts. Regarding them did David say, "My heart is astir with a good theme" (*Tehillim* 45:2).

כג כסלו
23 KISLEV / CYCLE 1

כד סיון
24 SIVAN / CYCLE 2

SEFER CHOFETZ CHAIM
TOELES: Relationships

⮜Suggesting A Relationship

We have seen that it is forbidden to attempt to involve someone in a situation that the person would not want, would he be aware of certain facts.

If an acquaintance is seeking a person with years of experience with whom to start a business, one may not recommend someone who appears to be experienced but, in fact, is not — unless the acquaintance is told this. This holds true even if the person possesses natural talent which seems to compensate for his lack of experience.

Often, people feel that they know what their friend is "really looking for" far better than the friend himself does, and feel justified in deceiving the friend by providing inaccurate information about a perspective *shidduch* or employee, with the aim of seeing the *shidduch* or hiring realized.

It is presumptuous and arrogant for one to think that he has the right to make others' life decisions for them.

Moshe strove to make peace with those who brazenly opposed him.

Furthermore, it should be understood that the human personality is complex. Logically, one may seem to have found the perfect match for his friend. Nevertheless, if one's friend has developed an attitude — irrational though it may be — that he or she will only marry someone who meets a particular specification, hiding the truth about a prospective mate could have lifelong repercussions.

(Continued on Page 408)

לע"נ מרדכי מאיר ע"ה בן יצחק ישכר מנחם מענדיל זילברברג ז"ל · 23 Kislev
נקטף בדמי ימיו
לע"נ הרב אהרן ישעי' בן 24 Sivan · Rabbi Aaron Yeshia Shapiro
ר' יעקב יצחק זצ"ל
Dedicated by Rabbi & Mrs. Jeruchom Leib Shapiro and family

❧The Way of Moshe

A son is required to totally remove himself from his father's feud when he sees himself as powerless to resolve it. However, in a situation where a father has high regard for his son's opinion and would allow him to bring the matter to a peaceful resolution, the son is obligated to become involved.

Tanna D'Vei Eliyahu Rabbah (ch. 21) states: "One cannot stand silently as his father and mother speak forbidden talk. If he will remain silent, the lives of all three may be cut short."[1]

It is a *mitzvah* for every Jew to make peace between feuding parties. As the Mishnah states (*Pe'ah* 1:1), this is one of the deeds whose "fruits" one enjoys in this world but whose "principal" [i.e. primary reward] remains for the World to Come. Even if one side is clearly wrong and is deserving of punishment for having initiated the dispute, and one has the power to bring this punishment upon this person, nevertheless, he should do everything in his power to resolve the matter peacefully. Such was the way of Moshe, who strove to make peace with Dasan and Aviram, though he had the power to bring punishment upon them for their having brazenly opposed him. Thus does the Torah relate, "Moshe stood up and went to Dasan and Aviram" (*Bamidbar* 16:25), to which the Sages comment, "From this we derive that one should not remain steadfast in dispute" (*Sanhedrin* 110a).

Because Moshe went to the tents of Dasan and Aviram to make peace, he merited to save four righteous individuals, Ohn ben Peles and Korach's three sons, from the sufferings of *Gehinnom*.

---

1. Of course, he should intervene respectfully, in consonance with the stringent rules of *kibud av v'em* (honoring one's father and mother — see *Shulchan Aruch, Yoreh De'ah* ch. 240).

כד כסלו
23 KISLEV / CYCLE 1

כה סיון
24 SIVAN / CYCLE 2

SEFER CHOFETZ CHAIM
TOELES: Relationships

~When Facts May be Concealed

There are times when a *rav* may permit suggesting a *shidduch* and temporarily concealing information which could prevent the *shidduch* from coming about.

Occasionally, a situation exists as a result of which people might be reluctant to even consider a *shidduch* with a particular person or family, though, in fact, the situation need not warrant such reluctance.

It is in such a case that a *rav* may permit an initial meeting (and at times even a series of meetings) without the pertinent fact being mentioned, so that when it finally is revealed, the person stands a chance of being judged fairly.

However, it is forbidden to conceal the information until after the other party has developed strong, positive feelings concerning the *shidduch,* for at that point, the party will be denied the opportunity to reach an objective decision, and will have been the victim of dishonesty and manipulation.

Needless to say, such decisions are not to be made by a *shadchan* (matchmaker) and certainly not by the family involved. Only a qualified Torah authority should decide such matters.[137]

If one does not succeed in making peace on his first or second attempt, nevertheless, he should not abandon his pursuit of this sacred achievement.

לע"נ נעימה בת מנשה וחנה פנירי · 24 Kislev
Dedicated by her daughter Orna Gabay and Natalie Michal,
Rivka Na'ama, Nethanella Rachel Hadassa
25 Sivan · Yaakov ben Amar לע"נ יעקב בן קמר
Dedicated by his dear brother & his loving children and grandchildren

☙Perseverance

David declared: "Seek peace and pursue it" (*Tehillim* 34:15). The Sages comment (*Vayikra Rabbah* 9:9): "Seek peace for your loved ones and pursue it for your enemies; seek peace where you live and pursue it elsewhere; seek peace with your body and pursue it with your resources; seek peace for yourself and pursue it for others; seek peace today and pursue it tomorrow."

This final exhortation means that one should never despair of making peace; rather, he should pursue it today, and then tomorrow, and the next day ... until he attains it.

If thick ropes which pull a wagon are strained regularly, they will become weak, and eventually will tear. So it is with strife. If one does not succeed in making peace on his first or second attempt, nevertheless, he should not abandon his pursuit of this sacred achievement. Ultimately, his words will accomplish. If he will have no effect at all upon the prime quarrelers, because they have become overpowered by the appetite for triumph and are blind to the truth, he may be able to influence those who have been drawn into a quarrel that is not their own. In this way, he will save them from the bitter retribution which results from strife, in the way of Moshe, who saved Ohn and Korach's sons.

✎*Suggesting a Shidduch: The Balance*

In light of the prohibition of misleading one's fellow (see Days 79-80), one may be reluctant to suggest *shidduchim* (marriage matches) altogether; others may feel it necessary to mention every possible shortcoming of the person so as not to be guilty of misrepresenting the truth.

Few acts of *chesed* (kindness) can compare with that of helping to build a Jewish home. One who thinks that a certain young man may be a suitable match for a certain young woman is not responsible to investigate the two and their families before proposing the match. That is the responsibility of the parties involved and their parents.

However, the prohibition against misleading one's fellow requires that one not suggest a *shidduch* unless:

(1) He believes that given what he knows of their personalities, the two could be a good match, and he is unaware of any reason the relationship should cause pain to either one.

(2) In his opinion, there is reason to believe that their meeting will ultimately result in an engagement. (It is wrong to waste a person's time, energy and emotions!)

(3) He is not aware of any medical, emotional, or character deficiency that would render one party unfit for marriage.

The ability to restrain oneself from speaking when the situation warrants silence is, indeed, precious.

(Continued on page 409)

---

25 Kislev · In memory of our beloved mother and grandmother
לע״נ בילא בת יצחק
Dedicated by the Golombeck, Chesner and Kirschner families
26 Sivan · Naomi Shoshana bas Gavriel לע״נ נעמי שושנה בת גבריאל

✒The Quality of Silence

R' Yitzchak said: Which craft should man pursue in this world ?
He should make himself like a mute (Chullin 89a).

R' Yitzchak's description of the quality of silence as an אומנות,
craft, conveys a number of important lessons:

If a person who is unfamiliar with a certain trade seeks to create
a product of that trade with his own hands, he will find the task exceedingly difficult, regardless of how simple he may have imagined
it to be. To become skilled in a given craft requires a period of training and experience.

So it is with the art of silence. The ability to restrain oneself from
speaking when the situation warrants silence is, indeed, precious.
With the quality of silence, man is protected from the many sins
which are related to speech; without it, it is exceedingly difficult to
refrain from verbal transgression.

A person who exercises restraint in speech only when the possibility of forbidden speech seems likely, but at all other times speaks
whatever comes to mind, will be unable to avoid transgression.
Such a person is simply not accustomed to restraining himself in this
area, and is totally unprepared when the moment of trial arrives.

Therefore, one should train himself, like someone learning a craft,
to exercise restraint in speech. One must reach the point where such
restraint comes naturally to him. *Which craft should man pursue in
this world? He should make himself like an* אלם, *mute.* Then he will
surely refrain from forbidden speech and avoid any such sin.

כו כסלו
26 KISLEV/ CYCLE 1

כז סיון
27 SIVAN / CYCLE 2

SEFER CHOFETZ CHAIM
TOELES: Relationships

⮜*Advice*

The previous rules apply to the initiator of a *shidduch,* employment or business partnership. *Halachah* classifies such a person as an advisor and requires that he not make the suggestion if he has reason to suspect that it may not be in the best interest of either party.

A similar set of rules applies to one who did not make the suggestion, but whose advice is sought by one of the parties. He too must not be guilty of misleading the people involved. In fact, his responsibility is even greater than that of the *shadchan* (matchmaker). Whereas the *shadchan* merely suggests that the *shidduch* be considered, the advisor often states a definitive opinion regarding the proposed relationship which may profoundly influence the party's final decision.

Giving advice is not a matter to be taken lightly. One does not give guidance unless he believes he understands the situation, and has the insight and life experience necessary to properly direct his petitioner. One should never encourage a match he knows nothing about for the sake of seeing to it that the person "finally gets married." One may encourage a match only if he sincerely believes that it is good for both parties.

(Continued on page 409)

> *Hashem has given man something which He has not given any other earthly creature — a speaking soul.*

26 Kislev · Hershel Pleskin לע"נ אליעזר צבי בן יעקב מענדל ז"ל
Dedicated by the family of the late Shimon Leib Pleskin ז"ל
27 Sivan · לע"נ אסתר בת יוסף ע"ה
Dedicated by her children Rabbi & Mrs. Aharon Yona Piller
and family, Wickliffe, OH

ᐃ*Debt of Gratitude*

We can suggest another explanation of R' Yitzchak's teaching: "Which craft should man pursue in this world? He should make himself like a mute."

Suppose a person suddenly suffers a loss of speech. All the city's doctors are summoned to suggest a cure, but all fail. Finally, a renowned specialist is brought in from another city. He succeeds in curing the patient and refuses any offer of payment for his services. Imagine the love and gratitude which the patient would feel toward the doctor! His gratitude would be readily apparent; he would run to do the doctor's every bidding. For the patient to speak a negative word about the doctor would be unthinkable.

Hashem has given man something which He has not given any other earthly creature — a speaking soul through which he can study Torah and perform other *mitzvos*, thus earning for himself eternal reward. By the strict measure of justice, a person who has used his tongue hundreds of times to speak the forbidden should awaken one morning to find that he has lost his power of speech. However, Hashem, Whose compassion is boundless and Who is slow to anger, continues to grant this priceless gift as He awaits the person's repentance.

How can such a person persist in speaking *loshon hora* and other forms of evil speech? Is this how one expresses gratitude to the One Above?

Which craft should man pursue in this world? He should make himself like a mute. A person who has been guilty in the past of speaking the forbidden should forever bear in mind that it is only through the kindness of Hashem that he has not awakened one morning to find himself a mute. Through such reflection, one will forever feel indebted to Hashem for His unceasing kindness and will surely refrain from forbidden speech.

כז כסלו
27 KISLEV / CYCLE 1

כח סיון
28 SIVAN / CYCLE 2

SEFER CHOFETZ CHAIM
TOELES: Relationships

✑*Providing Information*

U nlike the *shadchan* (matchmaker) or advisor, a
third party who is approached with specific
questions about one of the parties is not offering advice. His primary concern, therefore, is not the sin of
misleading others. His main responsibility is to be
honest, and to refrain from speaking that which
might constitute *loshon hora.*

If asked whether the other party has a specific,
relevant shortcoming, it is certainly correct to tell
the truth. For example, if one is asked about the person's character, and is aware that he has an
uncontrollable temper, this must be told, *l'toeles* (for
a constructive purpose). Of course, the preconditions for relating such information are required
(second-hand information must be presented as
such; constructive intent is required; and one may
relate only that which is accurate and necessary).

If, however, one is approached for information
that on an objective level is irrelevant but in the eyes
of this party is important, one is faced with a
dilemma. To provide the information is, in effect, assisting in the unjustified abrogation of a potentially
successful *shidduch.* On the other hand, one does
not have the right to mislead the party by way of
false information, and in so doing, decide the person's future for him without his knowledge. The
Chofetz Chaim suggests that in such cases one defer
by saying, "I don't know." (Why this does not constitute falsehood will be discussed later.)[138]

(Continued on page 409)

*Not
always is
silence
desirable.*

27 Kislev · Rabbi Yitchok Lubin ל ר' יהושע העשיל ל ר' יהושע העשיל
Dedicated by Shmuel & Suri Lubin and family, Lakewood, NJ
28 Sivan · Mrs. Tama Mirel (Munci) Fried לע"נ טעמא מירל בת יצחק
Dedicated by her daughter Brucha Blima

❧Study the Laws

There is another meaning to the description of the art of silence as an אמנות, *craft*. One who seeks to become a craftsman must study and train until he has mastered the skills of a given craft. There is no other way to become a true expert at one's trade.

With regard to speech, one might be inclined to think: "Why must I study the laws of *shmiras haloshon* in all their fine details? I will simply train myself to avoid conversation. That way, I will surely not transgress!" This is a mistake, for not always is silence desirable. In fact, there are even times when the *halachah* requires that one relate negative information about a given individual! Therefore, one must study and know well the laws of speech in all their details, so that he will truly master the art of silence.

The Sages were very exacting in stating, "Which craft should man pursue in this world?" For one might mistakenly think: "It has been my way for many years to be careful in avoiding forbidden speech. I have more experience in this 'craft' than a real craftsman has in his particular expertise! *Shmiras haloshon* is by now second nature to me; there is no longer any need for vigilance."

To preclude this false notion, the Sages state: "Which craft should man pursue *in this world*?" to indicate that all man's days in this world he must be alert to the pitfalls of forbidden speech.

כח כסלו
28 KISLEV / CYCLE 1

כט סיון
29 SIVAN / CYCLE 2

SEFER CHOFETZ CHAIM
TOELES: Relationships

⁕*Matters of Opinion*

Subjective questions about people are most diffi-cult to answer:

"Is he a *talmid chacham*?" "Is she intelligent?"

Each of these terms is relative, for at what point does a student of Torah become a *"talmid chacham,"* and how does one measure intelligence? Lack of a definitive barometer is a problem with most character traits as well, making accurate evaluations in these areas extremely difficult.

Furthermore, we have seen that one may not provide information that could prevent a match from materializing unless the information provides valid basis for this. How can one really be sure that the factors in question cast doubt on the appropriateness of the match? How, then, does one correctly provide information when asked?

It is clear that it is unwise for a party to approach an acquaintance with a request for such information. In fact, the Chofetz Chaim says that such inquiries warrant no response. However, one may bring such questions before a *rav*, *rosh yeshivah*, or seminary dean, etc., who has the wisdom and experience to evaluate a situation properly and offer an appropriate response. Others who are approached with such questions may direct the person to the proper authority.[140]

The Sages were the wisest of men and surely did not engage in pointless conversation.

לע"נ ר' אברהם בן עזרא ורינה גיינדי ע"ה· 28 Kislev
Dedicated in loving memory by his son Isaac Guendi and family
29 Sivan · Moshe Reisman לע"נ משה פתחיה בן אברהם
Dedicated by the Fixler family

∾Best of All

Shimon his [Rabban Gamliel's] son says: "All my days I have been raised among the Sages and I found nothing better for oneself than silence" (Avos 1:17).

R' Shimon is, in effect, saying: "I was reared among the Sages and had the opportunity to glean from all their precious, sacred qualities. And of all those qualities, the art of silence is most outstanding."

Alternatively, R' Shimon may have meant the following: The Sages were the wisest of men and surely did not engage in pointless conversation. Nevertheless, there was nothing, aside from speaking words of Torah, which they found more beneficial to themselves than silence.

R' Shimon was precise in saying: ולא מצאתי לגוף טוב, which literally means, *and I found nothing better for the body ...* Man's corporeal existence in this world makes it virtually impossible for even the purest of souls to ensure that his every utterance is without flaw. This is why silence is so desirable.

If such was true of the generation of R' Shimon, whose Sages were accustomed to speaking only words of true wisdom, then what of ourselves, whose minds are preoccupied with matters devoid of substance and meaning? If one's mouth will not be restrained by the harness of silence, then invariably it will speak in the way that it has been accustomed since one's youth, and the loss will outweigh the gain many times over.

◆Vital Information

One who knows of a *shidduch* in the making and has negative information about one of the parties has a responsibility — in certain cases — to offer this information without waiting to be asked.

The commandment *Do not stand aside while your brother's blood is shed* (*Vayikra* 19:16) requires one to volunteer information if he is aware that one party in a proposed match has severe physical, psychological, or spiritual shortcomings, which by objective standards can be expected to interfere with the marriage, and that this information is being concealed from the other party.[141]

Once again, the conditions which permit speaking negatively for a constructive purpose must be fulfilled:

(1) The information must be firsthand, or clearly stated as secondhand and not verified.

(2) It must clearly be a problem by objective standards (e.g. a debilitating disease in the person, or in the family if it is hereditary; severe psychological disorders; violent tendencies; major problems in *hashkafah* [outlook on basic issues of Jewish life]; an immoral lifestyle) and not a matter of personal opinion — even if one feels certain that this is not what the other party wants. It must also be clear that the information is being concealed from the other party.[142]

(Continued on page 410)

When this month has only 29 days, the lesson for 30 Kislev should also be studied today.

When one responds to verbal attack, the result is worse verbal attack.

29 Kislev · Bessie Bernstein ע"ה לע"נ גילה פעשא בת שלמה ע"ה
Dedicated in loving memory of our beloved mother and grandmother
by the Krugman family
30 Sivan · Rabbi Benjamin Lapidus לע"נ הרב בנציון שלמה בן
הרב חיים אריה ז"ל
Dedicated by his wife and children

☙A Matter of Life and Death

By exercising verbal restraint, one is saved from many sins: *loshon hora,* flattery, mockery and lying. He is also saved from verbal attack. There are numerous inestimable benefits of developing the quality of silence.

People confide their private matters to a person who is known to guard his tongue, for he can be trusted to keep such information to himself.

A wise man once said: "When I hear someone speak evil of me, I remain silent, for I fear that would I respond in kind, I would then hear abuses that are worse than the previous ones." Whenever a person is verbally attacked and responds in kind, the result, invariably, is worse verbal attack.

"Death and life are in the tongue's power" (*Mishlei* 18:21). The tongue can cause harm in a way that the sword cannot. The sword can kill only through direct contact with its victim, while the tongue can bring about the ruination of someone who is miles away. Man was created with two eyes, two ears, two nostrils, but only one mouth, to indicate that he is obligated to limit his speech, for transgression through speech can occur quite easily, and with far-reaching consequences.

ל כסלו
30 KISLEV/ CYCLE 1

א תמוז
1 TAMMUZ / CYCLE 2

SEFER CHOFETZ CHAIM

TOELES: Relationships

✍Shidduchim and other Relationships: A Summary

Returning now to our original three situations (Day 78), we may conclude that if one is aware of a negative factor that by objective standards renders the proposed relationship a mistake, he is obligated to speak up. However, if by objective standards the factor does not lead to such a conclusion, but it may adversely affect the future of the people involved, one should not volunteer information about it, but one would have to respond truthfully when questioned specifically regarding the topic under which that factor falls.

If by objective standards the factor would have no bearing on the relationship, but it is clear that the other party would see it as an issue, one should not volunteer information about it and should avoid telling of it even if asked, but is not permitted to suggest that the relationship be pursued.

As a concluding note to this section, one must understand that the possible situations of constructive negative speech that could arise in the settings of family, friends, community, business, employment, education, etc. are endless. No book can possibly give explicit instructions for dealing with them all. One's only recourse is to become fluent in the principles, develop an understanding of the concepts, and accustom himself to consulting a *rav*, so that he can meet the challenges that such situations bring with them.

When this month has only 29 days, the lesson for 30 Kislev should be learned together with 29 Kislev.

One's mouth can be the source of his ruination and the movements of his lips can endanger his soul.

---

30 Kislev · Esther Hoffman לע"נ אסתר בת יהודה
Dedicated by Rabbi Leib Hoffman, Baltimore, MD
1 Tammuz · לע"נ אלימלך גבריאל בן גרשון ז"ל
Dedicated by the Tress family

Protective Fence

DAY 90

"The best medicine of all is silence" (*Megillah* 18a). "A protective fence for wisdom is silence" (*Avos* 3:17). Silence is good for the wise, and surely for the unwise. One should guard his tongue like the apple of his eye, for one's mouth can be the source of his ruination and the movements of his lips can endanger his soul. Thus it is written, "One who guards his mouth and tongue guards his soul from tribulations" (*Mishlei* 21:23).

Better to be told, "Speak! Why are you so quiet?" than for others to find one's prattling burdensome and ask that he be silent.

Scripture states: "From that which lies within your bosom [i.e. your soul], guard the portals of your mouth" (*Michah* 7:5). The use of the term *portals* in reference to the mouth is instructive. An entrance to a house must be opened when necessary, but it cannot be left open all day and all night; to do so would mean to leave the house open to thieves. Similarly, one cannot allow his mouth to be open indiscriminately.

A person's most prized possessions are usually kept in a special vault, hidden away in an inner room and carefully guarded. As man's most prized function, the power of speech must be guarded with great care, and its greatest protection is the quality of silence.

א טבת
I TEVES / CYCLE I

ב תמוז
2 TAMMUZ / CYCLE 2

SEFER CHOFETZ CHAIM

Listening to Loshon Hora

✦When Listening is Lowly

Not only is *speaking loshon hora* a lowly act not befitting the Divine image in which man was created, but to *listen* as someone else speaks *loshon hora* is lowly as well. The Torah states לא תשא שמע שוא, *Do not accept a false report* (*Shemos* 23:1). The Chofetz Chaim is apparently of the opinion that merely paying attention to *loshon hora* being spoken constitutes giving it some degree of credence, and is in violation of this prohibition.

Just as it is wrong to select the shortcomings of others as subject matter for one's own speech, so too it is wrong for one to focus his attention on negativity being expressed by others.

Just as it is wrong to cause harm to others by way of speech, so too it is wrong to serve as a listener as potentially harmful information is being conveyed.

In short, derogatory or harmful speech should never earn one's attention.[144] Listening to *loshon hora,* even if one does not believe it, is in violation of Torah prohibition.

One should never praise his fellow excessively, for praise will inevitably lead to criticism.

I Teves · Abraham Schwimmer לע״נ אברהם בן יעקב
Dedicated by Yaffa Blum, Yaakov Tuvia Schwimmer and Miriam Firestone
2 Tammuz · Chaim Yishai Wiener לע״נ חיים ישי בן דוב בעריש ז״ל
Dedicated by the Pinchas & Sherie Gross and family,
Yitzchak & Marsha Kasdan and family, Silver Spring, MD

DAY 91

❧The Need To Talk

People who find themselves inclined towards melancholy feel a need to speak freely to others and are, understandably, afraid to focus themselves on developing the quality of silence. Should this be the case, one should at least accustom himself to not speak about others, whoever they might be; his friendly conversations should focus on *matters* of interest, and not on people of interest. When he does find it necessary to discuss others, he should be as brief as possible.

I have heard it said regarding the great Torah genius, Rabbi Raphael of Hamburg, that he resigned his post as rabbi four years prior to his passing. From that time and on, he would ask of those who visited him that as long as they were within the confines of his home, they should not speak about other people. I have also heard regarding another leader of his generation that he was exceedingly careful never to discuss others.[1]

Certainly one must be careful not to discuss a storekeeper with his competitor, nor a craftsman with other members of his craft. Such conversations often lead to *loshon hora,* especially when the storekeepers or craftsmen are known to bear ill will toward one another.

This restriction applies not only to singing the storekeeper's praises, regarding which our Sages warned: "One should never speak the praises of his fellow [excessively], for praise will inevitably lead to criticism" (*Arachin* 16a).[2] One should refrain *entirely* from discussing an individual with that person's competitor, for the listener will quite possibly steer the conversation in a direction that will allow him to vent his negative feelings. If one finds it absolutely necessary to engage in such discussion for some constructive purpose, he should keep the conversation as brief as possible; otherwise, it will inevitably lead to *loshon hora.*

---

1. Toward the end of his life, the Chofetz Chaim was visited by someone who broached the subject of a dispute in his home town. The Chofetz Chaim interrupted him, "For years, I have avoided the sin of *loshon hora.* Do you wish that I now be caught in its web?"

2. When one praises another excessively, it is inevitable that the speaker or someone else present will point out one or more of the subject's faults (*Rashi* ad loc.). See *Sefer Chofetz Chaim* Part I, ch. 9.

ב טבת
2 TEVES / CYCLE 1

ג תמוז
3 TAMMUZ / CYCLE 2

SEFER CHOFETZ CHAIM
Listening to Loshon Hora

✄The Speaker's Accomplice

In addition to violating the prohibition against listening to *loshon hora*, every listener of *loshon hora* is, in effect, making it possible for the speaker to relate his forbidden words, and therefore is an accomplice in his sin.

In the case of a lone listener, the prohibition *Before a blind person do not place a stumbling block* (*Vayikra* 19:14) would surely apply, for included in this verse is a prohibition against causing another Jew to sin. We will see that in certain instances listening to *loshon hora* is forbidden not because of the primary prohibition against such listening, but because of the prohibition against causing another Jew to sin.[145]

One should abruptly change the subject in the same way he would spit out non-kosher food.

לע״נ נעטל בת הרב ר׳ אברהם זאב ז״ל   2 Teves · Nety Beeber
Dedicated by Robert J. Beeber, Sarah, Avrohom Zev, Brocha Beeber
לע״נ ר׳ אברהם אשר בן ר׳ משה יוסף Abe Miller · 3 Tammuz
Dedicated by the Katlowitz family

DAY
92

◄Non-Kosher Conversation

If one begins speaking with Reuven concerning Shimon and in the course of conversation becomes aware that Reuven bears Shimon ill will, he should either bring the conversation to an end or divert it to some other subject. Similarly, if one begins to speak and suddenly realizes that his own words are leading toward *loshon hora*, he should muster his spiritual strength and abruptly change the subject — in the same way that he would spit out the food he was chewing were he to become aware that it was non-kosher. If this will cause him discomfort or embarrassment, he should bear in mind the Sages' words: "Better to be considered a fool all one's days [in this world], and not be considered wicked even for a moment before the Omnipresent" (*Mishnah Ediyos* 5:6).

As already mentioned, the restriction against discussing an individual with that person's adversary applies only when one feels himself unqualified to make peace between the two. However, when one can play the role of peacemaker, it is a *mitzvah* to listen to each party's grievances in order to settle their feud.[1]

---

1. See rules of *toeles*, constructive purpose, in Laws section.

ג טבת
3 TEVES / CYCLE 1

ד תמוז
4 TAMMUZ / CYCLE 2

SEFER CHOFETZ CHAIM
Listening to Loshon Hora

✒Admonishing the Speaker

The commandment הוכח תוכיח את עמיתך, *You shall reprove your fellow* (*Vayikra* 19:17), requires a Jew to inform a sinner that his behavior is improper, and attempt to convince him to mend his ways. In voicing his disapproval, one must be prepared to endure embarrassment and insult and should continue to voice his disapproval so long as the forbidden act is being repeated. Even if one sees little or no chance that his words will be heeded, he must nevertheless continue to protest. Only in a case where one knows that his reproof would cause the sinner to react by committing more serious offenses is he to refrain from speaking up.

(Reproof must be administered with respect and understanding, and should be done in private whenever possible — see *Rashi* to *Vayikra* 19:17).

Even one sinner can ruin an entire group.

Generally speaking, one is required to interrupt and reprove the speaker of *loshon hora*, and do his best to ensure that he put a halt to his sinful speech. As mentioned, this does not apply when the speaker would likely react by expressing yet greater negativity towards the person he was speaking about, as a way of defending his sinful talk.[146]

Another situation where reproof would be out of place is when:

(Continued on page 410)

---

3 Teves · May today's learning be a זכות for נ״י גרשון בן גרשון מיכאל נתן
4 Tammuz · Vivian Mizrahi וגבריאלה ויויאן חיה בת יהודה לע״נ
Dedicated in loving memory by Solomon & Lauren Shalam and family

DAY 93

✍Choose Your Company

One should avoid association with a given group unless he knows that its members are careful to avoid forbidden speech. If circumstances demand such association, one should limit it to a minimum, and maintain silence whenever possible. Even one sinner can ruin an entire group and make it necessary to avoid being in its company.

Sefer Rosh HaGivah writes:

> Be alert, my son, regarding that which King Shlomo said: "In the ears of a fool do not speak, lest he disparage the wisdom of your words" (*Mishlei* 23:9). Beware of a gathering of one hundred men among whom is found even one scoffer or fool, and certainly if [one of the fools] is a wise man in his own eyes, for he is the quintessential fool ...¹ Strengthen yourself to sit in silence at such a gathering, do not discuss anything at all. Even if you will speak all sorts of wisdom, they [the scoffers and fools] will best you and grant you disgrace, as it is written, "Iniquity appears and disgrace follows" (ibid. 11:2).
>
> If you wish to converse [at such a gathering] with a man like yourself, be careful that your words not reach their [the scoffers'] ears. Thus does Scripture advise: "In the ears of a fool do not speak," rather than, "Do not speak with a fool."

---

1. See *Mishlei* 26:12. A fool who considers himself wise has no hope of acquiring wisdom, and thus is the greatest fool of all (*Metzudos* ad loc.).

ד טבת
4 TEVES / CYCLE 1

ה תמוז
5 TAMMUZ / CYCLE 2

SEFER CHOFETZ CHAIM
Listening to Loshon Hora

❧*Group Reproof*

We have seen that one must reprove the speaker of *loshon hora* even if it is highly unlikely that the reproof will be effective.

When several people are involved in a discussion that includes *loshon hora*, one must speak up and caution them that what they are discussing is forbidden. However, unlike the case of an individual who speaks *loshon hora*, if the people ignore the reproof, one should not persist in his rebuke unless he feels that his words might ultimately achieve a positive result. In an unreceptive group setting, it is wise to refrain from excessive reproof.[148]

An exception to this rule is when one finds himself in a community where the prohibition of *loshon hora* has long been disregarded. Widespread disregard calls for more than ordinary reproof. It demands persistent protest, calling for an awareness of the severity of speaking *loshon hora*, and knowledge of what constitutes *loshon hora*.[149]

With the passage of time, one will find loshon hora repulsive — like anything else which the Torah prohibits.

4 Teves · Regina Lapidus לע״נ רבקה בת ישראל הכהן
Dedicated by Debbie
5 Tammuz · Rosa Bamberger (née Schweizer) לע״נ רייסכא בת החי ר׳ משה
Dedicated by her children and grandchildren

❧Step-by-Step

One who seeks to attain the quality of *shmiras haloshon* should use the very opposite approach of the gossiper. The gossiper makes it his habit to sit among groups involved in conversation, in the hope that he will hear some bit of information that he can ridicule or spread to others. The gossiper is forever in search of "the latest news" in his town, so that he will have no lack of material to relate all day and night.

The quality of *shmiras haloshon* should be attained gradually. The first step is to accustom oneself to avoid groups involved in idle conversation and to train oneself not to inquire about the latest gossip. One should train himself, little by little, until he reaches the point where he does not even want to be informed of any gossip. With the passage of time, Hashem will help him so that *shmiras haloshon* will become a part of his very nature. He will find it incredible that others can transgress the sin of speaking *loshon hora*, which to him has become something repulsive, like anything else which the Torah prohibits.

ה טבת
5 TEVES / CYCLE 1

ו תמוז
6 TAMMUZ / CYCLE 2

SEFER CHOFETZ CHAIM
Listening to Loshon Hora

◆ *Proper Reaction*

B ased on the previous rules, it is clear that upon hearing *loshon hora* one should promptly interrupt the speaker and reprimand him for his words. In a case where doing so would cause the speaker embarrassment (i.e. others are present), it is preferable that one tactfully change the subject, thus preventing the further speaking of *loshon hora*, and offer reproof later (in private).[150]

If one finds himself unable to change the subject, he should walk away. While incapable of fulfilling his obligation to reprove, one must, nevertheless, avoid transgressing the sin of listening to *loshon hora*. If one feels uncomfortable leaving, the least he should do is try his best to ignore what is being said, and use facial expression to show disapproval. Certainly, he should not appear as though he is enjoying the conversation.[151]

It is only initially that refraining from loshon hora is difficult.

One must train himself to defend his values, to be more concerned with truth than with his personal pride. Ultimately, one will find that the less he fears scorn and derision of scoffers, the more his self-esteem will grow — and his stature will grow in the eyes of others as well.

5 Teves · Mr. Zev Benedek לע"נ זאב בן יצחק ע"ה
Dedicated in loving memory by the family
6 Tammuz · Bina Machla David ע"ה לע"נ בינה מחלה בת יהודה ברוך ע"ה
Dedicated by the Bina Machla Tzedakah Fund

❧Silencing the Gossipmongers

It is a proven fact that to restrain oneself from speaking and listening to *loshon hora* is difficult for only the first few weeks. As others come to realize that an individual will not speak or listen to *loshon hora*, mockery or other forbidden speech, they will refrain from relating such talk to him, and will peddle their "wares" elsewhere. They will come to understand that such talk does not raise their esteem in this man's eyes; to the contrary, he considers them nothing more than gossipmongers and scorners. He will hardly have to guard himself from hearing *loshon hora*, for the gossipmongers themselves will avoid telling their stories in his presence, lest he belittle their words before others who are present.

What is needed is an initial firm resolve to acquire this sacred quality. Regarding such spiritual striving do our Sages say, "One who reflects upon his ways in this world merits and sees salvation from the Holy One, Blessed is He" (*Moed Katan* 5a).

ו טבת
6 TEVES / CYCLE 1

ז תמוז
7 TAMMUZ / CYCLE 2

SEFER CHOFETZ CHAIM
Listening to Loshon Hora

⸎*Whom to Rebuke*

In situations where reproof is required (see Day
93), one is obligated to interrupt even his own
parent who is speaking *loshon hora* and respectfully explain that he or she should not be speaking
in this manner.[152] A *rav*, as well, should not be allowed to speak *loshon hora*. However, it is
disrespectful to accuse a *rav* of speaking *loshon
hora*. Instead, one should ask the *rav* for assistance
in understanding why it was permissible for him to
make a given statement.[153]

Children are not included in our obligation to reprove a fellow Jew who has sinned. However,
parents, as well as teachers, are obligated in the
mitzvah of *chinuch,* educating their charges in
proper *mitzvah* observance. Thus, parents and
teachers must train children from an early age to
refrain from speaking or listening to *loshon hora*.[154]

*The more
one judges
others
favorably,
the less
loshon
hora he
speaks.*

6 Teves · Reb Shea Gutwein לע״נ יהושע בן יהודה
Dedicated by the Gutwein family
ר׳ חיים מאיר בן דינה לרפואה שלמה · 7 Tammuz

ᴥJudge Others Favorably

The Torah states: "With righteousness shall you judge your fellow" (*Vayikra* 19:15), which our Sages interpret as a commandment to give one's fellow the benefit of the doubt (*Shevuos* 30a). This precept is among those whose fruit one enjoys in this world and whose principal reward is preserved for the World to Come (*Shabbos* 127a). Development of this trait is crucial for perfecting the quality of *shmiras haloshon.*

To give one's fellow the benefit of the doubt is to decide in one's mind that someone who is said to have committed a misdeed did so either unwillfully, out of ignorance, or correctly (i.e. that, in fact, a sin has not been committed). When the report does not lend itself to any of the above interpretations, one should consider the possibility that the speaker added or omitted details which completely alter the nature of the report.

To judge others favorably is also to bear in mind the teaching: "Do not judge your fellow until you have reached his place" (*Avos* 2:5).

The more one accustoms himself to judge others favorably, the less he will transgress the sin of *loshon hora.*

ז טבת
7 TEVES / CYCLE 1

ח תמוז
8 TAMMUZ / CYCLE 2

SEFER CHOFETZ CHAIM
Listening to Loshon Hora

✒Whom Not to Rebuke

The obligation to reprove one's fellow Jew does not apply to a non-observant Jew who is in the category of a *mumar* (one who is aware of halachic requirements and ignores them — see Day 14).[155] However, a non-observant Jew who sins out of ignorance must be instructed gently regarding *loshon hora*. The beauty of *shmiras haloshon* can be appreciated even by those whose observance level is minimal, and should be shared with them at the earliest opportunity.

Nevertheless, one does not rebuke a non-observant person with whom he does not have a relationship. It is obvious that such reproof will not convince the person to refrain from speaking *loshon hora* in the future, and will only serve to anger him. This would be similar to the situation (in Day 93) where reproof would cause worse sin to occur and is therefore inappropriate.

One who judges his fellow favorably is judged favorably by Heaven.

This rule holds true for an observant Jew as well. It is wrong to offer rebuke to someone with whom one has no real relationship, if it is clear that he will not change his ways and that he will be offended by the person's meddling in his affairs.[156]

Rebuke in such a case would cause hatred and, possibly, even more *loshon hora*.

7 Teves · לע"נ חיים אלטר בן הרה"ג ר' ישראל גרשון ז"ל
Dedicated by his children
8 Tammuz - לע"נ אברהם מרדכי הלוי ז"ל בן חיים שלמה הלוי נ"י
הונצח על ידי אחיו נפתלי אלי הלוי פאללאק ומשפחתו,
מאנטריאל ,קוועבעק

◢◣A Classic Illustration

The following incident, recorded in the Talmud (*Shabbos* 127b), illustrates the extent to which a Jew must judge his fellow favorably:

A man from Israel's Upper Galilee hired himself out for three years to someone living in the southern portion of the Land. At the end of the three years, on the eve of Yom Kippur, the worker requested his wages so that he could return home and feed his family.

His employer responded, "I have no money."

"Then pay me with fruit," said the worker.

"I have none," came the reply.

"Pay me with land."

"I have none."

"Pay me with livestock."

"I have none."

"Pay me with pillows and blankets."

"I have none."

The worker slung his pack over his shoulder and headed home, bitterly disappointed.

At the conclusion of Succos, the employer appeared at his worker's door, with money in hand, along with three donkeys, bearing food, drink and delicacies. The food was brought inside and the two enjoyed a hearty meal together. Afterwards, the employer paid the worker in full.

The employer then asked, "When you asked for your earnings and I replied that I had no money, what did you think?"

The worker replied, "I thought that perhaps a deal that you could not pass up had come along and you had used all your cash for that."

"And when I said that I had no land?"

"I thought that perhaps all your land had been leased to others."

"And when I said that I had no fruit?"

"I thought that perhaps your fruits had not yet been tithed."

(Continued on page 410)

✒️Pertinent Information

The prohibition, "Do not accept a false report" (see Day 91), teaches us that *loshon hora* should not be listened to and must not be accepted. However, when the information being conveyed is important to know for constructive reasons, it merits one's attention and may be listened to. Just as relating negative information *l'toeles*, for a constructive purpose, is not considered speaking *loshon hora*, so too is listening for a constructive purpose considered responsible and proper.

Information that one may listen to includes anything that might help to prevent or correct undue harm to any individual, be it the listener, the speaker, the person spoken about, or another party. It would also include information that could help prevent or correct damage that is physical, financial, emotional or spiritual.

Each person's merits are weighed against his sins.

It is correct to listen to a person's claim against someone else if one thinks that he can be of help in rectifying the situation, or if the listener or someone else might be vulnerable to similar treatment by the person being spoken about. It is permissible to listen to information about a person with whom one is planning to collaborate in a joint venture, if the information is pertinent to that relationship. In all of the above instances, the information is being listened to for a constructive purpose, and hence is not considered *loshon hora*.[157]

8 Teves · Jack Schwartz לע״נ יעקב בן מאיר ע״ה
Dedicated by the Birnbaum family, Brooklyn, NY
9 Tammuz · Elliot Brown לע״נ אליהו בן משה
Dedicated by Kenny & Frida Brown

DAY 98

❧ *The Day of Judgment*

The way in which an individual tends to judge others can well determine his own status as a *tzaddik* (righteous person) or *rasha* (wicked person) for all eternity.

The Sages teach that whether or not an individual is deemed meritorious is determined by weighing the sum of his merits against his sins.[1] The Sages further state regarding the great Day of Judgment at the time of the Resurrection of the Dead: Three Books will be opened — one for the completely righteous; one for the completely wicked; and one for those in between. The completely righteous will immediately be inscribed for eternal life; the completely wicked will immediately be inscribed for *Gehinnom;* and those in between will descend to *Gehinnom* and [after enduring a period of retribution] will then ascend (*Rosh Hashanah* 16b).

If Hashem will judge an individual by the measure of strict justice, then even if that individual had performed countless good deeds through the course of his lifetime, he will nevertheless be left with very few merits by the time his judgment has ended. Many of his deeds will have been found lacking in proper detail or method, while those whose performance was wholesome might not have been accompanied by proper love of God, awe of Him, or were devoid of the joy with which a *mitzvah* should be performed. Thus, most good deeds will be found blemished in some way. The individual's remaining good deeds will be far outweighed by his sins, and thus he will be deemed a *rasha* for eternity.

---

1. See *Rambam, Hilchos Teshuvah* 3:1-2.

✒A Matter of Intent

While listening to negative information for constructive purposes is not a violation of the prohibition against accepting *loshon hora*, before taking the liberty of listening to such information one must be sure that he will not be guilty of causing the speaker to sin.

We have seen that in order to convey pertinent information that would otherwise be considered *loshon hora* several conditions must be met. For example, the speaker's intent must be to bring about a positive result. If the speaker does not have constructive intent, his words are *loshon hora*, despite the fact that the information is important for the listener to hear. In such a case, being a listener would be a transgression of, "Before a blind person do not place a stumbling block" (*Vayikra* 19:14).

If one is privately doing business with someone and then, by coincidence, a friend begins speaking *loshon hora* about that very individual, one is required to interrupt him or walk away! Since the speaker is unaware that the listener is doing business with this person, the speaker is talking *loshon hora* and must be stopped. After interrupting him, one may tell him that the information he had begun to relate may be important to the listener, and that he may continue speaking provided that he can honestly relate it for that constructive purpose only.[158]

Hashem's Attribute of Compassion can cause the sum of one's sins to be diminished.

לע"נ פרידא בת שמעון 9 Teves · Mrs. Frieda Fiacre
Dedicated by Eli & Mechi Yarmish
לע"נ אלטער יחיאל בן אלטער יחיאל הלוי 10 Tammuz · Mr. Yechiel Scheiner
Dedicated by Yitzchok & Miriam Scheiner and family

❧Meriting Divine Favor

However, if Hashem will judge the person with compassion and seek to find him meritorious, the sum of his good deeds will remain intact. Moreover, if the person will merit the full measure of Hashem's Attribute of Compassion, then the sum of his sins will be diminished, for many of them will be found to have been carried out unwillfully or will be attributed to some outside factor for which the sinner will not be held responsible.

In summation: Heaven has infinite ways through which to find an individual meritorious. Through such consideration, the individual's good deeds will outweigh his sins, thus granting him the eternal status of a *tzaddik*.

The way in which Heaven judges an individual is reflective of the way in which that individual acts toward his fellow on this earth. If it is his way to judge others favorably, then Heaven will judge him favorably. However, if it is his way to view others critically and to express his views to others, then the Heavenly angels will speak of him in the same fashion.[1]

Thus, one must always bear in mind that at the moment when he expresses a judgment of his fellow's actions, he is determining the way in which he himself will be judged by the Heavenly Court.

---

1. *Midrash Mishlei* 11:5.

⚭Inquiries

In light of the above, if one must inquire about a person, family, community, or school in order to make an important decision, but does not want others to know what he is contemplating, he may not engage people in casual conversation with the aim of obtaining pertinent derogatory or harmful information. Unaware that his speech is constructive, the speaker is guilty of speaking *loshon hora*, and the listener who drew him into conversation has caused him to sin.

Thus, when soliciting necessary information, one must make it clear to the other person that circumstances permit this and that his response, therefore, will not constitute *loshon hora*.[159]

A common practice in such situations is not only to refrain from divulging the purpose of the inquiry, but also to inquire about several people at once, so as to conceal the fact that it is a particular individual about whom one is seeking information. This is absolutely forbidden. The desire to protect one's privacy does not justify soliciting irrelevant negative information and causing others to speak *loshon hora*.[160]

To love one's fellow Jew as oneself is to help him avoid situations which would result in his suffering shame or criticism.

10 Teves · Mr. Elias Davidman לע״נ אליהו בן שמוא־ל אלעזר
Dedicated by the Rosenblatt family
11 Tammuz · Mrs. Ruchie Friedman לע״נ חיה רחל בת הר״ר מנחם מנדל ע״ה
Dedicated by her children

❧*Love Your Fellow Jew*

Fulfillment of the *mitzvah* to judge one's fellow favorably and de- velopment of the quality of *shmiras haloshon* both hinge on the fulfillment of "You shall love your fellow as yourself" (*Vayikra* 19:18). If one truly loves his fellow Jew, surely he will not speak negatively of him; to the contrary, he will seek any possible merit for his ac- tions, as he would for himself.

If one were to commit an act which appeared improper, and he were to learn that his action was being talked about by others, surely he would fervently hope that someone would speak up in his de- fense and explain that, for whatever reason, he was not at fault. This is exactly what one should do when someone else's behavior comes under scrutiny.

Moreover, to love one's fellow as oneself is to help him avoid sit- uations which would result in his suffering shame or criticism.

Let us suppose that one finds himself for an extended period of time in a city whose customs are foreign to him. He would seek out a loyal friend in that city who could familiarize him with local cus- toms and inform him privately when his behavior might evoke negative feelings among the city's inhabitants. In this way, he would be forewarned of anything which could possibly cause him distress or embarrassment. One should act toward his fellow in exactly this manner. If one sees another Jew doing that which could ultimately lead to his distress or embarrassment, he is obligated to warn him of this.

יא טבת
11 TEVES / CYCLE 1

יב תמוז
12 TAMMUZ / CYCLE 2

SEFER CHOFETZ CHAIM
TOELES: Constructive Listening

∞Soliciting Information: Preconditions

A s it is forbidden to cause another Jew to transgress, one may not solicit information unless it is clearly permissible for the other person to offer such information. Thus, in order to solicit information, the following conditions must be met:

(1) The person from whom information is being sought is not known to fabricate stories about others, to read into their behavior in an unjust manner, or to draw hurried conclusions about their character; and

(2) the person is not known to exaggerate in his descriptions of events; and

(3) it can be assumed that when informed that the information is necessary, he will not speak out of malice toward the subject; (thus, one may not seek information from a person who is not on good terms with the subject);[161] and

(4) it is clear that the information is necessary for a constructive purpose, and that there is no alternative to soliciting such information.[162]

Rebuking one's fellow Jew privately, with love and respect, is a fulfillment of two mitzvos.

❧With Love and Respect

We find that the Sages willingly brought shame upon themselves in order to save another person from being shamed:

> It happened once that Rabban Gamliel said: "Awaken seven judges for me and have them come to the attic." The next morning, Rabban Gamliel awoke and found eight judges in the attic. He declared, "Whoever ascended without permission should descend." Shmuel *HaKattan* arose and said, "I am the one who ascended without permission." ... It was not really Shmuel *HaKattan* who ascended without permission, but someone else. It was only because of the embarrassment that person would have suffered that Shmuel *HaKattan* made his admission (*Sanhedrin* 11a).

Surely, then, one should help his friend correct any improper behavior that could lead to his embarrassment. Certainly if one sees his fellow acting in a manner which is contrary to *halachah,* he is obligated to inform him of this privately and, if necessary, rebuke him. In so doing, one fulfills both the commandment to reprove one's fellow (*Vayikra* 19:17) and the commandment to love one's fellow as oneself.

When one helps his fellow Jew to improve his Divine service, he brings great satisfaction, as it were, to Hashem. Conversely, when one disparages his fellow before others for his having behaved incorrectly, what does the One Above gain from this?

יב טבת
12 TEVES / CYCLE 1

יג תמוז
13 TAMMUZ / CYCLE 2

SEFER CHOFETZ CHAIM
TOELES: Constructive Listening

✒Irrelevant, But Permissible

In the cases discussed thus far, the determining factor in making it permissible to listen to negative speech was relevance. If the information is important, in a constructive sense, for the listener to hear, it is proper for him to give his attention to what is being spoken, and at times to even solicit such information.

There are times when *halachah* permits listening to negative information which is of no relevance to the listener or any of his acquaintances. Where the speaker feels the need to express his anger or frustration for relief of emotional pain, one is doing an act of *chesed* (kindness) by hearing the person out and expressing understanding of his feelings. If the listener feels that the speaker can be made to understand how he misjudged the person responsible for his frustration, he is obligated to do so.[163] (Often, however, a person expressing his frustrations is in need of empathy and is not open to logic. At a later point, after the speaker has calmed down, the listener could approach him and attempt to explain how he may have misunderstood the situation.)

Care must be taken to keep the speaker from wandering from the matter at hand, and speaking irrelevantly about other faults of the one whom he feels has wronged him. Furthermore, one listening in such a situation must take care not to accept what he hears as fact.

Hashem rejoices at our joy, and is pained at our suffering.

ᴥA *Father's Pain*

Picture the following: A boy has done something improper. One of the boy's companions announces to a crowd what the boy has done. Present at this announcement is the boy's father who, understandably, is quite upset. He tells the one who publicized his son's iniquity: "Had you rebuked my son in private, with no one else present, I would have been deeply grateful to you. Why did you have to make known his deed to the public? What you have accomplished is to make him an object of ridicule and disgrace. It seems to me that your intentions were not honorable. You were not out to correct my son's behavior; rather, you sought to damage his reputation and rejoice over his disgrace."

Such is the way of Hashem concerning the Jewish people, of whom it is written, "You are children to HASHEM, Your God" (*Devarim* 14:1). Hashem, as it were, rejoices at our joy, and is pained at our suffering. When a Jew rebukes his fellow in public, in the presence of our Father in Heaven, Whose glory fills the earth, can He take any pleasure from this?

One should be forever cognizant of *Rambam*'s statement that one is required to be as concerned for another Jew's possessions and honor as he is for his own (*Hilchos Aveil* 14:1).

❧*Between Husband and Wife*

We have already seen that there are no grounds for sharing gossip with one's spouse (Day 16). To view withholding *loshon hora* from one's spouse as a breach of harmony and trust is mistaken. (A husband and wife who seek to have the Divine Presence dwell in their midst should build their home on the foundations of *halachah* and avoid conversations which promote strife and dissension among Jews.) Moreover, sharing negativity (e.g. information, feelings, etc.) does not help create a healthy, positive relationship.[164]

Nevertheless, when a husband or wife is in need of emotional support in dealing with difficulty, it is only natural to look to one's spouse for assistance. Speaking or listening under such circumstances is constructive and is clearly permissible.[165]

When possible, one should attempt to help one's spouse understand the situation in a way that would relieve his or her anger or frustration.[166]

If one finds that his or her spouse is forever in need of "letting off steam," it is important to try to bring about a general change of attitude through discussion, reading or audio material, or suggesting a meeting with a rabbi or other qualified individual.

A word of caution: While one must be prepared to hear out a spouse and offer emotional support when necessary, one must be ever vigilant not to be drawn into a conversation of *loshon hora* for no constructive purpose. It is often the case that couples fail to draw this distinction, and consequently totally ignore the laws of *shmiras haloshon* when conversing.

What Hashem seeks of us is that we love one another, honor one another, and respect one another.

13 Teves · In memory of Esther Bibi
14 Tammuz · Mr. Joseph Fruhman לע"נ יוסף בן ר' חיים ז"ל
Dedicated to our beloved father and zayde by the Fruhman & Saltzman families

DAY
103

⮜The Way of a Jew

Tanna D'Vei Eliyahu Rabbah (ch. 28) states:

> The Holy One, Blessed is He, said to Israel: My beloved children! Is there anything I lack that I should have to ask of you? All I ask of you is that you love one another, that you honor one another, that you respect one another. In this way, no sin, robbery, or base deed will be found among you, so that you will remain undefiled forever. Thus it is written, "He has told you, O man, what is good, and what HASHEM seeks of you — only the doing of justice, loving kindness, and walking humbly with HASHEM, your God" (*Michah* 6:8).

If it happens that one's fellow acted improperly towards him, one must not take revenge or bear a grudge. Rather, one must erase the matter from his heart, and seek to do good in every way with that person, just as he would with any other Jew, as if nothing negative had ever come between them. This is what the Torah requires of us, as it is written, "You shall not take revenge and you shall not bear a grudge against the members of your people; you shall love your fellow as yourself" (*Vayikra* 19:18).

Zohar states (*Parashas Mikeitz* p. 201b):

> Note the following: Not only did Yosef not repay his brothers in kind [for their having sold him], but he acted toward them with kindness and truth. Such is always the way of the righteous. Therefore, the Holy One, Blessed is He, forever watches over them, in this world and in the next.

יד טבת
14 TEVES / CYCLE 1

טו תמוז
15 TAMMUZ / CYCLE 2

SEFER CHOFETZ CHAIM
TOELES: Constructive Listening

◈Children

It is a parent's responsibility to sensitize his or her child to the evils of *loshon hora* and help the child to develop self-control in this area. At the same time, it is a parent's responsibility to provide his or her child with emotional support and assistance. The overzealous parent can cause a child irreparable harm by forever scolding when reassurance is in order; however, failure to discipline one's child is no less harmful. One must learn to discern between situations where a child is relating an incident because he needs his parent's help, and when he is speaking *loshon hora* for no good reason.

A child should be taught that if interesting events of the day include negative facts about others, then names should be omitted. To relate how a certain child misbehaved in class is to speak *loshon hora,* even if what that child did was clever and amusing. Conversely, it is perfectly correct for a child to reveal the identity of a boy who interferes with his own activity or disrupts him during class time.[167]

All Jews are one in a very real sense.

14 Teves · Rochel Miller לע״נ מרת רחל בת ר׳ צבי הירש
Dedicated by the Katlowitz family
15 Tammuz · Mr. Yaakov Kasten לע״נ ר׳ יעקב בן ר׳ יהושע חיים
Dedicated by the Kasten family, Brooklyn, NY

❧*The Unity of the Jewish People*

T he following sublime insight is found in *S'mag* (9); its source is
Talmud Yerushalmi (*Nedarim* 9:4):

Suppose a man were walking along a path and one of his feet
would trip over the other, causing him to fall to the ground and suffer cuts and bruises. Would he seek revenge of the "guilty" foot and
refrain from trying to heal its wounds? Would he harbor any ill will
toward that foot? Obviously not, for his feet, hands, face, etc. are all
parts of one body — his own. If anything, he might reflect upon his
deeds, and view his sins as the true cause of his mishap.

Similarly, if a neighbor refuses to do a favor that one has asked of
him, or even if he has caused one heartache or has shamed him in
any way, one should not seek revenge or bear a grudge against him.
For who is "oneself" and who is "one's fellow"? — both stem from
the same source, as it is written, "And who is like Your nation, Israel,
one nation on earth?" (*I Divrei HaYamim* 17:21).

The Torah states: "All the souls of the house of Yaakov who came
to Egypt, seventy" (*Bereishis* 46:27). The Hebrew word for *souls* is
נפשות. Yet in this verse, the singular form, נפש, is used, alluding to
the fact that in Heaven, the souls of the people of Israel are like one.
Each Jewish soul, while part of one whole, is distinct and unique, like
a person whose body is a single unit comprised of many individual
parts, each with its own distinct and unique function. All Jewish
souls will eventually be gathered in to one source, beneath the
Heavenly Throne, as it is written, "And the soul of my master shall
be bound in the bond of life" (*I Shmuel* 25:29).[1]

It is only in this world, where each soul is clothed in its own physical body and is involved in its own personal matters, that one sees
himself as a distinct entity, apart from his fellow Jew. In truth, however, all Jews are one in a very real sense.

---

1. See *Shabbos* 152b.

טו טבת
15 TEVES / CYCLE 1

טז תמוז
16 TAMMUZ / CYCLE 2

SEFER CHOFETZ CHAIM
TOELES: Constructive Listening

◈The Non-Observant

As we have seen, it is forbidden to listen to negative information in any situation where the speaker is transgressing by relating the information. As it is not permissible to speak *loshon hora* about a non-observant Jew unless he is classified as an *apikores* (heretic), it is forbidden to listen to *loshon hora* that is being spoken about him. As has already been noted, today the average non-observant Jew is classified as a *tinok shenishbah* (lit., child who was taken captive), a victim of ignorance and circumstance and not, God forbid, an *apikores*.[168]

As mentioned above, to discuss the life-style of a particular non-observant Jew in order to teach others not to learn from his ways is considered speaking *l'toeles*, for a constructive purpose, and is permissible. It is therefore also permissible to listen to such a discussion.

Similarly, when an individual's improper behavior is publicized as a way of pressuring him to mend his ways, it is correct to listen, for the goal will never be achieved if everyone chooses to ignore what is being said of the person.[169]

When one exacts revenge from his fellow Jew, it is himself whom he is hurting.

לע"נ אבינו מורינו ר' משה יוסף בן שלמה הלוי זצ"ל · 15 Teves
Dedicated by your beloved daughters, Scharne, Minnie, Eva, Shirley, Rachel
16 Tammuz · Philip Segal לע"נ פסח בן בנימין
Dedicated in memory of our beloved grandfather by his grandchildren

◆The Folly of Revenge

The Sages teach that a single Jew's sin adversely affects the entire Jewish people. This is because, as mentioned above, all Jews stem from a single source and are like one. When one organ of a body is injured, the entire body is affected.

The *Midrash* states (*Vayikra Rabbah* 4:6):

> "A scattered sheep is Israel" (*Yirmiyahu* 50:17). When one of a sheep's organs become afflicted, all its organs are affected [i.e. they become inflamed, which is not the case with other creatures — *Maharzu*]. Similarly, all of Israel can suffer retribution because of one Jew's sin.
>
> R' Yishmael taught: This can be likened to a group traveling aboard a ship. One of the travelers begins to drill a hole in the floor beneath him. His companions cry out: "What are you doing?!" "What do you care?" he responds. "I'm drilling only beneath my seat!" "But the boat will become flooded and all of us will drown!" the others retort.

Therefore, be exceedingly careful not to exact revenge from your fellow Jew or bear a grudge towards him, for it is you yourself whom you are hurting! Rather, tell yourself that Heaven has brought this distress about as a result of your sins, and what difference is there if it came about through this person or through someone else? If you will accept what has happened as an expression of Divine will, it will atone for your sins.[1]

(Continued on page 411)

---

1. In explaining the prohibition against taking revenge, *Sefer HaChinuch* writes: "Among the roots of this *mitzvah* is that a person know and take to heart that whatever happens to him, whether for good or for bad, is brought about by Hashem, Blessed is He, for nothing can occur that is contrary to His will. Therefore, when one is pained or annoyed by another, he should realize that his sins have caused this and that this has been decreed by Hashem. Thus he should not turn his thoughts to revenge, for this person is not the real cause of his hurt; rather, sin is the cause."

This explanation does not discount the fact that the one who caused hurt did so of his own free will and will be held accountable for his misdeed.

טז טבת
16 TEVES / CYCLE 1

יז תמוז
17 TAMMUZ / CYCLE 2

SEFER CHOFETZ CHAIM

Believing Loshon Hora

◈Secondhand Information

The commandment לא תשא שמע שוא, *Do not accept a false report* (*Shemos* 23:1), prohibits the acceptance as fact of any negative statement concerning a person or group of persons. Accurate interpretation of a person's actions and/or words demands thorough knowledge of the setting in which the action occurred and the events which led up to it, an understanding of the person's mindset and manner of speech, and much sensitivity. This is obviously impossible unless one has witnessed the action and accompanying remarks. Reliance on the sensitivity, objectivity, integrity and wisdom of an alleged observer of an improper act is rejected by the Torah as foolish and wrong. Certainly, if the speaker is committing the sin of speaking *loshon hora*, his integrity is suspect and one cannot accept his words as true and accurate. By Torah law, only the testimony of two valid witnesses accepted by a *beis din* (rabbinical court) can be believed as fact.[170]

Whatever character development the Torah requires of us is obviously within our reach.

16 Teves · May today's learning be a זכות for our משפחה
Dedicated by Peretz B. Eichler and family, Lakewood, NJ
17 Tammuz · Elayne Hyman לע״נ חי׳ רבקה בת העשל
Dedicated by Yaakov & Esther Craven, Chicago, IL

DAY 106

➤A *Change of Attitude*

*Y*ou *shall not take revenge and you shall not bear a grudge against the members of your people; you shall love your fellow as yourself — I am HASHEM (Vayikra 19:18).*

What does the concluding *I am HASHEM* represent?

Ostensibly, the commandments in this verse present great difficulty. Suppose that one desperately needs his neighbor's help in a certain matter. The neighbor, who is in a position to provide that help, refuses to lend a hand, and instead does something to upset the person. Can the person really be expected to bear no grudge toward his neighbor, and even to love him as oneself?!

Since the Torah does require this of us, then obviously such character development is within our reach. The way to attain it can be explained with a parable:

Reuven bore ill will toward his neighbor, Shimon, and made a habit of speaking disparagingly of Shimon. One day, Yehudah, a respected man known for his truthfulness, tells Reuven: "I was recently present when Shimon paid a visit to R'_____, a leading Torah sage of the generation, who is known for his great wisdom and piety. The sage accorded Shimon great honor and showed him genuine love. After witnessing this, my friend, I must conclude that your opinion of Shimon is grossly incorrect."

After digesting this information for a few moments, Reuven responds, "It may well be that I am mistaken. My conviction that Shimon has wronged me may be due to man's natural inclination to see himself as correct in any dispute. On the other hand, it may be that Shimon is so clever and deceiving that he is able to deceive even a sage into thinking that he is an upright individual.

"In other words, your report has given me reason for thought, but I'm not fully convinced. In any case, I'll cease from speaking disparagingly of Shimon, at least for the time being."

Reuven's response indicates only the beginning of a change in attitude. As our parable continues, we shall see how, with a proper outlook, it is possible for one's attitude towards others to undergo a complete transformation.

~Vigilance Without Acceptance

The fact that a derogatory statement was made for a constructive purpose does not permit the listener to accept it as fact. It is permissible to listen to negative information for *toeles*, a constructive purpose; however, it is not permissible to believe such information.[171] One may act upon such information on the possibility that it might be true.[172]

It is for this reason that the first precondition for speaking constructively (Day 50) is that one have firsthand knowledge of the negative information he is conveying. Since one cannot believe derogatory information as fact, he cannot present it to others as such. In situations where it is permissible to relate secondhand information one is required to say that he heard it from others and could not be sure of its accuracy (See Day 71).[173]

Just as Hashem has a deep unwavering love for every Jew, so too must we develop a deep unwavering love for each other.

17 Teves · Ethel Shayovich לע"נ עטיא פייגא בת ר' מרדכי ע"ה
Dedicated by Mr. & Mrs. Mark Kutoff and family, Minneapolis, MN
18 Tammuz · לע"נ ביילא רבקה איטא בת פרומע עלקא ע"ה
In memory of a very special נשמה. May you be a מליצת יושר for our משפחה.

◄The View from Above

Thus far, our parable has shown how Reuven has ceased to speak disparagingly of Shimon after hearing that Shimon is held in high esteem by a leading Torah sage. The parable continues:

Some time later, Yehudah tells Reuven, "I was privileged to be present when Shimon met with the Sages of the Mishnah — Rabbi Yehudah HaNasi, Rabbi Meir, and others — men endowed with Divine inspiration, who are akin to angels and cannot possibly be deceived! I saw how they too accorded Shimon great honor and showed him deep love and admiration."

A shaken Reuven responds, "I have erred. Obviously, it was my evil inclination which caused me to bear ill will toward Shimon."

Yehudah then adds one last point, "The Sages of the Mishnah are often visited by the prophet Eliyahu. They mentioned that Eliyahu had related how he had heard the Holy One, Blessed is He, express his deep love for Shimon."

"Woe is me!" exclaimed Reuven. "I have harbored ill will and spoken against someone who is loved by Hashem! I now see things in a different light. Either I was mistaken in thinking that Shimon had wronged me, or I was correct but had failed to attribute his actions to an inadvertent error on his part, for surely he would not have wronged me intentionally! I have sinned grievously in speaking disparagingly of such a man.

"I deeply regret my feelings and actions and will strive to develop a true love for Shimon."

Scripture states: " 'I loved you' said HASHEM" (*Malachi* 1:2); and "You are children to HASHEM, your God" (*Devarim* 14:1). This is the intent of the phrase "I am HASHEM," at the conclusion of the verse which prohibits harboring ill will and commands us to love our fellow Jew. Just as Hashem has a deep unwavering love for every Jew, so too must we develop within ourselves a deep unwavering love for each other.

(Continued on page 411)

⚜*A Proper Approach*

The Talmud (*Niddah* 61a) makes it clear that although negative information should not be accepted as fact, one can and should act to protect himself and others on the chance that it may be true. Just as it is naive and wrong to believe the *loshon hora* one hears, so too it is naive and irresponsible to totally ignore a report which could save oneself or others from possible harm or anguish.

On a personal level, one's relationship with the subject of the negative report should not change. Chances are the statement was inaccurate, if not altogether false. One's behavior towards the individual should, therefore, not be affected at all, and one should continue to show him kindness and assist him as in the past. On a practical level, one should investigate the matter and protect himself against any possible harm that could result should the report prove to be true.

If, for example, one hears that an acquaintance is dishonest, it is forbidden to think of him as such — but one should keep his wallet in a safe place when that person is around! If one is told that a person who accepts charity is actually well-to-do, one should not stop assisting him until the matter has been investigated and it has been determined beyond doubt that he is not deserving of assistance.[174]

To speak disparagingly of the Jewish people as a community is an extremely grave sin.

לע"נ ר' שלמה בן ר' נפתלי ז"ל · Carlebach · 18 Teves
גולדא בת חנה שתחי' Dedicated by
לע"נ בנש"ק ר' אליעזר ז"ל בן הרב משה העשיל ז"ל הי"ד · 19 Tammuz
Dedicated by his family

DAY 108

ᴴDisparaging the Community

In previous chapters, we discussed the severity of speaking *loshon hora* against an individual. To speak disparagingly of the Jewish people as a community is a sin of far greater severity.

Regarding the verses, "Do not inform on a servant to his master ... A generation which curses its father and does not bless its mother" (*Mishlei* 30:10-11), the Talmud expounds: "Even if a generation curses its father and does not bless its mother, do not speak against it before its Master, the Holy One, Blessed is He" (*Pesachim* 87b).

When the prophet Yeshayahu was shown God's glory in a Heavenly vision, he declared, "Woe is me! — for I am a man of impure lips, who sits among a people of impure lips" (*Yeshayahu* 6:5). Yeshayahu's intent was not to disparage his people, but rather to express his feeling of unworthiness upon experiencing a lofty vision. Nevertheless, Scripture continues, "And one of the *seraphim* [angels] flew towards me and in his hand was a glowing coal ... and he touched it to my mouth and said '... your iniquity shall be removed and your sin shall be atoned for' " (vs. 6-7). The Sages state that the word רצפה, *glowing coal,* is a contraction of רצוץ פה, "*Break the mouth* of the one who slandered My people" (*Yalkut Shimoni* 406). It was this sin which ultimately brought about Yeshayahu's death (see *Yevamos* 49b).

יט טבת
19 TEVES / CYCLE 1

כ תמוז
20 TAMMUZ / CYCLE 2

SEFER CHOFETZ CHAIM
Believing Loshon Hora

⊷*Prefatory Remarks*

We have seen that a derogatory statement about someone is not to be believed as fact even for a constructive purpose. One is to take the necessary precautions without changing his attitude towards the subject.

We have also learned that to cause another Jew to transgress is to violate the prohibition לפני עור לא תתן מכשל, *Before a blind person do not place a stumbling block* (*Vayikra* 19:14).

Consequently, when one relates negative information for a constructive purpose, he must be careful not to cause the listener to sin by believing the information as fact.

The proper way to convey negative information for a constructive purpose is to preface it with a statement such as, "Don't take my word for it — I may be mistaken — but do take the matter seriously."[175]

He who likened his generation to that of the Flood did not merit to benefit from the generation's salvation.

---

19 Teves · May today's learning be a זכות for our משפחה
Dedicated by Yehuda Levine & family
20 Tammuz · Jacob Lewin - יעקב צבי בן שלמה
לע״נ
Dedicated by his wife Miriam and children Shlomo, Leah, Moishe, Debbie, Rivke and their families

---

⌐Measure for Measure

S cripture relates how the prophet Eliyahu was forced to hide in a cave to escape the designs of the wicked King Achav and his queen, Izevel. When God appeared to Eliyahu in a vision, the prophet said: "I have been exceedingly zealous for HASHEM, the God of Legions, for the Children of Israel have abandoned Your covenant ..." (*I Melachim* 19:10). It was because of this indictment of his people that the role of transmitting the Divine word to the generation was transferred from Eliyahu to his disciple Elisha (*Yalkut Shimoni* 217).

Years later, when Elisha prophesied the end of a famine, an officer of the king declared, "Behold! If HASHEM makes windows in the heavens, can such a thing be?" (*II Melachim* 7:2). The *Midrash* (cited by *Sefer Charedim* 47:23) understands the officer's words as meaning: "Surely it is within God's power to bring this about. However, the generation is like the generation of the Flood, regarding which it is written, 'And the windows of heaven were opened' (*Bereishis* 7:11). How can it be that a generation so wicked should merit a miracle so great?" Because he spoke this way of the Jewish people, the officer was told by Elisha, "You will yet see the miracle occur, but you will not eat from the food that will result from it."

⌒Expressing Frustration

We have learned that speaking negatively for the sake of one's own emotional well-being is an acceptable form of constructive speech. It is reasonable for one to express anger and frustration about an individual to one's parent, spouse, or mentor to obtain sympathy, reassurance and advice, and it is the obligation of the listener to provide such support.[176]

However, even in such situations, the listener may not decide in his own mind that the report is true, for as far as he is concerned, the information is only secondhand. It is therefore imperative that the following understanding exist between those who take part in such discussions:

Halachah permits one to occasionally "let off steam" and express his frustrations to someone else. However, it is obvious that one who is involved in a disagreement to the point of anger, or considers himself the victim of verbal abuse, lacks the ability to be objective. Any negativity expressed under such circumstances is to be understood as a description of the speaker's feelings and not as an accurate account of what actually took place.

In this way, a husband and wife or close friends can rely on one another for emotional support without transgressing the laws of proper speech.

Our generation is one of abundant merit, and one should seek to awaken Divine mercy on its behalf.

20 Teves · May today's learning be a זכות for
Mr. Menachem Shayovich and family, Brooklyn, NY
Dedicated by his children and grandchildren
21 Tammuz · Louis Borinsky לע״נ לויס בן אברהם
Dedicated by Yehudit Weinberg in memory of her father

DAY 110

✦A Heartfelt Plea

T*anna D'Vei Eliyahu*[1] (I, ch. 19) states:

Master of the Universe! Take note of our suffering ... and allow the disgrace which we endure at every hour to rise up before You. Remember the many heads of families among Israel who have no livelihood, yet toil in Torah each day, continually. Remember the many poor among Israel, who have their flesh torn from their bodies by the nations of the world [through taxes and other monetary demands], yet toil in Torah each day, continually. Remember the youth among Israel who know not their right from their left [i.e. who are pure and unsullied by sin — *Yeshuos Yaakov*], and toil in Torah each day, continually. Remember the many aged men and women among Israel, who arise early to enter the houses of prayer and Torah study, and who yearn, crave and hope each day for Your salvation.

My Father in Heaven! Remember the covenant which You established with the three righteous Patriarchs, Avraham, Yitzchak and Yaakov. And you have written in Your Torah, "And if your brother will become impoverished ... you shall strengthen him" (*Vayikra* 25:35) [so, too, strengthen us so that we will not falter].

My Father in Heaven! Remember the many crippled and blind among Israel who do not have sufficient food, yet hire teachers to study Torah with their children.

My Father in Heaven! Remember Israel, Your possession in this world, as it is written, "Is He not your Father, your Possessor?" (*Devarim* 32:6); and "HASHEM acquired me at the beginning of His way" (*Mishlei* 8:22).

My Father in Heaven! Remember the many widows and orphans among Israel, who toil in Torah and *mitzvos* each day, continually.

(Continued on page 411)

---

1. *Tanna D'Vei Eliyahu* is a collection of teachings revealed by the prophet Eliyahu to the Talmudic sage R' Anan. It contains numerous pieces which speak the praises of the Jewish nation and are designed to awaken Divine compassion on its behalf.

כא טבת
21 TEVES / CYCLE 1

כב תמוז
22 TAMMUZ / CYCLE 2

SEFER CHOFETZ CHAIM
Believing Loshon Hora

☙Between Teachers and Student

Loshon hora initiated by children and accepted as fact by their believing parents is often a cause of major injustice. It happens all too often that one or two key students in a class arbitrarily take a disliking to their teacher and stories are exaggerated and circulated. Well-meaning parents accept their children's accounts of the goings-on at school and before long the teacher finds himself struggling to defend his position.

As every adult knows, student dissatisfaction is not necessarily an indication of a teacher's inadequacy as an educator. The students' version of a situation must be considered but not accepted as fact. A thorough and discreet investigation — one which does not cause the teacher embarrassment — must be conducted before a teacher is declared at fault.

One who seeks merit for the Jewish people becomes endowed with a spiritual light.

A teacher, too, must avoid believing accusations directed by students against one another. Here, too, an investigation is called for, and unless the facts can be established, no action should be taken.[177]

לע"נ יעקב בן מנחם מאניס זאב ע"ה ‎21 Teves · Mr. Jacob Freeman
Dedicated by the Freeman, Brecher & Shapiro families
לע"נ ר' יעקב בן ר' שמואל זנוויל ז"ל ‎22 Tammuz · Yakov Kraus
Dedicated by Mr. & Mrs. S. Halpern, Manchester, England

➳*Meriting the Light*

The Torah states: "... and they [the judges] shall judge the people with righteous judgment" (*Devarim* 16:18). *Midrash Tanchuma* comments:

> R' Yehudah ben R' Shalom said: [This teaches] that the judges should strive to find merit for their people before the Holy One, Blessed is He. From whom do we learn this? From Gidon ben Yoash. In his days, Israel was in distress and God sought someone who could speak their merit [and thereby arouse Divine compassion for them] but no one could be found, for the generation was poor in its fulfillment of *mitzvos* and performance of good deeds. As soon as Gidon was deemed worthy of having found merit for them, a Heavenly angel revealed himself to him. Thus it is written, "And an angel of HASHEM appeared to him ... and he said, 'Go with this strength of yours' " (*Shoftim* 6:12-14), meaning, "with the strength of the merit which you found for My children."
>
> This, then, is the meaning of "... and they [the judges] shall judge the people with righteous judgment," i.e. that they should strive to find merit for the generation.

The above, too, underscores the greatness of finding merit for the Jewish people before Hashem. One who does so becomes a receptacle for the spiritual light of the sacred Heavenly sanctuary which is called the Sanctuary of Merit, for it is there that the merits of Israel are mentioned, as stated in *Sefer Chareidim.*

כב טבת
22 TEVES / CYCLE 1

כג תמוז
23 TAMMUZ / CYCLE 2

SEFER CHOFETZ CHAIM

Believing Loshon Hora

❧*Rumors*

Halachah allows for certain rumors to be reckoned with, but never are they to be accepted as fact.

It is important to note the halachic qualifications which distinguish a rumor that may have some credence from that which is mere character assassination. If the subject is known to have enemies in the community who are very possibly the rumor's source, it may not be granted any legitimacy. Even if everyone in the community has a favorable opinion of the subject, the rumor would have to circulate throughout the community for one and a half days without losing strength before it could be taken seriously.[178]

When a rumor does seem to have validity, *halachah* allows for it to cast doubt on the status of the person(s) involved; e.g. where the report concerns the subject's status as a *Kohen* or similar issues of lineage.

Condition yourself to tolerate distress and be forgiving of insult.

The unfortunate reality is that rarely is a rumor anything more than wide-scale *loshon hora*. Even when *halachah* grants a rumor some degree of validity, it cannot be accepted as fact.[179]

לע"נ הרבנית רחל בת ר' אהרון ע"ה · 22 Teves
23 Tammuz · Rav Abraham Weintraub בן אברהם צבי בן לע"נ ר'
הרב גרשון מונש
Dedicated by his children, grandchildren and great grandchildren

❧The Quality of Acceptance

In striving to develop the quality of *shmiras haloshon,* one must place great emphasis on reacting toward any situation with *savlanus,* that is, to be tolerant of whatever negativity is thrown one's way. In the words of *Avos D'R' Nosson* (41:11): "Condition yourself to tolerate distress, and be forgiving of insult." Through such character development, the quality of *shmiras haloshon* is easily attainable. Conversely, one who lacks *savlanus* will forever be torn by the need to relate the wrongs which others have done against him. At times, he will prevail in this struggle; other times, he will fail.

A *savlan* is capable of bearing insult in silence. He tells himself that whatever occurs is an expression of Divine will, and that in reality his own sins are the true causes of his being shamed.[1] When one accepts disgrace in this way, totally and sincerely, Hashem surely elevates his stature in this world and in the next.

---

1. See Day 105.

✌*Exception to the Rule*

We have already seen that one may not believe even his spouse or close confidants when they relate negative information about others. At most, he may consider the possibility that the information might be true.

The Talmud states that one exception to this rule is where the listener considers the speaker to be a man of unusual integrity whose words are weighed very carefully. Such a person can be trusted to relate an incident exactly as it happened, to the extent that the listener can consider himself as having witnessed it, and thus may accept the report as fact. Nevertheless, since the decision that the speaker is trustworthy is a personal one made by the listener, he cannot pass the information on to others as if he had witnessed it — even for a constructive purpose.[180]

The Chofetz Chaim is of the opinion that today no one can claim to have the degree of integrity necessary for his words to be accepted as fact, and it is therefore forbidden for anyone to believe a negative statement on the basis of someone else's report.[181]

Bearing insult in silence and without ill will is indicative of one's sanctity of soul and deep-rooted faith.

---

23 Teves · May today's learning be a זכות for Dr. Michael Shallman
and family, Long Beach, CA

24 Tammuz · לכבוד הרב יוסף קאלאצקי שליט״א ותלמידיו
כולל יד אברהם Yad Avraham Institute

❧Three Levels

*T*hose who are insulted and do not insult, who hear their disgrace and do not respond, who act out of love and are happy in their affliction, regarding them does Scripture state (*Shoftim* 5:31): "But they who love Him shall be like the sun going forth in its might" (*Shabbos* 88b).

The commentators understand this passage as enumerating three distinct levels of reaction to insult:

(1) *Those who are insulted and do not insult,* but they do respond in some way.

(2) *Those who hear their disgrace and do not respond* at all, lest their response evoke further insult and disparagement. In their hearts, though, they harbor bitterness toward their abuser.

(3) *Those who act out of love and are happy in their affliction,* meaning, whose love of Hashem impels them not to respond to insult and to accept their affliction [i.e. disgrace] with gladness.

It is when a person attains this third and highest level that he merits the great reward with which the passage concludes. Such attainment is indicative of his sanctity of soul and pure faith in Hashem, Who guides the happenings of mankind, as it is written, "For His eyes are upon the ways of man" (*Iyov* 34:21). It is with recognition of Hashem's involvement in all man's affairs, and belief that whatever difficulties one encounters are ultimately for the good, that a person is able to bear insult without ill will and with a happy heart.

כד טבת
24 TEVES / CYCLE 1

כה תמוז
25 TAMMUZ / CYCLE 2

SEFER CHOFETZ CHAIM
Believing Loshon Hora

✺*"Innocent" Remarks*

There are times when *halachah* accepts as fact "innocent" remarks, i.e. statements made in passing without the speaker being aware of the consequences of his words. As a rule, people do not lie unnecessarily, so that when a person does not realize that he is saying something of significance, it can be assumed that he is telling the truth.

Halachah grants such statements the status of testimony in two instances:

(1) Where it is certain that ultimately the true story will be revealed to all. People do not fabricate tales when it is clear that their lies will be revealed as such.

(2) To establish that an individual is no longer alive.

"Innocent" negative statements are not granted any such legitimacy. They are *loshon hora* and one is not permitted to believe them.[182]

Suffering draws one close to Hashem.

24 Teves · Mr. Simcha Bryks לע״נ שמחה בן נפתלי פאליק הלוי
Dedicated by Howie & Chanie Bryks
25 Tammuz · לע״נ ר׳ יעקב חיים בן ר׳ יחזקאל
Dedicated by משפחת פאנאטה

DAY 114

◄Growth Through Tribulation

The Sages teach:

> Rabbi Eliezer ben Yaakov said: One should feel a sense of gratitude toward the Holy One, Blessed is He, when suffering comes upon him. Why? Because suffering draws a person close to Him, as it is written, "Hashem reproves the one whom He loves" (*Mishlei* 3:12).
>
> When suffering comes upon a person, he should accept it and withstand [the test], for its reward is infinite (*Midrash Tanchumah, Parashas Ki Seitzei* 2).
>
> "Wait silently for [the salvation of] Hashem, and wait longingly for Him" (*Tehillim* 37:7). Place your hope in the Holy One, Blessed is He. If He brings afflictions upon you, do not demonstrate disdain; rather, accept your lot like [one would accept] musical instruments [התחולל, *wait longingly,* can homiletically be related to חללין, *flutes*] (*Yalkut Shimoni, Tehillim* 729).

To accept insult without bitterness, with the knowledge that all that transpires is an expression of Divine will, is to accept a form of affliction, as the passage above states: [Those who are insulted and do not insult ...], *who act out of love and are glad in their affliction.*[1] The reward for such acceptance is without measure.

---

1. Once, the *tzaddik* R' Zalman of Volozhin (disciple of the the Vilna Gaon) was traveling with his brother, R' Chaim. When they arrived at a certain inn, the innkeeper spoke harshly to them and refused to grant them a room for the night. Later, as they resumed their journey, R' Chaim noticed his brother crying. "Why are you crying?" he asked. "Did you then pay attention to the innkeeper's words? I ignored them completely!" R' Zalman replied: "Heaven forfend that I should cry over being insulted. I am crying because I sense a slight inner hurt as a result of his words. I cry that I have not yet attained the level of 'Those who are insulted ... and are glad in their affliction' " (from *Sefer Toldos Adam*).

כה טבת
25 TEVES / CYCLE 1

כו תמוז
26 TAMMUZ / CYCLE 2

SEFER CHOFETZ CHAIM
Believing Loshon Hora

❧Confirming Suspicions

The Torah does not accept circumstantial evidence as proof of a person's guilt. Thus, when one suspects an individual of improper behavior, he may not decide that his suspicions are correct based on the person's reaction to accusations or other strange behavior that strongly points to his guilt.

Nevertheless if, in addition to the circumstantial evidence, such suspicions are subsequently supported by someone else's claim to have actually witnessed the person engaging in such behavior, one does have the right to believe that his suspicions are correct.[183]

However, to whatever degree possible, the listener is still obligated to judge the perpetrator favorably; he must seek to understand his motives and should not be swift to condemn him.[184]

Moreover, one may not pass on the information without fulfilling the preconditions for relating negative information for a constructive purpose.[185]

Humiliation in this world is certainly preferable to retribution in the next world.

---

25 Teves · Joseph ben Zakiye Shehebar לע"נ יוסף בן אברהם וזכייה
Dedicated in loving memory by his wife Fortune and his entire family
26 Tammuz · Reb Moshe Hilsenrath לע"נ ר' משה בן איסר יהודה ז"ל
Dedicated by the Hilsenrath children and grandchildren

DAY
115

❧Dealing With Humiliation

The author of *Sefer Chareidim* writes:

> Whenever someone insults or humiliates me in public, I place a scale before my eyes: On one side are my sins, on the other side are the insults and humiliations which have been directed toward me. I see the side of my sins weighing down lower and lower, and I choose to bear my disgrace in silence and tell myself that I deserve it. I do this whenever faced with any sort of distress, be it through another's word or deed (*Sefer Chareidim* 4:5).

The average person would prefer to suffer humiliation if this will prevent him from suffering monetary loss, as when his property is threatened by fire or other means of devastation. How much more should one be willing to suffer humiliation if this will save his soul from punishment. Certainly, then, one should react to humiliation with silent acceptance.

✦*The Habitual Sinner*

The prohibition of accepting *loshon hora* does not apply when the subject is known to regularly engage in the negative behavior under discussion. Thus, if on a number of occasions one has personally witnessed an individual commit a particular sin, he would be permitted to believe that the person committed that sin again. The Chofetz Chaim seems to suggest that one would even be permitted to believe that the person has committed a different sin. When a person is known to totally disregard the Torah and its *mitzvos* one may certainly accept a report that he committed any sin.[186]

If one is known to regularly transgress a particular sin out of temptation, one would be allowed to believe that he transgressed it again, but would be required to reject a claim that this time it was done maliciously.[187]

"Whose sins does Hashem forgive? One who overlooks the wrong committed against himself."

26 Teves · Ida Danzger לע״נ חי׳ בת יוסף ארי׳ הכהן
Dedicated by Reuven & Malkie Danzger and family
27 Tammuz · Johanna Hertz לע״נ העindעלע בת גרשון ע״ה
Dedicated by Kurt & Edith Rothschild and family

DAY 116

⚓*Forgive and Forget*

Even if all that one would gain through silent acceptance of humiliation is a lessening of punishment for a single sin, it would be well worthwhile. In fact, the gain is far greater, as stated in the Talmud:

> Rava said: Whoever refrains from exacting his measure [i.e. from responding to the hurt caused him], [the Heavenly Tribunal] removes from him all his sins, as it is written, "He forgives transgressions and passes over sins" (*Michah* 7:18). Whose sin does He forgive? One who passes over sins [committed against himself] (*Rosh Hashanah* 17a).

Rava taught that even פשעיו, one's willful sins committed in a state of spiritual rebellion, find atonement when one refrains from "exacting his measure." However, to be worthy of such atonement, one must demonstrate a corresponding degree of forgiveness; that is, he must bear no ill will towards those who have caused him hurt, even when he knows for a fact that the hurt was inflicted maliciously.

Of course, such atonement is dependent upon the individual's sincere resolve to refrain from committing these sins in the future.

כז טבת
27 TEVES / CYCLE 1

כח תמוז
28 TAMMUZ / CYCLE 2

SEFER CHOFETZ CHAIM

Believing Loshon Hora

✒Repentance

The standard order of *teshuvah* (repentance) for sins between man and God is: confession, regret, and resolution never to repeat the act in the future. One who willfully listened as someone related *loshon hora* is required to engage in this process.[188]

If one actually believed the *loshon hora*, then the above steps must be preceded by a successful effort at convincing oneself that the information was not accurate. This applies even when *halachah* permits listening to the information for a constructive purpose but does not permit believing it as fact.[189]

Generally, sins between man and his fellow require that one ask forgiveness. However, this does not apply when one has accepted *loshon hora*. So long as the listener has not acted on the basis of the report in a way that was harmful to the subject, there is no need to approach the person for forgiveness.[190] In fact, the person should not be informed that *loshon hora* was spoken about him, as it would serve no purpose other than to hurt his feelings, and may involve *rechilus* (speech which causes hatred — See Day 118).

The Sage was granted new life because he overlooked the wrong caused him.

27 Teves · Dovid Miltz לע"נ ר' דוד טעביל בן ר' יהושע
Dedicated by the Miltz and Mann families
28 Tammuz · Mr. Leon Faigenbaum לע"נ יצחק אליעזר בן פנחס ז"ל
Dedicated לזכרון עולם by the Rosenthal family of New York &
the Faigenbaum family of Cleveland, OH

DAY
117

◆New Lease on Life

At times, the willingness to overlook and forgive can cause a person's life on this world to be extended, even after Heaven has decreed that his time has come. The Talmud relates (*Rosh Hashanah* 17a):

> R' Huna, the son of R' Yehoshua, fell ill. R' Pappa went to visit him. Upon seeing that he was unconscious, R' Pappa told them [R' Huna's attendants], "Prepare provisions for him [i.e. ready his burial shrouds]." In the end, R' Huna recovered. They [R' Huna's attendants] asked him [R' Huna], "What did you see [while unconscious]?" He told them, "Indeed, that is how it was [that death had been decreed upon me]. But the Holy One, Blessed is He, instructed them, 'Because he does not exact his measure, therefore, do not be exacting with him.' As it is written, 'He forgives transgressions and passes over sins' (*Michah* 7:18) — whose sin does He forgive? One who passes over sins."

Therefore, one should cling to this sacred attribute constantly. In this way, it will be good for him in this world and in the World to Come.

❧*Rechilus: A Definition*

While the verse לא תלך רכיל בעמיך, *Do not go as a gossipmonger among your people* (*Vayikra* 19:16), prohibits all forms of *loshon hora*, the term רכיל, *gossipmonger*, refers specifically to רכילות, (*rechilus*), information that potentially can cause ill will between Jews. Whereas *loshon hora* that is derogatory can cause others to lose respect for the subject, *rechilus* can cause damage to relationships between the subject and his fellow Jews.[191]

It is forbidden to tell someone that an individual: did something to harm him; spoke *loshon hora* against him; doesn't like him; or doesn't respect him, since such statements would, in all probability, cause the listener to feel ill will towards that individual.

Trust in Hashem is vital for proper shmiras haloshon.

28 Teves · May today's learning be a זכות for our משפחה
Dedicated by Yehuda Levine & family
29 Tammuz · In memory of Victoria Gindi

☙ *Trust in Hashem*

In developing the quality of *shmiras haloshon,* one must strive to forever strengthen himself in matters of *bitachon,* trust in God. *Bitachon* is a sacred and vital component of Divine service as a whole, and is crucial for proper observance of the laws of *shmiras haloshon.*

For example, let us suppose that someone does something to slight someone else's honor or affect his livelihood in some way. The victim's heart burns with a strong desire to make known the wrong done to him. He finds it difficult to quell this desire. Then, he begins to reflect upon the Sages' teaching that no one can affect that which has been Divinely ordained for his fellow, be it a financial gain or mark of honor, even by a hairsbreadth (*Yoma* 38a). His desire is quelled.

David said: "Trust in Hashem and do good, that you may dwell in the land and nourish [yourself] with faithfulness" (*Tehillim* 37:3). David first exhorts us to trust in Hashem and only then to do good, for Divine trust is a solid foundation upon which any good endeavor should be established.

∾*When an Act is Justified*

Speaking *rechilus* is prohibited even when it is made clear that the act committed was totally justified. It is therefore forbidden to tell someone that another person spoke negatively of him for a constructive purpose (*l'toeles*). Moreover, it is forbidden to tell someone that another person spoke negatively of him upon the advice of a *posek* (halachic authority). People tend to bear ill will towards those who speak against them even when it is obvious that the speaker was justified in doing so.[192]

The evil inclination attempts to draw the Jew away from Torah study by way of a simple argument.

29 Teves · May today's learning be a זכות for Elimelech Michoel Goldstein and family, Baltimore, MD

1 Av · In honor of our dear children שיחיו לכבוד בנינו ובנותינו היקרים
Dedicated by Yankie & Esther Rosenberg

DAY
119

◄The Man of Trust

Hashem has commanded us to study Torah at every available moment; at the very least, we are to set aside a fixed portion of time each day for its study. We are also commanded to set aside a portion of our earnings for *tzedakah* (charity), and fulfill other *mitzvos* which ostensibly seem to deplete one's resources or prevent him from adding to his income. The evil inclination incites the Jew to be lax in his observance of these *mitzvos* by way of simple arguments: "What will you be left with in the end if you give away so much money which could be used toward lucrative investment?" Or, "Now is a most opportune time for a business trip; you might never have an opportunity like this one! Your studies will have to wait for another time." In this way, one feels compelled to give less charity or to sacrifice his fixed learning session for the sake of the business opportunity which "cannot be missed."

To counter this, David declares: "Trust in Hashem" (*Tehillim* 37:3) — trust that He will surely grant you whatever has been decreed for you; "and do good" — through such trust you will find yourself ready to carry out all the good which the Torah seeks of you.

Talmud Yerushalmi (*Sotah* 9:13) relates that a businessman was once studying Torah when some customers approached him, demanding that he show them his merchandise. The man replied: "I will not interrupt my fixed study period. If this profit has been decreed for me, then inevitably it will be mine."

✎Committees and Courts

The prohibition against speaking *rechilus* is highly relevant when a committee meets to consider an individual for possible enrollment in a school, employment in a firm, or appointment to a communal or organizational position. Whether or not the final outcome is in the person's favor, it is forbidden to divulge the identity of anyone who expressed an opinion against the person. It is wrong for a member of the committee to tell the candidate, "I was on your side but was outvoted by my colleagues."

The same would apply when a *beis din* (rabbinical court) considers a case and comes to a decision against a party. It is forbidden for any of the judges to state that the ruling was unanimous, or which judges sided with which party, or to even say, "I voted in your favor but was outnumbered," for it is natural for people to harbor ill will toward those who ruled against them.[193]

Surely one cannot hope to improve his situation by contravening the will of Hashem.

I Shevat · Cantor David Baum לע״נ מנחם דוד בן שמוא־ל בנימין
Dedicated by Dovid Davis and family, Baltimore, MD
2 Av · Chana Engel לע״נ חנה בת אהרן שלמה הלוי ע״ה
Dedicated by Moshe Yehuda Engel, Meir Engel & Goldie Golding

❧ *The Inconceivable*

DAY 120

It is inconceivable that one's livelihood should suffer because he refuses to interrupt his fixed study period to engage in business. Can it be that Hashem would subtract from the amount of sustenance that has been decreed for an individual on Rosh Hashanah because that person faithfully adheres to his schedule of Torah study?!

If one's steadfastness in this area results in the loss of a business opportunity, this should not be cause for concern. The Omnipotent has infinite ways of bringing profit to one's door. If it will not be here today, it will be here some other day. One thing is certain: by the time the year ends, whatever income has been decreed in Heaven will be his, as our Sages have taught: "All of a person's income is fixed [each year] from Rosh Hashanah until Rosh Hashanah" (*Beitzah* 16a), and all the effort and business acumen in the world will not gain him one cent more.

Surely one cannot hope to improve his situation by contravening the will of Hashem and disrupting his Torah study in order to earn profit, or by giving less *tzedakah* than a man of his means should give. Only the wicked improve their material existence in this world by transgressing God's will, as it is written, "And He repays His enemies in his lifetime, to make him perish" (*Devarim* 7:10).

ב שבט
2 SHEVAT / CYCLE 1

ג אב
3 AV / CYCLE 2

SEFER CHOFETZ CHAIM
The Many Forms of Gossip

✺Negative Opinions

As *rechilus* includes any statement that might cause ill feelings between Jews, it is forbidden to inform a manufacturer or distributor that a certain individual dislikes his product. This is true even if the product is generally unpopular. Similarly, one may not tell a speaker that a certain person or persons did not enjoy his lecture, nor may one tell a writer or artist that certain people do not appreciate his work (unless this is absolutely necessary for a constructive purpose).

One who seeks a life of fulfillment and tranquility should heed David's call.

2 Shevat - L'zichron Olam our son Ezra Witkin ז"ל לע"נ חזקיהו עזרא ז"ל
בן רב ברוך יבלח"ט
Dedicated by Rabbi Boruch & Gittel Witkin & family, Elizabeth, NJ
3 Av - Rosenthal לע"נ משה בן יחזקאל הכהן ז"ל
Dedicated by Rabbi Shlomo & Miriam Leider, Monsey, NY

❧Stealing One's Own Time

At times, people totally ignore their obligation to study Torah, and yet become very successful in business. However, if one will carefully follow the fortunes of such individuals, he will discover that in many instances, circumstances beyond their control cause them to lose significant amounts of their hard-earned money. This may be Heaven's way of taking away that which rightfully belonged to someone else, as it is written, "One who accumulates wealth, but not with justice, in half his days it will forsake him" (*Yirmiyahu* 17:11). Or it may be that the person accumulated some of his wealth during time that was not his own, meaning, time which should have been dedicated toward the study of Torah and other *mitzvos*.

Avos D'R' Nosson (29:2) states: "Whoever disrupts himself from studying words of Torah will have disruptions cast his way [which will interfere with his daily affairs]. For example, a lion, or leopard ... or armed bandits may come, surround his property and exact retribution from him, as it is written, "... there is indeed a God Who judges in the land" (*Tehillim* 58:12).

The above punishment is measure for measure. Because the person neglected his obligation to study Torah and instead strained to amass material wealth, therefore circumstances will force him to turn his attention away from the endeavors in which he has wrongfully chosen to toil.

The Sages state: "If a person sees affliction come upon him, he should examine his ways. If he examined them and they are not lacking, he should attribute [his suffering] to disruption of Torah study" (*Berachos* 5a).

In conclusion: The world and its fullness belongs to the Holy One, Blessed is He. He fashioned all of creation for His honor, as it is written, "All that is called by My Name and for My honor, have I created" (*Yeshayahu* 43:7). Therefore, one who seeks a life of fulfillment and tranquility should heed David's call: "Trust in HASHEM and do good."

☙*Friends and Relatives*

It is reasonable to assume that people dislike those who speak badly of their friends or relatives. Therefore, to tell an individual that someone has spoken negatively of his friend or relative is to speak *rechilus.*

An important application of this law is in the case of children. We have learned that one may speak of a child's mischievous behavior if neither the speaker nor the listener will think any less of the child as a result of the incident. Since the Torah deems children culpable for their actions only in a limited sense, their misbehavior is considered shameful only if people view it as such. Nevertheless, it is common for a parent or grandparent to feel ill will toward someone who tells others of his child's or grandchild's misbehavior. Therefore, to inform a parent or grandparent that someone told of their child's misbehavior is to speak *rechilus.*[194]

Even in a time of Divine concealment, one should forever trust in Hashem's power to provide him with his every need.

3 Shevat · Monroe Fragin לע״נ משה אהרן בן אברהם
Dedicated by Avrohom Moshe & Mimi Fragin, Harrison, NY
4 Av · Yocheved (Jolan) Rosenberg לע״נ יוכבד בת
ר׳ ישראל משולם (פייש) ע״ה
Dedicated by the entire Treitel family

❧The King and His Bird

"Trust in HASHEM forever, for in God, HASHEM, is the strength of the worlds" (*Yeshayahu* 26:4). The term עֲדֵי עַד, *forever,* alludes to the current situation, when the happenings of this world are guided from Above with a degree of *hester panim,* Divine concealment [as opposed to earlier generations, such as the Temple era, when God's involvement in the world's affairs was plainly apparent]. Even in our day, when Hashem seems hidden from us and many have strayed from the ways of their ancestors, nevertheless, one should trust in Hashem.

We can compare this to the situation of a king who possessed great wealth and power, and ruled over his kingdom in grand style. One day, news reached the royal palace that a small, insignificant village had rebelled against the king's rule. While the king's advisers were debating what sort of punishment should be dealt the rebels, the king went for a stroll in his garden. He came upon a beautiful bird chirping in a very sweet way. A servant obeyed the king's order that the bird be brought to the royal palace so that the king and his family could enjoy its chirping. As the bird was being carried to its new home, it began to chirp a lilting song. Someone said aloud, "How lovely are you, and how lovely are the songs that you sing! How I worry that you may go hungry, now that some of the king's subjects have rebelled and refuse to give of their produce for the royal family and its pets."

A servant of the king replied: "You foolish, ignorant man! Need a king, who rules over scores of provinces and whose storehouses overflow with abundance, worry about a few grains that his bird needs for sustenance? How foolish can one be?!"

The message of this parable is clear, as we shall see.

✑Cynicism

It is forbidden to relate to a member of a community, family or organization that someone spoke cynically of his group; to do so is to speak *rechilus*. This is true even when members of that community, family, or organization regularly joke about themselves. It is common for people to poke fun at themselves, yet be offended when others make similar comments.

The same applies regarding a school. Students who regularly joke about their school or class are often offended when outsiders make similar comments. Therefore, mentioning to students that someone spoke negatively of their school is speaking *rechilus*.

[It should be noted that joking about one's own school generally involves *loshon hora*, or at least *avak loshon hora*.]

We are children of the King, and need not worry that we may go hungry.

4 Shevat · Mr. Zoltan Reisman לע"נ יהודא זונדל בן יעקב ז"ל
Dedicated by the Reisman family, Brooklyn, NY
5 Av · Irene Siegal לע"נ שרה בת ר' יחזקאל יהודה
Dedicated by her family, Los Angeles, CA

ᴥ*Children of Hashem*

Denial of God's glory is possible only in this world. Only in his earthly existence can man, with his corporeal desires, be drawn away from His service and thus deny that which is true and sacred. In the upper world, however, all the Heavenly angels perceive Hashem's glory, recognize how He sustains and guides them, and declare His praise and bow before him, as it is written, "And the hosts of Heaven bow before You" (*Nechemiah* 9:6).

In truth, this world is not even like a tiny seed when compared to the totality of worlds Above, where countless Heavenly contingents exist, each consisting of an infinite numbers of angels, as it is written, "A thousand thousands serving Him, and myriad myriads standing before Him" (*Daniel* 7:10). Thus, the wicked's flouting of His will in this world is of little significance when viewed within the scope of creation in its entirety.

In this world, the Holy One, Blessed is He, takes pleasure in the Jewish people, who are so beloved to Him that they are called "Children of Hashem" (*Devarim* 14:1). He takes pleasure, as it were, in the voice of their prayer and study, as it is written, "Let Me hear your voice" (*Shir HaShirim* 2:14). Shouldn't we be ashamed *not* to trust in the One Who gives life to all the worlds and the myriads of angels? How can man fret and worry, "Whence will come my sustenance, the fulfillment of my needs?" Indeed, such worry and concern is cause for greater wonder than the concern of the fool in the above parable, who worried that the rebellion of an insignificant village would deprive the king's bird of its sustenance!

It is incumbent upon us to strengthen ourselves spiritually, to concentrate on fulfilling God's will — and not to worry about our material situation. As "Children of Hashem" we are like children of a king, who need not worry that they may go hungry.

ה שבט
5 SHEVAT / CYCLE 1

ו אב
6 AV / CYCLE 2

SEFER CHOFETZ CHAIM
The Many Forms of Gossip

◆Parties at Odds

As *rechilus* is defined as any statement that may cause ill feelings between Jews, one might think that statements where ill feelings already exist would be excluded from this category. In fact, this is not the case. It is forbidden to strengthen existent animosity or even to remind someone of his negative feelings towards his fellow.[195]

All of creation continues to exist only by way of Hashem's unceasing will that it be so.

לע"נ אהרן צבי אביגדר בן משה יצחק פיש · 5 Shevat
Dedicated by the Fish Family
לע"נ רויזא בת עובדי' Rose Brill · 6 Av
Dedicated by her children & grandchildren

⊸The Strength of His Worlds

Our above discussion is capsulated in a single verse cited above:

בטחו בה' עדי עד ,כי בי-ה ה' צור עולמים
Trust in HASHEM forever, for in God, HASHEM, is the strength of the worlds (Yeshayahu 24:6).

"Trust in HASHEM forever ..." Even after the Temple has been destroyed and the Jewish people finds itself in exile while the wicked prosper, nevertheless, *trust in Hashem* and He will help you, for His power is infinite and eternal.

All of creation continues to exist only by way of Hashem's unceasing will that it be so, as the Sages formulated in the morning prayer, "and in His goodness renews daily, perpetually, the work of Creation"; and as Scripture states, "And You give them all life" (*Nechemiah* 9:6). Hashem's involvement in this world is unchanging and He continues to watch over those who place their trust in Him. Therefore, the above verse concludes: כי בי-ה ה' צור עולמים , *for in God, HASHEM, is the strength of the worlds.* Hashem created His worlds with the Name י-ה; the upper world with the letter י, and this world with the letter ה. His will, as represented by the letters of His Name, continues to be the צור, *strength*, of His worlds.

ו שבט
6 SHEVAT / CYCLE 1

ז אב
7 AV / CYCLE 2

SEFER CHOFETZ CHAIM
The Many Forms of Gossip

✍*Ultimate Result*

Included in the prohibition against speaking *rechilus* is relating information which might ultimately cause ill will if it were to be passed on to a certain person or persons.

Therefore, it is forbidden to say anything to anyone that might cause animosity between any two people. One must assume that whatever is told to even one person is likely to be repeated to others —and could ultimately be heard by just about anybody. Only if the listener is warned not to tell anyone what he is about to hear, and can be trusted to heed this warning, would it be permitted to share such information with him (provided, of course, that the information is not of a derogatory nature; otherwise, it would be *loshon hora*).[196]

To abstain from strife out of concern that Hashem's Name not be desecrated is a source of infinite merit.

לע"נ התינוקת בתיה לאה ע"ה בת אברהם 6 Shevat · Batya Leah Feld
שמחה פעלד נ"י
Dedicated in loving memory by the family
לע"נ יעקב בן יהודה ארי' · 7 Av
Dedicated by Avrumie & Elisa Taub

~Infinite Merit

As mentioned above, one who seeks to acquire the quality of *shmiras haloshon* must strengthen his *bitachon,* trust in Hashem, so that he will not become upset if someone will cause him any sort of hurt or loss. With proper *bitachon*, one will refrain from speaking negatively in such instances and will refrain, as well, from feuding with or shaming the guilty party. Rather, he will be confident that Hashem will replenish his losses in the way that He sees fit.

The Talmud states: "Whoever places his trust in the Holy One, Blessed is He, will merit that He will be a refuge for him in this world and the next" (*Menachos* 29b). This assurance is granted even to those whose trust is not predicated on a desire to honor God's Name. Surely, then, one will merit this reward if he refrains from argument out of concern that he might utter that which the Torah prohibits. Moreover, one who refrains from "exacting his rightful measure"[1] out of concern that Hashem's Name not be desecrated, and instead places his trust in Him, will surely merit infinite reward.

---

1. See Day 116.

ז שבט
7 SHEVAT / CYCLE 1

ח אב
8 AV / CYCLE 2

SEFER CHOFETZ CHAIM
The Many Forms of Gossip

✍*Old Information*

The prohibition against speaking *rechilus* may apply even if the listener is already aware of the information being conveyed. *Rechilus* includes any statement which may foster animosity; repeating how someone maligned or acted against the listener might make the listener better aware of details that would be cause for added hatred. Moreover, if the listener had not yet given much thought to the information, repeating it could be cause for animosity to form.[197]

Through proper trust, one pursues the path of peace— and can merit yet greater success in his financial endeavors.

7 Shevat · Rabbi Yisroel Meir Heiman לע"נ ר' ישראל מאיר בן
דב צבי היימאן
Dedicated by Sara Heiman, Far Rockaway, NY
8 Av · May today's learning be a זכות for בת מיכל הענדעלע
מיכאל נתן שתחי'

⋘Recipe for Success

The infinite benefit of avoiding strife in financial matters through proper *bitachon*, trust in Hashem, can be understood with the following parable:

A father distributed portions of food to his sons who were gathered around his table. One son reached over and snatched his brother's portion. When the victim saw that his portion would not be returned, he went to the head of the table and told his father what had happened. "I am sure, Father," said the son, "that you do not want me to fight with my brother. That is why I am requesting another portion for myself." Upon hearing this, the father kissed his son on the head and handed him a larger portion than before. The father said, "Let your foolish brother keep your original portion. The next time we eat together, you will receive a double portion, while he will get nothing."

Now, what would the father's reaction have been had the victimized son yelled at his brother and attacked him physically until he succeeded in retrieving his portion? Surely the father would have been very upset. He would have told the victim, "I would have gladly given you another portion rather than have you and your brother come to blows with one another. What utter foolishness you have demonstrated!"

When a Jew adversely affects another's financial affairs and refuses to honor a request that he cease his wrongful practices, and the victim pleads before Hashem that He replenish his losses—surely he will find favor Above for demonstrating his trust in Hashem and pursuing the path of peace. And his trust will be rewarded with yet greater success in his business endeavors.

However, if one chooses to feud with the person who has done him wrong, he will not find favor before Hashem, like the victimized son in our parable who upset his father by taking matters into his own hands.[1]

---

1. Of course, the victim has every right to seek restitution in a Jewish court of law or pursue other avenues which are sanctioned by *halachah*.

ח שבט
8 SHEVAT / CYCLE 1

ט אב
9 AV / CYCLE 2

SEFER CHOFETZ CHAIM
The Many Forms of Gossip

◈Overt and Covert

A s with other forms of *loshon hora*, *halachah* does not differentiate between *rechilus* that is stated explicitly or merely inferred. A statement in which names are omitted is still *rechilus* if the listener can deduce the identities of the people involved.[198] Also, it is forbidden to communicate *rechilus* through body motion, sign language or any other means. Likewise, it is forbidden to make available written or recorded material if awareness of its contents could create ill feelings between individuals.[199]

Dishonesty will not earn a person one cent more than what has been decreed for him on Rosh Hashanah.

פרידה בת רבקה עטי׳ שתחי׳ שתזכה לרפואה שלמה · 8 Shevat
מה״ש בתושח״י
לע״נ חיים יעקב בן אלכסאנדר זישע ע״ה 9 Av · Grandpa Mr. D.

☙The Folly of Dishonesty

Above, we spoke of the great reward for avoiding strife in situations where one has clearly been wronged. And what of the one who committed the wrong, who profited at the expense of his neighbor's loss? He acted wickedly and foolishly, for his sinful tactics will not earn him one cent more than what has been decreed for him on Rosh Hashanah. By denying his neighbor that which was rightfully his, he will ultimately be denied that which had been decreed for himself. In the end, his wrongful gain will cause his rightful earnings to become lost as well, for, as the Sages teach, the punishment for forcing one's personal burden upon another Jew is the loss of one's possessions (*Succah* 29b).

The Sages further teach: "If you take that which is not your own, your own will be taken from you" (*Derech Eretz Zuta* ch. 3). To be dishonest in financial matters is to exchange the channel of sustenance that Heaven provides for one that is sinful. Hashem declares: "It is not enough that the wicked rob, but they even inconvenience Me to return the money to its rightful owner" (*Sanhedrin* 8a).[1]

The above is illustrated in the episode of Yaakov and Lavan. Before fleeing Lavan's house, Yaakov was shown in a prophetic dream that the birth of unusually colored sheep in his flock was Divinely decreed compensation for Lavan's ill treatment of him. As *Rashi* explains, an angel had brought colored sheep from Lavan's flock to Yaakov's so that this would occur. As justification for such Divine intervention, Yaakov was told in his dream, "... for I have seen all that Lavan is doing to you" (*Bereishis* 31:12). And as Yaakov later told Lavan directly, "I served you fourteen years for your two daughters and six years for your flocks, and you changed my wages a hundred times" (ibid. v. 41).

---

1. Obviously, nothing is difficult for Hashem to do. "They inconvenience Me" means that the settling of accounts might require changes in the natural course of events (see *Maharsha, Ben Yehoyada*).

❧*Ambiguities*

A statement which can be interpreted by the listener to mean that one party acted or spoke against another is *rechilus* even though this was not the speaker's interpretation of that which he recounted. Such information may be related only if the speaker makes it clear that no harm was intended AND the listener is not known to be one who is likely to draw his own negative conclusions.[200]

If someone finds Torah observance unfulfilling, the fault lies with him, not with the Torah.

9 Shevat · Chana Miriam Schmell לע״נ חנה מרים בת בן־ציון
Dedicated by friends in the Memphis Jewish community
10 Av · לע״נ פנחס בן משה
Dedicated by יוסף פיינבערג

◆Verbal Remembrance

A method through which one can motivate oneself to avoid the sin of *loshon hora* and its bitter punishment is alluded to in the juxtaposition of two verses in the Torah:

> *Beware of a tzaraas affliction, to be very careful and to act; according to everything that the Kohanim, the Levi'im shall teach you, as I have commanded them, you shall be careful to perform (Devarim 24:8).*[1]
> *Remember what HASHEM, your God, did to Miriam on the way, when you were leaving Egypt (ibid. v. 9).*[2]

Sifre expounds: " 'Remember what HASHEM, your God, did to Miriam ...' This cannot mean to remember in one's heart, for the [previous] verse, 'Beware of a *tzaraas* affliction ...' already teaches this sort of remembrance [for, as *Sifre* expounds, this verse instructs us to always beware of the sin of *loshon hora*, for which *tzaraas* is a punishment]. What, then, does 'Remember' imply? That we remind ourselves of this [Miriam's punishment] verbally."

Regarding the positive commandments, the Torah states: "...that you may ... remember all the commandments of HASHEM and perform them" (*Bamidbar* 15:39). In the same way, verbal remembrance of the severity of *loshon hora* is a prime way of avoiding its transgression.

One may wonder: How is it that people recite the verse, "Remember what HASHEM, your God, did to Miriam on the way, when you were leaving Egypt," each morning, and yet they speak *loshon hora*? Moreover, there are individuals who commit this sin *immediately* after reciting this verse!

(Continued on page 411)

---

1. This verse prohibits any attempt to cut away the physical symptoms of *tzaraas*.
2. This verse is expounded upon at length in Days 45-47.

❧*Upon Request*

As with any Torah prohibition, one may not speak *rechilus* even when he was asked to do so by someone who will be upset by his refusal to comply and has the power to do him damage. One must be prepared to suffer embarrassment, jeopardize his social status, or even lose his job in order to avoid speaking *rechilus*.[201]

As with other forms of forbidden speech, one may not speak *rechilus* upon the request of a parent, teacher, or *rav*, except when it is necessary *l'toeles*, for a constructive purpose (see below).[202]

When one has a tendency toward a particular form of negative behavior, he must determine its root cause and eradicate it.

✒Root Causes

Verbal remembrance of Miriam's affliction will inspire a person to refrain from *loshon hora* only if he is not in the habit of transgressing this bitter sin. However, one who has developed such a habit, and thus finds it difficult to refrain from speaking and listening to forbidden talk, must deal with his spiritual malady as he would treat a physical one. To cure a physical condition, one must determine the condition's source and then administer the appropriate medication. Similarly, when one is afflicted with a penchant for a particular form of negative behavior, he must determine its root cause and eradicate it.

The root causes of *loshon hora* are alluded to in the words כל גיהנם (lit., *All Gehinnom*). These words are an acronym for: כעס, *anger*; ליצנות, *scoffing*; גאוה; *arrogance*; יאוש, *despair*; הפקר, *without rule or regulation*;[1] נרגנות, *negativity*; and אומר מותר, *saying it is permissible*. We shall elaborate upon each of these traits.

There are those whose frequent transgression of the laws of forbidden speech is rooted in the trait of anger. These people are by nature quick-tempered, and their anger flares at the slightest provocation. In a fit of anger, they find it impossible to control their tongues, speaking whatever comes to mind. There is no hope for such people to develop the quality of *shmiras haloshon* unless they learn to overcome their tendency toward anger.

---

1. Lit., *ownerless*.

יא שבט
II SHEVAT / CYCLE I

יב אב
12 AV / CYCLE 2

SEFER CHOFETZ CHAIM
The Many Forms of Gossip

✍*For the Sake of Peace*

There are situations where refusal to answer a question would itself be a transgression of the prohibition against speaking *rechilus*. When, for example, one is asked whether or not a certain individual was the guilty party in a certain incident, remaining silent is no less revealing than an explicit "yes." Here, *halachah* requires one to conceal the facts, and simply say "no."[203]

The obvious question is: Why is lying preferable to speaking *rechilus* when both are prohibited by the Torah? To answer this, we must gain a better understanding of the commandment מדבר שקר תרחק, *Distance yourself from falsehood* (*Shemos* 23:7).

The Talmud (*Shevuos* 31a) notes that rather than command us, "Do not lie," the Torah instructs us to distance ourselves from "falsehood." In determining whether or not a given statement is "falsehood," one must examine its end result more than its technical accuracy. A "little white lie," for example, which is technically correct but intentionally misleading, is falsehood.

Maharal explains that the Torah views personal animosity as a form of falsehood. This attitude is clearly expressed by the Sages' classic term for animosity: *sinas chinam*, baseless hatred.

(Continued on page 412)

> **One should flee the trait of anger like one would flee a fire.**

II Shevat · Burech Mechl Wieder   לע"נ ר' ברוך יחיאל בן ר' שמואל ז"ל
Dedicated by his children
12 Av · Leigh Zulberg   לע"נ לאה בת יוסף הכהן
Dedicated by Allan & Linda Zulberg, Johannesburg, South Africa

DAY 130

≈Like from a Fire

Anyone of even minimal intelligence should understand that one should flee the trait of anger like one would flee a fire. He should realize that without a doubt a tendency toward anger will ensure his condemnation on the Day of Judgment when he departs this world.

One whose sins exceed his merits is deemed a *rasha,* wicked person, and as our Sages state, "Whoever is given to anger surely has more sins than merits, as it is written (*Mishlei* 29:22), 'And the master of anger has much sin (פשע)' " (*Nedarim* 22b). In Scripture, the term פשע, *sin,* denotes willful sin with the intention of rebelling against and angering God. The term is used here regarding the man of anger, because in the heat of rage one has total disregard for Torah and *mitzvos.* Thus do the Sages state, "Whoever is given to anger has no regard even for the Divine Presence" (ibid.); and, "Whoever rips his clothing, smashes his vessels or disperses his money in a fit of rage should be in your eyes like an idol worshiper ... Which verse alludes to this? 'There shall be no strange god within you' (*Tehillim* 81:10). Which 'strange god' is *within* the body of man? The evil trait of anger" (*Shabbos* 105b).

יב שבט
12 SHEVAT / CYCLE 1

יג אב
13 AV / CYCLE 2

SEFER CHOFETZ CHAIM
Avak Rechilus

❧*Definition*

One who does not exercise proper caution in matters of speech may find himself inadvertently fanning the flames of hatred. It is forbidden to mention an incident or other piece of information which might remind the listener of a situation where he was wronged by someone. To relate such information is to speak *avak* (lit., the dust of) *rechilus.* The speaker transgresses even though he has no intent of causing the listener to recall the wrongdoings; the Sages hold the speaker responsible for not having exercised proper caution in mentioning that which might reawaken ill feelings.[206]

By gauging an individual's anger, one can determine what sort of person he is.

~Choose Your Company

Scripture states: "Withdraw yourselves from the man whose life's breath is in his nostrils, for with what is he deemed worthy?" (*Yeshayahu* 2:22). *Zohar* comments (*Parashas Tetzaveh*):

> With these words, the Holy One, Blessed is He, commands and cautions man to guard himself from those who have turned away from the path of good to that of evil, who have contaminated their souls ... And how is man to know whose company he should seek and whose he should avoid? By gauging an individual's anger, one can determine what sort of person he is. If when anger comes upon a person, he guards the sanctity of his soul and does not allow it to be uprooted and replaced by that "foreign god" [that is anger], then he is a person whom it is fit to be near. However, if he does not guard the sanctity of his soul, allowing it to become uprooted so that the "other side" can dwell in its place, surely he is a person who rebels against his Master, and it is forbidden to seek his company ... He is the person who "tears apart his soul in his anger" (*Iyov* 18:4); he tears apart and uproots his soul because of his anger, and allows a foreign god to dwell within himself.
>
> Regarding such a person it is written, "Withdraw yourselves from the man whose life's breath is באפו [lit., *in his nostrils*]," [meaning,] whose sacred soul is torn apart and contaminated באפו, *by his anger* ..[1]

Thus, it is imperative that one rid his heart of anger so that he will be saved from *Gehinnom* and will merit entry into the World to Come.

---

1. In Scripture, the term חרון אף denotes outwardly displayed, flared-up anger. The expression metaphorically refers to *flaming nostrils* (see *Rashi* to *Shemos* 15:8).

יג שבט
13 SHEVAT / CYCLE 1

יד אב
14 AV / CYCLE 2

SEFER CHOFETZ CHAIM
Avak Rechilus

❧Rechilus When Attempting to Avoid Rechilus

It is forbidden to tell someone, "I'd rather not tell you what so-and-so said about you," for this is implying that "so-and-so" said something negative about the listener. If the speaker honestly — though naively — intended to avoid speaking *rechilus,* he violated only the rabbinical prohibition of *avak rechilus.* However, if the implication was intentional, then the remark is classified as outright *rechilus* and he has transgressed the Scriptural prohibition.[207]

Scoffers are one of four groups that will not merit to greet the Divine Presence.

לע"נ מרת פעסל בת ר' שלום · 13 Shevat
Dedicated by the Kasten family, Brooklyn, NY
14 Av · Rabbi Shmuel Steinhart לע"נ שמוא־ל בן משה הלוי
Dedicated by Yocheved, Rochel and Rivky Steinhart, Philadelphia, PA

✒Scoffing

O ne of the root causes of *loshon hora* is ליצנות, *scoffing*. Some people are accustomed to scoffing at anything, and attach themselves to people who are of their own kind. It is natural for such people to scoff at others who are outside their circle and to speak degradingly of them. Therefore, one who seeks to cleanse his soul should ponder the terrible sin of such behavior.

Our Sages teach that scoffers are one of four groups that will not merit to greet the Divine Presence (*Sotah* 42a). In addition to his own sins, a scoffer is guilty of causing others to join him in his ridicule. It is well known that to cause others to sin is an extremely grave offense, and prevents the perpetrator from being granted Heavenly assistance to repent (*Avos* 5:18).

Aside from all of the above, to idle one's time away, even not in a sinful way, is to waste precious time that could be used for studying Torah and accruing reward for the World to Come. According to one Talmudic opinion, the verse "... for he scorned the word of HASHEM" (*Bamidbar* 15:31) applies to one who squanders the opportunity to study Torah.

How ashamed, then, should one be to have spent hour upon hour in the company of scoffers! Moreover, were they to restrain themselves from speaking the forbidden, they would thereby merit eternal life, for, as the *Midrash* states, for each moment that a person refrains from speaking the forbidden, he merits a hidden light that no angel can fathom.

SEFER CHOFETZ CHAIM

Avak Rechilus

✒ *Praise*

When sincerely praising an individual's generosity in the presence of others, one should not do so in a way that may cause his family or business partner to be upset with him for having been charitable at their expense. Acknowledging a major donation in the presence of the donor's spouse or offspring may arouse feelings on his or her part that the family's money is being mishandled. If the recipient had good intentions only, he would be guilty of speaking *avak rechilus.*[208]

"Praise-worthy is the man ... that sat not in the company of scoffers."

14 Shevat · The Manchester Rosh Yeshiva לע״נ הגאון הצדיק הרב
יהודא זאב בן הגאון הצדיק הרב משה יצחק הלוי סג״ל זצוק״ל
Dedicated by Shlomey and Nomi Klor, London, England
15 Av · Chaim Rosenthal לע״נ ר׳ חיים משה בן החבר ר׳ יונתן רוזנטל ז״ל
Dedicated by his family, Gateshead/London, England

✑Loser of Two Worlds

A ליץ, *scoffer,* is liable to suffer retribution in this world for his sinful behavior. As the Talmud states (*Avodah Zara* 18b): "Whoever scoffs will have affliction visited upon him, as it is written, 'And now, do not scoff, lest your retribution intensify' (*Yeshayahu* 28:22). Said Rava to the rabbis, 'I ask you not to engage in scoffing, so that affliction not come upon you.' " The Talmud further states (ibid.) that scoffing causes one to be denied his material needs.

Scoffers bring punishment upon the entire world, as the Talmud (ibid.) states, "Whoever scoffs brings about destruction in the world." It is forbidden even to sit in the company of scoffers, as it is written, "Praiseworthy is the man ... that sat not in the company of scoffers" (*Tehillim* 1:1).

The Vilna Gaon writes in his famous letter:

> To the verse, "All man's toil is for his mouth" (*Koheles* 6:7), the Sages comment (*Midrash Koheles* ibid.) that all the *mitzvos* and Torah study of a person are not sufficient to negate that which he utters [sinfully] with his mouth. They further state: "Which craft should man pursue in this world? He should strive to emulate a mute [and avoid evil talk] (*Chullin* 89a), and press his lips together like two millstones [which grind against one another].

Therefore, one must distance oneself from scoffers so that he will not learn from their ways; rather, he should sit where Torah is being spoken. Praiseworthy will he be, in this world and in the World to Come.

טו שבט
15 SHEVAT / CYCLE 1

טז אב
16 AV / CYCLE 2

SEFER CHOFETZ CHAIM

Avak Rechilus

❧Seeking Assistance

When seeking a person's assistance, be it financial or otherwise, one may not mention that he knows of others who received similar assistance from this individual — unless the individual is known to appreciate the publicizing of that fact.

This rule is based on the concern that a person may not want his charitable acts to become public knowledge, as this could bring about an endless barrage of requests for his assistance. By mentioning his having made a contribution to a certain person, one reveals that the recipient shared the information with others — which may cause the donor to be upset with that recipient.

When reference to the recipient is made to bolster one's own request and not to cause animosity, it is categorized as *avak rechilus.*[209]

When a person persists in seeking fame for himself, the opposite occurs.

לע"נ פריידא בת ר' יצחק אייזק · 15 Shevat
Dedicated by Yosi & Chavi Salgo
16 Av · Matis Zelman לע"נ מתתיהו ע"ה בן משולם זישא הלוי יבל"ח
Dedicated in loving memory by his entire משפחה

DAY 134

❧Arrogance

A mong the root causes of *loshon hora* is גאוה, *arrogance*. The arrogant person views himself as a man of wisdom and stature, and he looks down upon everyone else. It is therefore only natural that he will ridicule others. The arrogant person is also filled with jealousy and enmity toward anyone in his community who is accorded greater honor than he. He tells himself, "Were it not for him, *I* would be the recipient of all that honor!" This attitude brings him to delve into the other person's history until he finds something derogatory to say about him, be it true or false, so that he can heap scorn and shame upon that individual and lower his stature among people.

The Talmud states (*Sotah* 42b) that four groups will not merit to greet the Divine Presence: חנפים, *flatterers;* שקרנים, *liars;* מספרי לשון הרע, *[habitual] speakers of loshon hora;* and לצנים, *scoffers.*[1] Arrogance can cause a person to belong to all of the above groups. He will speak disparagingly of his fellow so that the person will be shamed while he will be honored; he will scorn and mock him; he will falsely boast of personal qualities which he does not possess; and he will flatter the wicked and refrain from reproving them, so that they will not hate him and seek to diminish his honor.

Therefore, one who wishes to purify his soul of arrogance should forever ponder the shamefulness of this bitter sin. How can man be arrogant when he was created from a putrid drop and will ultimately go to a place of dust, worms and maggots?[2] One should also ponder the severity of this sin, which is one of the 365 negative commandments,[3] as it is written, "... and your heart will become haughty, and you will forget HASHEM, your God" (*Devarim* 8:14); and "Take care, lest you forget HASHEM, your God" (ibid. v. 11).

When a person persists in seeking fame for himself, the opposite occurs. His reputation gradually becomes diminished and he becomes an object of disgrace in the eyes of others.

---

1. The Chofetz Chaim notes that the word חשמל (a type of angel) is an acronym for these four groups.
2. See *Avos* 3:1.
3. See *S'mag* 64.

טז שבט
16 SHEVAT / CYCLE 1

יז אב
17 AV / CYCLE 2

SEFER CHOFETZ CHAIM
Avak Rechilus

❧Sensitivities

To cause outright animosity between Jews is to speak *rechilus*; to effect a minor degree of ill feeling between Jews is to speak *avak rechilus*. An example of the latter is where one relates that someone spoke about the listener in a manner which is neither derogatory nor harmful, but which may cause the listener to be disappointed with that individual. The classic example of this is where Hashem spoke critically to Avraham of Sarah for her having expressed incredulity upon hearing an angel (disguised as a wayfarer) say that she would bear a child. Hashem said, "Why did Sarah laugh, to say, 'Shall I in truth bear a child, though I have aged?' " (*Bereishis* 18:13). In fact, Sarah had said, "And my husband is old." (V.12). *Talmud Yerushalmi* (*Pe'ah* 1:1) states that to repeat such a statement would be to speak *avak rechilus*. Now, to say that a man of ninety-nine is old is neither derogatory nor damaging. However, it is a bit discomforting for a person of advanced age to hear that his spouse speaks of him as "an old man"; therefore, to report such a remark is to speak *avak rechilus*.[210]

Instead of pondering the fact that he will ultimately lie in the earth, the arrogant person acts as if he will enjoy prominence forever.

16 Shevat · Rabbi Eliyahu Shapiro לע"נ ר' אליהו בן שמואל הכהן ז"ל
Dedicated by his son Shmuel Shapiro & family
17 Av · Mr. Ephraim Sorkin לע"נ אפרים בן ר' חיים זעליג
Dedicated by the Sorkin family, Brooklyn, NY

ᕦMore Points To Ponder

One should ponder the severe retribution, both in this world and the next, which is liable to result from arrogance. The Talmud states that arrogance causes one's properties to become ruined (*Succah* 29b) and one's resources to become depleted (*Sotah* 5a). The Sages further state (ibid.) that regarding an arrogant person, Hashem says, "He and I cannot dwell together in the world." Rabbi Elazar said: "Whoever is arrogant will not awaken at the time of the Resurrection" (ibid.). This last punishment is measure for measure. Instead of pondering the fact that he will ultimately be laid to rest in the earth, the arrogant person acts as if he will enjoy prominence forever, living a life of stature in which he will always be a notch above everyone else. Because of his sinful attitude, when his body will become part of the dust of the earth, it will lack the power to come back to life. When everyone else will return to life, he will remain asleep, underneath the feet of the people above whom he had glorified himself.

Furthermore, arrogance makes one repulsive before Hashem, as it is written, "Despicable to HASHEM are all who are arrogant of heart" (*Mishlei* 16:5).

ין שבט
17 SHEVAT / CYCLE 1

יח אב
18 AV / CYCLE 2

SEFER CHOFETZ CHAIM
Avak Rechilus

❧Secrets

The most severe form of *avak rechilus* involves statements that reveal information which one was told in confidence. (Sharing confidential information to save someone from harm will be discussed later.) Divulging secrets breeds a lack of self control in speech-related matters which leads to actual *rechilus*.[212]

When publicizing a secret could prove damaging, doing so would constitute speaking both *avak rechilus* and actual *loshon hora*. Even when no damage was foreseen, the mere violation of confidentiality renders one a הולך רכיל, *gossipmonger*.[211]

Upon honest reflection one will realize that he has utilized only a fraction of the potential with which he has been Divinely endowed.

לע״נ חי׳ ראדה בת הרהח׳ חיים · 17 Shevat
18 Av · May today's learning be a זכות for our משפחה
Dedicated by Yehuda Levine & family

DAY
136

✒ *Lost Opportunities*

When one ponders his great poverty in Torah study and performance of other *mitzvos,* he realizes that he has nothing to be arrogant about. As the Sages put it, "If you lack knowledge, then what have you acquired?" (*Bereishis Rabbah* 1:6). And if one does have a bit of Torah and *mitzvos* to his credit, nevertheless, honest reflection will result in the realization that he has utilized only a fraction of the potential with which he has been Divinely endowed.

This last point is illustrated by the following parable:[1]

A businessman sent two of his employees, David and Yaakov, to a faraway land to buy precious gems. To David, the businessman gave one thousand gold coins; to Yaakov, he gave one hundred. On the way, the two squandered much of their money on worthless merchandise. By the time they arrived at their destination, David had two hundred coins remaining, while Yaakov was left with forty.

One day the two became embroiled in a dispute. In his rage, David shouted, "You are but a pauper compared to me, for I possess five times the amount of money that you have!"

An outsider who had been listening to the argument spoke up, "What are you boasting about, you fool?! Everyone knows that the money which you have with you is not your own. In fact, you are far poorer than Yaakov. Both of you have squandered away your employer's money. However, you have wasted eight hundred coins, while Yaakov wasted only sixty. What will you do when your employer will demand an accounting of all the money he gave you? You will find yourself burdened with an enormous debt and will be filled with shame — far more shame than the man to whom you are boasting!"

(Continued on page 412)

---

1. Cited in the preface to *Zichru Toras Moshe* by Rabbi Avraham Danzig.

יח שבט
18 SHEVAT / CYCLE 1

יט אב
19 AV / CYCLE 2

❧*Constructive Speech*

As in the case of *loshon hora*, the prohibition of *rechilus* involves meaningless or destructive gossip only. Reporting to a person concerning what someone else said or did against him *l'toeles*, for a constructive purpose, is not considered speaking *rechilus* and may, in fact, be considered a *mitzvah*.

However, a clear understanding of the conditions which make such reporting permissible, complemented by a generous dose of objectivity, are absolute prerequisites for conveying such information.

Hashem does not make excessive demands of His creations.

18 Shevat · May today's learning be a זכות for Yitzchok Meir Goldstein, Yerushalayim
19 Av · May today's learning be a זכות for Shmuel Borger and his family

DAY
137

✒️*Despair*

A nother primary reason why people speak *loshon hora* is יאוש, *de-spair*, meaning that they despair of being able to live by the Torah's laws of proper speech. There are those who convince themselves that anyone who interacts with others in normal business and social relations cannot possibly live by these laws. To support this contention, they cite the Talmudic statement that "everyone is guilty of *loshon hora*" (*Bava Basra* 165a). Of course, they are grossly mistaken.

It is a known axiom of Jewish belief that Hashem does not make excessive demands of His creations. If the Torah places a certain obligation upon us, then surely its fulfillment is within our reach. Would adherence to the laws of *shmiras haloshon* be an inordinately difficult achievement, then it would be optional, a matter for the exceedingly righteous who strive to perfect themselves in ways that others never attempt. In fact, to refrain from speaking *loshon hora* is required by the Torah, and involves numerous commandments. Obviously, the Creator has endowed every Jewish soul with the ability to observe these laws.

"A God of faith without iniquity" (*Devarim* 32:4) — God created man to be righteous, not wicked (*Sifre* ad loc.). This means that Hashem endowed each Jew with the ability to observe all of His commandments, for if not, it would be unfair to hold him accountable for their transgression.

יט שבט
19 SHEVAT / CYCLE 1

כ אב
20 AV / CYCLE 2

SEFER CHOFETZ CHAIM
Laws of Toeles

◆Constructive Intent

People who speak *rechilus* usually have some motive in mind which they consider a positive one. The Torah's view, however, is that unless the motive is clearly constructive, the speaker is doing nothing more than gossipmongering and his words are strictly forbidden.

The most common constructive motive that would permit relating such information is to forewarn a person of someone else's intent to harm him so that the person can protect himself;[213] to inform a person that someone is *presently* harming him, so that he can put an end to the situation; or to tell a person that someone *has already* harmed him, so that he can seek restitution for the damage (if it is monetary) or at least prevent any further damage.

Hashem has given man the ability to subdue his evil inclination.

לכבוד משפחת זליחובסקי · 19 Shevat
Dedicated by Levi Yitzchok & Rivkie Zelishovsky
לע"נ דוב בער בן חיים פנחס ז"ל · 20 Av
Dedicated by משפחת קורלענדער, New York & Cleveland

DAY
138

✤In Man's Hands

God has made man upright, but they sought many intrigues (Koheles 7:29).

The Holy One, Blessed is He, Who is upright and righteous, created man in His image so that he too would be upright and righteous. One may ask: If so, then why did God create the evil inclination, as it is written, "The imagery of man's heart is evil from his youth" (Bereishis 8:21)? If God Himself refers to this inclination as "evil," then who can possibly transform it into something good?

God responds: "It is you who has made it evil! As a child, you did not sin — it is when you matured that you sinned! There are many items in this world more rigid and bitter than the evil inclination, yet you make them sweet. There is nothing more bitter then *turmusin,* yet you diligently cook it seven times until it turns sweet ... surely then, you can do the same with the evil inclination that is given over into your hands" (Midrash Tanchuma, Bereishis 7).

The intent of the above *Midrash* is clear. Hashem has given man the ability to subdue his evil inclination, so that it can be utilized in accomplishing his spiritual goals, as it is written, "... yet you can conquer it [the evil inclination]" (Bereishis 4:7). It is man alone, through his ways and deeds, who determines who will be the victor in this crucial struggle.

כ שבט
20 SHEVAT / CYCLE 1

כא אב
21 AV / CYCLE 2

SEFER CHOFETZ CHAIM
Laws of Toeles

✎Nothing to be Gained

In a situation where a person has been caused damage, it is forbidden to inform him of the perpetrator's identity unless there is a reasonable chance that this will serve a constructive purpose. The fact that one personally observed an improper act does not automatically justify informing the victim. If restitution seems unlikely and there is no possibility that the victim will unsuspectingly be vulnerable to further harm, nothing positive will be accomplished by telling the victim who was responsible; to reveal the perpetrator's identity is to speak *rechilus.*

Any Jew can acquire the golden quality of shmiras haloshon.

20 Shevat · Yankel Zimmer לע״נ אברהם יעקב בן אהרן אליעזר ע״ה
Dedicated by Mrs. Marilyn Zimmer and family
21 Av · Mr. Franklin D. Hettinger לע״נ אברהם בן פרנקל
Dedicated by the Hettinger family

DAY
139

✍*Within Everyone's Reach*

A ny Jew who reflects upon his ways regularly, and resolves to scrupulously refrain from speaking the forbidden, will surely succeed in attaining the quality of *shmiras haloshon*. As our Sages teach, one who seeks to purify himself is granted Heavenly assistance (*Shabbos* 104a). They further state that if a person sincerely strives to be a *tzaddik* (righteous individual), then Hashem will assign him an angel who will treat him as a *tzaddik*; and if he will sincerely strive to be a *chassid* (exceedingly righteous individual), then Hashem will assign him an angel who will treat him as a *chassid* (*Tanna D'vei Eliyahu Zuta* ch. 3).

The Talmud qualifies the statement, "Everyone is [guilty of speaking] *loshon hora*" (*Bava Basra* 165a) by saying that this refers not to actual *loshon hora*, but to *avak loshon hara*[1]; that is, statements which can lead to *loshon hora* being spoken or from which negative information can be inferred.[2] Moreover, *Maharsha* (ibid.) comments that "everyone" refers only to a person who is not careful in matters of speech, and speaks whatever comes to mind. Such a person will surely be guilty of speaking *avak loshon hora*. The Sages did not, Heaven forfend, mean that it is impossible for *anyone* to be free of this sin. With knowledge of the relevant laws and proper zealousness, any Jew can acquire the golden quality of *shmiras haloshon*.

---

1. Lit., *the dust of loshon hora;* see Laws, Day 33.
2. As an example, it is forbidden to praise someone in the presence of his enemies, as his enemies will probably respond by voicing their criticism of him.

כא שבט
21 SHEVAT / CYCLE 1

כב אב
22 AV / CYCLE 2

SEFER CHOFETZ CHAIM
TOELES: Seven Conditions

✍*Fact or Hearsay*

For a statement to be excluded from the realm of *rechilus* and be classified instead as constructive, several conditions are necessary.

Condition #1:

Most important is that one ascertain that the information is fully accurate. This involves both verification of facts as well as a clear understanding of the situation (as was discussed regarding conveying negative information for a constructive purpose). [216]

The commandment לא תעמד על דם רעך, *Do not stand aside while your fellow's blood is being shed* (*Vayikra* 19:16), obligates us to report constructive information if our knowledge of it is firsthand.[217] Should one choose to speak of an alleged occurrence that he did not personally witness in order to save his fellow Jew from possible harm, it must be clearly stated that the information is based on hearsay and is not to be accepted as fact.[218]

Who is a greater healer of the spirit than King David?

21 Shevat · Allen Kane לע"נ אברהם יצחק בן חיים מעכל ז"ל
מאת מיכאל נתן בן גרשון
22 Av · Mr. Alex Schmookler לע"נ ר' אליקים בן ר' ישראל הכהן
Dedicated by his wife and children, New York

❧*Without Rule or Regulation*

A primary cause of speaking *loshon hora* is that people consider matters of speech as הפקר, *without rule or regulation*. Tragically, many do not even consider speaking *loshon hora* a sin. Such blatant disregard for this severe prohibition weakens the resolve of those who might otherwise be cautious with their words.

The following parable is a fitting response to the above situation:

A sizable portion of a city's inhabitants contracted a dreaded disease. All the city's doctors despaired of curing the stricken. One day, a world-renowned physician appeared who was known for his ability to restore the seriously ill to their original health. The illness that had swept through the city was viewed as incurable, and thus many doubted that even this doctor could save them. One sick man, however, hurried to the doctor's lodgings at the first opportunity. "Where are you rushing?" one of his friends asked. "No one else seems to be in a hurry to see this doctor."

"Foolish man," the patient replied. "A wise person understands that when one's life is at stake, even the most remote possibility of a cure must be pursued. In this case, the possibility is not at all remote. This doctor has earned himself a reputation as being able to heal when no one else can. He has cured people who were at death's door. Should I neglect to seek his expertise because so many fools ignore this opportunity for salvation?"

If the above argument is true regarding physical health, how much more so does it apply regarding spiritual health. King David declared, "Go, O sons, heed me ... Which man desires life, who loves days of seeing good? Guard your tongue from evil, and your lips from speaking deceit" (*Tehillim* 34:12-14). Who is a greater healer of the spirit than King David, of blessed memory? One who ignores David's advice will remain spiritually ill eternally, and will suffer retribution in this world as well, as explained above. Surely, then, one should pay no heed to those who make light of this most severe sin.

כב שבט
22 SHEVAT / CYCLE 1

כג אב
23 AV / CYCLE 2

SEFER CHOFETZ CHAIM

TOELES: Seven Conditions

✦*Thorough Understanding*

Condition #2:

Even when one has personally witnessed a situation, he must avoid hastily concluding that one party has harmed, or is about to harm, another. Often, it is impossible to fully understand the attitude and behavior of one person towards another without a thorough knowledge of their relationship until this point. What appears to be a sinister plot might actually be a plan of self defense. Exposing the "plotter" in such a case might leave the real victim vulnerable and defenseless.

Some people are wont to complain and find fault at every opportunity.

22 Shevat · The Manchester Rosh Yeshiva לע״נ הגאון הצדיק הרב
יהודא זאב בן הגאון הצדיק הרב משה יצחק הלוי סג״ל זצוק״ל
Dedicated by his children and grandchildren
Batya Zakheim Brecher לע״נ בתיה רחל בת משה יוסף
Dedicated by her parents Moish & Venezia Zakheim
23 Av · Dr. Yitzchok Golfeiz לע״נ אבינו יצחק בן אג׳א צאלח ז״ל
Dedicated by the Golfeiz family, Baltimore, MD

DAY 141

⚖Negativity

Yet another primary cause of speaking *loshon hora* is נרגנות, *neg-ativity*, as it is written, ותרגנו באהליכם ותאמרו,בשנאת ה' אתנו הוציאנו..., *And you spoke very negatively in your tents and said, "Because of Hashem's hatred for us did He take us out of [the land of Egypt]* (*Devarim* 1:27). There are people who are wont to complain and find fault at every opportunity, to criticize the ways and words of their fellow even when, in fact, he acts toward others with sincerity and has not caused them the slightest bit of harm. Such people never give others the benefit of the doubt; they assume every unintentional wrong to be deliberate, and are certain that it was done with malice. Whoever is afflicted with this terrible trait will speak *loshon hora* regularly, for he will view whatever others say or do as intended against himself.

One who seeks to rid himself of this destructive trait should contemplate its various ill effects; through such reflection, he will ultimately succeed in viewing others in a favorable light.

כג שבט
23 SHEVAT / CYCLE I

כד אב
24 AV / CYCLE 2

SEFER CHOFETZ CHAIM

TOELES: Seven Conditions

⚭*Real or Fantasy*

What may appear to be a plot-in-the-making, that should be exposed before it materializes, may sometimes be nothing more than meaningless talk. If one overhears others plotting to harm someone, he may not inform the potential victim unless there is sound basis for assuming that the plotters are serious.

Occasionally, people deal with anger and frustration by fantasizing, plotting and threatening with no real intent of translating their words into action. In such situations, the well-meaning bystander who conveys information is guilty of speaking *loshon hora, rechilus* and *hotzaas shem ra* (slander).[219]

Baseless hatred was the sin which brought about the destruction of the Second Temple.

23 Shevat · Mrs. Celia Kurzman לע״נ טשרנא בת צבי
Dedicated by her grandchildren & great-grandchildren, the Kopolovics family
24 Av · In appreciation of all those who support the program
Dedicated by Shmiras Haloshon, South Africa

DAY 142

✎Sin Breeds Sin

A s mentioned above, the way to rid oneself of נרגנות, *negativity*, is to ponder its ill effects:

Such an attitude makes it impossible to fulfill the commandment "You shall love your neighbor as yourself" (*Vayikra* 19:18). Usually this trait leads to *sinas chinam,* baseless hatred, which is a transgression of the commandment "You shall not hate your brother in your heart" (ibid. v. 17). Baseless hatred was the sin which brought about the destruction of the Second Temple (*Yoma* 32b). Moreover, the Talmud states that because of baseless hatred, strife abounds in one's home and tragedies may befall him (*Shabbos* 32b).

This trait also leads to transgression of "With righteousness you shall judge your fellow" (*Vayikra* 19:15), which our Sages understand as a requirement to grant one's fellow the benefit of the doubt (*Sanhedrin* 34b). *Sefer Chareidim* (66:39) writes that one who judges his fellow critically becomes attached to one of the spiritual forces of impurity.

Judging others hypercritically causes one to suspect the innocent of wrongdoing. Our Sages teach: "One who suspects the innocent is afflicted physically" (*Shabbos* 97a). Inevitably, he will also transgress the sins of causing hurt through words, embarrassing one's fellow, and causing strife — whose punishment is particularly severe.[1]

Thus, one who seeks a life that is good, both in this world and the next, should distance himself from this terrible trait.

---

1. See Days 70-74.

❧*When Rebuke is in Order*

Condition #3:

W e have seen that with regard to *loshon hora,* one may not speak negatively about someone for a constructive purpose without first discussing the matter with that person. An exception to this rule is a case where speaking to the person could prevent the desired result from being achieved (See Days 45, 72).

With regard to *rechilus,* the exception may be more common than the rule. When an individual has already harmed someone or is about to harm someone, one should not enter into a discussion with him concerning the matter if this could make it more difficult for the victim to protect himself or attain restitution.

In other situations of *rechilus*, *tochachah* (rebuke) toward the perpetrator is a prerequisite for relating *rechilus* for a constructive purpose. A discussion with the person could preclude the need to speak *rechilus* concerning him, and dispel suspicions regarding the speaker's true intentions. (Rebuke is further discussed in Days 152-153.)

Serious study of the relevant laws is the primary means for avoiding the sin of loshon hora.

---

24 Shevat · The Manchester Rosh Yeshiva הרב הצדיק הגאון לע"נ
יהודא זאב בן הגאון הצדיק הרב משה יצחק הלוי סג"ל זצוק"ל
הונצח על ידי תלמידיו דוב ובנימין שטראה ומשפחתם, לונדון, ענגלאנד
25 Av · Mrs. Betti Heyman פעסל בת יצחק ע"ה לע"נ

❧The Primary Deterrent

**DAY
143**

A mong the root causes of speaking *loshon hora* is אומר מותר, *one says it is permissible,* meaning that one convinces himself that a given statement is not *loshon hora* when in fact it is. Or he assures himself that it is permissible to disparage a certain individual — and that it may even be a *mitzvah* to do so! — when in fact such is not the case.

Most people who speak or listen to *loshon hora* do so out of ignorance of the relevant laws. Thus there is no alternative to studying these laws, as put forth in *Sefer Chofetz Chaim.* Every Jew must be fluent in the fine details of the laws of proper speech, in order to know exactly what may or may not be spoken, and so that one can perceive the far-reaching effects of negative speech.

Serious study of the relevant laws is the primary means for avoiding the sin of *loshon hora.* In fact, any time a person feels dominated by his evil inclination with regard to a specific sin, his best hope for improvement is through study of the laws of that particular commandment. He should study the relevant laws in great depth, in all their fine details, and ponder them many times. In this way, the laws will become embedded in his mind, and the strength of his evil inclination will dissipate. As the *Midrash* states (*Bamidbar Rabbah* 14:4): "If you toil exceedingly in their [the commandments'] words, then the Holy One, Blessed is He, will remove the evil inclination from you."

The above is alluded to in the verse, "... that you may see it [the *tzitzis*] and remember all the commandments of HASHEM and perform them" (*Bamidbar* 15:39). As *Rashi* comments, remembrance of the commandments leads to their performance.

כה שבט
25 SHEVAT / CYCLE 1

כו אב
26 AV / CYCLE 2

SEFER CHOFETZ CHAIM
TOELES: Seven Conditions

✎*Accuracy*

Condition #4:

As with *loshon hora,* one may not exaggerate *rechilus* even for a constructive purpose. If a person harmed, or is planning to harm, someone else and the victim must be informed, one may not give him an exaggerated account of what has transpired or is about to occur.[220] This applies even if the person being warned does not take the danger of the situation seriously.

Furthermore, one may relate only as much information as is necessary for the purpose to be accomplished. To relate any additional information would be a transgression of the prohibition of *rechilus.*[221]

Hashem has endowed man with sensitivity, especially with regard to matters of personal speech.

25 Shevat · Isador Hyman לע״נ יצחק בן יוסף
Dedicated by Eugene & Ida Haber
26 Av · לע״נ חיים יוסף בן שמואל שניצלער ומשפחתו הי״ד
הונצח על ידי בנו משה אליעזר וחנה פערל שניצלער וב״ב

DAY 144

✒ *Sensitivity in Speech*

Even if one has become so accustomed to speaking *loshon hora* and so overcome by his evil inclination that forbidden talk pours from his lips without his even realizing what he is saying, nevertheless, he should not despair. Through proper study and review of the relevant laws, a dramatic change for the better will occur. His very nature will change, and he will find himself carefully weighing his own words as he speaks. Even if he will speak but *avak loshon hora* (words which can lead to *loshon hara*[1]) he will take note of it, and will be careful not to repeat his mistake.

Hashem has endowed man with sensitivity, especially with regard to matters of personal speech. This ability is a great asset in the study of Torah, for when a student enunciates his thoughts, he can better perceive whether or not they are correct. As the Sages state, "For they [words of Torah] are life to those who express them with their mouths " (*Eruvin* 54a). This ability to discern is true regarding other areas of speech as well.

However, such sensitivity is exceedingly weakened through habitual involvement in idle conversation and according little thought to what one is saying. However, when one studies the laws of proper speech and, as a result, becomes cognizant of his own verbal expression, this sensitivity returns little by little, until it attains its original strength.

---

1. See Laws, Day 33.

כו שבט
26 SHEVAT / CYCLE 1

כז אב
27 AV / CYCLE 2

S E F E R   C H O F E T Z   C H A I M
TOELES: Seven Conditions

✎*Pure Intent*

Condition #5:

By commanding us, "Do not go as a gossipmon-ger among your people" (*Vayikra* 19:16), the Torah is teaching us that to derive pleasure from spreading gossip runs contrary to the mature, dignified character expected of a Jew. Thus, one who derives pleasure from spreading gossip has violated this commandment even when his report brings about a constructive result.

Relating what would otherwise be considered *rechilus* for a constructive purpose is permissible only if one's intent is *solely* to accomplish that purpose. Deriving satisfaction from being "involved in the action," or from aborting the plans of someone who is not well liked, is forbidden.

Nevertheless, improper motivation cannot free one of his obligation to impart information for a constructive purpose. The Torah demands that we develop a correct mind-frame and come to the aid of our fellow Jew out of sincere concern.[222]

Unless one is certain that a given statement is not in the category of forbidden speech, he should not utter it.

לע"נ פיגא בת יהודה לייב ע"ה
26 Shevat · Rosenthal
Dedicated by Rabbi Shlomo & Miriam Leider, Monsey, NY
לכבוד הרב יוסף קאלאצקי שליט"א ותלמידיו · 27 Av
כולל יד אברהם Yad Avraham Institute

✒A Cardinal Rule

Generally speaking, unless one is certain that a given statement is not in the category of forbidden speech, he should not utter it. Even if he is inclined to think that it is a *mitzvah* to utter the statement and that he will receive reward in the World to Come for it, nevertheless, he should refrain from doing so. In this way, he will be saved from Divine retribution.

For example, if in fact one was obligated to speak critically of a certain individual and did not do so out of uncertainty, he will be able to come before the Heavenly Court and say, "I was not sure whether or not I was permitted to criticize him to others; therefore I chose to remain silent." Conversely, if he will speak critically of the person when in fact this was wrong, or if he will mistakenly initiate a quarrel out of the conviction that it is a *mitzvah* to do so — how will he exonerate himself before the Heavenly Court? How will he excuse his having spoken the forbidden and having been the cause of strife? He will not be able to say that his uncertainty impelled him to speak, for if he was uncertain he should not have spoken.

כז שבט
27 SHEVAT / CYCLE 1

כח אב
28 AV / CYCLE 2

SEFER CHOFETZ CHAIM

TOELES: Seven Conditions

~Constructive Result

In Day 145, we learned that one may relate *rechilus* for a constructive purpose only if his intent is pure and unsullied by personal motivation. Indeed, constructive intent is what distinguishes a concerned, responsible individual from a *rachil,* gossipmonger.

However, proper intent alone is not sufficient to make such talk permissible. Unless there is a reasonable chance that the intended purpose will be accomplished, the speaker — though well-meaning — is guilty of gossipmongering.

Occasionally, one finds himself advising friends who are victims of physical or emotional abuse, whether in a family, social or work setting. At times, the victim has yet to grasp the severity of his problem, or does not realize who the responsible party is. Clarifying these matters for the person and advising him how to deal with the other party would appear to be a true act of kindness, a genuine *mitzvah.*

In many such situations, however, the victim lacks the courage to defend himself, and will do little or nothing to improve his lot. When dealing with such a person, it is forbidden to show him how someone else is causing him agony, as that would be purposeless gossip. Sad as it is, one may not make a person better aware of his own situation if he will not make constructive use of such clarification and advice.[223]

One should strive to uproot these deficiencies little by little and supplant them with traits that nurture interpersonal relationships.

**DAY
146**

~Curing the Malady

The above lends insight to the verse, "One who guards his mouth and tongue, guards his soul from tribulations" (*Mishlei* 21:23). Why does this verse stress the negative, that through *shmiras haloshon* one's soul is saved from retribution? Why does it not mention the infinite reward of one who avoids forbidden speech as stated in the well-known verse, "Which man desires life, who loves days ... guard your tongue from evil ..." (*Tehillim* 34:13)?

We may suggest that the first verse alludes to the necessity of guarding one's tongue at times when he feels that a derogatory remark *might* be in place and that its being uttered *might* even be a *mitzvah*. Scripture warns us that unless we are absolutely certain that such a remark is called for, we should not express it. Following this approach, we will "guard [our] soul from tribulations"; that is, from the Divine retribution that will be forthcoming if in fact the remark is unwarranted. Conversely, a person who will not exercise restraint in such situations will ultimately suffer punishment, instead of the reward he was anticipating for what he mistakenly considered a *mitzvah*.

This concludes our discussion of the primary factors in which speaking *loshon hora* is rooted: *anger, scoffing, arrogance, despair* [of abiding by the relevant laws], [considering speech] *without rule or regulation*, *negativity* and *saying that* [a given statement] *is permissible* [when, in fact, it is not]. One who has been accustomed to speaking *loshon hora* and seeks to cure himself of this severe malady should begin the process by searching within himself to discover which of the above-mentioned traits are at the root of his problem. He should strive to rid himself of these deficiencies little by little and supplant them with traits that nurture interpersonal relationships and discourage negative talk.

כח שבט
28 SHEVAT / CYCLE 1

כט אב
29 AV / CYCLE 2

SEFER CHOFETZ CHAIM

TOELES: Seven Conditions

✑Weighing the Options

Condition #6:

As with *loshon hora,* one may not relate *rechilus* for a constructive purpose if this purpose can be accomplished through other means (See Day 46).

Of course, easiest of all is the direct approach — informing the potential victim of what is being plotted and allowing him to fend for himself. The Torah, however, views this avenue as a last resort. If the option exists, one must protect the victim without his even suspecting that someone is attempting to harm him. (This option does not apply where it is important for the potential victim to be on guard should the other party attempt to harm him at a later point in time.)[224]

Obviously, there is a limit to how much effort one is required to invest in protecting his fellow Jew from harm when the person is fully capable of protecting himself. If, in order to avoid involving the potential victim, one would have to dedicate an unreasonable amount of time and energy, it would be permissible to inform the person so that he can protect himself.[225]

> *One who takes action against others for committing a sin, and later commits that very sin, is considered as if he had acted against innocent people.*

28 Shevat · Rabbi Isaac Kalman Sachs לע״נ הרב יצחק אייזיק קלמן
בן יעקב זאקס ז״ל
Dedicated by the Sachs and Ryp families, New York
29 Av · May today's learning be a זכות for בת אלישבע עטיא
מיכאל נתן שתחי׳

⮞Retroactive Guilt

One should ponder the fact that at the moment he speaks *loshon hora*, the Heavenly angels announce his own sins (*Roke'ach*, *Aggadas Mishlei* 11:27).

Riva (cited by *Semak* 283) states that if one kills someone who is attempting to commit a capital crime against his fellow (and, as such, should be killed if that is the only way to ensure that the crime will not be committed) and later is guilty of that very same offense, then retroactively, he is considered as if he had shed innocent blood. As proof, *Riva* cites the episode of King Yeihu who, in killing the members of King Achav's household, was fulfilling the Divine will as transmitted through prophecy. Yet because Yeihu too was guilty of a degree of idol worship — though his infractions did not approach the heinous acts of Achav — he was held responsible for murdering Achav's household, as it is written, "And I shall bring to account the blood of [Achav who was killed in] Yizrael upon the house of Yeihu" (*Hoshea* 1:4).

The same applies to any sin between man and his fellow. If one rightfully attacks someone physically (to prevent him from committing a crime), or embarrasses him (for his having publicly disgraced Hashem's Name), or speaks negatively about him (to prevent him from causing someone else harm), and has committed or later commits that very same offense, then he is considered as if he had acted or spoken against an innocent man. Consequently, he will be subject to Divine retribution as if he had acted or spoken against a Jew whose service of Hashem is wholesome and beyond reproach.

כט שבט
29 SHEVAT / CYCLE 1

ל אב
30 AV / CYCLE 2

SEFER CHOFETZ CHAIM
TOELES: Seven Conditions

❧No Revenge

Condition #7:

The final condition necessary to permit speaking what would otherwise be *rechilus* for a constructive purpose is that conveying the information does not cause undue harm to the subject. Constructive intent does not justify causing harm to another person.

Therefore, one cannot inform a person that someone else is about to harm him if the person will respond by harming the plotter. This applies not only to physical or financial retaliation, but even to retaliation in the form of *loshon hora* in a manner prohibited by *halachah*.[226]

The wicked rejoice over the failings of others and incite others to feud.

❧A Study in Contrasts

In summation: A Jew must strive to develop positive character traits, especially with regard to traits that have a major impact on interpersonal relationships. One must strive to assist his fellow to the best of his ability and overlook his fellow's faults just as he would want others to overlook his own faults. If one's friend has expressed his anger toward someone else, he should do his best to soothe that anger through reason and explanation — a demonstration of true wisdom and inner strength.

A wicked person behaves in the very opposite way. He seeks to damage others, to reveal their unintentional misdeeds and claim that they were committed willfully. The wicked person rejoices over another's failings, and incites others to feud. He prides himself over his success in such endeavors, as he considers this an indication of his wisdom and might — but of course he is wrong.

Midrash Shochar Tov (ch. 52) cites the episode of Doeg's treachery against David and Achimelech, the *Kohen Gadol* (High Priest). At a time when King Shaul was in pursuit of David and seeking to harm him, Doeg told Shaul that Achimelech had intentionally helped David to flee from Shaul, which was a lie. Doeg's slander brought about Achimelech's death (see *I Shmuel* chs. 21-22).

As the *Midrash* relates, David told Doeg, "Is a man truly mighty when he sees his fellow at the edge of a pit and pushes him in, when he sees his fellow on top of a roof and pushes him off? On the contrary, a man deserves to be called a mighty warrior when his fellow is about to fall into a pit and he grasps his hand to prevent his fall or when he lifts the fallen man from the pit. But when you saw that Shaul was angry at me, you persisted in vilifying me." Thus did David say, "Why do you pride yourself with evil, O mighty warrior?" (*Tehillim* 52:3).

SEFER CHOFETZ CHAIM

TOELES: A Contrast of Loshon Hora vs. Rechilus

~Rechilus and Loshon Hora

The conditions for a statement to be considered proper, constructive speech, rather than prohibited *rechilus,* are almost identical to those which permit communicating information that would otherwise be considered *loshon hora* (i.e. information that is derogatory or harmful). In fact, a study of the situations which permit *rechilus l'toeles* (for a constructive purpose) will reveal that virtually every case involves *loshon hora* as well.

As discussed above, among the reasons which permit speaking *rechilus* for a constructive purpose are the prevention or termination of harm, or gaining restitution for harm caused by the subject. Such statements invariably incriminate the subject, and are therefore *loshon hora.* Thus, for *rechilus* to be spoken for a constructive purpose, all conditions which permit speaking *loshon hora* for a constructive purpose must be met as well.

Conversely, not all motives that justify negative speech qualify as constructive purpose to permit speaking *rechilus.* While one may publicize the wrongdoings of an individual if social pressure could bring about a change in his behavior, one could not do so if the victim is as yet unaware of the individual's identity. The evils of causing animosity between victim and villain outweigh the possibility that social pressure will yield concrete constructive results.[227]

> *To rejoice over another's failures is to direct the Attribute of Judgment against oneself in a powerful way.*

30 Shevat · In honor of our esteemed משפיע Horav Shimon Winegarten שליט"א
Dedicated by Shmiras Haloshon Shiur and Mishmeres, Golders Green, England
1 Elul · לע"נ אבינו היקר מאיר בן דוב
Dedicated by his sons Mordechai Yehuda & Yisroel Yakov Amsel

DAY 149

↞*"When Your Enemy Falls ..."*

How careful must a Jew be not to rejoice over his fellow's downfall or disgrace! As Scripture states, "When your enemy falls be not glad, and when he stumbles, let your heart not be joyous. Lest HASHEM see it and it displease Him, and He will turn His wrath from him [to you]" (*Mishlei* 24:17). To rejoice over another's failures is to direct the Attribute of Judgment toward oneself in a powerful way. Moreover, this sin has the destructive power of idol worship. The Sages relate (*Midrash Eichah* 1:21) that at the time of the First Destruction the soul of the Patriarch Avraham entered the Temple ruins. "What is My beloved doing in My house?" asked Hashem. Responded Avraham, "Why have my descendants been cast into exile among the nations of the world?" Hashem answered, "Because they worship idols and rejoice over each other's downfall." Thus, Hashem equates these two sins.

One should forever reflect upon his own spiritual failings so that he will be reminded that he too is deserving of shame and scorn. It is the merits of his ancestors, coupled with other factors for which he can take no credit, that Hashem, in His mercy, spares him from shame. With this outlook, one will truly empathize with those who experience failure and disappointment in their personal lives.

SEFER CHOFETZ CHAIM

TOELES: A Contrast of Loshon Hora vs. Rechilus

❧Secondhand Information: A Distinction

We have seen (Day 140) that secondhand information which would ordinarily be considered *rechilus* may be communicated for a constructive purpose provided that it is not presented as fact. Regarding *loshon hora,* however, communicating secondhand information for a constructive purpose was prohibited in most cases (see Day 43).

The Chofetz Chaim explains that while achieving a positive result on the basis of firsthand information is justified even when the chances for success are minimal, secondhand information may be used only when one can assume that the intended result will almost certainly be achieved. Consequently, one may inform one party in a prospective *shidduch* (marriage match) or business partnership of possible major problems regarding the other party (See Day 83) on the basis of hearsay, since such information will probably be taken very seriously. For the same reason, one may warn a potential victim of impending danger on the basis of secondhand information. Conversely, one cannot publicize the alleged unethical behavior of an individual with the hope that social pressure will encourage him to change his ways or reimburse his victims; this would be permissible only when one was witness to such behavior. The effectiveness of social pressure in persuading people to change their ways is far too limited to justify relating secondhand negative information — even if it is clearly stated that the information has not been verified.[228]

> *An abudance of spiritual reward can be lost due to scorn, slander and strife.*

1 Adar · May today's learning be a זכות for Mr. Kurt Rothschild and family, Toronto, Canada
Dedicated by his children and grandchildren
2 Elul · May today's learning be a זכות for Chaim Boruch Goldstein and family, Passaic, NJ

☙Squandering One's Wealth

In the Book of *Mishlei* (Proverbs), we read, "There is one who is [apparently] rich, but [in truth] has nothing" (*Mishlei* 13:7). To understand this proverb, let us imagine that a person has made business investments which earned him huge profits. To everyone, including himself, the man seems on his way to achieving great wealth. Later, however, the man makes a thorough accounting of all his endeavors and discovers that, to his dismay, the losses of certain investments all but nullified the huge profits that other investments had earned for him. *There is one who is apparently rich, but in truth has nothing.*

The lesson is clear: A person can spend a lifetime accruing merit through the performance of *mitzvos* and the study of Torah. Yet he can come to the Next World and find that his merits have been nullified by his negative attitude towards others. The bounty of spiritual reward that had been awaiting him was washed away by the waves of scorn, slander and strife which poured forth from his lips.

ב אדר
2 ADAR / CYCLE 1

ג אלול
3 ELUL / CYCLE 2

SEFER CHOFETZ CHAIM

TOELES: A Contrast of Loshon Hora vs. Rechilus

◆Accuracy vs. Justification

O bviously, the requirement that one be certain of the accuracy of his information applies to all situations where *loshon hora* or *rechilus* is to be spoken for a constructive purpose. There is, however, an aspect of this requirement that does not apply in all cases.

We have seen (Days 52-54) that the Torah requires us to judge our fellow Jew favorably and refrain from concluding that he has sinned when an alternative way of explaining his behavior can be found. As noted, even when it is clear that the person has sinned, one must consider the possibility that this may have been the result of ignorance or unusual circumstances.

While the Torah does insist that we give people the benefit of the doubt, this should not be done at the expense of others. Consequently, if one has witnessed one person harming or attempting to harm another, the need for accuracy does not require an attempt at justifying the perpetrator's motives. Even if the act is out of character it must be rectified, and one may, therefore, inform the appropriate parties.[229]

Instead of planting seeds of spiritual attainment, his "field" had become overgrown with the "thorns" of idle chatter and fruitless endeavors.

2 Adar · Ezra Polen לע״נ עזרא בן הרב דוד שמעון
Dedicated by Shalom & Naomi Polen, Baltimore MD
3 Elul · Carrie Ann Kass לע״נ חיה חנה בת ר׳ חיים
Dedicated by the Pearl, Auman, & Whitman families, New York & Memphis

DAY 151

ᕽᐧ*Two Failures*

I passed by the field of a lazy man, and by the vineyard of a man devoid of understanding, and lo! It had become overgrown with thorns, briars had covered it over, and its stone fence had been destroyed. I perceived this and considered it well, I looked upon it and took from it a lesson (Mishlei 24:30-32).

These verses describe two individuals who took divergent paths, both ending in failure. *I passed by the field of a lazy man* — a man whose laziness caused him to neglect the study of Torah, or to forget what he had already learned. The owner of the vineyard was *a man devoid of understanding* — a foolish man who did not take care to hold on to those *mitzvos* which he had accomplished through much time and effort. The first man, instead of planting seeds of spiritual attainment, allowed his field to *become overgrown with thorns,* the thorns of idle chatter and fruitless endeavors. As for the second man, the sacred words of Torah study and prayer which he had uttered with fervor and devotion, which could have ascended Heavenward as a song of praise to the One Above, had become unrecognizable — *briars had covered it over* — the briars of spiritual impurity wrought by evil speech.

SEFER CHOFETZ CHAIM

TOELES: A Contrast of Loshon Hora vs. Rechilus

‎⮜When Rebuke is not Required

We have seen that at times reproof may be coun-terproductive and is therefore out of place (See Days 45, 72 and 143). There are several other factors which must be considered when determining whether or not it is necessary to approach an individual privately before speaking against him.

In a case where an individual has regularly violated a given commandment, and means are being sought to encourage his repentance and to prevent others from following in his ways, the need for reproof as a first step is obvious. There is no justification for publicizing a person's negative behavior if a meaningful discussion with him could convince him to change his ways. Even if it is obvious that the person will not respond to rebuke, failure to approach him directly before speaking about him could be misconstrued by others as insincere *chanufah,* flattery — an approach where the speaker deliberately exhibits tolerance in the perpetrator's presence to gain his favor, while speaking negatively of him behind his back (see Day 58).

If, however, the person being discussed has harmed someone, and the purpose of publicizing his actions is to correct the situation, one need not fear suspicions of insincerity. In such a case, rebuke would not be a prerequisite unless there is reason to believe it will achieve results.

(Continued on page 412)

Man is naturally bent toward speech and it is to refrain from speech which requires effort.

3 Adar · Chaim Yitzchok Druck ‏לע"נ חיים יצחק ב"ר יעקב גרשון‏
Dedicated by the Druck family
4 Elul · Reb Yehudah Dovid Feuer ‏לע"נ רב יהודה דוד בן רב שלמה‏
Dedicated by Eli Meir Feuer

✥Torah Study vs. Loshon Hora

The Talmud states (*Arachin* 15b): "R' Chama bar Chanina said: If one has spoken *loshon hora*, how can he rectify his sin? If he is a Torah scholar, he should toil in Torah study, as it is written, 'A healing for the tongue is a tree of life' (*Mishlei* 15:4). Torah is the 'tree of life,' as it is written (ibid. 3:18), 'It is a tree of life to all who grasp it.' "

"Death and life are in the power of the tongue" (ibid. 18:21). Evil speech can deny one the eternal bliss of the Next World. One who seeks to heal his tongue of this terrible malady should partake of the tree of life that is Torah. At the same time, he must be on guard to avoid repeating past sins.

This can be likened to a person who is being treated for food poisoning. It is not enough to take the necessary medicines; one must also be careful to avoid eating more contaminated food.

The Talmud further states that immersion in Torah study is itself a preventive measure against speaking *loshon hora*. As Scripture states, "For man was born to toil" (*Iyov* 5:7). The Talmud (*Sanhedrin* 99b) understands "toil" as a reference to speech, specifically the speech of Torah study. The Talmud is teaching us that man's tongue differs from his other limbs in a very important way. Use of man's other limbs requires energy. If man is lazy, his limbs will not be put to maximum use. Such is not the case with the tongue. Man need not overcome any innate laziness to engage in conversation. To the contrary, he is naturally bent toward speech and it is to refrain from speech which requires effort. Thus do the Sages state that "man was born to toil" refers to the toil of speech.

It is for the toil of Torah study that man was born. However, man has free choice to decide what the nature of his speech will be. If he will not use his natural inclination toward speech for the study of Torah, then inevitably he will speak other matters and will transgress the laws of forbidden speech.

∾Exaggerations

The rule that slander cannot be justified, even for a constructive purpose, would seem to be without exception. The Chofetz Chaim, however, speculates that if one cannot bring about a given constructive result without exaggerating, then it may be acceptable. The case he cites is where one is attempting to dissolve a friendship between two children, one of whom is a bad influence upon the other. If the victim will not be influenced to end the relationship unless the evils of his friend are exaggerated, this may be permissible.

The guidelines for such an exemption are very sensitive and one cannot rely upon it without prior consultation with a competent *halachic* authority.[231]

> *If one sanctifies himself a little, they sanctify him a great deal from Above.*

4 Adar · May today's learning be a זכות for Lillian Solomon, Hollywood, FL
5 Elul · Reb Yehudah Dovid Feuer לע״נ רב יהודה דוד בן רב שלמה
Dedicated by Eli Meir Feuer

DAY 153

✑*Sanctity upon Sanctity*

D*o not contaminate yourselves through them lest you be-*
come contaminated through them. For I am HASHEM your
God — you are to sanctify yourselves and you shall become
holy, for I am holy (Vayikra 11:43-44).

In commenting on the above, the Sages state:

> If a person contaminates himself a little, they contaminate
> him a great deal; [if he contaminates himself] below, they
> contaminate him Above; [if he contaminates himself] in this
> world, they contaminate him in the World to Come.
> [Conversely,] if a person sanctifies himself a little, they sanc-
> tify him a great deal; [if he sanctifies himself] below, they
> sanctify him Above; [if he sanctifies himself] in this world,
> they sanctify him in the World to Come (*Yoma* 39a).

Zohar states that when a person utters forbidden speech a *ruach hatumah,* spirit of impurity, is manifest upon his words. Spiritual forces of
destruction then take this spirit of impurity and use it to contaminate
words of Torah and prayer that this person has uttered. Thus, *if a person contaminates himself a little, they contaminate him a great deal*.

Conversely, Hashem, Whose lovingkindness is boundless, seeks
to uplift us with an abundant flow of *kedushah,* sanctity. He calls to
each and every Jew, as it were, "Open for me an aperture like the eye
of a needle and I will open for you an opening like that of a hallway"
(*Shir HaShirim Rabbah* 5:3). When a Jew overcomes his evil inclination and fulfills the Divine will, a spirit of sanctity is drawn upon his
soul. *If a person sanctifies himself a little, they sanctify him a great deal*.

✒Violating Confidentiality

As stated above, disclosure of an item told in confidence is prohibited as *avak rechilus* (see Day 136). An extremely sensitive area not discussed in the *Sefer Chofetz Chaim* is that of disclosing confidential information for a constructive purpose.

It is obvious, however, that if *halachah* requires a person to disclose a matter to a particular individual and he discloses it to a different person instead, while insisting that it remain confidential, his wishes should not be respected. If, for example, a person involved in a *shidduch* (marriage match) confides in a friend that he suffers from a chronic serious ailment, it is the responsibility of the friend to ensure that the other party is informed. One cannot demand confidentiality when the Torah requires him to disclose such information.

A second situation where it is clear that one must reveal a secret that has been shared with him is where one has been told by a person of his secret plan to harm someone. One cannot demand confidentiality in order to harm others.

People come to loathe the gossip-monger and keep their distance from him, lest he speak evil of them.

---

5 Adar · Mr. Alexander (Sender) Francis לע"נ אבי מורי אלכסנדר חיים בן
ר' שלום ז"ל
In loving memory of our father by Rabbi & Mrs. Moshe Francis, Chicago IL
6 Elul · לזכות הרוצה בעילום שמו לישועה קרובה
Donated anonymously as a *zechus* to receive a *yeshuah* shortly.

356　□　CHOFETZ CHAIM

DAY
154

❧Lesson of the Serpent

The first slander ever spoken was uttered by the Serpent who, through cunning and deceit, prevailed upon Adam and Eve to partake of the Tree of Knowledge. "The serpent said to the woman, 'You will surely not die [by partaking of it]; for God knows that on the day you eat of it your eyes will be opened and you will be like God, knowing good and bad' " (*Bereishis* 3:4-5).

R' Yehoshua of Siknin said in R' Levi's name: "The serpent began speaking slander of his Creator, saying, 'He [God] ate of this tree and created this world. He therefore ordered you not to eat thereof so you will not create other worlds, for every craftsman hates his competitors' " (*Bereishis Rabbah* 19:4).

The result of this slander was the decree of death upon mankind. As for the serpent, it was punished measure for measure. "I will put enmity between you and the woman, and between your offspring and her offspring. He will pound your head, and you will bite his heel" (*Bereishis* 3:15). The serpent caused death, therefore man seeks to kill him. The serpent claimed that God felt threatened by man and had enmity for him, therefore man hates the venomous serpent who seeks to do him harm.

And so it is with the gossipmonger. As people become aware of his wicked nature, they come to loathe him and keep their distance from him, lest he find cause to speak evil of them.

ו אדר
6 ADAR / CYCLE I

ז אלול
7 ELUL / CYCLE 2

SEFER CHOFETZ CHAIM
TOELES: Personal Information

⋙Lawyers and Therapists

The commandment לא תעמד על דם רעך, *Do not stand aside while your fellow's blood is being shed (Vayikra* 19:16), presents a major dilemma for the professional whose effectiveness, reputation and livelihood rest on the confidence placed in him by his clientele. Often, a client will reveal to his lawyer or therapist information that is being withheld from someone unjustly.

Whenever possible, a therapist must convince his client that he has a moral obligation to divulge such information to the proper party. Where appropriate, the client should be made to understand that despite the consequences, he will experience a sense of relief after having revealed the information. Moreover, by being honest and open in his personal life, one is able to develop a more positive self-image.

Should the client persist in his refusal to divulge such information to the proper party, the lawyer or therapist may be faced with the painful choice of either allowing a destructive relationship to materialize, or possibly jeopardizing his livelihood and reputation. Consultation with a competent *halachic* authority is a must in such situations. This would also apply to a physician who is aware that his chronically ill patient is seeking to marry. When bringing such matters before a *halachic* authority, one should not mention the names of the parties involved unless absolutely necessary.[232]

Does the gossip-monger expect a tzaddik's blessing to outweigh the strength of his sinful ways?

6 Adar · Mrs. Golda Berger שמחה ברוך 'ר בת גאלדא נ"לע
Dedicated by the Berger & Hochman families
7 Elul · Selma Borinsky יוסף בת סלמה נ"לע
Dedicated by Yehudit Weinberg in memory of her mother

❧The Blessing
and the Curse

The serpent was cursed, "... upon your belly you shall go, and dust shall you eat all the days of your life" (*Bereishis* 3:14). Similarly, the gossipmonger is punished with poverty, as stated in *Sefer HaKaneh*.[1]

I am truly amazed by the fact that people who regularly speak evil of others nevertheless do not hesitate to request blessings and *segulos* (auspicious omens) from *tzaddikim* for success in earning a livelihood. Do they expect a blessing to outweigh the strength of their sinful ways? The Torah states, "Accursed is one who strikes his fellow stealthily" (*Devarim* 27:24), which the Sages interpret as a curse upon one who speaks *loshon hora*. This curse was uttered in the presence of the entire Jewish people, who collectively answered "Amen" to its pronouncement. Can the blessing of even a *tzaddik* outweigh the power of this curse?

Would such a person seek my advice for material blessing, I would tell him to be exceedingly careful to avoid the sin of *loshon hora*. In this way, he will merit the blessing, "Blessed is one who does not strike his fellow stealthily" (see *Sotah* 32b). Additionally, he should avoid any form of robbery, usury, or any other act that might result in another's monetary loss. Such zealousness will surely bring blessing to one's endeavors.

---

1. See Day 43.

ז אדר
7 ADAR / CYCLE 1

ח אלול
8 ELUL / CYCLE 2

SEFER CHOFETZ CHAIM
TOELES: Personal Information

❧*Improper Behavior*

A lawyer may not assist a client in committing an injustice. A lawyer may not represent a client in a lawsuit to attain payment which the client admits is not due him. Thus, a lawyer may not present medical bills which the client has informed him are fictitious. A lawyer, too, should seek the guidance of a halachic authority so that he will conduct his practice in strict adherence to Torah law.

Similarly, a therapist may not assist a client in living an immoral lifestyle. Jewish therapists must be guided in their work by qualified *rabbanim* who are well versed in the relevant areas of *halachah.*

Without fear of God, one's wisdom will do him little good.

7 Adar · Dedicated by משה מאיר ואסתר סנדלר ומשפחתם Lakewood, NJ
8 Elul · Mrs. Minnie Hamburger לע"נ מינדל בת ר' יעקב ע"ה
Dedicated by Rabbi & Mrs. Eliezer Hamburger

☙Fear of God

In the Book of *Tehillim* (Psalms), King David declares: "The beginning of wisdom is the fear of HASHEM" (*Tehillim* 111:10). In the Book of *Mishlei* (Proverbs), David's son, Shlomo, declares: "The beginning of wisdom is to acquire wisdom [i.e. the wisdom of Torah]" (*Mishlei* 4:7). This is no contradiction, for as our Sages have taught, "If there is no fear of God, there is no wisdom; if there is no wisdom, there is no fear of God" (*Avos* 3: 21).

Elsewhere, Sholmo teaches: "If you seek it out like silver, and search for it like buried treasures, then you will comprehend the fear of HASHEM and knowledge of God you will find" (*Mishlei* 2:4-5). Those who search for silver or other precious items do not engage in such pursuits for a day or two. They pursue their quest relentlessly until discovery, and then begin the search for more. So it is with fear of Hashem. A Jew who forever ponders his Creator's greatness and the good which He continuously showers upon man will forever attain yet higher levels of awe for the One Above.

Without such growth, one's wisdom will do him little good. A person lacking in fear of Hashem will be uninspired to fulfill the *mitzvos* in all their details, no matter how well he has studied them. Moreover, his faculties will be unattuned to those laws which govern their use. Fear of Hashem inspires a person to guard his tongue, in accordance with the laws which he has studied. A lack of such fear causes one to ignore these laws.

ח אדר
8 ADAR / CYCLE 1

ט אלול
9 ELUL / CYCLE 2

SEFER CHOFETZ CHAIM
TOELES: Personal Information

❧ Teachers

We have already detailed the laws of *loshon hora* as they apply to a teacher who wishes to discuss his or her students with others (see Day 60). An additional concern for a teacher is that of *giluy sod,* sharing information that was related in confidence by a student.

A common situation, especially among teachers of younger children, is where the student divulges information concerning his family that his parents would certainly not want anyone to know. Under no circumstances may the teacher believe such information if it involves negativity or if its becoming known could cause the family harm; obviously, the teacher may not relate to others what was said by the child. Moreover, to inform the parents of what the child said may be *rechilus* (as it may cause ill will between parent and child) or *onaas devarim,* causing hurt through the spoken word. In certain situations, it may be correct for the teacher to speak to the parents, so that they can caution the child not to repeat such information again.

If, however, the child mentions something that is cause for alarm, the teacher's involvement may be necessary. This is especially true when the information involves abuse. The matter must be investigated, and — when necessary — the proper authorities should be contacted.[233]

(Continued on page 413)

Torah study that is comple- mented by genuine fear of God is exceed- ingly beloved to Hashem.

8 Adar · Kaila Malinowitz לע"נ קילא בת ר' חיים זאב
Dedicated by her children
9 Elul · Jacqueline Ray Rosenberg רחל בת אברהם לע"נ ינקלא
Dedicated by Mitchell & Lori Rosenberg, Mark & Lauren Rosenberg

DAY 157

❧The Stained Volumes

O ur Sages teach (*Tanna D'Vei Eliyahu Zuta* ch. 24) that when a person comes to the next world, his every deed and word is shown to him and he is judged accordingly.

Picture a man who all his life zealously studied one page of Talmud each day. He anticipates that after his death the thousands of pages that he has studied will be brought before the Heavenly Court and will earn him much reward. However, when that time does arrive and the pages are brought out, he discovers that, much to his dismay, each page is enveloped in a *ruach hatumah*, spirit of impurity, that resulted from his disregard of the prohibitions against speaking and accepting *loshon hora*. How great his anguish will be when he sees how his carelessness in this crucial area caused him the irreplaceable loss of his hard-earned wealth!

This point can be illustrated by the parable of a man who purchased what seemed to be a most exquisite set of Talmud. The cover of each volume was made of leather, embossed with beautiful gold design and bound with the finest heirloom binding. The seller had assured the buyer that the inside of each volume was as beautiful as its outside and thus there was no need to open and inspect it. The buyer had taken him at his word and paid in full, after which the seller left town for some undisclosed destination. How utterly dismayed the buyer was when he later discovered that the pages of each volume were stained by thick grime! How angry the buyer was — at himself! — for not having inspected the volumes before purchasing them.

And so it is with the habitual gossiper. Even if he will study the entire Talmud many times, in the end not a single tractate will shield him at his time of judgment. Each volume will be enveloped in impurity and will be repulsive to look at.

A wise man considers the ramifications of his actions and acts accordingly. Therefore, while one strives to live by the verse, "The beginning of wisdom is to acquire wisdom," he must also strive to live by its companion verse, "The beginning of wisdom is fear of Hashem." Such an approach is the key to a good life in both worlds, for Torah study that is complemented by genuine fear of God is exceedingly beloved to Hashem.

◦*Constructive Speech: In Conclusion*

Having discussed the laws of constructive speech regarding both *loshon hora* and *rechilus,* it becomes obvious that there are no shortcuts in deciding whether or not to speak up for a constructive purpose. Silence when in doubt may be true of non-constructive situations, but when someone else's life — or quality of life — hangs in the balance, one may be *required* to become involved. One must be well versed in proper applications of the seven conditions for constructive speech listed above (Day 50) or at least be in contact with an authority who is well versed in these matters.[234]

One should approach every mitzvah in the way that he approaches the mitzvah of blowing the shofar.

9 Adar · Hendl Rosengarten לע״נ האשה הענדל בת ר׳ יחזקאל שרגא ע״ה
Dedicated by her children
10 Elul · May today's learning be a זכות for Yonah Refael Goldstein and family, Har Nof, Yerushalayim

☙"Turn from Evil and Do Good"

In this work, we have focused on King David's words, "Which man desires life, who loves days of seeing good? Guard your tongue from evil, and your lips from speaking deceit" (*Tehillim* 34:13-14). Let us now examine the next verse, "Turn from evil and do good, seek peace and pursue it."

There is a basic distinction between the reward or punishment for *mitzvos* that are between man and God and those that are between man and his fellow. The primary reward or punishment for the former is reserved for the World to Come. Such is not the case with *mitzvos* between man and his fellow. As performance of these commandments betters one's fellow's lot in this world, a significant portion of one's reward is bestowed in this world, measure for measure. Conversely, by transgressing these *mitzvos,* one worsens his fellow's lot in this world. Therefore, a significant degree of retribution is exacted in this world.

In the above verse, the terms רע, *evil,* and טוב, *good,* refer to matters between man and his fellow. Thus, David informs us that one who seeks a good life in this world and the next must be especially zealous in the fulfillment of his interpersonal obligations as expressed in the Torah. *Turn from evil* refers to the full gamut of actions prohibited by the Torah: robbery, usury, lending with interest, causing hurt or embarrassment, etc. *Do good* includes the giving of *tzedakah* (charity), performing acts of kindness, offering financial assistance to a struggling businessman, burying the dead, visiting the sick, hosting guests, returning a lost object, paying a worker's wages on time, etc.

Hearing the blowing of the shofar on Rosh Hashanah is a *mitzvah* which everyone makes every effort to fulfill. In the same way, one should strive to fulfill every *mitzvah*, and to rejoice in its fulfillment. As we say each night in the *Ma'ariv* prayer, "Therefore, HASHEM, our God, upon our retiring and arising, we will discuss Your decrees and we will rejoice with the words of the study of Your Torah and with Your commandments ..."

❧The Prohibition

A s in the case of *loshon hora,* one must do his best to ignore someone who is about to begin or has already begun to speak *rechilus.* If someone begins talking of how one person has wronged another, to willfully listen as he continues to speak is, according to the Chofetz Chaim, in violation of לא תשא שמע שוא, *Do not accept a false report* (*Shemos* 23:1). Just as it is lowly to speak gossip, so too it is not befitting a respectable human being to listen to gossip.[235]

Each mitzvah provides its own unique spirituality and is vital to the soul's well-being.

לע״נ משה בן בערל · Milton Blavin · 10 Adar
Dedicated in loving memory by Neil & Lynn Blavin and family, Southfield, MI
לע״נ רעכיל חוה בת גבריאל מנשה · Chavi Baum Weingarten · 11 Elul
Dedicated by all the girls whose lives she touched at Manchester Sem.

❧ *The Whole of Man*

In summation: One must strive to fulfill each and every *mitzvah*, be it between man and God or between man and his fellow, for each is an expression of Hashem's will. Thus does the Torah state: "Apply your hearts to all the words... with which you are to instruct your children, to be careful to perform all the words of this Torah. For it is not an empty thing for you, for it is your life..." (*Devarim* 32:46-47). Let no one think that even a single *mitzvah* is extraneous, a matter left to those who seek exceptional refinement of character or spiritual attainment. *For it is your life.* No part of the human body is extraneous; each serves an important function without which the body would be unsound. Similarly, each *mitzvah* provides its own unique spirituality and is vital to the soul's well-being.

Thus do we conclude the reading of the Book of *Koheles*: "The sum of the matter when all is considered: Fear God and keep His commandments, for that is the whole of man" (*Koheles* 12:13). To be the *adam hashaleim,* man of spiritual perfection, one must *fear God* so that he will refrain from doing that which the Torah prohibits, and he must *keep His commandments,* that is, all positive commandments. *That is the whole of man.*

יא אדר
ll ADAR / CYCLE 1

יב אלול
12 ELUL / CYCLE 2

SEFER CHOFETZ CHAIM
Listening to Rechilus

✍The Subject

It is forbidden to listen to gossip when it involves others, and even more so when it involves how others dislike the listener himself. (When there is a constructive purpose in the listener knowing such information, listening may be permissible. This will be discussed later.) It is forbidden to listen to accounts of how others have spoken negatively about one's family members or friends. Such listening usually serves no constructive purpose and causes the listener to dislike the person mentioned.

One who denies the authenticity of even a single letter of the Torah is considered as if he had denied the entire Torah.

לע״נ אליהו בן שמוא־ל ודבורה אסתר · 11 Adar - Mr. Al Epstein
Dedicated by his loving wife Zelda Epstein, children and grandchildren
12 Elul - Zakiye bat Bahiye Shomer לע״נ זכייה בת יצחק ובהייה
Dedicated in loving memory by her children, grandchildren and
great grandchildren

**DAY
160**

✍Two Tablets

For a Torah scroll to be kosher and endowed with proper sanctity, it cannot be missing a single letter. Even an imperfection in one letter can render a scroll invalid. In a similar vein, a Jew is considered a believer and is worthy of a portion in the World to Come only if he believes that every letter contained in the Torah is God-given. If, Heaven forfend, one denies the authenticity of even a single letter in the Torah, it is as if he has denied the authenticity of the entire Torah.

We are all *ma'aminim b'nei ma'aminim*, believers sons of believers. All of us believe that every letter of the Torah was received by Moshe from Hashem. How then is it possible for a person to approach even a single *mitzvah* without proper reverence? This is not an indication of faulty belief; rather, it points to habitual transgression of a commandment which results in one viewing the forbidden as something permissible: "Once a man has been guilty of transgression and repeats it, it becomes to him like something permissible" (*Kiddushin* 40a).

The Torah states: "He [Hashem] gave Moshe the two Tablets of Testimony" (*Shemos* 31:18). The Torah omits the *vav* from the word לוחות, *Tablets,* so that the word can be read as if it is the singular לחת, *Tablet. Rashi* (citing *Tanchuma*) writes that this teaches that the Tablets were identical in dimension with supernatural precision so that they appeared as if they were one.

The commandments inscribed upon the first Tablet concern man's relationship with God, while those on the second concern man's relationship with his fellow. The Tablets were made identical to teach that all *mitzvos* are vital and it is the totality of their spiritual light within a single individual that produces the man of spiritual perfection.

יב אדר
12 ADAR / CYCLE 1

יג אלול
13 ELUL / CYCLE 2

SEFER CHOFETZ CHAIM
Listening to Rechilus

✒Ignore and Rebuke

As in the case of *loshon hora,* it is forbidden to listen to *rechilus* spoken by one's parents, siblings or spouse. Familial closeness is not a reason to share information that promotes strife and ill will among Jews.

When subjected to gossip, one is required not only to distance himself from the conversation, but must also reprove the speaker for violating a Torah commandment. Only when rebuke will cause the gossiper to speak with greater malice should one not offer rebuke.

If one's employer or colleagues are prone to gossip, one must ignore their conversations. (One is not required to offer reproof if this might cause him to lose his job. Fulfillment of a positive commandment [such as the *mitzvah* to offer reproof] does not require a monetary risk of such magnitude. However, one should attempt to voice disapproval at some point so as not to be guilty of *chanufah,* false flattery.)

In all situations, the listener must do his best to stop the gossip — perhaps by tactfully changing the subject.[237]

Nothing less than daily pursuit of spiritual accomplishment will suffice.

לע״נ הרב ירחמיאל רפאל שאול בן יוסף צבי זצ״ל 12 Adar · **Rabbi Shaul Miller**
Dedicated by Reuven Moshe & Cori Grant
13 Elul · לע״נ יוטא בת צבי פרנקל ע״ה
מאת משפחת פרנקל

❧Daily Pursuit

It is imperative that one uproot a complacent attitude toward certain *mitzvos*. Doing so is crucial if one is to fulfill his obligations toward his Creator and toward his fellow man.

"Hillel used to say: If I am not for myself, who will be for me? And if I am for myself, what am I? And if not now, when?" (*Avos* 1:14). If Hillel was wont to repeat this maxim, surely it must contain teachings which are fundamental to one's Divine service and purpose in life. In fact, Hillel is awakening us to approach Torah and *mitzvos* with alacrity and zeal, each and every day.

When a man is seen refraining from day-to-day involvement with earning a livelihood, the logical question is: How does he support his family? A variety of possibilities exists:

He may own a factory which is staffed by dependable workers, so that periodic involvement on his part is sufficient.

He may be a highly skilled professional who earns enough in a few hours of work to provide his family with their weekly needs.

He may be a merchant who does business only at the regional market, which is open for a few weeks at a time at regular intervals during the year.

In the above-cited Mishnah, Hillel teaches that with regard to Divine service none of the above-mentioned possibilities exists. Nothing less than daily pursuit of spiritual accomplishment will suffice.

יג אדר
13 ADAR / CYCLE 1

יד אלול
14 ELUL / CYCLE 2

SEFER CHOFETZ CHAIM

Listening to Rechilus

✑In a Group Setting

From the wording of the verse which requires a Jew to reprove his fellow when he sins (*Vayikra* 19:17), the Sages derive that one must do so without embarrassing the sinner. Thus, when a person is relating gossip in the company of others, it is preferable that a listener tactfully change the subject and later rebuke the speaker privately. One may openly protest gossipmongering in a way that causes the speaker discomfort only if there is no other way to bring his monologue to an end.[238]

Spiritual light and contentment cannot be purchased; they can be attained only through toil and striving.

☙Light and Contentment

"Hillel used to say: If I am not for myself, who will be for me?" The spiritual world is not like the world of business where one can rely on trusted workers to do his work for him. The term *myself* refers to one's soul, which is nourished only through one's own efforts in the sphere of Torah and *mitzvos*. Hillel is saying: "If I will not expend effort for my soul's sake, then *who* will nourish it with light and contentment?" These are not things that can be purchased; they can be attained only through one's own toil and striving.

And, Hillel continues, the spiritual realm is unlike the physical one where a highly skilled craftsman can earn a livelihood working but a few hours a day. As the Mishnah says elsewhere, "The day is short and the task is abundant" (*Avos* 2:20). Thus does Hillel say: "And if I am for myself, what am I?" If I were to dedicate my every moment to *myself,* that is, for my soul's benefit, could I claim with certainty that I have done enough to earn eternal life in the World to Come?

The Talmud relates that when the sage Mar Ukva examined his impressive charity records before his death, he reflected, "The way is long, but the provisions are small" (*Kesubos* 67b).

Thus, a man of wisdom will dedicate every available moment toward the service of his Creator.

יד אדר
14 ADAR / CYCLE 1

טו אלול
15 ELUL / CYCLE 2

SEFER CHOFETZ CHAIM
Listening to Rechilus

◈When the Speaker Cannot be Stopped

When one finds himself in the company of someone speaking *rechilus* and finds it difficult to interrupt the speaker, he must leave. If one cannot bring himself to actually walk away, he must, at the very least, not pay attention to what is being said and must make it clear through facial expression that he disapproves of the discussion.[239]

Let no one delude himself with the notion that a bit of Torah study, and a mitzvah here and there, is sufficient.

14 Adar · Pesach Kruler לע״נ יחזקאל פסח בן שרה
Dedicated by Sholom Dov & Iris Rothman and family
15 Elul · לע״נ מרת יסכה בת ר׳ משה רודער ז״ל
Dedicated by her children and grandchildren, Eretz Yisroel, England and Canada

~No Time To Spare

The message of Hillel's question *And if I am for myself, what am I?* goes further. If the average person were to make an accounting of how his regular day is spent, he would see that only a small part of his time is free for spiritual pursuits. How then can he allow these precious moments to slip by without using them to acquire for himself Torah and *mitzvos,* an eternal acquisition?

When a person works to provide his wife and children with their needs and pay for his children's Torah education, his efforts bear great fruit. He will receive reward not only for his hours of Torah study, but for his efforts at earning a livelihood as well, for all his strivings were directed toward one essential purpose — fulfilling Hashem's will.

Such is not the case, however, when one strives for a lifestyle of luxury, to live in an expensive home with lavish decor, and to dress his family in rich taste. In truth, such a person is not really toiling for *himself*, that is, for his soul's benefit — for whose will is he seeking to fulfill, if not his evil inclination? What good will such striving accomplish for his soul? The same can be said of those who labor until their old age so that they can leave a generous inheritance behind for their loved ones. Such effort does not benefit the soul.

Hillel exhorts us to use our precious time on this world wisely, and not to let the hours slip by without accomplishment. Let no one delude himself with the notion that a bit of Torah study, and a *mitzvah* here and there, is sufficient.

טו אדר
15 ADAR / CYCLE 1

טז אלול
16 ELUL / CYCLE 2

SEFER CHOFETZ CHAIM
Listening to Rechilus

❧Avoid the Gossipmonger

There are, unfortunately, people who forever gossip, perhaps as a result of their inactivity and their need for social involvement. Unless one honestly feels that he can help such a person to mend his ways, he should avoid his company entirely. If contact with such a person is unavoidable, it should be minimized to whatever degree possible.

One must also avoid settings that are prone to discussions of gossip. Ideally, one should find a way to permanently change the nature of conversation at such settings so that those present will be spared the evils of *rechilus*.[240]

In the spiritual realm, this world is the "market" and every day is "market day."

15 Adar · Mrs. Florence Falik ע"ה לע"נ פייגא בת שלמה אבא ע"ה
Dedicated by her children
16 Elul · Rabbi Chaim Okrongly Ben-Zev ז"ל לע"נ הרב חיים אריה בר' זאב דוב ז"ל
Dedicated by his wife Hannah Ben-Zev תבלחט"א,
children and grandchildren יבלח"ט

DAY
164

❧Market Day

A merchant who conducts all his business at the regional market has plenty of time off during the long intervals when the market is closed. But can he vacation while the market is open? Certainly not — that is, if he intends to earn a decent livelihood so that he can provide for his family.

In the spiritual realm, this world is the "market" and every day is "market day." It is in this world that one must acquire the merits which will earn him the light of the World to Come. If one approaches Torah and *mitzvos* with laziness and allows his days to pass by with little accomplishment, what will he bring with him when his days on this world are over?

Shlomo exhorts us: "Whatever you are able to do with your might, do it. For there is neither doing nor reckoning nor knowledge nor wisdom in the grave where you are going" (*Koheles* 9:10). A Jew must serve Hashem with the full strength of his spirit, and accomplish whatever is within his power, for the next world is the place of reward where the opportunity for accomplishment is no more. As the Sages comment to the verse, "You shall observe the commandments... that I command you today, to perform them" (*Devarim* 7:11): *today* — in this life — is the time to *perform* the commandments, while their primary reward is reserved for *tomorrow* — that is, for the World to Come (*Avodah Zara* 4b).

How much there is to accomplish! One is not seeking to provide for himself for a few months' time or even for a few years, but for eternity! Of course, guiding one's children along the path of Torah is part of providing for oneself in the next world, and this too should be approached with great dedication and care. One who does not have the opportunity to raise children of his own in the way of Torah should strive to help educate other Jewish children. Whatever the nature of one's mission on this earth, let him go about fulfilling it in the best possible way.

[Hillel said:] *"And if not now, when?"*

טז אדר
16 ADAR / CYCLE 1

יז אלול
17 ELUL / CYCLE 2

SEFER CHOFETZ CHAIM
TOELES: Constructive Listening

❧Constructive Listening

Just as it is not lowly to speak (what would otherwise be considered) *rechilus* for a constructive purpose, so too it is not wrong to listen to *rechilus* if the listener honestly believes that it is important for him to be aware of the information. This includes any discussion that could help the listener protect himself from others who plan to harm him, or to protect others from damage about to be inflicted upon them. It is also permissible to listen to information that could be of help in rectifying damage already done to oneself or others.

In these cases, the discussion is not labelled as "gossip"; rather, it is constructive speech.[241]

Each day is a gift for itself; if squandered, it is lost forever.

16 Adar · Mrs. Evelyn Golding לע"נ האשה חוה בת ר' יעקב
Dedicated by her sons, Shimon Gedalia, Yosef Chaim,
Dovid Nachman & Yisroel and their families
17 Elul · Kalman Katlowitz לע"נ הרב ר' קלמן בר' שלמה הירש
קאטלאוויטץ הי"ד
Dedicated by the Katlowitz family

❧The Lazy Traveler

King David pleaded, "I am a sojourner in the world, hide not Your commandments from me" (*Tehillim* 119:19). Man is but a sojourner on this earth; the World to Come is his eternal home. Realizing that his days of Torah study were numbered, David begged Hashem to reveal to him the wisdom inherent in His commandments.

Iyov declared, "There is a fixed service-term for man upon earth" (*Iyov* 7:1). A person's life-span on this earth is allotted to him with exacting precision. Therefore, one cannot tell himself that he will compensate for having wasted one day by making constructive use of the next day. Each day is a gift for itself; if squandered, it is lost forever.

This can be illustrated with a parable: A man who had been unable to earn a livelihood sailed to a faraway land in the hope of finding some way to provide for his family. He remained there for some twenty years, accomplishing nothing in all that time. Lazy by nature, he spent his days strolling here and there, surviving on an occasional handout.

One day, he was surprised to meet a neighbor from his hometown. "I can't believe that you've spent all these years doing nothing!" the neighbor exclaimed. "Didn't you come here to find a proper livelihood for yourself?"

"Oh, I'm quite aware of that," the man responded, "but I still have plenty of time for that — I've only been here twenty years!"

"Have you lost your mind?" the neighbor retorted. "Even if you would be a permanent resident of this land, it would be ridiculous for you to have wasted so many years of your life. The facts being what they are make your story most incredible. For you came to this land temporarily, *for the express purpose of providing for your family*. How, then, could you have spent so many years accomplishing nothing?!"

(Continued on page 413)

יז אדר
17 ADAR / CYCLE 1

יח אלול
18 ELUL / CYCLE 2

SEFER CHOFETZ CHAIM
TOELES: Constructive Listening

❧*Informing the Speaker*

For one to listen to *rechilus* within the framework of *halachah,* it is not sufficient that the listener be justified in paying attention to the information being conveyed; the speaker, too, must have constructive intent. If the speaker is unaware that the information he is relating is of significance to the listener, then he is guilty of speaking *rechilus.* The listener, then, is cause for the speaker's transgression and has violated the prohibition "Before a blind person do not place a stumbling block" (*Vayikra* 19:14), which prohibits one from causing another Jew to sin.

Thus, it is the responsibility of the listener to explain to the speaker that the information is important for him to hear and is therefore not considered gossip.

If the speaker was already in the process of relating the gossip to others when a person to whom the information is relevant appeared on the scene, he would not be guilty of causing the speaker to transgress. Even so, it is proper for the listener to explain why he is listening, so that the others will realize that he is not transgressing and that he considers their non-constructive listening a sin.[242]

In the sphere of Torah study, a half hour plus a half hour does not equal one hour.

17 Adar · Mrs. Margie Schlanger לע״נ שרה מחלה בת ר׳ מרדכי
Dedicated by the Snow family, Brooklyn, NY
18 Elul · Alfred Hertz לע״נ אהרן בן יוסף ז״ל
Dedicated by Kurt & Edith Rothschild and family

◈The Waters of Torah

It is clear that through *shmiras haloshon* one saves himself from transgressing thousands of sins each year — literally. Moreover, in place of these potential sins, one earns for himself thousands of merits.

Let us suppose that a given individual begins to exercise caution in matters of speech and thus refrains from speaking (on the average) ten forbidden words per day which he otherwise would have spoken. This means that each year he exercises self-control in not expressing more than three thousand forbidden words. The Talmud states, "One who sits and does not commit a sin is given reward equivalent to that of one who performs a *mitzvah*" (*Kiddushin* 39b). Above, we have cited a *Midrash* quoted by the Vilna Gaon that the reward for refraining from speaking the forbidden is beyond the comprehension of angels.

For one who has a fixed daily Torah study session, the quality of *shmiras haloshon* can ensure that his learning is not interrupted by idle chatter. Aside from the sin of speaking *loshon hora*, the sin of *bitul Torah*, unwarranted disruption of Torah study, is most severe. To disrupt one's Torah learning shows a lack of regard for this greatest of *mitzvos* and causes one's learning to be fractured and lack the power and accomplishment of continuous study. In the sphere of Torah study, a half hour plus a half hour does not equal one hour.

Torah study is a prime antidote against the impurity wrought by sin, including that of *loshon hora*. *Sifre* (*Devarim* 11:22) likens Torah study to the waters of a *mikveh*, which purify. It follows then that just as the *mikveh* purifies from an impurity which encompasses the entire person, so too does Torah purify even if one's being is totally immersed in the morass of sin.

However, just as the *mikveh* purifies only when there is no *chatz-itzah,* interposition, between the person's body and the water, so too can the purifying effects of Torah elevate the person only when he is totally immersed in its study.

❧ Soliciting Information

Not only may one listen to *rechilus* that is important for him to hear, he may even approach someone and request information that would otherwise be considered *rechilus*. Obviously, the solicitor must make it clear that his solicitation is sanctioned by *halachah*.[243]

One must also be careful to request only pertinent information and nothing more. Should the person from whom the information was requested begin relating unnecessary gossip, he should be stopped immediately.

"If you forsake me for one day, I will forsake you for two."

DAY
167

✒Day After Day

Torah is also likened to bread, as it is written, "Come partake of my bread" (Mishlei 9:5). Now, if man does not eat bread for a day or two, he becomes weakened; if he goes a week without bread (or a comparable substitute), he becomes extremely weak and it is difficult for him to regain the strength that he has lost. This is exactly the way of Torah study, which is sustenance for the soul. If a Jew lets a few days go by without study, his soul becomes weakened; if he lets an entire week slip by, his soul grows extremely weak.

One must be extremely zealous not to allow even a day to pass without Torah study. Such interruptions have a negative impact on the Torah study that will follow, as the Sages state, "If you forsake me [the Torah] for one day, I will forsake you for two" (*Yerushalmi Berachos* 9:5).

If extenuating circumstances cause a cancellation of one's daily study session, the student should consider this as "borrowed time" that must be repaid. He should strive to repay his debt quickly, in the way of the Talmudic sage who "borrowed by day and paid back that night" (*Eruvin* 65a).

As mentioned above, one must ensure that his study sessions not be marked by interruptions. Diligent uninterrupted study causes a spirit of sanctity (רוח של קדושה) to become manifest upon the student; such is not the case with study marked by disruption.

✎Lending An Ear

There are instances where one may listen to *rechilus* although the information is not at all pertinent to him.

When an individual is experiencing sadness or extreme anxiety and is in need of someone with whom to share his frustration, it is considered an act of kindness to lend a sympathetic ear and listen to his troubles. One must be certain, though, that the circumstances do, in fact, demand this. Also, such expression should not become a regular occurrence for the speaker. Finally, care must be taken that the speaker not wander from the matter at hand and offer negative remarks which are not relevant.

One may also listen to *rechilus* if his intention is to make the speaker understand that his perception of the situation, and of those of whom he speaks negatively, is mistaken.[244]

Fulfillment of a given mitzvah with total dedication and precision is a catalyst for earning the great reward of the World to Come.

לע״נ ברײנא בת בן ציון · 19 Adar
Dedicated by her children
20 Elul · Joseph Braun לע״נ יוסף צבי בן שמעון
Dedicated by the Braun & Brecher families, Brooklyn, NY

DAY
168

৶Taking Hold of the Tree

The Torah is called a "tree of life for those who grasp it" (*Mishlei* 3:18). The way to grab onto a tree is to take hold of one its branches; in so doing, one has attached himself to the entire tree of which this branch is a part. So it is, explains *Sefer Chareidim* (ch. 61), with Torah. The way to attach oneself to the 613 *mitzvos* is by fulfilling one particular *mitzvah* with exacting precision and total dedication. Dedication and attachment to a single commandment will cause one's soul to become united with Hashem and His Torah and will lead to the proper fulfillment of other *mitzvos* as well. Thus do we find, "Rav Nachman said: I will be rewarded [in the World to Come] for having [zealously] fulfilled [the *mitzvah*] to eat three meals on Shabbos. Rav Sheishes said: I will be rewarded for having [zealously] fulfilled the *mitzvah* of *tefillin*" (*Shabbos* 118b). The Talmud goes on to cite similar statements of other Sages and offers illustrations of how meticulously each sage fulfilled the *mitzvah* of which he spoke. *Sefer Chareidim* also cites *Talmud Yerushalmi* which states that fulfillment of a given *mitzvah* with total dedication and precision is a catalyst for earning the great reward of the World to Come.

Thus, the above can be added to all the great benefits of *shmiras haloshon* of which we have already spoken. One who will dedicate himself to the meticulous observance of these laws in all their fine details, in all situations and under all conditions, will thereby take hold of a branch of the Tree of Life and merit reward that no angel can fathom.

כ אדר
20 ADAR / CYCLE I

כא אלול
21 ELUL / CYCLE 2

SEFER CHOFETZ CHAIM
Believing Rechilus

❧Believing Rechilus

The prohibition which forbids acceptance of *loshon hora* or *rechilus,* לא תשא שמע שוא, which we have translated *Do not accept a false report,* uses the term שוא, which literally means *vain* or *meaningless.* Clearly, the inference is that negative speech is not to be given credence.

It is often difficult, if not impossible, for a speaker to convey every detail and all background information that is crucial for an accurate understanding of a given occurrence. Certainly, if the speaker is violating *halachah* by relating *rechilus,* one dare not assume that he is being careful to speak only the truth. Therefore, as in the case of *loshon hora,* belief of secondhand information in a way that could cause ill feelings among people is unjustified and prohibited.[245]

If a mitzvah lies in disgrace, it is our obligation to strengthen ourselves in its observance.

20 Adar · The Manchester Rosh Yeshiva לע״נ הגאון הצדיק הרב
יהודא זאב בן הגאון הצדיק הרב משה יצחק הלוי סג״ל זצוק״ל
Dedicated by Rachel Charitable Trust
21 Elul · George Braunstein לע״נ שמחה גאדל בן אברהם יצחק
Dedicated by his children

DAY 169

⌒Lying in Disgrace

The obligation to bury a *meis mitzvah,* unattended corpse, rests upon all Jews without exception. The Talmud (*Berachos* 19b) states that even a *Kohen Gadol* (High Priest), a *nazir,*[1] or someone who is on his way to the Temple to bring a Pesach offering must attend to a *meis mitzvah.*

Sefer Chareidim (105:261) writes that a *mitzvah* which the current generation is neglecting is akin to a *meis mitzvah.* When no one pursues a given *mitzvah* — pursue it! Otherwise, that *mitzvah* ascends before the Heavenly Throne and complains, "How lowly I am, for I am all but forgotten from among the people."

What is an actual *meis mitzvah*? A lifeless corpse. The Torah is stringent regarding its burial, not because of what it is now, but because of what it once was — an abode for a Jewish soul. It is thus that the Torah requires that a *Kohen Gadol* — who is not permitted to attend to the corpse of even his own father or mother — attend to a *meis mitzvah*, so that it not lie in disgrace. Surely, then, if a *mitzvah* of the Torah — which is more precious than gems (*Mishlei* 3:13) and is the "daily delight" of the One Above (ibid. 8:30) — is lying in disgrace, it is our obligation to strengthen ourselves in its observance, so that it not be cause for indictment of our generation before Hashem.

To our misfortune, the concept of *loshon hora* is woefully ignored by many in our generation, thus making it a *"meis mitzvah"* of our day. How great then is the reward of those who rescue this *mitzvah* from disgrace by faithfully adhering to the laws of *shmiras haloshon.*

---

1. The voluntary vow which makes a person a *nazir* (lit., *one who is separated*) requires him to abstain from eating grapes or their derivatives; from cutting his hair; and from coming in contact with a human corpse (see *Bamidbar* ch. 6).

כא אדר
21 ADAR / CYCLE 1

כב אלול
22 ELUL / CYCLE 2

SEFER CHOFETZ CHAIM
Believing Rechilus

≈*Believing Constructive Information*

Unlike listening to *rechilus,* which is justified when the information is pertinent, believing *rechilus* is not permissible regardless of one's purpose. Even if one must inquire about a person with whom he is considering entering into a relationship, he may not believe as fact any negative information that has been told about the person. Never may one develop feelings of hatred towards a person on the basis of information heard about him — even though the information was obtained in a permissible manner.[246]

There is no mitzvah in our time that is dis-regarded more than the sin of loshon hora.

21 Adar · Dedicated by Shmuel & Esther Rieder and family
22 Elul · Abe Frost · לע״נ אברהם בן חיים שמואל
Dedicated by David & Fruma Frost, Savannah, GA

❧*Most Neglected*

A bove, we referred to *shmiras haloshon* as a *meis mitzvah*, a *mitzvah* which is woefully ignored by many who do not reckon it as a *mitzvah* at all. Though this needs no proof, we will nevertheless demonstrate that it is true.

There are people who find nothing wrong with saying the most derogatory remarks about others, for no good reason. When asked, "Why do you speak *loshon hora*?" they respond with dozens of reasons as to why their words are not *loshon hora* at all! If the questioner then responds with irrefutable proof that, indeed, the statements voiced *do* constitute *loshon hora,* they respond, "Well, it's not *loshon hora* when said about So-and-so — it's a *mitzvah* to speak ill of him!" The more one tries to convince them that they err, the more they heap calumny upon the subject of their ill-spoken words.

Does this happen with other sins? Does an otherwise observant Jew who has been caught eating something forbidden respond to his reprover by grabbing another piece of the food and stuffing it into his own mouth? Certainly not. Why then does this occur with the sin of *loshon hora* which, as we have shown in previous chapters, is among the worst sins in the Torah? The answer is that this very serious matter has become *hefker,* disregarded, and trampled upon by many. We speak not only of habitual gossipers. There are many people who are not given to gossip, yet do not consider *loshon hora* as serious as most other sins. Therefore, they turn a deaf ear when told to refrain from speaking the forbidden.

There is no greater *meis mitzvah* in our time.

כב אדר
22 ADAR / CYCLE 1

כג אלול
23 ELUL / CYCLE 2

SEFER CHOFETZ CHAIM
Believing Rechilus

∝Divisive Insights

I f a person was present when a statement was made or an act was committed by an individual, and then someone else who was present points out to the person that the act was intended to hurt him, he may not believe this interpretation of what had transpired. Not only is it wrong to believe a report that is *rechilus,* it is also prohibited to accept an insight that transforms an innocent occurrence into a malicious act.[247]

The gossiper clearly believes that every letter of the holy Torah is true — why then does he totally disregard these verses in practice?!

לע"נ הניא בת מאיר ע"ה 22 Adar · Hanna Shayovich
Dedicated by Mr. & Mrs. Menachem Shayovich and family
לע"נ ר' חיים יהודה בן נחום ז"ל 23 Elul · Rabbi Leo H. Shayovich
Dedicated by Mr. & Mrs. Menachem Shayovich and family

⋘A Contradiction

The gossiper should be filled with shame over his blatant disregard for the transgressions which he regularly commits, for surely he believes that every letter of the Torah is true and God-given.

Imagine that the gossiper were called to the Torah and the portion to be read contained one of the verses which prohibits *loshon hora*, such as "Do not go as a gossipmonger among your people" (*Vayikra* 19:16); "Accursed is one who strikes his fellow stealthily" (*Devarim* 27:24); "Remember that which HASHEM, your God, did to Miriam (*Devarim* 24:9); "Do not accept a false report" (*Shemos* 23:1); etc. As the gossiper looks at the scroll's words before reciting the opening blessing he notices that one of the letters in one of the above verses is missing a point, rendering it invalid. Surely he would not recite the blessing, for he knows that in order to be valid the Torah scroll must be complete, and that not a single letter may be deficient in any way. The gossiper clearly believes that every letter of the holy Torah is true. Why then does he totally disregard these verses in practice?!

As mentioned above, a person should choose at least one *mitzvah* to which he will dedicate himself with utmost devotion. There is particular benefit in selecting the *mitzvah* to guard one's tongue as one's singular *mitzvah.* We can liken this to earning a livelihood. The average person would prefer to have a steady livelihood which earns him a modest but predictable profit, as opposed to a business which may bring him large profits, but without any sort of regularity or predictability. The *mitzvah* of *shmiras haloshon* can accrue merit day and night in virtually any situation. Whether one is at home, in the study hall, market, or at a social gathering, he is forever presented with opportunities to refrain from speaking and listening to the forbidden. And as the Sages teach, "One who sits and does not commit a sin is granted reward equivalent to that of one who performs a *mitzvah*" (*Kiddushin* 39b).

כג אדר
23 ADAR / CYCLE 1

כד אלול
24 ELUL / CYCLE 2

SEFER CHOFETZ CHAIM
Believing Rechilus

❧Necessary Precautions

In light of the prohibition against believing *rechilus,* one might ask: How can we ever consider such information to be constructive and permit listening to it? What purpose could there be in listening to information which one is not permitted to believe?

The answer to this is found in the *halachah* which differentiates between acceptance of *rechilus* as fact, which is prohibited, and the taking of appropriate precautions on the chance that the report may be true, which is proper. To believe *rechilus* is foolish and wicked; to ignore it is naive and irresponsible.

While one must not allow his relationship with the person to be affected by what was said about him, one must protect himself from the possibility of harm.[248]

A single congregation can merit to bring about the Final Redemption by internalizing the quality of peace.

לע"נ לאה בת חיים שמחה 23 Adar · Lillian Shatz
Dedicated by the Rothman family
24 Elul · לע"נ מרן רבינו החפץ חיים ר' ישראל מאיר בן
ר' ארי' זאב הכהן זצוקלל"ה
24 Elul · לע"נ חי' מלכה בת יעקב שלמה הכהן שכטר
מאת משפחת פרנקל

DAY
172

~It is in Our Hands

The Talmud states (*Yoma* 9b) that the Second Temple was destroyed because of *sinas chinam,* baseless hatred, to which *loshon hora* is a prime contributing factor. If this sin had the power to destroy an existing Temple, surely it has the power to prevent a new Temple from being built. Therefore, one who will strengthen himself regarding *shmiras haloshon* and will inspire others to do the same will surely earn for himself inestimable merit.

The coming of *Mashiach* is literally in our hands, for *Zohar Chadash* states (*Parashas Noach* 23:3) that a single congregation can merit to bring about the Final Redemption by internalizing the quality of peace in the desired way. It is impossible to merit the quality of peace without first ridding oneself of baseless hatred and *loshon hora*. Whoever will strive to rid himself of these sins will have a share in the building of the Third Temple.

Were we to be granted the opportunity to build the Temple today and all that were lacking was money, surely each one of us would come forth and contribute generously. Who would not want a share in the Temple's construction? In truth, it is not money that is needed; rather, what each of us must do is uproot baseless hatred from within himself, refrain from speaking *loshon hora*, and acquire the quality of peace.

How exalted will be those who merit these accomplishments, for when *Mashiach* will appear and the Temple will be built, it will become known that they played an important role in bringing this about.

כד אדר
24 ADAR / CYCLE 1

כה אלול
25 ELUL / CYCLE 2

SEFER CHOFETZ CHAIM
Believing Rechilus

↚Relative Reports

It is forbidden to believe *rechilus* even if the speaker is someone very close to the listener and would not want to draw him into a feud unnecessarily. Even though it is clear that the speaker has only the good of the listener in mind, his account of the story may not be accepted as fact.[249]

If one finds it difficult to convince himself that the report is totally false, he must, at the very least, assume that the speaker's interpretation of the incident is mistaken and that no ill will was intended by the subject. (As stated above, if the report was intended to save him from harm, he must, of course, protect himself on the possibility that it may be true.)

Those who teach others regarding shmiras haloshon bring themselves and their fellow Jews great merit.

24 Adar · May today's learning be a זכות for our משפחה
Dedicated by Jerry & Anita Ghanooni
25 Elul · Israel Aronovitz לע"נ ישראל נתן בן חיים ז"ל
Dedicated by David & Fiona Aronovitz, Johannesburg, South Africa

◄Inspire Others

In essence, it is every Jew's desire to fulfill Hashem's will. It is ignorance of *halachah*, lack of awareness of the matter's severity,
and a feeling of helplessness as to how to change oneself in this
area, which are the root causes of widespread disregard for *shmiras
haloshon*. One who will attempt to guide others in this matter will
surely find his words well received, and will bring great merit to his
fellow Jews.

Zohar Chadash states (*Lech Lecha* 25a): "Rav Avahu said: 'Take
note of the great reward that awaits one who inspires another Jew
to repent. From where is this derived? From the words, "And
Malkitzedek, King of Shaleim, brought out bread and wine" '
(*Bereishis* 14:18). R' Chiya Rabbah taught: 'When the soul of a righteous person who inspired others to repent departs this world, the
angel Michael, who brings the souls of the righteous before their
Creator, goes forth to greet him, as it is written: *And Malkitzedek* —
this refers to Michael, head of the keepers of the Gates of *Tzedek*
(Righteousness); *King of Shaleim* — this refers to the Jerusalem of
Heaven; *brought out bread and wine* — he goes forth to welcome the
righteous man, saying: Peace unto you!' "

Elsewhere, *Zohar Chadash* states (ibid. 62a): "A Heavenly call goes
forth each day: 'Meritorious are those who toil in Torah, who draw
others close to Torah, and who overlook the hurt caused them.' "

כה אדר
25 ADAR / CYCLE 1

כו אלול
26 ELUL / CYCLE 2

SEFER CHOFETZ CHAIM
Believing Rechilus

✎*Public Revelations and Suspicious Silence*

One may not believe *rechilus* even if it was re-lated in public. The fact that a person is unafraid to publicly relate information that is cause for ill will is not proof of its authenticity and certainly not of its accuracy.[250]

Furthermore, even if an accusation is made in the presence of the subject and the accused fails to respond, one may not interpret his silence as self-incrimination. The person may have been flustered and at a loss for words, or he may have chosen to remain silent rather than cause an escalation of the verbal abuse hurled at him.[251]

Let us follow in the ways of our ancestors, to do kindness with one another and faithfully uphold our covenant with Hashem.

✺The Way of Our Ancestors

The *Midrash* states that four sources of merit figured prominently in the redemption from Egypt: The Jews did not adopt Egyptian names, did not speak in the way of the Egyptians, were not guilty of immorality and did not speak *loshon hora* (*Vayikra Rabbah* 32:5).

Tanna D'Vei Eliyahu Rabbah (ch. 23) relates:

> When the Jews were in Egypt, they assembled and sat down together, for they were united as one. They established a covenant to do kindness with one another; to safeguard in their hearts the covenant of Avraham, Yitzchak and Yaakov; to serve their Father in Heaven alone; not to forsake the language of their father Yaakov's house; and not to learn the language of the Egyptians, so as not to follow the ways of idol worshipers.
>
> The Egyptians would ask them: "Why do you not serve our gods, for if you did, your workload would be lightened?" The Jews responded: "Did our forefathers forsake our Father in Heaven, that we should now do the same?"
>
> When the Jews circumcised their sons, the Egyptians suggested, "Perhaps if you do not observe this law, your difficult labor will be lightened." The Jews responded: "Did our forefathers forget the covenant into which they entered with our Father in Heaven, that we should now do the same?"
>
> When Jews would marry and celebrate the Seven Days of Feasting that follow, the Egyptians asked, "Why do you celebrate? Soon you will be forced to perform your slave labor!" The Jews responded, "We shall celebrate — you can do with us as you please. Those who are destined to die, shall die. Those who are destined to live, shall live."

(continued on page 413)

כו אדר
26 ADAR / CYCLE 1

כז אלול
27 ELUL / CYCLE 2

SEFER CHOFETZ CHAIM
Believing Rechilus

~Beyond Reproach

Halachah does recognize that there are individuals who are so precise, both in perception as well as in their conveying of facts, that hearing their account is tantamount to witnessing the act in person. One would be permitted to believe even *rechilus* told by such individuals, but could not share the information with others.[252]

As stated in the laws of *loshon hora,* the Chofetz Chaim contends that no one today can claim to possess this degree of integrity; therefore, one should not rely on this *halachah* in practice.[253]

One is obligated to instruct his children regarding the severity of speaking loshon hora.

לע״נ רחל טובא ע״ה בת פנחס יוסף יבל״ח Rochelly Lazar · 26 Adar
Dedicated by her loving family
לע״נ אהרן בן יוסף שמריהו Aaron Silbermintz · 27 Elul
Dedicated by Nechama Silbermintz

➳*A Public Appeal*

Through the kindness of Hashem, I have now attained the age of "strength" (the eighties - see *Tehillim* 90:10), and virtually my entire life I have not diverted my mind from pondering the matter of speech, which involves numerous positive and negative commandments. To our misfortune, many among the multitudes have no regard whatsoever for the matter of *shmiras haloshon*; to their minds, it is nothing more than a matter of custom and propriety for those who wish to be zealous in it.

I direct my words to those who have some understanding of the Torah's precepts, people whose hearts would undoubtedly be distressed for months on end were they to mistakenly eat meat that is unkosher. It is rare that these same people would feel such distress upon realizing that they have accepted as fact malicious talk about a certain individual, thereby transgressing the Torah prohibition against believing *loshon hora*. The reason for this apparent contradiction is that this prohibition is not taken seriously by the multitudes...

Ramban understands the commandment to recall the episode of Miriam's affliction (*Devarim* 24:9) as an obligation to admonish one's children and transmit to future generations how exceedingly shameful is this sin. In this way, the prohibition against speaking *loshon hora* will be fluent upon their lips. For this sin is great and brings with it many bad things — and people tend to transgress it regularly.

Moreover, inspiring others regarding the seriousness of this sin goes a long way toward insuring that one will himself refrain from speaking the forbidden (from a letter of the Chofetz Chaim, Iyar 5686 [1926]).

כז אדר
27 ADAR / CYCLE 1

כח אלול
28 ELUL / CYCLE 2

SEFER CHOFETZ CHAIM
Believing Rechilus

❧*Innocent Remarks*

When someone makes an innocent statement without realizing the consequences of what he is saying, people tend to accept his word as fact. *Halachah,* too, accepts such statements as fact in certain specific instances. (These are: as testimony regarding a man's death in order that his wife be permitted to remarry; in determining the status of food that had been suspected of being non-kosher by rabbinic law; or where the facts will eventually come to light in any case.) *Rechilus,* however, cannot be accepted as fact even when a statement was made off-handedly.[254]

When speaking loshon hora, one may violate one or more of seventeen negative commandments.

27 Adar · In memory of Leon (Yehudah) Schemo
28 Elul · Shloime Dunner לע״נ ר׳ שלמה ז״ל בן הרה״ג
ר׳ יוסף צבי הלוי שליט״א
Dedicated by his family, London, England

⟡Negative Commandments

In his introduction to *Sefer Chofetz Chaim,* the Chofetz Chaim enumerates 17 negative commandments which one may violate when speaking or listening to *loshon hora.* Below are the negative commandments most commonly transgressed:

1) לא תלך רכיל בעמיך, *You shall not be a gossipmonger among your people (Vayikra* 19:16).

2) לא תשא שמע שוא, *Do not accept a false report (Shemos* 23:1), which prohibits both speaking and accepting *loshon hora (Pesachim* 118a).

3) השמר בנגע הצרעת לשמר מאד ולעשות, *Beware of a tzaraas affliction, to be very careful and to act (Devarim* 24:8), which *Sifre* explains as a reference to *loshon hora* for which *tzaraas* is a punishment.

4) לפני עור לא תתן מכשל, *And you shall not place a stumbling block before the blind (Vayikra* 19:14), by causing others to sin.

5) השמר לך פן תשכח את ה' אלהיך, *Take care, lest you forget HASHEM, your God (Devarim* 8:11) through arrogance *(Sotah* 5a) — a prime cause of *loshon hora.*

6) ולא תחללו את שם קדשי, *You shall not desecrate My holy Name (Vayikra* 22:32).

7) לא תשנא את אחיך בלבבך, *You shall not hate your brother in your heart (Vayikra* 19:17).

8) לא תקם, *You shall not take revenge ...*

9) ולא תטר, *and you shall not bear a grudge (Vayikra* 19:18).

10) לא יהיה כקרח וכעדתו, *That he not be like Korach and his assembly (Bamidbar* 17:5), who caused strife among the Jewish people.

11) ולא תונו איש את עמיתו, *Each of you shall not aggrieve his fellow (Vayikra* 25:17) through hurtful words.

12) (הוכח תוכיח את עמיתך) ולא תשא עליו חטא, *(You shall reprove your fellow) and do not bear a sin because of him (Vayikra* 19:17) by embarrassing him in the course of your reproof.

(The five remaining negative commandments are found in *Shemos* 22:21; 23:2; *Vayikra* 19:14; *Bamidbar* 35:33; and *Devarim* 19:15.)

◆*Circumstantial Evidence*

As in the case of *loshon hora,* the one instance where *rechilus* may be believed as fact is where the report confirms a suspicion already supported by evidence which would be insufficient on its own. If, for example, someone's strange behavior is a clear indication of his having done something wrong, and a person then claims to have witnessed the act, one may believe the person's account. This does not, however, permit sharing the information with others, unless there is a halachically acceptable constructive purpose in doing so.

In summation, *rechilus* may be spoken and listened to for a constructive purpose, but it may be believed only when supported by circumstantial evidence.[255]

*On 29 Elul, the lesson for Day 178 should be learned together with today's lesson.

When speaking loshon hora, one may violate one or more of fourteen positive commandments.

28 Adar · Morris (Moshe Aaron) Zarecki לע"נ משה אהרן ב"ר חיים סענדר
Dedicated by the Zarecki family, Montreal, Canada
29 Elul · The Manchester Rosh Yeshiva לע"נ הגאון הצדיק הרב
יהודא זאב בן הגאון הצדיק הרב משה יצחק הלוי סג"ל זצוק"ל
Dedicated by Shuly and Feigy Lerner, London, England

DAY 177

ﬤPositive Commandments

In his introduction to *Sefer Chofetz Chaim*, the Chofetz Chaim enu-merates 14 positive commandments one may violate when speaking or listening to *loshon hora*. The commandments most commonly transgressed are:

1) זכור את אשר עשה ה' אלהיך למרים בדרך בצאתכם ממצרים, *Remember what HASHEM, your God, did to Miriam on the way, when you were leaving Egypt* (*Devarim* 24:9 — see Days 44-48).

2) ואהבת לרעך כמוך, *You shall love your fellow as yourself* (*Vayikra* 19:18).

3) בצדק תשפט עמיתך, *With righteousness shall you judge your fellow* (*Vayikra* 19:15).

4) הוכח תוכיח את עמיתך, *You shall reprove your fellow* (*Vayikra* 19:17), which includes the obligation to reprove one who is speaking *loshon hora*.

5) את ה' אלהיך תירא, *HASHEM, your God, shall you fear* (*Devarim* 10:20).

6) מדבר שקר תרחק, *Distance yourself from falsehood* (*Shemos* 23:7).

7) והלכת בדרכיו, *And you shall go in His ways* (*Devarim* 28:9), a requirement to emulate the ways of Hashem.

(The seven remaining commandments are found in *Shemos* 20:12; *Vayikra* 19:30,32; 21:8; 25:35; and *Devarim* 6:7, 10:20.)

ᴥRepentance

One who has either spoken *rechilus,* listened as someone else spoke *rechilus,* or believed a statement that is classified as *rechilus,* must engage in the *teshuvah* process appropriate for his transgression.

One who spoke *rechilus* should preferably approach anyone who was present when he made the statement and explain that it was inaccurate. Otherwise, he must approach the subject of his remark and beg forgiveness for having spoken *rechilus* concerning him.

One who listened to *rechilus* need not ask forgiveness of the person spoken about even if he had believed the statement. However, if he did believe the statement, he must convince himself that the information may have been totally inaccurate and taken out of context.

In all of the above situations, one must confess before Hashem for having violated a Torah commandment, express regret for what he did, and resolve to avoid repetition of his misdeed.

During Hebrew leap years, Adar I has 30 days. During those years, the lesson for 29 Adar should be learned again today.

"Even those of wholesome character will feel a positive effect from studying these works."

29 Adar · Morris Lapidus לע״נ חיים משה בן ישראל זאב
Dedicated by Debbie
30 Adar · Mrs. Bella Orlen לע״נ בלהה בת אהרן
Dedicated in memory of a beloved wife and mother, by her husband Shmuel and her daughter Sivia

ᔆThe Peddler's Potion

It happened that a certain peddler was making his way through the towns near the city of Tzippori, calling out as he went, "Who wishes to purchase a life-giving potion?" People crowded around him [to obtain what he was offering].

R' Yannai was sitting on his balcony studying Torah. Upon hearing the peddler's announcement, R' Yannai called down, "Come up here and sell me your potion." The peddler replied, "Neither you nor those like you need it." However, R' Yannai persisted until the peddler agreed to come up. The peddler opened the Book of *Tehillim* (*Psalms*) and read, "Which man desires life?... Guard your tongue from evil and your lips from speaking deceit. Turn from evil and do good..." (*Tehillim* 34:13-14). R' Yannai said, "Shlomo too declared, 'One who guards his mouth and tongue, guards his soul from tribulations' (*Mishlei* 21:23).

R' Yannai reflected, "All my life I read this verse, but never perceived its full meaning until this peddler came along"[1] (*Vayikra Rabbah* 16:2).

While on a visit to *Eretz Yisrael* in 1936, Rabbi Avraham Mordechai Alter, the *Rebbe* of Ger (and author of *Imrei Emes*), wrote the following in a letter to his followers in Poland:

> I also seek the following from you: As the tribulations befalling our nation have multiplied both within and without, and our Sages, with their trustworthy insight, have taught that the causes of this exile are *loshon hora* and *sinas chinam* (baseless hatred), I suggest that all of you study *Sefer Chofetz Chaim* and *Sefer Shmiras HaLoshon* ...

(continued on page 414)

---

1. R' Yannai had never understood why David taught this lesson in the form of a question and answer. After meeting the peddler, R' Yannai understood that because people so easily transgress the laws of proper speech, it is therefore necessary to draw their attention to this matter by making a public announcement such as the peddler did (*Maharzu*).

Continuations...

SEFER CHOFETZ CHAIM — *continued from page 96*

The Chofetz Chaim fails to find justification for such leniency; furthermore, he discourages reliance on *Rambam's* opinion with regard to *loshon hora* spoken in the presence of three, as most other commentators seem to disagree with his ruling.[39] Thus, one should never relate derogatory information, even when it was related to three or more listeners.

SEFER SHMIRAS HALOSHON — *continued from page 129*

The Torah states: "And the person with *tzaraas* ... his garments shall be torn, the hair of his head shall be unshorn, and he shall cloak himself up to his lips;[1] he is to call out: 'Contaminated, contaminated!' " (*Vayikra* 13:45).

The purpose of this proclamation was to warn people to stay away from him lest his *tumah* contaminate them,[2] and to inform others of his anguish so that they would pray for him.[3] The *metzora's* isolation and disgrace would humble him and inspire him to regret his sin. He would resolve that from then on he would refrain from committing this bitter sin, and he would beg forgiveness of those of whom he had spoken disparagingly in the past.

SEFER CHOFETZ CHAIM — *continued from page 130*

Nevertheless, the Chofetz Chaim refers to derogatory statements made for a constructive purpose as *"loshon hora l'toeles"* seemingly for lack of a better term. We, too, have made use of the term *"loshon hora (or rechilus)* for a constructive purpose'' at various points in this work.

A great deal of sensitivity, objectivity, and knowledge of *halachah* is required in order to distinguish between genuine

---

1. He dresses and acts like a mourner, so that he will be influenced to repent the behavior that brought this affliction upon him (*Ibn Ezra*).
2. *Rashi* ad loc.
3. *Moed Katan* 5a.

constructive speech and what amounts to nothing more than rationalized *loshon hora*. The Chofetz Chaim lists several conditions necessary for a statement to be deemed one of *toeles*, constructive purpose, as opposed to *loshon hora*.

The conditions for a statement to qualify as *constructive*— soon to be discussed here— must be studied carefully before taking the liberty of making a statement that would otherwise be considered *loshon hora*. It would also be wise to discuss the matter with a competent *rav*, as an incorrect decision could result in irreparable harm.

SEFER CHOFETZ CHAIM — *continued from page 158*

It is permissible to publicize that a Jew regularly violates a particular *halachah* if it is clear that he is aware of the *halachah* and has chosen to ignore it, and it stands to reason that publicizing his behavior will induce him to change. This applies even if he transgresses the law out of temptation. However, one must be certain that all the conditions of *toeles,* constructive speech, including purity of intent and lack of an alternative, apply.[94]

SEFER CHOFETZ CHAIM — *continued from page 162*

However, he is not considered עֲמִיתֶךָ, *your fellow*, and consequently the prohibition of *onaas devarim,* causing hurt through the spoken word (*Vayikra* 25:17), will not apply in his case. Social pressure may be used to encourage observance even if he will suffer embarrassment in the process, provided that all the conditions of constructive speech are met. Non-constructive speech that is either derogatory or harmful would constitute *loshon hora.*[98]

(3)The classic *apikores* (heretic) who is knowledgeable but rebels is considered neither *your brother* nor a part of *your people*. If there exists such a person today, one may speak about him without any preconditions.[99]

SEFER CHOFETZ CHAIM — *continued from page 168*

A teacher must make every effort to fully understand the behavior of each student; he must not be swift to condemn. It is essential that a student feel comfortable about expressing his true feelings to his teacher (in a respectable manner, of course). *Conditions 1-4* of constructive speech (see Day 50) necessitate a good heart-to-heart talk with the student before reporting a problem (unless one suspects that serious danger may be imminent).

SEFER CHOFETZ CHAIM — *continued from page 196*

Finally, one should consider why he deems it necessary to relate the information altogether. Perhaps it would be better not to get involved and refrain from any action which would affect the storekeeper's income.[122]

SEFER CHOFETZ CHAIM — *continued from page 204*

The Sages teach that Korach's argument as rooted in jealousy, resulting from his having been passed over for the position of prince of his Levite family.

Before embarking on an ideological campaign against others, one must ask himself: "Am I honestly promoting the cause of truth, or am I involved in a personal feud disguised as an ideological debate?"

Ideological disagreement should never lead to personal animosity. When Torah scholars disagree, their dispute is over ideals, and is never personal. When a scholar is involved in a dispute, his followers must be careful not to become involved in a matter that is not their own, and certainly should avoid character assassination and personal hatred towards his opponent.

SEFER CHOFETZ CHAIM — *continued from page 212*

(1) Objectively speaking, it may not be good for the people involved, or (2) it does not satisfy the subjective needs and tastes of both parties.

Not only is it cruel to subject people to situations that are bad for them, it is also wrong to involve the unsuspecting in relationships they would not have wanted had they known the facts.[135]

Examples of this rule will be discussed below.

SEFER CHOFETZ CHAIM — *continued from page 214*

Upon discovering the truth after the wedding, the person might spend the rest of his married life feeling that he settled for second best. Even if he was told the truth right before the wedding and nevertheless went through with it, feelings of disappointment might surface later.

Such practices, though well intended, constitute giving bad advice and are in violation of "Before a blind person do not place a stumbling block."[136]

SEFER CHOFETZ CHAIM — *continued from page 218*

(4) He does not feel that either party will have a negative influence upon the other.

(5) He is not aware that one party lacks something that the other is insistent upon, or has something to which the other has explicitly expressed strong objection.

Should there be any doubt as to whether any of these conditions have been met, the counsel of a *talmid chacham* should be sought.

SEFER CHOFETZ CHAIM — *continued from page 220*

Thus, while the advisor's first obligation is to the party he is advising, it is forbidden for him to encourage a *shidduch* that he clearly knows is bad for the other party. This would be considered speaking *loshon hora* in the form of speech that causes harm.

It is forbidden for an advisor to discourage a relationship unless his disapproval is based on firsthand information that was carefully analyzed.

Finally, if an advisor encouraged his petitioner to pursue a given *shidduch* but his advice was ignored, he may not draw the conclusion that the person "just doesn't want to get married," is "incapable of making commitments," or has "unrealistic expectations." To make such statements would be to speak *loshon hora* and perhaps *hotzaas shem ra* (slander).

SEFER CHOFETZ CHAIM — *continued from page 222*

In summation, then, if, for example, an eligible young man is insistent that the woman he marries be at least four years younger than he, should never have failed an exam in elementary school, or comply with some other stipulation of seeming irrelevance, one who is asked concerning such matters should simply say, "I don't know." However, a *shadchan* may not suggest someone who does not meet these terms without first consulting a *rav* (Days 79, 80).[139]

SEFER CHOFETZ CHAIM — *continued from page 226*

(3) If it is possible to convince the party that is concealing the information to come forth with it, that would be preferable.[143]

(4) The information is not to be exaggerated and only that which is necessary may be told.

(5) One's intent must be to prevent a harmful situation from coming about and not to denigrate the party spoken about. Moreover, there must be a real possibility that the information conveyed will not be ignored, so that the constructive purpose will be realized.

(6) No realistic alternative to conveying the information directly can be found.

(7) No undue harm will be caused by informing the party of the problem. Should there be reason to suspect that the party, upon learning that it has been deceived, will denigrate the other party or seek revenge in some other way, one should not get involved.

SEFER CHOFETZ CHAIM — *continued from page 234*

(1) The speaker does not realize that the information he is conveying is *loshon hora*, or is totally unaware that *loshon hora* is prohibited by the Torah; and (2) it is obvious that the speaker will continue speaking *loshon hora* even after being told that this is forbidden.

In such a case, reproof would transform the speaker from an inadvertent sinner into one who sins intentionally. Hence, it is better not to reprove him.[147]

SEFER SHMIRAS HALOSHON — *continued from page 243*

"And when I said that I had no pillows or blankets?"

"I thought that perhaps you had dedicated all your possessions to the Temple."

The employer exclaimed, "I make an oath that that is exactly what happened! ...Just as you judged me favorably, so too should the Omnipresent judge you favorably."

And indeed, the Sages teach, "One who judges his fellow favorably is judged favorably [by Heaven]" (ibid.).

SEFER SHMIRAS HALOSHON — *continued from page 259*

Such was the attitude of David when Avishai ben Tzeruyah sought to take revenge from Shimi ben Geira for his having cursed David Commanding Avishai to refrain from this, David said, "HASHEM told him [i.e. permitted him to — *Ralbag*] 'Curse!' " (*II Shmuel* 16:10). The Sages state that it was because of this acceptance of the Divine will that David merited to be one of the "supports" of the Divine chariot (*Shevet Mussar* 20:27 citing *Midrash*).

SEFER SHMIRAS HALOSHON — *continued from page 263*

On this earth, a person sees others clothed in their physical garb, and thus tends to look down upon them and focus on what he perceives as their faults. Hashem, however, sees the essential holiness of every Jewish soul, which, as often stated in the holy *Zohar,* is awesome. Hashem's love and regard for each soul is predicated on this knowledge, and thus is exceedingly great.

SEFER SHMIRAS HALOSHON — *continued from page 269*

The above should inspire each of us to arouse compassion before Hashem on behalf of the Jewish people, for in our day, the sources of merit cited in *Tanna D'Vei Eliyahu* are still to be found. The material status of the Jewish people in our time is far from good; yet wherever one turns, he finds Jews who study Torah, observe *mitzvos,* support Torah study, do kindness with others and give charity to the poor.

SEFER SHMIRAS HALOSHON — *continued from page 305*

The answer to this is obvious. The Torah states: כי לא דבר רק הוא מכם, *for it is not an empty thing for you* (*Devarim* 32:47). Midrashically, this means that the Torah is not, Heaven forfend, empty. If you find it to be unfulfilling, then the failure stems מכם, *from you*. The fault is *in you*, not in the Torah.

To our misfortune, we have fulfilled the prophet's words, "Because this nation has approached Me, honoring Me with their mouths and lips, but their heart was far from Me, and their fear of Me was by force of habit" (*Yeshayahu* 29:13). We declare זכור, *Remember*,with our lips, but we do not take its message to heart. It is clear that when a person *does* take its message to heart, the effect is profound.[1]

SEFER CHOFETZ CHAIM — *continued from page 308*

Thus, a statement of *rechilus* which could be cause for *sinas chinam* is a potential cause of falsehood — and concealing or altering the facts to avoid *rechilus* is an advancement of the cause of truth. In the Sages' words, מותר לשנות מפני השלום, *One may alter the facts for the sake of peace* (see *Rashi* to *Bereishis* 50:16).[204]

It must be noted, however, that under no circumstances may one swear falsely — even for the sake of peace.[205]

SEFER SHMIRAS HALOSHON — *continued from page 321*

Every soul that descends to this world is an emissary of Hashem, endowed with a mission to perfect his soul in accordance with its Divinely endowed abilities. It is foolish for a person to feel proud that he has been blessed with superior intellect, for his intellect is not his own acquisition. Rather, it has been granted him by Hashem so that he can accomplish his unique purpose in this world. Therefore, one should ponder how he has used his inborn gifts, how he has spent each of his days, and how much valuable time he has squandered. It may well be that the man of superior intellect and talent has used but a small fraction of his inborn abilities. As such, he certainly has nothing of which to be proud.

SEFER CHOFETZ CHAIM — *continued from page 352*

In the case of a prospective business or marriage relationship, where certain aspects of the subject's history cast doubt on the correctness of the proposed relationship, rebuke would not affect matters and is therefore unnecessary. Even if the person would

---

1. It seems clear that to verbally recall Miriam's affliction is a Spiritual requirement. The Chofetz Chaim wonders why it is generally treated as an optional custom.

pledge to mend his ways, the other party would have to be warned of the possibility that he may return to his previous mode of behavior. However, one should attempt to encourage the person to inform the other party of his past, thus lessening the need for involvement of a third party.[230]

SEFER CHOFETZ CHAIM — *continued from page 362*

When older students share personal information with a teacher, the teacher may not pass the information on to others. If the advice of colleagues or supervisors is necessary, the student's identity should not be divulged. The teacher may reveal the information, along with the student's identity, only when a student discloses facts of which *halachah* requires him to inform others. This includes any medical condition or behavioral problem of which the school administration should have been informed (e.g. chemical imbalance). As in the case of the therapist or lawyer, a teacher should be in contact with a *halachic* authority in dealing with issues of confidentiality.

SEFER SHMIRAS HALOSHON — *continued from page 379*

Some people spend their younger years accomplishing little spiritually, content to enjoy what they perceive as the "good life" in this world. They know that life here is not forever, that it is the next world where the soul lives on eternally. However, they convince themselves that there will be time in their old age to concern themselves with matters of the spirit. And so, ten, twenty or more years swiftly pass, as the cycle of work and relaxation repeats itself again and again, with little earned for the long road that all men eventually travel. Those with such an attitude are like the man in our parable who failed to recognize the real purpose of his journey.

Let us make the most of our years, days and hours. The potential for accomplishment is without limit.

SEFER SHMIRAS HALOSHON — *continued from page 397*

Let us follow in the ways of our ancestors, to do kindness with one another and faithfully uphold their covenant to serve no one but Hashem. Let us pay no heed to enticements and arguments to the contrary, just as the Jews paid no heed to the Egyptians' words.

May we merit the fulfillment of the prophecy, "As in the days when you departed Egypt, will I show him wonders" (*Michah* 7:15) — speedily and in our time.

A POSTSCRIPT — *continued from page 405*

Heaven and earth bear witness that upon completing the above-mentioned works I felt within myself a positive effect. Even those who are of wholesome character will feel a positive effect from studying these works.

Though the peddler told R' Yannai that "Neither you, nor those like you, are in need of this potion," R' Yannai troubled the man to come up to him, to demonstrate that everyone is in need of it.

מקורות מספר שמירת הלשון

מקורות והערות לספר חפץ חיים

ידועים דברי החת״ס שגם אחרי סידור המשנה והתלמוד לא הותרה כתיבת תושבע״פ אלא משום עת לעשות (שו״ת חת״ס או״ח סי׳ ר״ח), אשר מדבריו יוצא שהדפסת ספר מוצדקת אך ורק במקום ובזמן שקיים חשש אמיתי לשכחת התורה או חלק ממנה.

גישה זו מורגשת בעליל בכל אחד מספריו הרבים של מרן החי״ח – ממחנה ישראל ונדחי ישראל ליהודים נדחים – ועד לליקוטי הלכות, חי״ח ושה״ל לחלקי התורה שהגדיר אותם החי״ח כמתי מצוה – ועל כולם ספר משנה ברורה אשר מפיו אנו חיים – כל משפט צועק ככרוכיא ״עת לעשות״ של ה,,הפרו תורתך.״

על רקע זה מובן היטב המבנה של ספר חפץ חיים אשר רבים מתקשים להסביר איך שגאון ישראל וממיטב מחבריריה שהצליח להבהיר לנו את הסוגיות המסובכות ביותר, השליך אותנו למצולות שיטות הראשונים באפי תלתא ואפי מרא עוד לפני שגמר להגדיר מה נכלל באיסור לה״ר!

אלא – שספר חי״ח לא נכתב כשו״ע גרידא לסדר בפנינו הלכות לה״ר ורכילות, אלא גם – ובעיקר – לגדור את פרצת הדור בחטא הלשון; ולכן ראה לנבון להקדיש את חלקו הקדמי של הספר לתיקון הטעויות המצויות שהיוו גורמים עיקריים לפרצה.

ובכן – כלל א׳ עוסק רובו ככולו בטעויות המצויות אצל ההמון עם – שלה״ר על האמת מותר (סעיף א׳), שאין בשמירת הלשון אלא משום מדת חסידות בלבד (סעיף ב׳, ג׳ וד׳ – וזוהי ג״כ מטרת הפתיחה), שמותר לספר לה״ר ע״פ בקשת אחרים – כולל הורים ומורים (סעיף ה׳), שמותר לספר לה״ר במקום הפסד (ס״ו, ז׳), שמותר לרמוז על לה״ר (ס״ח), שמותר לכלול את חבריו בגנות שמספר גם על עצמו (סעיף ט׳).

כלל ב׳ ותחלת כלל ג׳ עוסקים בטעויות שהיו מצויות אצל ת״ח שלמדו סוגיות בש״ס שכאילו התירו סיפור לה״ר באפי תלתא (כלל ב׳) ובאפי מרא (ריש כלל ג׳), ואח״כ מוסיף החי״ח עוד היתרים שלמדנים עלולים להמציא – שלה״ר מותרת כשאינו מספר דרך שנאה (סעיף ג׳), אם לא הזכיר את שם המדובר במפורש (ס״ד), או אם לא תגרום הגנות לשום נזק והפסד (ס״ה). בסוף כלל ג׳ עוסק החי״ח בחיוב לדון את חבירו לכף זכות אשר כידוע היא ההנהגה החשובה ביותר במלחמה נגד לה״ר, ורק בכלל ד׳ מתחיל החי״ח לפרש את מהותו של איסור לה״ר.

והנה, בדורנו זה זכינו ומאמצי החי״ח בענין שה״ל עשו פרי, וישנה ב״ה התעוררות רבה ורצון טוב בקרב בני ובנות ישראל ללמוד וללמד לשמור ולעשות למען שה״ל, אלא שלא כל א׳ מסוגל לרכוש ידיעה ברורה ביסודות איסורי לה״ר מתוך ספר חי״ח. הספר הנוכחי הוא נסיון לענות על צרכי הזמן – סידור יסודות באופן ברור ומהיר, בשפה המדוברת, עם ציורים מעשיים מתוך החיים היום-יומיים של יהודי בזמננו.

מן הראוי שספר שכזה יכתב ע״י בעל שיעור קומה בידיעותיו וטוהר מדותיו. אבל מההלכות של,עת לעשות׳ שאין חולקין כבוד לרב. ולמרות שהדינים מבוססים על ספר ח״ח ופסקי גדולי זמננו, בכל זאת אבקש מהקורא שיש לו מה להעיר, לשלוח את הערותיו, וע״י יובהרו העניינים ויתוקן מה שטעון תיקון.

ומד׳ אבקש שלא אכשל בדבר הלכה, והספר הזה וכל חלקיו יצליח לזכות את הרבים בשמירות הלשון, ומי ששכן את שמו על המקום הזה הוא ישכן בינינו אהבה ואחוה ושלום וריעות.

ירושלם ת״ו בין המצרים תשנ״ה

*כל מקום שנזכר ח״ח במקורות, הכוונה למקוה״ח הל׳ לה״ר אא״כ מפורש שהוא בהל׳ רכילות.

1. רמב"ם פרק ז' דעות הל' ב'
2. שם הלכה ה'
3. ח"ח כלל ג' סעיף ו'
4. שע"ת לרבינו יונה שער ג' מאמר רט"ז, בחירתו לחייב ולהרשיע את חביריו ושמחתו לאידם – ופשוט שאף שלהתרכז על חסרונותיו של חבירו היא המדה הרעה שבלה"ר, מ"מ לא עבר על הלאו אא"כ סיפר לאחרים.
5. רמב"ם שם
6. ח"ח כלל א' סעיף א'
7. ח"ח כלל ד' סעיף ב'. וכ"ז כשמכוין לגנותו דאל"כ אינו אלא אבק לה"ר.
8. שם, וכנ"ל
9. ח"ח כלל ד' סעיף ו'
10. ח"ח כלל ד' סעיף ט'
11. במ"ח ס"ק ל"ז
12. ח"ח כלל ה' סעיף ד' ובמ"ח ס"ק ח'
13. משמעות דברי הח"ח בבמ"ח כלל ד' ס"ק א' שלא התיר לגלות מעשי אבות לחכם צנע אלא באופן שהמסתפר לא התכוין לגנותו וגם מכיר שלא יתגנה בעיני השומע עבור זה. ועיין בספר זרע חיים על דברי הח"ח כלל ה' סעיף ב'.
14. כשכוונתו לגנותו ודאי אסור כנ"ל, ואם אין כוונתו לגנותו כלל אבל בכל זאת יתגנה עי"ז בעיני השומע הרי"ז לכה"פ בכלל אבק לה"ר.
15. ח"ח כלל ד' סעיף א'
16. ח"ח כלל א' סעיף ט'
17. ח"ח כלל ח' סעיף א', ב'
18. ח"ח כלל ד' ס"ק כ"ח. וכתב ע"ז הגאון ר' הלל זקס שליט"א בזה"ל: שמעתי מאבא מארי הגאון זצ"ל, ששאל ע"י את מרן חותנו הח"ח זצ"ל, ואמר לו שנסתפק בזה והי' דעתו נוטה להקל (הוא לא הכריע) אבל נמנע מלהעתיקו בספרו, שחשש שיצא מזה תקלה. ע"כ. ולכאורה צ"ע הרי כשלא נגרם היזק למדובר אי"צ לבקש ממנו מחילה על סיפור גנות משום חטא שבין אדם לחבירו – וא"י אין המדובר בעל דבר למחול.
19. עי' לקמן הערה מס' 38
20. ח"ח כלל ב' סעיף ב', וכלל ט' סעיף ג' בהגהה
21. ח"ח כלל ב' סעיף ב', וכלל ג' סעיף א'. ולכאורה לפמ"ש בכלל ט' ס"ג בהגהה שנורא בי פלניא הוא לה"ר גמור חזר בו הח"ח ממש"כ שלפי התוס' אין היתר בדבר המשתמע לתרי אנפין באפי תלתא אלא אם הפירוש השלילי אינו גנות גמור. וגם צע"ק למה לא כתב שאין היתר בא"ת כשמספר לפני יראי אלקים כמו שכתב בשיטת הרמב"ם.
22. בכלל ד' סעיף ז' העתיק הח"ח את דברי רבינו יונה בשע"ת שער ג' מאמר רי"ט שהמוסר יצא מכלל עמיתך – ומשמע שאף במוסר לתיאבון הדין כן, אלא שהח"ח מסיים שיש ליזהר שלא לשכוח פרטים אחרים המצטרכים לזה – ובבמ"ח הזכיר בין שאר התנאים שצריך שיתכוין לתועלת דהיינו כדי שיתרחקו בני אדם מדרך רשע ואולי הוא בעצמו ישוב עי"ז – וא"י מפורש שהוא עדיין בכלל עמיך ולא הותר לספר עליו אלא

לתועלת (וזה שיצא מכלל עמיתך היינו לענין אונאת דברים בלבד). ולכאורה כך היא משמעות רבינו יונה שם בשע"ת שאסר למי שנכשל באותן עבירות שהמומר (בלשון רי"י – החונף) המיר בהן לפרסם את מעשי המומר כי אין כוונתו לטובה כי לשמח לאיד. ואלו באפיקורוס כתב הח"ח בכלל ח' סעיף ה' שמצוה לגנותו ובבמ"ח ס"ק ח' פירש שא"צ להפרטים המבוארים בכלל י'. ושם במקוה"ח מפורש שאפיקורס אינו בכלל י'. (ודברי הח"ח בבמ"ח כלל י' ס"ק ל' שגם מומר לתיאבון יצא מכלל עמיך ועי' לקמן הערה 94).

23. ח"ח כלל ט' סעיף ט'
24. בן יהוידע סוף כתובות, וע"ש שאסור להתלונן אפי' על מזג האויר בא"י.
25. שע"ת לרבינו יונה שער שלישי מאמר רי"ז. ולכאורה ה"ה שאסור לגנות נכרי שלא לתועלת – ועי' מדרש רבה פ' תצא פיסקא ט' שאסור רק כדי שלא יתרגל בגינוי הבריות ויבא לגנות גם ליהודים (ועי"ע זרע חיים כלל ח' ס"ה אות ג').
26. ח"ח כלל ד' סעיף י'
27. ח"ח כלל ד' סעיף י"ב, ומפורש בח"ח וכן בבמ"ח ס"ק א"ו שאם לא נגרם שום נזק א"י לבקש מחילה מזה שדבר עליו.
28. רמב"ם פרק ז' דעות הל' ה'
29. הקדמה בבמ"ח לכלל ט' רכילות
30. ח"ח כלל ד' סעיף א'
31. בבמ"ח כלל ד' ס"ק א'. וגם משמע שאין בזה משום גילוי סוד, ורצ"ל שהמסמפר מכיר את עברו של הבע"ת ממקור אחר. שאילו הבע"ת עצמו הוא שגילה למספר שהוא בע"ת הי' אסור לו לגלות את הדבר אפי' לחכם צנוע אם יש קפידא מצד הבע"ת, ומכ"ה מדברי הח"ח כאן שאין אדם יכול לאסור על אחרים מלספר עליו דברים אמתיים שאין בהם משום גנות ונזק אא"כ הוא זה שגילה להם את המידע. ועי' בספר שבילי חיים כאן שמדת חסידות להמנע מלגלות שלא לתועלת.
32. ח"ח כלל ה' סעיף ב'
33. ח"ח כלל ה' סעיף ז'
34. הגהה סוף כלל ב'
35. כלל ט' סעיף ה'
36. במ"ח כלל ב' ס"ק כ"ח
37. רמב"ם פרק ז' דעות הלכה ה'
38. ח"ח כלל ד' סעיף ג', ותמהו עליו רבים איפה מצא דין זה ברמב"ם עי' בספר הזכרון למרן הגר"י הוטנר זצ"ל, ואג נדברו חלק ב' סי' ע"ד. ובקונטרס מרפא לשון ח"א.
39. ח"ח כלל ב' סעיף י'
40. עי' לקמן הערה 94
41. שבילי חיים כלל ח' ס"ק ד'
42. ח"ח כלל ד' סעיף ג'
43. ח"ח כלל ד' סעיף י"ב
44. במ"ח שם ס"ק מ"ח
45. ח"ח שם
46. ח"ח כלל א' סעיף ח'

47. במ״ח כלל א׳ ס״ק י״ד

48. ח״ח כלל י׳ סעיף ד׳

49. ח״ח כלל א׳ סעיף א׳

50. שם, ובזרע חיים ס״ק ב׳ העיר שאם השקר לא שינה את הסיפור לגריעותא אין זה בכלל מוצש״ר

51. ח״ח כלל ג׳ סעיף ג׳. ועי׳ בבמ״ח שם ס״ק ב׳ בשם יד הקטנה שהוא לה״ר גמורה ולא אבק, ואף שבהגהה לבמ״ח ס״ק ה׳ חולק עליו בשיטת הרמב״ם אסיק מה״ת מסיק שלפי רוב ראשונים אסור מה״ת

52. ח״ח כלל ט׳ סעיף א׳

53. ח״ח כלל ט׳ סעיף א׳. וא״כ אסור למסור רשימות תורמים לאנשים שאינם מהוגנים או למי שעלול למסור אותן לאנשים כאלה

54. ח״ח כלל ט׳ סעיף א׳

55. שם סעיף ב׳

56. שם סעיף א׳

57. שם

58. שם סוף סעיף ג׳

59. ח״ח כלל א׳ סעיף ד׳

60. ח״ח כלל ד׳ סוף סעיף י״ב

61. ח״ח כלל ט׳ סעיף ד׳

62. ח״ח כלל א׳ סעיף ו׳

63. שם סעיף ז׳

64. שם סעיף ו׳

65. שם סעיף ה׳

66. ח״ט אין פתיחה בקטע המתחיל ומה שציירתי

67. לשון החינוך מצוה רל״ו שנמנענו מרכילות שנא׳ לא תלך רכיל, והענין הוא שם נשמע אדם מדבר רע בחברו שלא נלך אליו ונספר לו פלוני מדבר כך וכך אע״פ תהי׳ כוונתנו לסילוק הנזקין ולהשבית ריב. עכ״ל. הרי שהגדרת רוכל הוא המספר שלא לתועלת. וכן מפורש בדברי החי״ח כלל י׳ סעיף ד׳, גם זה איננו בכלל לה״ר ולתועלת יחשב׳

68. ח״ח כלל ד׳ סעיף ה׳, ז׳

69. ח״ח כלל י׳ סעיף א׳

70. ח״ח כלל ט׳ רכילות סעיף ג׳

71. שם סעיף א׳

72. ח״ח כלל ח׳ סעיף ח׳

73. ח״ח כלל י׳ סעיף ד׳, וע״ע בבמ״ח כלל א׳ ס״ק י״ג שאם הסיפור (או המצב) ידוע לשומע מותר להשתמש בו כדוגמא בלימוד.

74. ח״ח כלל י׳ סעיף ב׳

75. במ״ח כלל ט׳ רכילות ס״ק ט׳

76. ח״ח כלל י׳ סעיף ב׳

77. ח״ח כלל י׳ סעיף ד׳

78. ח״ח כלל ט׳ רכילות סעיף ב׳ בסוגריים

79. ח״ח כלל י׳ סעיף ב׳

80. במ״ח כלל י׳ ס״ק כ״ב

81. ח״ח כלל י׳ סעיף ב׳

82. ח״ח כלל י׳ סעיף י״ד

83. במ״ח כלל ט׳ רכילות ס״ק ל״ה

84. עי׳ זרע חיים כלל י׳ אות ג׳ ובספר לשון חיים.

85. ח״ח כלל י׳ סעיף ב׳ ובמ״ח סוף ס״ק ט׳, וכלל ט׳ רכילות סעיף ב׳

86. ח״ח כלל י׳ סעיף ב׳, וכלל ט׳ רכילות סעיף ב׳

87. במ״ח כלל ט׳ רכילות ס״ק ג׳

88. ח״ח כלל י׳ סעיף ב׳, וכלל ט׳ רכילות סעיף ב׳

89. ח״ח כלל ג׳ סעיף ז׳

90. ח״ח כלל ד׳ סוף סעיף ד׳. ועי׳ בבמ״ח יד הקטנה פטור אפי׳ מלהוכיחו כי בודאי עשה תשובה, והחי״ח חולק עליו. (ועי׳ בהערה 91)

91. ח״ח כלל ד׳ סעיף ג׳. והנה לפי החי״ח מצות תשפוט מתחלקת לכמה ענינים: א. איך לפרש מעשה בן אדם כשיש צד להסתכל עליו כעל מעשה איסור אבל גם אפשר להסבירו באופן אחר ב. איך להבין את כוונתינו של מי שבוודאי עבר עבירה אבל ייתכן ומעשיו נעשו מסבת חוסר ידיעה ג. כשברור שנעשתה עבירה ביודעים, האם נחזיק את העובר לעבריין העומד ברשעתו או שמא יש להניח שחזר בתשובה ומהיום יש לו חזקת כשרות לכל דבר. בכל א׳ משלושת השאלות חייבים לעיין בהנהגתו של האדם בכללות כדי לקבוע את ה,צדק׳ בפירוש המעשה עליו דנים. מובן מאליו שאם אדם אין אין הנהגותיו מוכרות לנו עשה מעשה ולא ברור את הי׳ מעשה איסור או לא, אין ביכולתינו לשפוט את המעשה שהרי חסר לנו כל הרקע למעשה – וממילא הדבר נשאר אצלנו ספק, ובכל זאת יש ענין לדון כל אדם (שאנו לא מכירים) לכף זכות (פתיחה לחי״ח עשין ג׳ ע״פ הרמב״ם בפיה״מ לאבות פרק א׳ מ״ו) לא כן במי שהנהגותיו מוכרות לנו – כי ה,צדק׳ מחייב שנשפוט את מעשיו בתבונה – ולכן אם העבירה היא דבר שלפי ידיעותינו היהודי הזה לא נכשל בה עד היום והוא נזהר ממנה תמיד, אסור לנו לחשוד שעבר עליה עכשיו ואפי׳ אם המעשה נוטה יותר לכף חובה. (לגבי דין זה כשהראשונים מדברים על,צדיק׳ הכוונה למי שהוא צדיק בנוגע לעבירה שנחשד עליה – הגאון ר׳ הלל זקס שליט״א במרפא לשון, וכן הורה למעשה מרן הגרש״ז אויערבך זצ״ל). באדם בינוני הנזהר מעבירה זו בדרך כלל אבל נכשל בה לפעמים, אם עשה מעשה שאפשר לפרשו כעבירה וגם אפשר לפרש אותו אחרת ואינו נוטה לכאן יותר מלכאן, מה״ת חייבים לדונו לכף זכות – וכ״ש כשהמעשה נוטה לצד זכות. אבל כשכף חובה מכריעה, מעיקר הדין מותר לדונו לכף חובה, אבל מדה טובה להשאירו ספק (במ״ח כלל ג׳ ס״ק ו׳) ומדת חסידות לדונו לכף זכות (במ״ח שם בסוף – אלא שגם בזה השתמש בלשון, מדה טובה׳). וברשע – דהיינו מי שעובר בתמידות בעבירה שעכשיו נחשד בה – דנים אותו לכף חובה אפי׳ אם המעשה נוטה לצד זכות.

וכל זה כשאפשר לפרש את המעשה באופן שלא הי׳ עבירה. אבל כשאין מנוס מלפרש כמעשה איסור – אז באיש אשר לענין שאר איסורים הוא צדיק או אפי׳ בינוני – אם עשה את העבירה באופן שאפשר לפרש את מעשהו כשגגה חייבים לפרש כן, ואפי׳ אם ראינו איך שנכשל בה כמה פעמים עדיין חייבים לומר או

שלא ידע שהוא דבר אסור או שסבור שהוא חומרא בעלמא. ואם ברור שהעבירה נעשתה במזיד – כשהוא צדיק או בינוני לגבי שאר איסורים וגם לאיסור זה היתה לו חזקת כשרות עד היום – אף שבודאי חייב להוכיחו – מ״מ התורה לא הפקיעה אותו מפרשת אונאת דברים ואסור לפרסם עונו כדי להחזירו למוטב שמא כבר שב מעצמו. ואפי׳ אם הוא לץ השונא את מוכיחו, בכ״ז עדיין הוא בכלל ,עמיתך׳ שאסור לביישו ע״י פרסום המעשה ומותר רק לספר לרבו המאמין למספר כבי תרי או במקרה ויש ב׳ עדים בדבר יכולים להעיד בפני דייני העיר כדי שייסרו אותו. (כ״ז בח״ח כלל ד׳ סעיפים ג-ה ע״פ דברי רבינו יונה בשע״ת שער ג׳ מאמר רט״ז-ר״כ.

והיות ופסק החח״ח לקמן בכלל ו׳ רכילות סעיף יא׳ שאין בזה״ז מי שנאמן כבי תרי, וגם קבלת עדות בבי״ד כדי שהב״ד ייסר מישהו בצנעא לא שכיח, סתמנו שהרואה יוכיחנו איש׳ וי ספר לרבו הפקח שלא יאמין אבל יחוש לדברים וימצא איך לודא את הענין לעצמו או איך להוכיח למדובר על צד הספק מבלי לביישו. והגאון ר׳ הלל זקס שליט״א הקשה ע״ז ממעשה דזיגוד – שאם מותר גם לעד א׳ לספר כדי שיוכיחוהו על צד הספק כמש״כ כאן. למה נגדי׳ ר״פ. ואולי י״ל שמותר לומר רק ליחיד וזיגוד סיפר בפני בי״ד.)

92. רבינו יונה אבות פרק א׳ משנה ו׳, ושע״ת שער ג׳ מאמר רי״ח

93. כאן מדובר במי שעושה את העבירה בתמידות אבל לא ברור שהוא מזיד (עי׳ לעיל הערה 91)

94. ח״ח כלל ח׳ סעיף ז׳ ועי׳ לעיל הערה 22, והנה לקמן בבמ״ח כלל י׳ ס״ק ל׳ הוציא החח״ח את המומר לתאבון מכלל עמיתך – וא״כ לכאורה א״צ שיכוין לתועלת וזו סתירה גלוי׳ לדבריו בכלל ד׳, ושם בכלל י׳ כתב כן בשם רי״י בשע״ת והמעיין בשע״ת ימצא שלא הוציאו רי״י אלא מכלל עמיתך של אונאת דברים ולא מכלל עמך האמור בענין לה״ר. ובספר זרע חיים תירץ שהמומר יצא מכלל עמיתך במקצת – דהיינו שמותר לבזותו על העבירה שהמיר לה אבל לא הותר לבזותו בגנות אחרת – והניחו בצ״ע. ולכאורה יש מקום להעיר שלשיטת החח״ח אונאת דברים בכלל לה״ר נעי׳ בהגהה ריש כלל ב׳ שחולק על דברי מהר״ל בפ״ז מנה״ל שהמביש את חבירו בפניו לא השתמש בייחודיות שבלשון וכמו״י הי׳ יכול להכותו וממילא אין בו משום חטא הלשון – ועיי״ש בהגהה שהקשה על הנ״ע ממומעי״ר וממעשה מרים לפי הספרי – ועי׳ בספר פחד יצחק למרן הגר״י הוטנר זצ״ל לחג השבועות שתירץ את דברי מהר״ל – וגם י״ל שדברי מהר״ל לא נאמרו אלא לענין ההיזק שבלה״ר וכמו שמעינו בפסוק ארור מכה רעהו בסתר, אבל על בחירתו לספר בגנות חבירו עובר אפי׳ בפניו), וא״כ – לפי החח״ח – המיעוט של עמיתך באונאת דברים כולל גם החלק של אונאת דברים שבלה״ר.

95. ח״ח כלל ד׳ סעיף ז׳
96. שם סעיף ח׳

97. הב״י ביו״ד סי׳ קנ״ט הביא את דברי הנ״י בב״מ שמותר להלוות ברבית לבן המומרת כיון שאין אנו מצווין להחייותו, ואע״פ שהי׳ מקום לומר שהוא כאנוס מ״מ הואיל שעמד בין ישראל והולך ומדבק בחוקותיהם של גוים מן המורידים הוא, ורדה ב״י את דבריו ע״פ שיטת הרמב״ם בבני הקראים (כוונתו לרמב״ם פ״ג ממרים ה״ג – עי׳ מל״מ פ״ה מלוה ולוה ה״ב, וש״ך בנה״ך שם ביו״ד) שהוא כתינוק שנשבה ביניהם – ואע״פ ששמע אח״כ שהוא יהודי וראה היהודים ודתם הרי הוא כאנוס. ועפי״ז פסק בשו״י יו״ד קנ״ט סעיף ג׳ שאין לקראים דין מומרים ואסור להלוותם ברבית. אולם הש״ך בס״ק י׳ חולק על פסק השו״ע ופוסק כנמוקו בצירוף התשובות שהקראים בזה״ז אינם כקראים שבזמן הרמב״ם. וא״י יהודי בלתי שומר תו״מ שגדל בין נכרים ומומרים ולא הכיר יהודים שומרי מצוות לבע״ע דינו כתינוק שנשבה, ומי שכן מכיר יראי ד׳ אבל איננו מאמין באמיתיות התורה בגלל החינוך שקבל – לשו״ע יש לעיין אם רצה לפסק כנמוקו לגמרי או שרק בקראים הכריע כמותו בצירוף התשובות שמא. ובסוף ס׳ אהבת חסד הביא החח״ר מהג״ר מולין וממהר״ם לובלין שבזה״ז אין מי שידע להוכיח ובהגה״ה פ״ז דעות כתב שאסור לשנוא את הרשע אלא אחר שאינו מקבל תוכחה – וממילא בזה״ז מצוה לאהוב הרשעים. וע״י בחזו״א יו״ר סי׳ ב׳ סוס״ק כ״ח.
98. עי׳ לעיל הערה 94
99. ח״ח כלל ח׳ סעיף ה׳. ובכלל זה הכופר בא׳ מי״ג עקרים – ואפי׳ אומר על אות א׳ בתורה שמשה אמרו מעצמו.
100. ח״ח כלל י׳ סעיפים ז׳-ט׳
101. ח״ח כלל ד׳ סעיף י׳, וכ״ז כשהסיפור הוא לטובת המדובר עצמו
102. מכות ח׳ ע״א, רמב״ם פ״ה רוצח הל׳ ה׳, ו׳ (ואפי׳ כדי ללמדו אומנות)
103. מו״ק י״ז ע״א
104. מדברי החח״ח ריש כלל י׳. ופשוט שמותר להעיד ביחידי בדיני ממנות, וכתב ע״ז הגאון ר׳ הלל זקס שליט״א: ומסתבר שמצוה רבה להגיד לניזק כדי שידע מי לתבוע ומה לתבוע, ואיני יודע אם יש בזה התנאי שיוכיחנו תחילה.
105. עי׳ רמ״א חו״מ סי׳ שפ״א סוף סעיף ז׳
106. גיטין פ״ב ע״ב, שו״י חו״מ סי׳ כ״ז ס״א
107. ח״ח כלל ד׳ סעיף ח׳
108. עי׳ ח״ח כלל ט׳ רכילות סעיפים ה׳-ו׳, ואפי׳ שנים שראו את הדבר בעצמם נקראים מסייעים לדבר עבירה אם יעשה מעשה ע״י (שלא ע״י בי״ד)
109. ח״ח כלל ו׳ סעיף ח׳ בהגהה
110. החח״ח בכלל ו׳ סעיף יא׳ אסר לספר ברבים איך שפלוני גזל ממנו דמסתמא אינו מכין לתועלת, ואילו בסעיף י״ג התיר לספר למי שתוכחתו תשפיע עליו. ומשמע שההבדל הוא ענין של כוונה בלבד; אבל במציאות יש עוד הבדל – שהמספר ליחיד יש לו השפעה על המדובר ינסה לברר אם הוא אכן אשם או יוכיחנו דרך חשש, אבל המפרסם על מישהו שרימהו רוצה שהציבור יאמין לדבריו ואולי ישתדלו להכריחו

לשלם ע"פ דיבורו בלבד, ועובר אלפני עור — או לכה"פ מס"ע וכנ"ל בהערה 108

111. ע"פ ח"ח כלל ט' רכילות סעיף י"ג קטע המתחיל ועם החמשה

112. במ"ח כלל י' ס"ק י"ד

113. ח"ח כלל י' סעיף י"ד בהגהה. והנה בספר זה השלחן הה"א כתב בשם הגה"צ ר' שמואל הומינר זצוק"ל שבספרו עיקרי דינים השמיט את דברי ההגהה מפני שהח"ח לא כתבו אלא בתורת אפשר והדבר גורם למכשולים, אלא מיבעי ליה ליתובי דעתי'. אולם בנתיב חיים כתב שמדברי הח"ח משמע שנוטה בזה להקל וכן מובא בקונטרס מרפא לשון שכ"מ שהח"ח חידש הלכה ולא מצא מקור מפורש לדבריו כתבה בלשון אפשר. ושבם מרן הגר"י הוטנר זצ"ל שמעתי כדבר פשוט שמהמשעבודים המוטלים על הבעל — להגרים את אשתו מדאגותיה, ולא ייתכן שיהא אסור לה להטעין בפניו. ופשוט שמותר רק עם קיום תנאי תועלת — כולל שיכוין לתועלת ולא ידבר מתוך שנאה.

114. ח"ח כלל ה' סעיף ג' בהגהה (אלא ששם התועלת היא להשקיט המריבה)

115. ח"ח כלל ה' סעיף ו', וכלל ט' רכילות סעיף ג'

116. במ"ח כלל ט' רכילות ס"ק ט'

117. שם בהגהה

118. ח"ח כלל ט' רכילות סעיף ג'

119. במ"ח כלל י' ס"ק כ"ה, וע"י גם במ"ח כלל ט' רכילות ס"ק י"ד

120. ע"י ח"ח כלל ט' רכילות סעיף י'

121. ע"י ח"ח כלל ט' רכילות סעיף י"א בהגהה דכ"ז אם לא ברור ממש שהוא רמאי, אבל אם מכיר את טבע בעל החנות שהוא מרמה את לקוחותיו תמיד מותר לגלות כדי לפרסם את החנפים.

122. ע"י כ"י בזרע חיים לכלל ט' רכילות סעיף י' (מסיק שם שאם נשאל באיזו חנות כדאי לקנות מותר להמליץ על היותר זולה, אבל ליעץ למי שלא שאל — אף שאין בזה משום לה"ר ורכילות — מ"מ אסור מדין מאי חזית אא"כ הוא קרובו או עני'. וכתב ע"י הגאון ר' הלל זקס שליט"א: מהח"ח משמע שאם שמע אחד רוצה ליכנס לחנות, אסור לומר לו שהשני מוכר בזול יותר אא"כ יותר משתות וכו', רצ"ע.

123. ע"י פרק כ' מסילת ישרים (משקל החסידות)

124. ח"ח פרק י' סעיף י"ז וכלל ט' רכילות סעיף י"ד

125. במ"ח כלל י' ס"ק מ"ג הניחו בצ"ע

126. ח"ח סוף פרק י'

127. פתיחה לספר ח"ח לאוין י"ב

128. ח"ח כלל ח' סעיף ח'

129. במ"ח כלל א' ס"ק י"ג

130. זרע חיים על כלל ח' סעיף ה', אות ב'

131. ח"ח כלל ד' סעיף י'

132. במ"ח שם ס"ק מ"ג

133. ח"ח שם סוף סעיף י'

134. הח"ח הביא דיני שיתוף ושידוך בסוף הלכות רכילות — ולכאורה דבר זה מעורר תמיהה, שהרי האיסור בסיפור חסרונותיו של צד א' לשני הוא לשון

הרע — דהיינו גנות וגרימת נזק, ואף שתוכל לצאת מזה גם שנאה — וממילא קיים גם חשש רכילות — עדיין תמוה למה תפס הח"ח את הטפל והניח את העיקר. אלא שכנראה סידר הח"ח את דיני פרסום עוולות בכלל י' לה"ר, ודיני סיפור לצד הנוגע בכלל ט' רכילות — שלה"ר היא דיבור האסור מצד עצם התוכן, ואילו רכילות אסורה מצד זהותו של השומע; וכן לענין התועלת — כלל י' רכילות עוסק בתועלת יותר כללית היוצאת מפרסום הדבר ואילו כלל ט' רכילות עוסק תועלת מעשית וממוקדת ע"י אספקת המידע לצד הנוגע. בכל זאת מצינו לנכון לכלול את כל עניני תועלת כאן בהל' לה"ר, ולקמן בהל' רכילות הדגשנו את ההבדלים בהלכה בין שני הסוגים של תועלת (ימים 149-153)

135. ח"ח כלל ט' רכילות סעיף ג'

136. בבמ"ח בציורים (סוף רכילות) ס"ק א' הסתפק איך להשיב כשנשאל על מצבו הכלכלי של חבירו ע"י מי ששוקל אפשרות של שיתוף עמו בעסק כשידוע לנשאל שהמדובר נמצא במצוקה כספית — אף שאין לו מצבו משום הוכחה לחוסר יכולת או כשרון — בכל זאת יש צד להתיר גילוי המצב כיון שהשואל גילה דעתו בפירוש שמקפיד ע"ז שיהא לו שותף בעל הון, ובסעיף ג' אסר ליעץ לחבירו להשתתף עם מי שיש לו שום רעותא — כולל ענוית — אם יודע בעצמו שאילו הי' הדבר נוגע לו הי' מתרחק מאנשים כאלו; ופשוט שקנה המדה שקבע הח"ח — שאילו הי' נוגע לו — פירושו אילו הי' במצב של חבירו — כולל תכונותיו של החבר וגם טעמו (שכן קבעה לנו התורה במצות צדקה — אשר יחסר לו ואפי' סוס לרכוב עליו — במי שירד מנכסיו). בכל זאת ישנם מקרים אשר אילו הי' מתעקש על דרישת טפשית הרי כשמשתתף כך עם חבירו אין לו בזה משום עצה שאינה הוגנת ולכן דבר הח"ח דוקא בציור כמו שיתוף עם עני — אשר יש בו הגון) אבל רק מי שיש לו רגישות פקחות ויראת שמים מוכשר להחליט בדברים כאלו (ראה יום 87).

137. מפי הגרש"ז אויערבך זצ"ל — והוא קבע שבדרך כלל מותר להעלים דברים מסויימים עד לפגישה שלישית ולא יותר — אבל, כמובן, הכל לפי הענין; וגם לאו כל ריעותא מותר להעלים.

138. במ"ח ציורים ס"ק א'

139. ע"י לעיל הערה 136

140. ח"ח ציורים סעיף ו' קטע המתחיל אבל אם החסרון, ובמ"ח ס"ק י'

141. ציורים סעיף ד'

142. שם סעיף ו', י'

143. ברור שלא שייך כאן חיוב תוכחה על החסרון שיש לו כתנאי להתיר סיפור — דלו יהא שיקבל תוכחתו עדיין א"א לסמוך ע"ז ולא להודיע לצד השני, שמא יחזור לקלקולו (וכמ"ש הח"ח בבמ"ח כלל ט' רכילות סוס"ק ט') ולפעמים לא שייך תוכחה כלל (כמו במקרה של מחלה), אבל אם קיימת האפשרות להשפיע על המדובר לגלות את החסרון בעצמו לצד השני — ברוב

המקרים יש לזה עדיפות מהרבה סיבות — כולל מניעת
איבה וחשדנות והצלת המדובר מעבירה (מרמה).
144. ח״ח כלל ו׳ סעיף ב׳
145. פתיחה לאוין ד׳
146. במ״ח כלל ט׳ ס״ק ט׳
147. כך הורה לנו מרן הגרי״ש אלישיב שליט״א ע״פ
דברי המשנה ברורה סי׳ תר״ח ס״ק ו׳ שמה שאין
אומרים מוטב שיהיו שוגגין בדאורייתא מפורש הוא
מטעם שבודאי אינם שוגגין, וא״כ כשברור שהמסַפר
הוא בדעה שענין שמירת הלשון הוא מדת חסידות
בלבד או שחושב — למשל — שלה״ר על האמת
מותרת, ודאי אמרינן מוטב שיהיו שוגגין (ושלא
כדברי החי״ח בבמ״ח הנ״ל סוס״ק ט׳. ואולי כוונת
החי״ח בבמ״ח שמן הסתם לא אמרינן מוטב, אבל בידוע
שהוא שוגג לא יוכיחנו (וכן הבין בשבילי חיים שם).
148. רמ״א או״ח סי׳ תר״ח סעיף ז׳
149. שיטה מקובצת ביצה דף ל׳ ע״א בשם ריטב״א
שהעיד בשם רב גדול מאשכנזים שהעיד בשם רבותיו
הצרפתים ובכללם ר״י ומהר״ם מרוטנבורג (מובא
במחצית השקל תר״ח)
150. מג״א תר״ח ס״ק ג׳ כתב שבעבירה בסתר יוכיחנו
בסתר ובעבירה שבגלוי יוכיחנו מיד שלא יתחלל ש״ש
— ומדוייק בלשונו שגם בעבירה שבגלוי הי׳ מוכיחה
בסתר אלא שאם יניח לגמור את הסיפור כדי להוכיחה
בסתר — בינתים ש״ש מתחלל ע״י המשך סיפורו
בגלוי, וא״כ כשאפשר להפסיקו מבלי לביישה עדיף
להתנהג כך ולהוכיחו אח״כ בסתר.
151. ח״ח כלל ו׳ סעיף ה׳
152. ח״ח כלל ח׳ סעיף י״ד
153. שו״ע יו״ד סי׳ רמ״ב סעיף כ״ב
154. ח״ח כלל ט׳ סעיף ה׳
155. ביאור הלכה סי׳ תר״ח סוף ד״ה אבל וע״ש
שמסתפק אם יש חיוב תוכחה למומר לתאבון
156. בה״ל שם ד״ה להוכיחה חייב בשם ספר חסידים
157. ח״ח כלל ו׳ סעיף ב׳
158. ח״ח כלל ד׳ סעיף י״א, ובמ״ח כלל ו׳ ס״ק ג׳
159. שם
160. הגהה תניינא כלל ד׳ סעיף י״א
161. בהגהה קמא כלל ד׳ סי״א אסר לדרוש את מהותו
של אדם אצל שונאו ואפי׳ אצל בן אומנתו (משום
חזקה אומן שונא בן אומנתו) גם מדין לפני עור וגם מפני
שעלול להגזים הגזים ואף לשקר לגמרי
162. ח״ח כלל ד׳ סעיף ו׳ שצ׳ את התנאים שבכלל ט׳
רכילות
163. ח״ח כלל ו׳ סעיף ד׳
164. ח״ח כלל ח׳ סעיף י׳
165. עי׳ לעיל הערה 113
166. ע״ח כלל ו׳ סעיף ד׳
167. עי׳ זרע חיים לכלל ט׳ סעיף ה׳
168. עי׳ לעיל הערה 97
169. אילו היתה השמיעה אסורה, הי׳ הסיפור אסור
משום לפני עור
170. ח״ח כלל ו׳ סעיף א׳, פתיחה לאוין ב׳

171. ח״ח כלל ו׳ סעיף ב׳
172. ח״ח כלל ו׳ סעיף י׳
173. במ״ח כלל ט׳ רכילות ס״ק ט׳
174. ח״ח כלל ט׳ סעיף י׳, י״א ובהגהה לסי״א
175. עי׳ זרע חיים כלל ו׳ ס״ב שאין בזה משום לפ״ע.
אבל מח״ח כלל ב׳ סעיף ו׳ משמע קצת כדברינו —
ובפרט אם מספר באופן שממנסה להוכיח את אמיתת
דבריו (ויש בזה חשש בל תאכילו).
176. עי׳ לעיל הערה 113
177. עי׳ שו״ת אגרות משה חלק יו״ד ב׳ סי׳ ק״ג
שאסור למלמד לדרוש מתלמידיו לגלות מי עשה דבר
מגונה
178. הגהה לבמ״ח כלל ז׳ ס״ק י׳
179. ח״ח כלל ז׳ סעיף ד׳
180. ח״ח כלל ז׳ סעיפים ז׳ וח׳
181. ח״ח כלל ז׳ רכילות סעיף ז׳
182. ח״ח כלל ז׳ סעיף ט׳
183. ח״ח כלל ז׳ סעיף י׳, וכ״ז כשהם דברים הניכרים
ממש וראה אותם בעצמו
184. שם
185. שם סעיף י״ב
186. בבמ״ח כלל ז׳ ס״ק י׳ חידש הח״ח שהעובר
בקריעות ובשאט נפש על איסור הידוע לכל כלל
ישראל יצא מכלל עמיתך ומותר לקבל עליו שעבר
עבירה שלא הוחזק עליה, ואילו בהגהה לכלל ו׳ סעיף י׳
אסר להאמין על מומר לתאבון שנעשה מומר להכעיס
— אע״פ שגם המומר לתאבון יצא מכלל עמיתך (עי׳
לעיל הערה 22). ובבמ״ח שם ס״ק ו׳ הסביר שהמומר
לתאבון לא יצא מכלל עמיתך לגמרי — ולכאורה
ההסבר כמבואר בהערה 22 שהמומר לתאבון יצא
מכלל עמיתך שבפרשת אונאה דברים שהתורה התירה
לבזותו כדי להחזירו למוטב ולגנות פעולי און — ובכלל
זה הותר גם לשמעים להאמין למה שנאמר עליו, אבל
מכלל עמך שכתוב בפרשת לה״ר לא יצא — וממילא
אסור להאמין שנעשה מומר להכעיס. ורק מומר
להכעיס יצא גם מכלל עמך ומותר לקבל עליו לה״ר
בכל ענין. והנה מתוך דברי במ״ח כלל ו׳ ס״ק כ״ח
משמע שאפי׳ במומר לתאבון יש להאמין שעבר
עבירה אחרת לתאבון וצ״ע מנין הוציא הח״ח דין זה.
187. שם בבמ״ח. ולכאורה משמע מכל דברי הח״ח
המובאים לעיל בהערה 186 שאסור להאמין על החוטא
בשוגג בקריעות שחטא עוד פעם בשוגג שהרי לא יצא
מכלל עמיתך — ואע״פ שהוחזק בדבר — כגון תינוק
שנשבה (עי׳ הערה 97) וצ״ע.
188. מדברי הח״ח בהגהה לכלל ו׳ סעיף ד׳ משמע שאם
משתדל להוציא מלבו כל מה ששמע, תיקן את הלאו
למפרע — וא״צ תשובה (עי׳ נתיב חיים שם).
189. ח״ח כלל ו׳ סעיף י״ב
190. במ״ח שם ס״ק ל״ד
191. ח״ח כלל א׳ רכילות סעיפים א׳ וב׳, ומפורש
בשע״ת לרבינו יונה שער ג׳ מאמר רכ״ב שמרבה שנאה
בעולם
192. שם סעיף ב׳

193. ח״ח כלל ב׳ (לה״ר) סעיף י״א ע״פ סנהדרין
כ״ט ע״א. וכתב ע״ז הגאון ר׳ הלל זקס שליט״א: לי
נראה שאם אמר שאחרי שכולם הביעו דעתם ודנו
בדבר, כולם הסכימו פה אחד נגדו. אין בזה משום
רכילות, ואולי אפי׳ מצוה איכא, ולכאורה כן משמע
מהח״ח.

194. ח״ח כלל ג׳ רכילות סוף סעיף ג׳
195. ח״ח כלל א׳ רכילות סעיף ד׳
196. ח״ח כלל ג׳ רכילות סעיף ג׳
197. ח״ח כלל ד׳ רכילות סעיף א׳
198. ח״ח כלל א׳ רכילות סעיף ט׳
199. ח״ח כלל א׳ רכילות סעיף י״א
200. ח״ח כלל ב׳ רכילות סעיף ב׳
201. ח״ח כלל א׳ רכילות סעיף ו׳,ז׳
202. ח״ח כלל א׳ רכילות סעיף ה׳
203. ח״ח כלל א׳ רכילות סעיף ה׳
204. נתיבות עולם למהר״ל נתיב האמת פרק א׳
205. שם בח״ח סעיף ח׳
206. כמו באבק לה״ר
207. ח״ח כלל ח׳ רכילות סעיף א׳
208. ח״ח כלל ח׳ רכילות סעיף ב׳
209. ח״ח כלל ח׳ רכילות סעיף ג׳
210. שם סעיף ד׳
211. שם סעיף ה׳
212. שע״ת לרבינו יונה שער ג׳ מאמר רכ״ה
213. ח״ח כלל ט׳ רכילות סעיפים ג׳ ו׳
214. שם סעיף י״א
215. שם
216. ח״ח כלל ט׳ רכילות סעיף ב׳
217. הגהה לבמ״ח כלל ט׳ רכילות ס״ק ט׳
218. במ״ח כלל ט׳ רכילות ס״ק ט׳
219. ח״ח כלל ט׳ רכילות סעיף ג׳, ובמ״ח ס״ק י״א וי״ב
220. ח״ח כלל ט׳ רכילות סעיף ב׳
221. ח״ח כלל י׳ (לה״ר) סעיף י״ד, ועי׳ במ״ח ס״ק ל״ח
שמצוה להוסיף פרט מעצמו שיקטין את הנזק
222. ח״ח כלל ט׳ רכילות סעיף ג׳, ובמ״ח ס״ק ג׳
223. ח״ח כלל ט׳ רכילות סעיף י״ב
224. ח״ח כלל ט׳ רכילות סעיף ב׳
225. עי׳ זרע חיים כלל י׳ לה״ר סעיף ב׳ אות ב׳
226. ח״ח כלל ט׳ רכילות סעיף ב׳ וסוף סעיף י״ב
227. ח״ח כלל י׳ (לה״ר) סעיפים ה׳,ו׳
228. ח״ח שם סעיף ב׳, ובמ״ח ס״ק ה׳, וכלל ט׳ רכילות
ס״ק ט׳

229. הצורך לדון לכף זכות מובא בכלל ד׳ (לה״ר) גבי
פרסום בעל עבירה למען קנאת האמת, ואילו בכלל י׳
לה״ר וכלל ט׳ רכילות כשמדובר בתועלות מעשיות לא
הביאו החי״ח כלל. ועי׳ בהקדמה לכלל י׳ לה״ר בנתיב
חיים

230. במ״ח כלל ט׳ רכילות סוף ס״ק ט׳
231. במ״ח כלל ד׳ (לה״ר) ס״ק מ״ג, ועי׳ שבילי חיים שם
232. עי׳ בחכמת שלמה לרש״ק על הגליון לשו״ע חו״מ
סי׳ תכ״ו ס״א שבזקן ואינו לפי כבודו פטור מלא תעמוד
כמו בהשבת אבידה. ולפי דבריו יש מקום לומר שאין
חיוב לסכן את פרנסתו ואת יכולתו לעזור לחולים
ונצרכים בעתיד כדי להציל יהודי משידוך שאינו הגון.
ובמקרה של פסיכולוג – אם יוודע שפסיכולוגים שומרי
תו״מ אינם שומרים על סודיות כבר לא יהי׳ מי שיתן
בהם אמון, ואין דוחין נפש מפני נפש. ולמעשה כל
מקרה טעון שאלת חכם בפני עצמו.

233. עי׳ חו״מ שפ״ח סעיף ט׳ שמותר למסור את הרודף
234. עי׳ במ״ח כלל ט׳ רכילות ס״ק א׳
235. ח״ח כלל ה׳ רכילות סעיף ב׳
236. במ״ח כלל ו׳ ס״ק ט׳
237. עי׳ ח״ח כלל ו׳ סעיף ה׳
238. עי׳ לעיל הערה 150
239. לעיל הערה 151
240. ח״ח כלל ד׳ (לה״ר) סעיף ד׳
241. ח״ח כלל ד׳ רכילות סעיפים ב׳ ו׳ ג׳
242. עי׳ לעיל הערות 158,159
243. לעיל הערה 159, ועי׳ גם הערה 161
244. לעיל הערה 163
245. ח״ח כלל ה׳ רכילות סעיף א׳
246. ח״ח כלל ה׳ רכילות סעיף א׳
247. ע״פ ח״ח כלל ד׳ רכילות סעיף א׳
248. ח״ח כלל ח׳ רכילות סעיף א׳
249. ח״ח כלל ח׳ רכילות סעיף ה׳
250. ח״ח כלל ח׳ רכילות סעיף א׳
251. ח״ח כלל ו׳ רכילות סעיף ב׳
252. ח״ח כלל ו׳ רכילות סעיפים ה׳, ו׳
253. שם סעיף ז׳
254. ח״ח כלל ו׳ רכילות סעיף ח׳
255. ח״ח כלל ו׳ רכילות סעיף ט׳
256. ח״ח כלל ד׳ רכילות סעיף ג׳, ובמ״ח סוף ס״ק ד׳.
עי׳ לעיל יום 28 מש״כ בשם ר׳ ישראל סלנטר זצ״ל.
257. ח״ח כלל ה׳ רכילות סעיף ז׳
258. שם

Vignettes From the Life of the Chofetz Chaim

from the memoirs of his son,
*Rabbi Aryeh Leib HaKohen Kagan**

Reflections

✒ In Two Worlds At Once

Those who knew my father and who were imbued with the light of his fear of G-d and Torah wisdom, recognize that his greatness was far beyond that which has been depicted by writers who have written about him since his passing. In truth, he was a unique individual; his essential greatness was that while his simplicity made him appear as one of us, nevertheless, his "head reached the very heavens."[1]

His many written works which have been disseminated among the Jewish people and which are studied in every *beis midrash*, bear witness to all that he accomplished. It is well known among our generation that my father was not only one who preached well, but also one who beautifully fulfilled — with alacrity and a sense of mission — all that he sought from his listeners. Many times I heard him say that the laws discussed in his various *sefarim* are all obligatory upon each and every Jew. Though my father personally adopted every good custom or mode of conduct that he had learned of, nevertheless, he never demanded of others that they accept such customs and ways upon themselves if they were not required by *Halachah*.

---

*These vignettes are excerpted from the memoirs found in the third volume of *Kol Kisvei HaChofetz Chaim HaShaleim,* and are written in the Chofetz Chaim's son's words.

1. A phrase borrowed from *Bereishis* 28:12.

✒ His Partner In Life

My father once remarked that one can never be sure where exactly lay his place of good fortune and contentment. He explained that before meeting my mother, he was offered *shidduchim* (matches) with young women from very wealthy homes; one prominent man offered him an enormous dowry. When his relatives heard that he had become engaged in the small town of Radin to the daughter of his stepfather,[1] who was of modest means and not of noteworthy lineage, they became agitated and their comments disturbed his peace of mind. My father, however, refused to even consider breaking the engagement. Reflecting upon his decision, my father told me, "Were it not for this small, tranquil town and the deeds of your mother, who knows if I would have been able to devote myself to the study of Torah rather than become overtaken by the preoccupations of daily living — as was the case with many of my peers?"

After his marriage, my father spent a few years studying in Minsk and Vilna before returning to Radin. My mother opened a general store which provided them with a meager income so that my father could devote himself to the full-time study of Torah. My mother had no formal education, but she was of superior intellect and was exceptionally good-hearted in extending help to the needy. She asked nothing from my father in the way of material needs; her only desire was that my father be able to dedicate himself totally to Torah study and the service of G-d. In material matters, she was satisfied with the bare minimum. Many times did I hear my father say, "The little Torah knowledge that I have is all thanks to your mother. She was always satisfied; she never desired a beautiful house, clothing or the like."

I recall that when she went with me to purchase my wedding suit, the proprietor wished me, "May you wear this suit in good health and become a rich, successful businessman." My mother became agitated and said, "Who asked you for such a blessing? Better bless him that he should become a Torah scholar and a G-d-fearing Jew."

---

1. The Chofetz Chaim was orphaned at age ten.

Between Man and His Fellow

✐ The Chofetz Chaim's Distress (I)

As a storekeeper, my mother was known for her integrity and gra-ciousness, both to Jew and gentile alike. Yet, all the years that she managed the store, my father was concerned lest they inadver-tently be guilty of a monetary infraction. Though he frequently checked that the weights and measures were accurate, he still wor-ried that perhaps a customer may have been wronged in some way. Toward the end of his life, he donated one hundred rubles to the community free-loan fund, so as to benefit any customer who may have been wronged in some way (for the Sages state that one who steals and does not know who his victim is, should contribute to a community cause).

My father's first public address was delivered in Radin's main syn-agogue and dealt with the various commandments relating to honesty in business. Afterwards, he visited every Jewish-owned store in the town to check that its weights and measures were ac-curate. Many years later, he authored a monograph on the topic of weights and measures and appended it to his work, *Nidchei Yisrael*.

⊰⊱

Once, on a Friday afternoon close to sundown, my father was seen running through the streets to deliver something. Unbe-knownst to my father, the man whom he had hired to print his next work had left the printing shop and gone home to prepare for Shabbos without receiving his pay. My father therefore hurried to pay him before Shabbos so as not to transgress the prohibition against being late with a worker's wages.[1]

---

1. *Vayikra* 19:13.

❦ The Chofetz Chaim's Distress (II)

For the last forty years of his life, my father sold his *sefarim* through emmisaries who traveled far and wide disseminating them to the masses. Whenever my father would receive his share of the sales, he would offer praise to Hashem that he no longer had to give of his precious time in order to sell his works.

I recall the time when a certain emissary wrote to my father with the good tidings that in a certain province, his sales had totalled one hundred rubles. My father's initial happiness later gave way to dismay, for the sales had exceeded the norm for that province. He was distressed over the possibility that the dealer had resorted to exaggerations or other distortions in convincing the people to purchase his wares.

In earlier years, he would arrive in a town with his *sefarim* and deliver an ethical discourse before the community. If ever, upon arriving in a town, my father would learn that he had been preceded by a visiting *rav* (rabbi), *maggid* (preacher) or *meshulach* (institutional fundraiser) who was planning on addressing the community, he would immediately leave the town without even opening his packages of *sefarim*. Even if my father had preceded the other visitor's arrival, he would quickly leave town so as not to hurt the other person's opportunities to speak and earn something for his own cause.

Once, he arrived in a certain town to find that a visiting *maggid* had preceded him. As my father prepared to head on his way, a distinguished delegation from the community approached him, imploring him to remain. They assured him that while they would not allow the *maggid* to address them, they would compensate him in full. My father, however, was not agreeable out of concern for the man's feelings. Then, the *maggid* himself came to my father and implored him to remain in the town; he assured my father that he already been compensated and that it was perfectly all right with him if my father would address the community. Reluctantly, my father agreed. He later told me:

"My sale of *sefarim* during that stay was quite poor. I saw this as Divine retribution for my having remained, for one should never cause anyone to be snubbed. Though the *maggid* was compensated, nevertheless, in his heart, he probably felt hurt that he had come to speak and was pushed aside in my favor.

"Thank G-d, I did not repeat my mistake. Later, when a similar situation occurred, I refused to accede to the community's entreaties. However, I promised to return at a later date. I did return, and thank G-d, my stay was very successful."

✍ Above Suspicion

As a young man, I had an interest in assuming the rabbinate in a certain town [and discussed this with my father]. As I recall, I wrote to the community leaders concerning the matter. One day, my father received a letter from a certain Torah scholar expressing his interest in ascending to that very position and requesting a letter of endorsement from my father on his behalf! My father responded that as a rule, he did not involve himself in matters pertaining to the rabbinate. At the same time, he ceased to entertain the possibility of my seeking the position, lest the scholar who had written him suspect that it was through his letter that my father became aware of the position's vacancy and apprised me of this — which, if true, would constitute a *chilul Hashem* (desecration of Hashem's Name).

✍ Doing For Others

A Jew's obligations toward his fellow was forever on my father's mind, both in important and in seemingly insignificant matters. I recall how as a child, I would look on as my father made his way among the *minyan* to find every poor person a place to eat when the Friday night prayers had ended. He would approach the members of the *minyan*, asking each one to host one poor person for the Shabbos meal. Whoever he could not place with someone would come to our home for the meal.

During the weekdays, it happened often that he would carry a pot of food to the synagogue in the morning and put it into the oven for the sake of a visitor who had arrived in town.

In my youth, a terrible plague struck a number of communities near our own. My father spoke with doctors concerning which medications should be used in the event that the plague would strike our town. He then collected money and purchased a large quantity of medications which he placed in a container in the synagogue should they be needed. Hashem, in His mercy, did not allow the plague to strike; not one person in our town died. I recall how people said that in was in my father's merit that the plague did not strike.

⋙⋘

While writing these memoirs, I was visited by a man who is advanced in years and who knew my father in his youth. I asked the man if he could relate something about my father's younger years and he told me the following:

As a young man, my father would spend many nights learning until late and sleeping in the *beis midrash*. When retiring, he would rest his head on two small pillows that he had with him from home. It happened then that a few women were making their rounds in the town collecting feathers to make bedding for a poor bride's trousseau. When my father learned of this, he gave away both of his pillows. No one knew of this until the next time my mother sent for the pillowcases so that they could be washed. It was only then that my father revealed that the pillows — and their cases — had been donated to *tzedakah*.

⋙⋘

Every embittered soul would come to my father to pour out his troubles; my father always felt the person's pain and sought to help however possible, whether with money, advice or moral support and encouragement. All this was done in the way of peace and without fanfare.

For her part, my mother would make her rounds of the town one day each week carrying a sack into which people would put food for the poor. She would distribute the food herself. Understandably, as time went on, every impoverished soul would find his way to my parents' house where he would seek assistance from my mother. She always came to the person's aid, whether he needed medicine for an ailment, food and clothing, money which which to make a child's wedding, help in starting a business or assistance in obtaining a loan. Never did she refrain from helping someone even if this meant borrowing money and becoming burdened with personal debt. When my mother passed away, my father hung a sign in the *beis midrash* stating that whoever had extended a loan to my mother should come to him and receive his money.

✎ *The Free-Loan Fund*

Already in his youth, my father turned his attention to the needs of the common laborers, a large percentage of whom were unlearned. In Radin, he established a nightly class for them in *Sefer Chayei Adam*[1] which he led. Of course, he spiced his words of *halachah* with comments concerning the awesome sanctity of Torah, fear of Heaven, etc. On Shabbos afternoon, he would teach the weekly Torah portion with *Rashi's* commentary. I recall that from time to time, he would also teach classic works of ethics and Divine service, such as *Sefer Chareidim* and *Yesod V'Shoresh HaAvodah*. With the passage of time, many of these ignorant laborers had become imbued with the awe of Hashem and were fluent in the laws of daily Jewish living (as set forth in *Chayei Adam*).

As a young man, my father was inspired to establish a free-loan fund in our town, which did not have one until then. The nucleus of the fund committee was the group of laborers who attended his daily class. Each member undertook to contribute a fixed sum to the fund each week; in a relatively short period of time, a sizable sum was raised and the fund was in working operation. My father composed a list of ordinances for the workings of the fund which he inscribed in the fund's record book and to which he added an introduction explaining the great importance of such a fund. He also instituted that each year, the committee should hold a special *seudah* (*mitzvah* meal) on the Shabbos of *Parashas Mishpatim*, the Torah portion in which is found the commandment to extend loans to one's fellow.[2]

≈)≈

---

1. By Rabbi Avraham Danzig, a disciple of the Vilna *Gaon*.
2. *Shemos* 22:24.

A wagon driver told me the following:

Once, he drove my father to a certain destination. My father, as was his way, spoke with the driver concerning man's purpose in this world. The wagon driver asked, "With what can an impoverished fellow like myself merit the World to Come?" My father replied, "Establish a free-loan fund." The wagon driver could not help but laugh. "Is the *Rav* serious? Why, I am a poor man!"

My father replied, "You are under the impression that to start a free-loan fund, one needs hundreds of rubles. It is not so. One needs only a few coins to start such a fund. Set aside one coin each week. After a few weeks, you will have enough set aside to extend one small loan to one individual. As the weeks pass, the sum will grow and in a matter of time, you will have saved up a sizable amount with which you will be able to extend a number of loans simultaneously. Your modest free-loan fund will be as precious before Hashem as those whose sums total many hundreds of rubles."

The wagon driver heeded my father's advice and in the course of time, was extending numerous small loans simultaneously on a steady basis.

◈ Ahavas Chesed

It was around the year 5646 (1876) that my father began work on his *Sefer Ahavas Chesed* (The Book of Love of Kindness) which is actually a companion volume to *Sefer Chofetz Chaim*, for both are based upon the same passage, "Which man desires life, who loves days of seeing good? Guard your tongue from evil and your lips from speaking deceit. Turn from evil and do good, seek peace and pursue it" *(Tehillim* 34:13-15). In the way of his work on proper speech, my father begins *Ahavas Chesed* with a lengthy introduction detailing the many positive commandments that involve doing kindness with others and the many prohibitions one is liable to transgress if he refrains from doing kindness.

The first eight chapters of the work discuss the *mitzvah* of extending interest-free loans to one's fellow. The remainder of the work discusses at great length the commandment to pay a worker on time, and the many *mitzvos* involving *chesed* (kindness) such as welcoming guests, visiting the sick, escorting the dead, comforting mourners, gladdening a bride and groom, giving *tzedakah* and apportioning a tenth of one's earnings for charitable causes.

Thousands of copies of this work have been disemminated throughout the world, and many synagogues have established groups which study it regularly. Its impact is beyond description. Based on the scores of letters which my father received over the years, the publication of *Sefer Ahavas Chesed* has resulted in the establishment of hundreds of free-loan funds and the forming of countless numbers of societies for welcoming guests and visiting the sick. Many of these groups requested of my father that he write an introduction to be inserted in their society's record book.[1]

Shmiras Haloshon

➜ *Unequaled*

With regard to *shmiras haloshon*, it is my feeling that my father surpassed his entire generation. Most incredible was the fact that he was not a man who refrained from talking, and he was the main speaker at every gathering. No one ever claimed to have heard my father say something improper or derogatory.

A distinguished rabbi told me that he came to my father in his later years to discuss a matter which involved the rabbi's interaction with a number of individuals [and the rabbi intended to name those

---

1. As his son notes, the Chofetz Chaim alludes to this on page 45 of *Ahavas Chesed* where he writes: "As this work is based on matters of kindness, and as is known, the term *chesed*, kindness, encompasses anything that one can do to benefit someone else, I said to myself that surely, there are people who are in need of an introduction for the record book of the sacred free-loan society in their community. Therefore, I have decided to perform a kindness for them in printing the introduction which appears in the record book of our community's free-loan society."

The Chofetz Chaim then refers the reader to the appropriate sections of his work for those who wish to write a introduction to a record book for other benevolent societies.

individuals and discuss their misdeeds]. When my father became cognizant of this he said: "It is now some sixty years that I have succeeded, thank G-d, in guarding my speech — and you want me to crawl into the mud now?" That ended the discussion.

⋟ Sefer Chofetz Chaim

I once asked my father why he published his work on proper speech, *Sefer Chofetz Chaim* [and its second part, *Sefer Shmiras Haloshon*] anonymously. He replied: "It was not in my merit that these works came to be published; it was in the collective merit of the Jewish people. For perhaps, through the dissemination and study of these works, we will see a diminishing of this sin [of *loshon hora*], which caused the death of the generation in the Wilderness, the destruction of the Second Temple, and our dispersion among the gentiles. Thus, the honor for publishing this work is not mine!"

My father was about thirty years old when he began writing *Sefer Chofetz Chaim*. He never told me what exactly inspired him to dedicate himself to clarifying this body of *halachah*. However, I do know that my father was not one to author a work without a compelling reason. At times, his pure soul, which was permeated with the awe of Heaven, could be aroused by a specific incident to go out towards his people and teach them the way of Torah.

It seems to me that one particular episode aroused his pure spirit to compose this work. When he was about twenty-four years old, a dispute erupted in our town between some members of the community and the *rav*. Ultimately, the *rav* was forced to leave the town and was appointed to the rabbinate elsewhere. As I recall, the *rav* passed away a few years later. It is said in our town that within a few years, the *rav's* antagonists fell victim to Divine retribution on this world.

It was not long after this that my father began to involve himself with the study and compilation of the laws of *loshon hora* and *rechilus*. It is my feeling that this dispute aroused his pure spirit to cease remaining hidden and instead, to shake heaven and earth regarding the terrible corruption of the power of speech that had become so prevalent.

My father was once speaking to me regarding personal safeguards which a person must make for himself, particularly regarding speech. He then related, "In my younger years, when strife raged in our city, I once visited Vilna and was confronted by some Jews who wanted to hear about the dispute. I told them curtly: "I have vowed not to discuss this.' They ceased to question me about the matter."

❧ Rabbi Yisrael Salanter

I recall that in my youth, not long after *Sefer Chofetz Chaim* was published, my father received a letter from R' Eliyahu Eliezer of Vilna,[1] in which he requested a copy of the work on behalf of his father-in-law, R' Yisrael Salanter. R' Yisrael's disciples would relate that in their teacher's final years, *Sefer Chofetz Chaim* was forever on his table.

My saintly brother-in-law R' Tzvi [Hirsh Levinsohn] was told by one of R' Yisrael's disciples that upon perusing my father's work, R' Yisrael declared that Providence had prepared a leader who would mend the hearts of his fellow Jews and renew their closeness with their Father in Heaven.

❧ Measure for Measure

Among those who would travel from town to town peddling my father's *sefarim* was a man who was a gifted orator. He was a very successful salesman and would sell my father's works in large quantities. However, when I had an opportunity to examine my father's ledgers, I discovered that this man owed my father many hundreds of rubles for *sefarim* which had already been sold. At first, the man tried to claim that he still had the books in his possession and owed nothing. However, when it became absolutely clear that the *sefarim* had already been sold, we ceased to deal with this man.

Later, I was informed that the man still traveled from town to town making good use of his oratory skills. I also learned that when people would ask him why he no longer sold my father's works, the man would reply that he had discovered that "in those works also,

---

1. He was the father-in-law of Rabbi Chaim Ozer Grodzensky and the grandfather of Rabbi Eliyahu Eliezer Dessler, author of *Michtav Me'Eliyahu.*

the truth is not to be found." Of course, we did not inform my father of this.

Around a year later, the man's wife appeared at my father's door and reported that her husband had become stricken with a severe ailment of the tongue. He had sent his wife to beg forgiveness of my father and to request help in covering his medical expenses. Though my father's financial situation was strained, he gave her twenty-five rubles and conferred his blessing.

~~~

My father would say that for sins between man and G-d, retribution is sometimes not meted out until the person departs this world. However, with sins between man and and his fellow, retribution is meted out on this world, measure-for-measure. He would relate incredible stories to which he was personally witness where individuals were Divinely punished with exacting measure for what they had done against their fellow. Sometimes many years would pass tranquilly until, ultimately, their punishment was administered.

✄ Suffering Souls

He was extremely careful not to respond harshly to the poor who would make their rounds in town, even though their words were sometimes cause for anger. He was concerned lest he trangress the prohibition, "You shall not cause pain to any widow or orphan" (*Shemos* 22:21),[1] which our Sages *(Mechilta,* ad loc.) apply to any suffering soul. He was extremely careful, and would caution others as well — not to cause pain to a widow or orphan.

My brother-in-law, R' Mendel (Zaks), related the following, which he heard from my father:

In my father's youth, it happened in our city that a widow rented an apartment from a Jewish laborer. In her poverty, she was unable to pay the rent, so the landlord attempted to evict her, but it was winter and she refused to leave. The landlord then proceeded to remove the roof that covered her dwelling. The entire city was in an

---

1. The Torah continues, "If you [dare to] cause him pain...! — for if he shall cry out to Me, I shall surely hear his outcry. My wrath shall blaze and I shall kill you by the sword, and your wives will be widows and your children orphans" (v. 22-23).

uproar over this wicked deed. However, the landlord payed no attention to this and forced the widow to leave at the height of the winter.

My father concluded: "Years passed and nothing happened; but I did not forget this despicable incident. I said to myself: "Can it be that life will go smoothly for this man, when G-d declares, (ibid. v. 22) "My wrath shall blaze against you..."?

"Some ten years later, the landlord was bitten by a mad dog. After a few days, he began to bark like a dog; his illness lingered for a few weeks until he died."

✒ Strife

In the years after I left my father's town of Radin, a dispute erupted among the members of the local *chevra kadisha* (burial society). The dispute actually led to physical blows in public. My father's efforts at making peace failed until he went before the *aron hakodesh* (holy ark) one day and said:

"Those of us who are alive today will one day leave this world. At that time, we will come before the Heavenly Court to account for all that we had done in the [relatively] few years alloted to us on this lowly world... One cannot imagine the exactness of that judgment; even our thoughts will not be overlooked ... Each one of us will be shown all that had transpired in his life, in the exact time and place. Each person will try desperately to find some source of merit for himself so that the judgment against him will be lightened somewhat."

My father then proceeded to enumerate the many sins which had been committed since the dispute had erupted. He listed numerous prohibitions which the disputants had trampled upon, including *chilul Hashem* (desecration of G-d's Name). He continued:

"When you will arrive in the next world and see how dark things will be for you, you may very well blame everything on me for lack of an alternative. You may want to claim: 'In our town there lived a *lamdan* (learned person) named Yisrael Meir. Had he shown us the severity of the sins that we were committing, we would have stopped!'

"Therefore, I tell you now before the *aron hakodesh*: You have strayed far in committing these terrible sins. If you will not take my words to heart, then there is nothing that I can do for you. However, I have saved myself by uttering this warning."

My father's words had their desired effect and peace soon reigned in Radin.

✑

Though every moment of time was very precious to my father, there were many instances where he would spend hours on end trying to make peace between feuding parties — especially if it was a community feud. I recall the sight of my father walking in the synagogue courtyard with his hand on the shoulder of a community member. Everyone knew that my father was not one to go for a leisurely stroll, involved in idle conversation. Rather, he was seeking to resolve a dispute, to soften a stubborn heart. He succeeded many times in melting even hearts of stone. How often was a disputant heard to say: "Were it not for the fact that I revere Reb Yisrael Meir..."

✑ *Pursue Peace*

On *Simchas Torah,* my father would ensure that every man had an opportunity to encircle the *bimah* with the Torah scroll, so that no one's feelings would be hurt. The children would dance carrying the scrolls of the Prophets and Writings. At times, the children would push one another as they struggled to snatch one of the scrolls out of the ark. Sometimes, they would hit one another. My father would calm me so that I would not fight. He gave me the *Sefer HaSemag*[1] to hold during the dancing, for he said that this printed volume encompassed both the Oral and Written laws.

Once, when I visited my father a few years before his passing, he summoned the family together and told us: "All my life, I was careful never to cause anyone to be pushed aside; to the contrary, I always allowed myself to be pushed aside for the sake of others — it is good to conduct oneself in this way."

It is told that my father was once walking on a narrow sidewalk in Grodno when an army officer came walking towards him. My father immediately stepped off the sidewalk to allow the officer to

---

1. On the six hundred thirteen commandments.

pass. The officer was amazed that a man so advanced in years would quickly make way for someone much younger than himself. When the officer asked my father about this he replied, "All my life, it has been my way to move aside for someone else. With this approach, one lives a happy life."

Between Man and His Creator

✑ No Taint of Sin

At the funeral of my father, of blessed memory, someone related the following in the name of his father-in-law, who had served as *Rav* of a certain town which my father visited in his younger years to sell his *sefarim*:

At the outset of that visit, my father gave the *rav* his money purse for safekeeping. After remaining in the town for a few days, my father prepared to travel on. He went to take leave of the *rav*, offered him his blessings, and then returned to his lodgings to gather his belongings. One of the *rav's* attendants came knocking on my father's door to report that the *rav* wished to see him before his departure. My father soon found himself before a very irate *rav*. "How can a person be such a *shlemazel* (i.e. scatterbrained and irresponsible)?" he shouted. "How could you have forgotten your money purse which you left with me?"

My father replied humbly that, in fact, he had not forgotten the money purse. However, he had realized that in leaving the money with the *rav* without witnesses or written proof, he had trangressed a rabbinic law. The Talmud (*Bava Metzia* 76b) states that proof is required when one leaves money with anyone, even a Torah scholar whose integrity is beyond reproach. This is out of concern that the scholar's preoccupation with his learning might cause him to forget what had occurred, thus causing him to deny that any money had ever been left with him. In such a scenario, the owner of the money would be guilty of causing another Jew to sin inadvertently.

My father continued, "You and I met a number of times over the past few days, and you never made any mention of the purse. I was concerned that you had forgotten that I had left it with you [and thus, would deny possession of it if were I to claim it]. Therefore, I decided to relinquish any claim to it. The money is yours and there is no need to return it to me."

The *rav* replied that he purposely had made no mention of the purse because he wanted to see whether his visitor was a *shlemazel* and would forget to ask for it. Upon seeing that my father was about to leave town without his money, he had sent the attendant after him.

The *rav* refused to retain my father's money and returned it to him as a gift.

In fact, my father was a very responsible individual, possessed of a wondrous memory and sharpness of mind. He understood thoroughly the wiles and schemes of people, yet he never rejected anyone because of this. All his days, he saw Hashem's Presence before him.

✒ Honor

In his last years, my father was in constant distress over the disgrace to Hashem's honor which the current political situation had brought about. In particular, he was anguished over the situation in Communist Russia.

When a man came before my father and requested a blessing that he be able to earn a proper livelihood and provide for his family, my father conferred his blessing. But when the man then asked for a blessing that he merit an abundance of material wealth, my father replied, "And is honor of G-d now found in abundance?"

Being accorded honor was anathema to him. Once, I asked him why in the text of the Blessing of the New Month, we ask for "a life of wealth and honor." My father replied that this refers to the honor of the Jewish people as a whole, which, in essence, is the honor of the One Above.

He once visited a certain city on behalf of the *Va'ad Hayeshivos*[1] and stayed at the home of my sister. The house was forever crowded with people who sought his advice or blessing, or who had come merely to gaze upon his countenance. My father told my sister, "I find all this honor repulsive and embarrassing, but for the sake of the Torah I must endure it."

❧ The Gift of Time

My father would spend only the minimum on household needs. He would even refrain from purchasing *sefarim* that were not essential for his current studies. He would say, "Earning money costs time, and time is life, and with life one can accomplish something for the honor of Hashem."

He once reflected: How precious is life, which cannot be prolonged for a minute more than is Divinely decreed, even by the mightiest king who has at his disposal all the remedies that are to be found in this world. How foolish are those who waste their precious years amassing fortunes which they will not take with them when their time comes.

❧ Torah Study

When R' Yaakov Brode, a wealthy and G-d-fearing Jew, passed away, R' Chaim Soloveitchik (of Brisk) and my father were asked to come to Warsaw to preside over the settlement of his will in which he had left one hundred thousand rubles to charitable causes. R' Yaakov had no children and some of the relatives who claimed his inheritance meddled over his will and wanted to declare it null and void. The matter dragged on for weeks; R' Chaim [who was advanced in years] grew weary and finally returned to Brisk while my father remained in Warsaw to resolve the matter. In the meantime, he was flooded with communications from many of the charitable

---

1. The *Va'ad Hayeshivos* (Council of Yeshivos) was founded by the Chofetz Chaim and Rabbi Chaim Ozer Grodzensky after the first World War. The *Va'ad* helped to ensure the financial survival of the impoverished yeshivos of Lithuania in the years between the two World Wars (see *Reb Chaim Ozer*, published by Mesorah).

institutions which R' Yaakov Brode had supported; they were desperate for a share of the will and had already distributed money to the poor which they had borrowed on the assumption that money from the will would be forthcoming. It took another few weeks before my father resolved the matter in a peaceful and correct way.

I was living in Warsaw at that time and often, my father would bemoan to me the precious weeks of time that he had been forced to give away in order that the matter of the will be settled. I noticed then, that my father was spending time writing a new monograph; as was his way, he would not reveal to me what its topic was until it was ready for publication. Later, I learned that this monograph was entitled *Toras HaBayis* (The Torah of the Home) and was based on the command, "and you shall speak about them [the Torah's commandments] when you sit in your home, when you walk on the way..." (*Devarim* 6:7), meaning, that in addition to his fixed sessions of Torah study, a Jew should occupy himself with Torah learning whenever possible. I am certain that my father's stay in Warsaw for weeks on end without being able to spend his time in a *beis midrash* studying, aroused his spirit to compose this essay, so that people would come to realize that even when they are preoccupied and unable to be in the *beis midrash*, they are, nevertheless, not free of the obligation to study Torah.

Though every *mitzvah* was precious to my father, he placed particular emphasis on spreading the study of Torah — the greatest of all *mitzvos* — among the masses.

❧ Mishnah Berurah

My father's method of Torah study was the same all his life: he studied each topic in great depth as he strove to arrive at a conclusion and deduce the *halachah*. He would begin with the earliest sources on a given topic. If it was rooted in Scriptural verses, he would first study those verses and the Sages' halachic derivations, as found in *Mechilta, Sifra* and *Sifre*. He would then study *Targum* and the commentaries of *Rashi* and *Ramban* before approaching the words of the *Mishnah*, Talmud and their commentaries.

In the summer of 5635 (1875), my father took me with him to the town of Lipnishak, some fifteen miles from Radin. He remained there for most of the summer and it was there that he began his work, *Mishnah Berurah*,[1] as he delved into the topics of *tefillin* and *tzitzis*.

Also there in Lipnishak was a Reb Yehoshua, who had sold his business in Vilna at age thirty and who would spend the remaining fifty years of his life in the diligent study of Torah. He and my father conversed often during that summer. In many of their conversations, my father would open a volume of the *Orach Chaim* section of *Shulchan Aruch* at random and raise a number of questions and related halachic queries on each paragraph that lay before them. My father told Reb Yehoshua, "These matters cannot be resolved unless one studies each topic beginning with its earliest sources; without such study, *Shulchan Aruch* remains a closed book... Now, *Shulchan Aruch* is a code of law written for every Jew — but it is enough to demand of the average Jew that he fulfill that which is clearly spelled out! We cannot burden everyone with the task of studying each topic beginning with its earliest sources in order to arrive at a halachic conclusion." This matter allowed my father no rest.

He once related to me that, before undertaking the arduous task of authoring a work on *Orach Chaim* that would contain halachic conclusions on all relevant issues and which could be understood and utilized by virtually anyone, he placed the matter before many prominent scholars, asking that they undertake the task. While they all agreed about the matter's urgency, each felt that he could not be the one to author such a work; one demurred because of his preoccupation with communal responsibilities, another because of his ill health ... With no alternative, my father approached this burdensome undertaking which, according to his own testimony, took twenty-eight years to complete.

One cannot depict the incredible effort that my father expended as he strove to clarify the *halachah* for the sake of his people and in numerous instances, decide between a number of varying opinions on a given issue. Never did he cite someone's else's opinion without re-

---

1. *Mishnah Berurah* is the Chofetz Chaim's classic multi-volume commentary to the *Orach Chaim* section of *Shulchan Aruch*. The Chofetz Chaim's opinion set forth in *Mishnah Berurah*, and its companion commentary *Be'ur Halachah*, are considered the final word on all matters relating to *halachah* of daily living. Many Torah luminaries are reported to have said that the Chofetz Chaim's exceptional *tzidkus* (righteousness) overshadowed his exceptional genius in Torah as is plainly evident from his *Mishnah Berurah* and *Be'ur Halachah*.

searching the matter thoroughly. In many instances, he spent weeks and even months immersed in a single chapter in *Shulchan Aruch.*

✒ A Refined Pen

In authoring *Mishnah Berurah,* my father was extremely careful not to offend the honor of any scholar whose opinion he quotes; this is true even where he contends with the opinion of a later commentator. In many instances, he refrained from inserting his refutation of a commentator's *pilpul* (interweaving of various sources to adduce a given point); only when absolutely necessary would he even write concerning such *pilpul:* "One is not bound by this [line of reasoning]."

Virtually all of *Mishnah Berurah* is free of any tangential *pilpul,* as is often found even in the works of luminaries. I am absolutely certain that had my father included in his *Mishnah Berurah* all that he propounded when researching the sources of the relevant laws, his work would have been many times larger than it actually is. Aside from the expense that publishing such a large work would have involved, it was not my father's way to offer lengthy digressions and make known to all his genius in study. It is precisely because he did not include such material in his work that *Mishnah Berurah* has become universally accepted, for everyone knows that this work contains nothing but pratical *halachah.*

✒ Publication

In the year 5644 (1884) the first volume of *Mishnah Berurah* was published in Warsaw. During the months of publication, my father stayed in Warsaw and visited the printer each day to ensure that the volume would be free of error. He explained that a work of practical *halachah* requires a heightened degree of care that it be error free. Moreover, he was concerned lest the volume contain mistakes such as missing lines or the like, and he would be guilty of robbery for having charged the price of an error-free volume. For this reason, he felt forced to suspend his daily study routine for a few months while publication was in progress.

From the year 5666 (1906) and on, when I lived in Warsaw, my father, for the most part, relied on me to oversee the publication of his works. Once, he wrote me that he had received a complaint from a purchaser who had bought a volume in which some pages in one section were reversed. My father wrote, "What have you done to me, my son? All my life I have been worried about how to avoid that which might even *smack* of robbery — I never dreamt that I would be guilty of *actual* robbery!" He instructed me to have that section reprinted correctly and then to place advertisements in Orthodox Jewish newspapers that anyone whose volume contains this error should write to us so that he could receive a corrected copy.

ᴥ Disseminating His Work

After the first volume of *Mishnah Berurah* was published and distributed in Warsaw, he journeyed to Mezritz and Lublin where many knew him well and where his works on *shemiras halashon* had already been widely distributed. The *rabbanim* in these cities revered my father and assisted him in disseminating his works among their communities. From these cities, my father would move on to distribute his newest volume in other places where people had already paid for their copy to help cover the cost of publication.

For the most part, my father traveled with his *sefarim* within the borders of Lithuania. The physical stress of these travels was enormous, for he traveled alone. He would hoist his packages of books onto the train without assistance and would take them off the train alone when arriving at his destination. At times, he would have no assistance when going from the train to a horse-drawn wagon and from the wagon to his lodgings. Never did he complain about this, though he was not cut out for this sort of physical work. The only bemoaning that escaped his lips was regarding the time he lost from his regular study schedule. He would rationalize aloud: "But what am I to do? I owe money [for the cost of publication]." He would often say. "We [who are considered Torah scholars] must be extremely careful to repay our debts. Any Jew who refrains from repaying a debt transgresses the prohibition, "You shall not cheat' (*Vayikra* 19:13). We, however, also transgress the prohibition, "You shall not desecrate My holy name' (ibid. 22:32), for people consider me a Torah scholar."

๛Arousing the Populace

His presence and public addresses left a deep impression upon the communities which he visited. Wherever he traveled, he addressed the people; his words drew many close to Torah and fear of Heaven. His address would usually last about an hour. He would not shout, dramatize or even use the familiar tune of the *maggidim* (preachers); occasionly, a groan would escape his lips. His main topic was the need to engage in daily introspection and take stock of one's spiritual standing. My father's words penetrated deep into the hearts of his listeners.

Someone related to me that he was present at one of my father's addresses more than fifty years ago. When the address had ended, some people stood chatting together and were heard praising the quality of my father's address. He approached them and said, "Please refrain from discussing the merits of my address — that is not important. What is important is that my words be taken to heart."

In Warsaw, where as mentioned above, my father spent many months in his younger years overseeing the publication of his *sefarim,* there lived a G-d-fearing young scholar named R' Yitzchak Grodzinsky. R' Yitzchak had founded a *chevra* (society) for laborers, who would gather together three times a day to study Torah. My father, who from his youth strove to disseminate Torah among the masses, particularly among the poor and unlearned, gave R' Yitzchak and his group much encouragement and inspiration. He would visit with them regularly and would encourage the laborers to strengthen their observance of *mitzvos* and character development. Eventually, R' Yitzchak's home became my father's regular place of lodging in Warsaw.

In time, R' Yizchak's *chevra* grew to the point where it was forced to rent a *beis midrash* for itself. The group founded its own *sefarim* library which included many copies of each of my father's works. R' Yitzchak studied my father's works with his *chevra* on a regular basis and this left a deep impression upon these laborers, both in matters between man and his fellow, and between man and his Creator. Many of these laborers developed into outstanding Jews, who were known for their awe of G-d and their eagerness to hearken to His calling.

After a period of time, R' Yitzchak founded a yeshivah with many classes, led by distinguished *roshei yeshivah*. His son-in-law, R' Yisrael Hirsh, founded a *chevra* of his own in a different part of the city which also made Torah study the focal point of its day. In time, similar groups were founded throughout Warsaw by disciples of R' Yitzchak. They also established committees for strengthening observance of Shabbos and the laws of family purity, and distributed hundreds of copies of my father's monographs on these vital matters.

The *tzaddik* R' Yitzchak passed away in 5681 (1921). It is not an exaggeration to say that he did not leave behind his equal in all of Warsaw, for the degree to which he spread Torah study and strengthened *mitzvah* observance throughout the city was unsurpassed. My father eulogized him and mourned his passing exceedingly. In truth, my father was at the center of all of R' Yitzchak's mighty deeds and projects.

✍ *The Face of Yehoshua*

(When reading of the sublime character traits and dedication to Torah of the Chofetz Chaim and other luminaries, one tends to feel far removed from their accomplishments and may find it difficult to relate to their exalted spiritual level. The following insight of the Chofetz Chaim, as related by his son, places matters in a somewhat different perspective.)

Our Sages relate that when Yehoshua, son of Nun, assumed the leadership of Israel following the passing of Moshe, the elders of the generation said, "The face of Moshe was like the sun, the face of Yehoshua is like the moon; woe to this disgrace, woe to this shame!" Ostensibly, the elders were lamenting how the nation's leadership had been diminished spiritually with the passing of Moshe. However, if this interpretation is correct, it is difficult to understand why the elders would use the terms "shame" and "disgrace" when referring to Yehoshua's leadership. He was, after all, a prophet who was imbued with G-dly wisdom! My father once offered his own interpretation of this passage by way of a parable:

A man was preparing to embark on a faraway journey to a land where precious gems were mined. He searched for someone in his city that would accompany him overseas, but could find only one volunteer. The two set out on their journey and were away from their families and friends for a number of years. Finally, they returned, carrying with them the fruits of their voyage. The primary voyager came laden with sacks of gems, while his companion brought with him considerable, though less, wealth. Upon seeing this, those who had refused the man's offer to journey with him became filled with envy toward the one who had accompanied him.

My father explained: Yehoshua's face did not shine like Moshe's, but it did, nevertheless, shine like the moon [whose light is a reflection of the sun's]. The elders looked at Yehoshua and expressed their dismay: "We have known Yehoshua since his youth — he was just like us! However, in the years that have passed since then, he has not left the tent of Moshe. Look how his face shines — our faces could be shining too, had we striven as he did. Woe to *our* shame, woe to *our* disgrace!"

✥ His Guiding Light

The Books of *Tanach*[1] (Scriptures) were my father's guiding light. Not only the commandments of the Torah, but all the happenings recorded in *Tanach* guided him as well. From these happenings, he gleaned a path of life for the Jewish people; their verses ignited a holy flame within him, inspiring him to instruct our people in what should be their proper course of action. From the words of *Tanach*, he drew Divine comfort and solace for every downtrodden and brokenhearted soul, and gave strength to the weakened to await Hashem's salvation.

Many of the stories which abound in Poland concerning the way in which my father awaited the arrival of *Mashiach* (the Messiah) are exaggerated. In truth, however, none of these exaggerations capture the essence of his unshakeable faith in *Mashiach's* ultimate arrival. For his faith was not based on mere allusions or even on Aggadic teachings which often are obscure and lend themselves to various interpretations. Rather, it was based on the clearly expressed words

---

1. תנ״ך *(Tanach)* is an acronym for תורה, נביאים, כתובים, *Torah, Nevi'im* (Prophets), *Kesuvim* (Writings), which contain the twenty-four books of Scripture.

of the Prophets, and even more so, the words of the *Chumash*.

Once, someone read to my father from the newspaper *HaMeilitz*, published by a group of *maskilim* ("the enlightened ones"), in which the hope was expressed that the Jews of Palestine would one day see their land become another Bulgaria, whose people had risen up against the Turks and gained their independence to become a nation like any other. My father began to weep, "Is this why Jewish blood has been spilled during the past eighteen hundred years — so that we could become another Bulgaria? Does not the Torah say, "HASHEM, your God, will bring you to the Land that your forefathers possessed and you shall possess it; He will do good to you and make you more numerous than your forefathers' (*Devarim* 30:5); '... when HASHEM will return to rejoice over you for good, as he rejoiced over your forefathers' (ibid. v. 9)? And does not the Torah foretell that the Jewish people will return to Hashem with all their hearts, as it is written, "You shall return and listen to the voice of HASHEM, and perform all His commandments that I command you today' (ibid. v. 8) ...?"

Virtually all his life, he kept a one-volume *Tanach* in his *tallis* bag. Never did he attempt to apply the words of *Tanach* to his way of thinking, to propound from them original insights — as is the way of many. Rather, he forever applied his way of thinking to the wisdom of Torah [to understand the plain meaning of each Scriptural verse]. It is not surprising, then, that he was possessed of powerful faith and mighty hope that not one word would remain unfulfilled of the glorious future for our people that the prophets foretell.

✍ Index of Laws by Day

Section One: *The Laws of Loshon Hora*

Concise Subject Index to the Laws*

Note: Numbers on this page refer to Day. (e.g. Ambiguous statements 12 = see Day 12)

*The *halachah* section of this work was written to provide an organized framework for understanding the principles of proper speech and was not intended for use as a definitive halachic reference. The serious reader will discover that accurate decision-making in matters of speech is impossible without a thorough knowledge of the pertinent concepts and laws. This concise index is intended merely to assist the reader in referring to specific situations he has already studied.

≈ Glossary

adam hashaleim — man of spiritual perfection

ahavas Yisrael — love of one's fellow Jew

apikores — heretic

arba minim — the four species which we are commanded to hold on the festival of Succos

av beis din — head of a rabbinical court

avak loshon hora — dust of loshon hora (See Day 33)

aveirah (pl. aveiros) — sin

b'tzelem Elokim — in the Divine image

ba'alei machlokes — men of strife

baal loshon hora — habitual speaker of loshon hora

baal teshuvah (pl. ba'alei teshuvah) — returnee to the path of Torah

Bamidbar — Numbers

bein adam la chaveiro — between man and his fellow

bein adam la Makom — between man and G-d

beis haknesses — synagogue

Beis Hamikdash — the Holy Temple

beis midrash — study hall

beis din — rabbinical court

Bereishis — Genesis

Bircas Kohanim — The Priestly Blessing

bitachon — trust in G-d

bitul Torah — disruption of Torah study

chanufah — flattery

chasid — exceedingly righteous individual

chatzitzah — interposition

Chazal — the Sages; a reference to the Sages of the Mishnaic and Talmidic era

chazzan — one who leads the prayer services

chesed — kindness

chillul Hashem — desecration of G-d's name

chinuch — child education and upbringing

chumros — halachic stringencies, above the letter of the law

Devarim — Deuteronomy

din Torah — litigation brought before a religious court and decided according to Torah law

Divrei HaYamim — Chronicles

Eretz Yisrael — the Land of Israel

Gehinnom — Purgatory

Geulah — redemption; often a reference to the Final Redemption

giluy sod — sharing information that was related in confidence

halachah (pl. halachos) — Torah law

halachic — pertaining to Torah law

Hashem — G-d

hashkafah — outlook on basic issues of Jewish life

hechsher — rabbinical endorsement, usually pertaining to the kashrus status of food

hefker — disregarded

hester panim — Divine concealment

Hoshea — Hosea

hotzaas shem ra — slander

Iyov — Job

Kaddish — the mourner's prayer

kashrus — kosher status of a food

kedushah — sanctity, holiness

kibud av v'em — honoring one's father and mother

Kiddush — prayer recited on the Sabbath and Yom Tov (usually over wine) in commemoration of the day.

Klal Yisrael — the Jewish People

Kohelles — Ecclesiastes

Kohen (pl. Kohanim) — lit. priest, a member of the priestly family descended from Aaron.

Kohen Gadol — High Priest

kollel — Institute of advanced Torah learning for married men

Levi — Levite

lulav — palm branch — one of the arba minim (see above)

Ma'ariv — evening prayer

machlokes l'sheim shamayim — a dispute for the sake of Heaven

machmirim — individuals who are stringent beyond the letter of the law

malshin — informer

malshinus — the act of being a malshin

Mashiach — the Messiah

meis mitzvah — unattended corpse

Melachim — Kings

metzora — one afflicted with tzara'as

midah k'neged midah — lit., measure for measure; used to describe G-d's method of reward and punishment

middah (pl. middos) — character trait

middas chasidus — measure of piety

mikveh — ritual bath

Minchah — the afternoon prayer

Mishlei — Proverbs

mitzvah (pl. mitzvos) — commandment

Moshe Rabbeinu — Moses Our Teacher

mumar — rebellious sinner

mussar — (a) rebuke; (b) ethical and religious teachings

nazir — nazarite

Nechemiah — Nehemiah

Olam Habah — the World to Come

ona'as devarim — causing hurt through the spoken word

Pesach — Passover

posek — halachic authority

psak — halachic ruling

rachil — gossipmonger

Rambam — Miamonides

rasha (pl. reshaim) — wicked person

Rashi — R' Shlomo ben Yitzchak; author of the primary commentary on the Scriptures and the Talmud

rav (pl. rabbanim) — rabbi

rosh yeshivah — dean of a Torah institution

Rosh Hashanah — Jewish New Year

ruach hatumah — spirit of impurity

savlan — tolerant person

savlanus — tolerance

segulah (pl. segulos) — auspicious omen

saraph (pl. seraphim) — a type of angel

Shabbos — Sabbath

shadchan — matchmaker

Shalos Seudos — the third Sabbath meal

Shavuos — Festival of Weeks

Shechinah — Divine Presence

Shemoneh Esrei — the Amidah

Shemos — Exodus

shidduch (pl. shidduchim) — marriage match

Shir HaShirim — Song of Songs

Shmuel — Samuel

shofar — ram's horn blown on Rosh Hashanah

Shoftim — Judges

Shulchan Aruch — Code of Jewish Law compiled by R' Yosef Caro in the sixteenth century.

sinas chinam — baseless hatred

siyata d'Shmaya — Divine assistance

Succos — Festival of Tabernacles

taharah — ritual purity

tahor — pure

talmid chacham — Torah scholar

tamei — impure

tefillah (pl. tefillos) — prayer

tefillin — phylacteries

Tehillim — Psalms

teshuvah — repentance

Tishah B'Av — Fast of the Ninth of Av commemorating the destruction of the Temple

tochachah — rebuke

tumah — ritual impurity

tzaddik (pl. tzaddikim) — righteous individual

tzara'as — an affliction which is discussed in great detail in the Book of Leviticus (ch 13 — 15). The term can refer alternatively to an affliction of the skin; head or beard; a garment; or house.

tzaras hanefesh — tribulation of the soul

tzedakah — charity

tzedek — righteousness

tzitzis — the fringes on a four — cornered garment worn by Jewish males

Vayikra — Leviticus

Yehoshua — Joshua

Yeshayahu — Isaiah

Yetzer hara — evil inclination

Yirmiyahu — Jeremiah

Yisrael — Israelite; or a Jewish male who is neither a Kohen or a Levi

Yom Kippur — Day of Atonement